The Cable and Satellite Television Industries

Patrick R. Parsons
The Pennsylvania State University

Robert M. Frieden
The Pennsylvania State University

Allyn and Bacon
Boston • London • Toronto • Sydney • Tokyo • Singapore

This work is lovingly dedicated from Patrick
to Susan, Judy, Mel, and Ginny,
and from Rob to Elizabeth and Alex

Vice President, Editor in Chief: Paul Smith
Series Editor: Karon Bowers
Editorial Assistant: Leila Scott
Marketing Manager: Kris Farnsworth
Editorial Production Service: Chestnut Hill Enterprises, Inc.
Manufacturing Buyer: Megan Cochran
Cover Administrator: Jennifer Hart

Library of Congress Cataloging-in-Publication Data
Parsons, Patrick.
    The cable and satellite television industries / by Patrick R.
Parsons and Robert M. Frieden.
        p.   cm.
    Includes bibliographical references and index.
    ISBN 0-205-20013-3
    1. Cable television--United States.   2. Artificial satellites in
telecommunication--United States.   3. Television broadcasting--
United States.   I. Frieden, Rob.   II. Title.
HE8700.72.U6P37   1997
384.55'5'0973--dc21   97-27532
                                                            CIP

Printed in the United States of Amerca

10 9 8 7 6 5 4 3 2 1   02 01 00 99 98 97

Contents

Preface

In 1965, most people with access to television watched three channels, NBC, CBS, and ABC. By the mid 1980s, a majority of the viewing public could choose among dozens of TV networks. By the dawn of the new century, viewers will have access to hundreds of channels and a wide array of program choices. Farther into the future, the concept of channels may disappear altogether, replaced by an interactive, on-demand television platform that gives people the ability to tailor their own viewing from a vast library of video choices. Driven by consumer preference for greater amounts and variety of television and made possible by new leaps in technology, television has changed steadily over the years. Whether one characterizes the change as gradual or dramatic, an evolution or a revolution, is perhaps a matter of perspective. However, its general contours and direction are clear: They include increasing capacity, increasing flexibility, and increasing choice. Moreover, the new systems of electronic communication that bring the viewer news and entertainment are now capable of delivering a variety of other services as well, including data communication and telephone service.

Leading this change are the cable and satellite television industries. Cable television was the first to begin expanding the number of channels and networks available to consumers, starting in the mid 1970s. By the mid 1990s, satellite-delivered consumer TV doubled and tripled cable's capacity. Currently, both cable and satellite operators are working to multiply their channel availability two- and threefold and to use it for a host of interactive consumer services.

For several years now the press, the public and the industries themselves have talked about "convergence." Telephone companies advertise a future in which they will provide interactive television service that includes video-conferencing *and* feature films. Cable companies today provide telephone service to businesses as well as selling HBO to consumers.

The Cable and Satellite Television Industries is different from many prior surveys of the television industry insofar as it looks at cable and satellite television in this larger context of converging services and technologies. It reviews the plans of the cable and satellite industries to offer home and business telephone service and data communication along with multichannel television, and it examines the potential for other telecommunications providers, especially the telephone companies, to do the same. In part, this text is about how cable and satellite television fit into the evolving Information Age. A number of electronic communications platforms are now capable of delivering traditional television programming and services such as wireless telephone, Internet access, paging, and, eventually, advanced interactive multimedia. This book is about these industries and the nature and causes of this change. It is about the structure and operation of the cable and satellite systems and several others that make up the larger television and telecommunications infrastructure. We will examine how these different systems work, what they do, and where they are headed. We also will consider the business of television, its programming, and program services. We will look at the history of cable and satellite communications and even a bit at the telephone business. Important technological and regulatory changes are at the heart of the changing nature of the television and telecommunications systems, and they will be considered closely.

The developing information infrastructure has been identified as key to our future economic well-being and central to our political and cultural health and development. It also has been cast as a potential threat to our privacy and freedom. We will examine a variety of perspectives on the implications of the emerging system. Whatever view one takes of the new communications technologies, however, no one can doubt their centrality to his or her life. On average, people spend more time watching television than almost anything else. Only work and sleep occupy more hours in our day. Television is our primary source of news, information, and entertainment. This book is about the current and changing nature of that medium.

THE PLAN OF THE BOOK

The book is divided into nine chapters dealing with history, structure, programming and services, operations, law and policy, international activities, and social issues in cable and satellite television. These are significantly interrelated categories, however. One cannot talk about the history of cable without referring to the development of law and regulation, and one cannot talk about technology without noting the influence of economics or programming. The chapters therefore can best be thought of as overlapping circles of interest that, as they do in the real world, blend significantly at the edges.

Chapter 1 presents an overview of the fundamental forces shaping the developing television system, including the digitization of electronic communication, recent changes in the law that have thrown cable and satellite industries into direct competition and with other telecommunications providers, and the business and social implications of the new media mix. Chapter 2 traces the history of cable and, to a lesser extent, satellite TV. The role of the telephone industry in cable evolution, primarily AT&T, is noted here as well. Chapter 3 details the technology of the existing and developing networks, looking at basics such as the electromagnetic spectrum and wireline conduits, including coaxial cable, telephone's copper twisted pair, and fiber optics. Old and new distribution architectures, including cable's "tree and branch" topography, as well as the newer "hybrid fiber coax" and "switched digital video" platforms, are also discussed and compared. There is a special emphasis here on the transformation from an analog to a digital world.

Chapters 4 and 5 look at the structure of the television and telecommunications marketplace. Multichannel television and its related components can be divided, conceptually at least, into the means of distribution, on the one hand, and programming and services, on the other. Chapter 4 examines the primary distribution networks in the context of their industrial organization. Each technology has evolved into a certain kind of industrial form with a given set of technical, business, and ownership characteristics. There is great overlap in many cases but important distinctions as well. The cable industry, the satellite industry, the telephone industry, and wireless cable will be considered, along with several lesser but nonetheless promising players. Chapter 5 considers the programming and services currently available and promised by the various providers discussed in Chapter 4. The largest part of the discussion will focus on traditional multichannel television programming and the nature and types of niche programming services, as well as traditional broadcast programming, local access, and similar familiar forms of TV. The chapter also will consider telephone service, especially as it may be offered by cable companies or via cellular and even satellite technologies. The chapter also will examine the provision of data communication, including on-line service and Internet access. Finally, it reviews the issue of ownership and control within and across both distribution and programming sectors.

Chapter 6 looks at the more detailed and basic issues of daily operations. It considers the organization and typical routines that characterize cable system operators, DBS companies, and programming networks. Customer service, programming strategies, tiering and pricing issues, the problems of start-up programmers, and the buying and selling of cable properties are among the topics addressed.

The law that had helped redraw the map of telecommunication and multichannel television, the Telecommunications Act of 1996, is one of the primary topics of Chapter 7. It also reviews more broadly the legal framework within which policy is developed, including the roles of the Federal Communications Commission, Congress, the Executive Branch, and the courts. First Amendment issues in cable and telecommunication will be examined along with problems of spectrum allocation, both domestically and globally.

Chapter 8 considers the developing international markets and the world of television without borders. One of the chief characteristics of the emerging system is its globalization. Broadband wired and wireless systems are coming together internationally in terms of technology, ownership, and programming. Transnational corporations are plumbing communications markets around the world. It was once said that the sun never set on the British Empire; the same might be said today about CNN and MTV.

Our communications systems have always been at the heart of our political and cultural life. Changes in the media systems ripple throughout the rest of the society. Chapter 9 looks at a variety of issues, both broadly philosophical and pointedly imminent, that are being raised by the changes occurring in the media world. Some people, for example, greet the Information Age with expectant joy and others with deep suspicion. Does technology enhance our lives, or trample our spirits? Does it expand our freedom, or enslave us and invade our privacy? Does multichannel television help alleviate our long-standing concerns about sex and violence on TV, or heighten the problems we already face? These and other questions are raised, although not necessarily answered.

CHALLENGES AND LIMITATIONS

There have been a number of challenges in writing the story of multichannel television today, the most daunting of which has been trying to keep pace with the changing landscape. It is common wisdom among many people writing about the Information Age that most of the words you type into your computer will be dated before they can be printed. Change occurs on a daily basis. In the year or so that it took to write this book, companies in the telephone industry committed millions of dollars toward establishing a delivery system to challenge cable TV, and then suspended those plans; cable companies positioned themselves to compete vigorously to deliver telephone service, and then changed their minds. As a result, large sections of this book have been written and rewritten several times in an effort to keep up. Despite the additional changes in ownership and corporate strategy that no doubt will take place in the next few years, we think that, overall, the book will help everyone better understand today's undulating landscape, the nature of the competing industries, where they have come from, what is at stake, and what forces drive and constrain them. For anyone seeking a detailed, integrated perspective on television and telecommunications industries today, this book is a good place to start.

In addition, we have been challenged, even overwhelmed, by the scope of this project. By necessity, this survey must encompass everything from technical aspects of electronic transmission techniques, to cash flow analysis, to First Amendment law, to media effects research. We hope that this book touches, at least to some extent, on everything you always wanted to know about cable and satellite television. Hundreds of facts, opinions, and ideas from business, law, technology, and sociology have been collected, sifted, and woven together into what we hope is a coherent whole. The material is as accurate and timely as we can make it given the limits of technology and our own abilities. Not everyone, of course, will agree on the stress we place on some elements over others, but we believe we have at least touched on all of the important issues and trends.

ACKNOWLEDGMENTS

We would like to acknowledge and thank the many people who have helped us gather all these facts and ideas, who have helped check and recheck the accuracy of our information and the clarity of our prose. Without their help, this book would have been much poorer, if it were possible at all.

First we would like to thank friends and colleagues at Penn State University who supplied expert information, careful proofreading and, continual moral support. They include E. Stratford Smith, who was literally there at the beginning of the industry and whose perspective was of great value; Richard Taylor, not only a wealth of information and insight but one of the best and fastest copy editors around; and Pamela Czapla, who never lost sight of the big picture, nor let us.

A number of people from the industries were very gracious and helpful in supplying information: David Pierce and his colleagues at the National Cable Television Association; Eric Rabe, Ginger Fisk, and Hud Manion at Bell Atlantic; Joe Rocco and Curt Kosko at TCI in State College; and, especially, Joe Aman of Cable TV, Inc. We also want to thank Warren Publishing, Intertec Publishing, and Paul Kagan Associates, Inc., for their generous permission to reprint material in this book.

Benjamin J. Bates, University of Tennessee; Thomas F. Baldwin, Michigan State University; Alan B. Albarran, Southern Methodist University; Ted Carlin, Shippensburg University; and Ron Rizzuto, University of Denver were kind enough to review the manuscript. We are grateful for the time and thought contributed by all of them. The work is stronger for their input. Charu Uppal, our always cheerful research assistant, wore out the steps between the office and the library, and we appreciate the long hours she worked. We would like to thank Al Greco, editor for The Allyn and Bacon Series in Mass Communications for giving us the opportunity to write this text, as well as Joseph Opiela, Joe Terry, Leila Scott, and Kate Sheehan at Allyn and Bacon for their support and encouragement. We are grateful to all who supplied information, ideas, and feedback. As always, the responsibility for any remaining mistakes or omissions is ours.

Finally, Patrick wants to thank Susan and the kitties for their unending patience, understanding, and support.

1

Converging Lines

Anik 2 hung invisibly in the morning sky, 22,300 miles above the equator. In Washington, D.C., the Speaker of the House of Representatives, Democrat Carl Albert, spoke into a camera. The electronic information that made up the television signal zipped through the East Coast transmission equipment and was "uplinked" to the orbiting communications satellite, which captured it and beamed it back to earth. It took only a half second for the Speaker's image to fly from Washington to California. On the West Coast, in Anaheim, California, an eight-meter wide satellite receiving dish stood in a hotel parking lot, its antenna pointed south. The receiving dish picked out the signal and fed it into a maze of circuitry that led to television sets on the floor of the Anaheim Convention Center. Among those who stopped to watch the telecast were some who knew they were seeing history in the making. Few, however, could have predicted the magnitude of the change that this event would foreshadow.

It was the first coast-to-coast satellite retransmission of a domestic television signal designed specifically for use by cable television systems. The day was Monday, June 18, 1973, and it was the opening day of the 22nd annual convention of the National Cable Television Association. The satellite demonstration had been arranged by Teleprompter Corporation, the nation's largest cable television company at the time, with the support of other cable operators. That night the satellite was used again to relay a championship boxing match between Jimmy Ellis and Ernie Shavers from Madison Square Garden in New York to convention rooms in the Disneyland Hotel. The telecast of the fight was produced by a fledgling pay television company called Home Box Office (HBO) and was the first sports event to use the satellite link.

The press called it an historic event.[1] Teleprompter, HBO, and others touted it as the transmission medium of the future.[2] Some in the industry were guarded in their optimism about the satellite's potential. The economics and the technology, they observed, were not yet proven. One or two even worried aloud about what would happen if the satellite fell down.[3]

No satellite lasts forever and some do eventually "fall down,"[4] but Anik 2 and the satellites that followed have shown sufficient durability and efficiency to change dramatically and forever our way of communicating. The marriage of cable and satellite communication restructured the television industry in the United States and abroad. Those who were cautious about the potential of the satellite link in 1973 had to wait only a few years before the technology began to prove itself. Up until the mid-1970s, cable television was, for the most part, a service dedicated to retransmitting existing commercial broadcast television, bringing network and independent television stations to homes that otherwise could not receive them. Satellites opened up the possibility of creating a national, cost-efficient, distribution system for cable television programming. It led to the creation of cable networks. Beginning in the mid-1970s and accelerating through the 1980s, a host of new television acronyms began working their way into our language—HBO, CNN, MTV, USA, ESPN. As the new networks emerged and found their way onto cable systems across the country, cable itself became a much more appealing service. Towns and cities that previously had no use for the medium because their over-the-air reception brought them all the television that was available were attracted by the new programming options: movies, sporting events, twenty-four-hour news channels, and entertainment forms, like music videos, that had not previously existed. People began subscribing to and watching cable TV. Viewership of cable programs climbed steadily while ratings for the commercial broadcast networks gradually sank.

Today about two-thirds of all U.S. homes subscribe to cable TV. Through programming services such as Cable News Network (CNN), Music Television (MTV), and C-SPAN, it has become influential in the nation's politics and culture. Cable and satellite television reshaped what has become known as our communications infrastructure; multichannel TV has grown to a multibillion dollar industry and plays a significant role in how we see the world and how we see ourselves.

Now, it is changing again. In a metamorphosis that may be every bit as fundamental as the one wrought in 1973, the television and telecommunications landscape is shifting once more. The change is far-reaching. It encompasses the technology of telecommunications, the economics and structure of several related industries, and the legal policies that help shape the electronic media system.

Technological advances, especially those in digital communication, have led to the creation of several different high-capacity systems, each capable of delivering a wealth of entertainment and information services, including multichannel television programming, telephony, computer communication, and related services such as paging and teleconferencing. The industries building these new information superhighways include cablecasters, satellite broadcasters, telephone companies, and terrestrial broadcasters.

Each of these industries is vying for public attention, as well as for consumer and investor dollars. The digital networks they are creating will increase the number of television channels from 40 or 50 to 400, 500, and more, perhaps in time abolishing the concept of "channels" completely, replacing it with a program delivery "platform." Subscribers will be able to select from hundreds of movie titles and determine for themselves when and how they want to watch. Satellite and terrestrial broadcasters, along with telephone companies, will offer what was previously thought of as cable television, while cable and satellite providers will sell telephone service and data communication as well as multichannel TV. Consumers will face an array of choices in the kinds of communication services they can receive, with a variety of packagers, prices, and providers.

A SNAPSHOT OF THE INDUSTRIES

This book is about cable and satellite television and the changes that will reshape these and related industries. We include related industries because cable and satellite TV cannot be understood outside the context of an increasingly diverse, yet integrated communication system that includes a number of other important players, the foremost of which is the telephone industry. As we shall see, telephone companies have received regulatory permission to enter the cable television business. Conversely, cable can now offer telephone service. Satellite companies, as well as some earth-based broadcast businesses, are offering both. This undulating landscape will be viewed largely from the perspective of the history and operations of the cable and satellite television business, but by necessity also will address the interacting forces of business, technology, and policy that touch on all the affected industries. While not specifically about the telephone business or traditional broadcast television, the book treats these subjects in their ongoing relationship with what we will call multichannel television.

This market is likely to be highly volatile over the next few years. How it sorts out the new competitors and which companies and approaches prove successful in the long run is, at best, a guessing game. Everyone agrees, however, that for the cable, satellite, and telecommunications industries, as well as for citizens and consumers, these are exciting times in what is being described as the Information Age.

The following offers a brief overview of the major industries that constitute the emerging and converging system. They include the cable and satellite television industries, the telephone industry, and the traditional and developing broadcast industries. Subsequently, the process of convergence, its primary characteristics and some of the principle forces that are driving it, will be considered in greater detail.

Cable Television

There are more than 11,000 cable television systems in the United States. Cable serves about 64 million homes, or 66 percent of all the homes in the United States that have television. It constitutes the primary mode through which our country views itself and the rest of the world. It is a multibillion dollar business with total revenues in 1996 of about $26 billion, including returns from system operators—those who own and run the local cable systems—and the programming networks such as CNN, MTV, and HBO.

The dominant ownership form in cable television is the Multiple System Operator, or MSO. MSOs range in size from companies that own only a handful of systems to those that own hundreds. The two largest MSOs in the country, and pre-eminent forces in the business, are Tele-Communications, Inc. (TCI) and Time Warner, Inc.

Cable TV has been around since the late 1940s and early 1950s, although its roots stretch back much farther, as the next chapter will explore. It began as a simple retransmission service extending the reach of early TV broadcasters and giving viewers access to more channels than they could receive with a home antenna. It was a small-town business and remained so throughout most of the 1950s and 1960s. Suppressive regulatory policies that favored the established system of local broadcast television acted to prevent cable from penetrating the large cities. Even without regulatory restraint, though, cable had few services to market in cities already saturated with network affiliate and independent television stations. The advent of satellite distribution, coupled with a change in regulatory philosophy, triggered the evolution of the medium from a Community Antenna Television System (CATV) to cable television.

The Cable–Satellite System

Just about all cable television systems have one or more earth stations receiving the satellite-delivered programming that most viewers now think of as cable TV. Video consumers want local and network broadcast signals, but they also expect a variety of specialty and premium channels as well. Satellites make it possible to generate the audience size needed for both advertiser-supported and pay cable television. Video programmers have been able to make a business case for national cable networks even though they do not achieve the kind of viewership typically delivered by broadcast networks. This is possible because cable enjoys a special advantage over broadcast television. Broadcasters make money only by selling advertising. Cable has twin revenue streams. It generates income through advertising and by direct payment from subscribers. In fact, as we will see, subscription dollars comprise the largest portion of cable revenue, and some programming networks, such as HBO and Showtime, survive and prosper on subscription income alone. At the same time, cable specialized program networks, those targeted to special kinds of audiences, may be particularly attractive to some advertisers. The demographic composition of the viewing audience may support a particular type of advertised message, such as beer ads to twenty-one- to thirty-five-year-old males who watch sports programming on ESPN. Aggregating such audiences on a national basis would not be possible without the reach that the satellite systems make possible.

When satellites engage in video program delivery, therefore, they enhance the value of cable television in three key ways:

- The point-to-multipoint delivery capability makes it possible to gather audiences and serve many cable systems with far lower costs than are possible with terrestrial options like microwave relays;
- They provide signal transport to places where terrestrial systems are unavailable, due to rugged terrain, separating bodies of water, harsh climates, technological limitations in the available media, or financial constraints;
- They promote diversification in program sources and competition by making it possible to serve narrow market niches and to export programming to foreign locations.

Satellites, in short, have substantially changed the content and composition of cable television by expanding the scope and reach of the available programming. Cable television viewers are no longer limited to what their system operators can pull off the air with high-gain antennas, or what they can import via costly point-to-point microwave relay facilities. Instead they can import a panoply of programming, originating anywhere within the "footprint" of a satellite, including sites of late-breaking news, sporting events, and sources of high quality entertainment.

The impact of satellites extends beyond simply reducing the cost of access. Satellites provide access to television and other services where oceans and other geographical barriers make it financially prohibitive or technologically impossible. Small communities in the Alaskan bush and other rural and remote areas far from a backbone microwave network can qualify for the same package of channels as viewers in more populated locales.

With the availability of satellite-delivered programming, cable television quickly migrated from a localized, self-contained, and somewhat sleepy distribution service to a nationally and globally connected infrastructure rich in diverse content.

Cable Programming

Today's cable services are familiar to most people. They include the local broadcast stations, which are picked up off the air (or fed directly from the station), then retransmitted via the cable. These stations usually include the affiliates of the major networks, NBC, CBS, ABC, and Fox. Systems also carry most local independent stations, those not affiliated with a major network, and may import the signals of distant stations that the local viewer could not normally receive. These stations, normally independents as well, are fed to the cable system by microwave or wire. Cable also carries "superstations," like WTBS in Atlanta, broadcasters who distribute their local signal nationally by satellite.[5]

Many cable systems provide local access channels for educational, government, and community groups. Sometimes these services are split to give the city its own channel, while offering a separate channel for individuals or groups to run material of local interest, or just to provide a community outlet for political and artistic expression. The cable system may have a separate institutional network to connect regional schools, hospitals, libraries, and similar agencies. Many systems provide channels for text services that feature news, weather, and sports information along with advertising for local businesses.

The bulk of what most people think of as cable programming comes in the form of the cable networks. They are chiefly of two types, advertiser-supported and pay-TV. The advertiser-supported cable nets include such well-established names as CNN, ESPN, MTV, the USA network, Black Entertainment Television (BET), Arts and Entertainment (A&E), the Weather Channel, and scores of other familiar and less familiar titles. There are dozens of cable networks and more are proposed every year, although, as we will see, not all of them are successful.

Cable systems usually offer the over-the-air channels, access channels, and most advertiser-supported cable networks in a bundled package. The local broadcast signals and access channels are typically grouped into a low-cost "basic tier" and advertiser-supported networks are added into a higher cost "expanded basic tier." This tier may also include the shopping channels and C-SPAN 1 and 2. The latter carry the proceedings of the U.S. House of Representatives and U.S. Senate, along with public affairs programs, and are supported by the cable industry through subscriber fees. The shopping channels, such as QVC and the Home Shopping Network, have become part of a multibillion-dollar catalog and at-home retail sales industry, and take a percentage of every telephone order.

The next highest level of service is the premium tier, which includes the pay cable channels. These are supported by a separate monthly subscription fee and primarily program films, although some offer a wider choice of material. The original premium service was Home Box Office (HBO). Its chief competitor for many years has been Showtime, and both have "sister services," Cinemax and The Movie Channel, respectively.

"Pay-Per-View" services, as the name implies, charge for each film or program ordered. Unlike HBO, which has a set schedule of films and programs, viewers have some choice in their selection of pay-per-view films. The degree of choice consumers have, as well as how much flexibility they can exercise in viewing the films at their convenience—watching when they want to watch—is contingent on the channel capacity and technical sophistication of the system. Direct-to-home satellite services currently offer more channel capacity and hence greater variety in films and convenience in viewing times, but other systems including cable are working hard to match and even exceed their capabilities.

Audio services have long been a part of cable's menu. Most systems run local and regional radio stations and many use satellite-delivered audio services. More recently, they have begun offering high-end, digital audio programming with CD-quality sound and dozens of specialized music channels. These digital services, such as DMX and Music Choice, typically charge a monthly fee.

The cable television industry created and for the past several decades has largely controlled the multichannel TV business. Cable's dominance in this area is now challenged by the rapid development of new technologies and new distribution networks. One of the first to exploit the dawning opportunities has been the satellite industry which, with its background as a part of the cable-distribution network, has been well positioned to begin delivering television directly to the home. In response, some cable operators have begun diversifying into data and telephony markets.

Satellite TV

Satellites joined the telecommunication mix in the mid 1960s, initially as government owned and operated projects. Partial deregulation of the industry in the early 1970s led to the development of commercial satellite systems and their entrance into the video market, initially for broadcast television program delivery and electronic newsgathering. Satellites joined the video program distribution business after almost twenty years of providing essential communication and information assistance to the defense and intelligence communities. The very technological features that made satellites such a key factor in command, control, communications, and information, are now paying commercial dividends. Depending on the installed electronics, a satellite can provide the military and intelligence communities with an "eye in the sky" for surveillance over a broad geographical area, or reliable, tactical telecommunications. With minor modifications and a change in frequency, operators can convert a government satellite blueprint into a commercial "bent pipe" for receiving and relaying video signals to receivers scattered across as much as one-third of the earth's surface.

The commercial exploitation of satellite technology followed a lengthy competition between the United States and Soviet Union for technological supremacy in space. Satellites and the launch vehicles needed to position them in orbit were considered a bellwether for assessing which political ideology, communism or democracy, could more quickly and successfully meet new challenges and conquer new frontiers. The Soviet Union hit political and public relations gold when in 1957 it launched the world's first artificial satellite, Sputnik, a tiny beeping transmitter that orbited the earth every ninety minutes.

Notwithstanding its primitiveness, Sputnik started to bring to fruition a vision of radio and television broadcasting first articulated by Arthur C. Clarke in 1945. Clarke hypothesized that three satellites could provide near ubiquitous access to space communications. He envisioned satellites operating as relays with spacing 120 degrees apart to secure maximum coverage. Clarke also suggested that these relays could hover in orbit above the equator, thereby providing a motionless target for receiving signals from Earth.

A U.S. satellite first provided this relay service in 1963, receiving a signal transmitted from Earth and sending it back, demonstrating the "transponder" function that makes satellites such an effective vehicle for delivering information. In 1964 Syncom 3 applied these capabilities by providing television coverage of the Tokyo Olympics. A year later, Early Bird, the first commercial geostationary orbiting satellite, created a live television link between the United States and Europe. That satellite had the capacity to retransmit one television signal or 240 telephone voice channels. Today's satellites have the capacity to support dozens of television channels and thousands of simultaneous telephone calls.

Point-to-Point Service

Two of the important early and continuing uses of satellites have been for "point-to-multipoint" communication, of the type described above, and "point-to-point."

A major point-to-point satellite application involves the delivery of video programming, including news and sports, from the event site back to a studio or distribution facility. Satellites, for example, provide remote newsgathering opportunities. Rather than videotape an event, rush it to a studio, edit the tape, and broadcast the package, broadcasters can provide live, on-the-scene coverage. While many sports coliseums have hardwired access to terrestrial telecommunication facilities, some programmers still prefer satellite distribution, particularly when cablecasters and broadcasters can directly tap into the live feed.

Satellites also provide transoceanic transmission. Until recently, submarine cables lacked the capacity to carry one or more television channels. While new fiber-optic submarine cables can handle video, satellites continue to have a comparative financial advantage when the receiving point lies some distance from coastal locations where a submarine cable makes landfall. Satellites usually provide a cheaper telecommunication service option when more than one location must be served. The same type of comparative advantage exists when the signal originates in a rural, or landlocked, interior location. The longer the terrestrial link from submarine cablehead, or the more remote the service locale, the more likely a satellite application can provide cheaper and more efficient service.

Point-to-Multipoint Service

The role of satellites in cable television has now evolved from a strictly supportive role as a key video program delivery mechanism to an active distribution competitor. At the onset of commercial satellite service, cable operators recognized the benefit of having access to a technology that would make it possible to use a single program delivery mechanism to serve the entire nation. The point-to-multipoint characteristic of satellite transmission means that programming uplinked to the satellite from a single source can be downlinked to numerous points anywhere within the footprint of the satellite, that is, anywhere an adequate signal illuminates the earth. Unfocused footprints covering as much as one-third of the earth's surface mean that a video programmer can establish a nationwide network of affiliates or partners who collectively can access and download programming from one or more satellite transponders.

Terrestrial point-to-point transmission networks have comparatively low startup costs vis à vis satellites, because the investments are made on an incremental basis as the network grows to serve additional points. On the other hand, satellites have large initial start-up expenses, to construct and launch the satellite, but serving an additional point of communication involves low incremental costs in the installation of another Earth station.

Before providing the first minute of revenue generating service, a satellite operator typically incurs over $300 million in expenses to construct, insure, launch, and manage a single satellite. Such substantial start-up costs create incentives for risk sharing, aggregation of demand, and joint ownership by several operators. In the international satellite marketplace, national governments executed a treaty-level document to create a global cooperative, the International Telecommunications Satellite Organization (INTELSAT) that would expedite the commercial exploitation of satellite technology and make it universally accessible. In many nations, despite vigorous deregulation and competition, a single government agency or private enterprise provides all satellite services. Even in the United States, where the Federal Communications Commission articulated an "open skies" policy and the grant of licenses to any qualified applicant, the number of commercial satellite service operators has never exceeded ten and currently has dropped to three: Hughes Communications, Inc., GE Americom, and Loral Space and Communications, Ltd.

Direct Broadcast Satellites

Developments in satellite technology make it possible to deliver video programming directly to homes equipped with easy to install and operate earth stations. The Direct To Home (DTH) and Direct Broadcast Satellite (DBS) industry blossomed when satellite transmitter and receiver technology evolved from the exclusive realm of trained engineers and hobbyists to the mass-market world of consumer electronics. This transition did not occur smoothly, nor has every part of the world responded equally. In the United States investors lost several hundred million dollars in the early 1980s because a mass-market DTH business was unsustainable. The services offered few channels, had limited access to programming options, and could not be received via low-cost, user-friendly terminals. At that time, satellite television was available primarily to technically savvy hobbyists who pieced together equipment typically costing $3,000 to $4,000. Now, mass-produced, pizza-sized terminals cost less than $200 and may soon come free to the consumer with the purchase of a DBS service package. These easy-to-use satellite terminals, a wealth of programming, advanced transmission technologies and aggressive marketing have made satellite TV a reality throughout the world.

DBS and DTH initially attracted viewers primarily unserved by cable television. Cable television now passes more than 90 percent of all households in the United States, but the unserved homes represent millions of prospective subscribers.[6] Moreover, the superior picture quality and larger inventory of channels and movies have proven attractive even for subscribers with cable television options. DBS in early 1998 had more than five million subscribers. Service includes all the major cable channels plus dozens of pay-per-view movie selections. The first major satellite television providers—PrimeStar (DTH), DirecTV, and U.S. Satellite Broadcasting (DBS)—were joined in 1996 by EchoStar. The competition helped drive down home equipment costs to consumers, and while monthly rates for satellite television vary widely, based on the level of service ordered, they are generally comparable to cable prices.

Finally, direct-to-home satellites are not restricted to commercial television service. The industry is preparing technology that will enable it to provide personal, worldwide wireless voice and data communication as well. These systems will allow you to talk to anyone in the world from anywhere in the world and to download computer software or to check your e-mail from your home, your car, or your backyard.

The Telephone Companies

Until the early 1980s, American Telephone and Telegraph (AT&T) dominated the telephone business and controlled nearly all the long-distance and local telephone traffic in the United States. AT&T agreed to divest its local operating companies in 1982 in exchange for the termination of a government initiated antitrust suit. The new companies created by the divestiture included seven regional Bell Operating Companies (RBOCs), which were restricted to providing local service in their areas, and AT&T, which focused primarily on long distance. The separate businesses have remained very lucrative, nonetheless. Revenues for local telephone service totaled about $100 billion in 1996. Long-distance revenues added another $40 billion.

The telephone industry was, for the most part, kept out of cable TV by force of government regulation, including the terms of the AT&T antitrust agreement and restrictions on the ownership of cable systems, until very recently. Telephone companies ("telcos") attempted to enter cable in the 1960s and in fact built, leased, and owned many cable systems. Action by the FCC blocked this activity, however, and, from cable's perspective, kept the much larger telephone industry at bay in all but some rural areas. The fear on the part of cable operators was that the size and power of the telephone industry, especially AT&T, would be more than sufficient to swamp small-town cable operators if the telcos got a toehold in the business.

In the early 1990s the telephone industry, led by the RBOCs, began challenging the legal restrictions that kept them out of the cable market. A series of favorable court decisions and a landmark piece of communications legislation opened the video business to the telephone industry in the mid-1990s. Multichannel television service is not currently the chief interest of the newly freed telephone companies. The law that allowed them to compete in video also removed the legal barriers that kept local and long-distance providers out of one another's businesses. It meant the RBOCs were free to offer long-distance and AT&T, along with other long-distance providers, were encouraged to enter the local service market. Because the telephone market, in terms of revenue, is two to three times larger than cable, and provision of voice communication is a business line more familiar to these companies than is television, the telcos have been positioning themselves to take advantage of voice (and data) delivery as their first priority. Nonetheless, the telephone industry is not ignoring its opportunity in television. The long-term goal of most of the larger phone companies is to build telecommunications systems that supply the full range of voice, computer data, and video services in competition with cable and the other multichannel providers. Like the other players in today's telecommunications contest, the telephone companies would like, in the long run, to be the one-stop shopping destination for the consumer's communication and information needs.

Terrestrial Broadcasters

The cable, satellite, and telephone industries are among the largest and most important participants in the emerging communications infrastructure, but they are not the only players. Terrestrial broadcasters are developing technologies that will allow them to compete in a multichannel environment. By terrestrial broadcasters, we mean television stations of the kind most people are familiar with, the local ABC, NBC, CBS, or Fox affiliate. Their expanding capacity may be used for additional channels of entertainment fare or a channel of High Definition TV, or data communications service, or some mix of all the above.

Even more powerful in terms of channel capacity are the "wireless cable" technologies. These are also known by the more formal term, "multichannel, multipoint distribution services," or MMDS. MMDS operators have been offering cable TV programming such as CNN and MTV for several years, usually configured in systems of twenty to thirty channels. Developing digital compression technologies, however, are expanding that capacity to several hundred channels, making MMDS and a few related multichannel broadcast platforms potentially competitive with cable and satellite services. Furthermore, like all of the emerging systems, they too can provide voice, data, and similar communications services in addition to video entertainment.

CONVERGENCE

In the mid 1970s people began speaking of *convergence.* It is a term that denotes the melding of developing telecommunications and computer technologies into a unified system, or at least an interrelated set of functions and distribution platforms. The concept of convergence has technological, regulatory, and business implications.

Converging Technology

Technologically, the notion of convergence suggests that information and communication functions previously restricted to separate distribution networks can now be performed collectively by any of several different network technologies. Furthermore, according to some theorists, because of the increasing utility of different distribution networks to provide the same functions, the logic of technology and the market will ultimately drive them to combine into a cohesive, integrated whole.

An example may help to illustrate. If you want to watch a recently released movie today, but you know you will have to stop and start it several times to make some telephone calls, you probably will rent a videotape and play it on your home VCR. You have physically brought the tape into the house and the "transport mechanism," so to speak, is your car. The telephone calls you receive are delivered over the telephone company's system of wires and switches. If you have a home computer and "surf the net," that is, explore the interactive computer network of the Internet and the World Wide Web, you will likely do that via a computer modem connected to the same telephone line. Should you want to shut down all these systems and watch the news on television, you will tie in to one of several other possible communication distribution platforms: standard, over-the-air broadcasting from your local TV station; a direct broadcast satellite service using a receiving dish in your back yard or on your roof; or the local cable TV system.

Convergence, in one sense, is the unification of all these systems into a seamless network of voice, data, and video services. In one scenario, all of the above information and communication activities would be provided by a single high-capacity wire coming into your home and linking you to the rest of the world. You would not have to go to the video rental store to get your movie. Like your telephone conversations and your Internet access, the film would come to your house via the cable, and you would retain the ability to stop and start or rewind and replay it just as if you had the physical tape in a VCR. The same wire could feed computer and World Wide Web material to the television set in your living room, allowing you to surf with friends from the comfort of your couch. At the same time, it would feed TV programming to the computer in the den, displaying live-action football games, news programs, or old game shows in one corner of the screen while you used the rest of the screen to talk with your sister across town, using the interactive videophone service the system also made possible. At the end of the month you would get one bill for the movies, the videoconferencing, the basic telephone, and television service.

In practice, there are several existing and evolving technologies that can provide some or all of these services, and it is not yet clear how they will ultimately sort themselves out in the marketplace. There are, nonetheless, some important technical characteristics that all the competing platforms share. They include a change from analog to digital technology and a related expansion of transmission capacity. Digital communication is the language of computers. We will explore the details of the digital revolution and its relationship to the older transmission format of analog communication later in this book. The point here is to note that digital methods vastly increase the power and flexibility of the communications system. Part of that power is in the ability to increase the capacity of the system so that communication circuits that once could carry one voice conversation or video program can now carry five, or ten, or more. All the previously mentioned network providers—satellite and terrestrial broadcasters as well as cable and telephone companies—are implementing digital methods and exploring their uses in a host of existing and new service areas. For the wire-based industries, cable and telco, an additional technology is aiding in this evolution, fiber optics. As we will see, fiber-optic lines provide a much bigger "pipe" through which information can flow. Telephone companies historically have had a very narrow electronic pipeline to the home; cable operators have had a much wider conduit in coaxial cable. Chapter 3 will look more closely at the telephone company's "narrowband" line and the cable industry's "broadband" wire. It also will examine the emergence of fiber and look at its characteristics and implications for greatly enhancing the capacity of cable and telephone.

There are, in short, several existing systems that could evolve into what has been called a "full service network." The industries associated with these systems are competing mightily to hold on to their existing markets and market share while at the same time expanding into others. At the industrial level, the outcome of this commercial struggle will define the business nature of the converging communications environment.

Convergence and Regulatory Policy

The entry of cable into telephone service and telephone in cable service would not have been possible without monumental changes in the law. Political change has been instrumental in altering the future of cable and satellite television, in fact the entire media universe. Cable, satellites, and telephone all have shared, to one extent or another, a history of fluctuating government regulation, greater or less public control over the past several decades. Most recently, attention has focused on "information age" services and rhetoric, and the political pendulum has swung forcefully toward the side of competition and free market economics.

In the early 1990s, Vice President Al Gore began heavy promotion of the concept of the "information superhighway" or, as the Clinton–Gore Administration labelled it, the "National Information Infrastructure" (NII). Terms like *information infrastructure* and *information highway,* popularized in the early and mid 1990s, largely in association with the Internet, have roots going back to the early 1970s[7] when authors like Ralph Lee Smith began talking about the potential of cable television to create an electronic society in his book, *The Wired Nation: Cable TV: The Coming Information Highway.*[8]

Some early efforts to regulate cable television, as we will see, were fashioned with an eye toward harnessing the medium for purposes of public discourse and electronic community interaction. The tenor of political philosophy has wavered significantly over the years, however, moving back and forth between attitudes that privilege strict government regulation as the best route to the information superhighway and those that prefer laissez-faire policies.

Currently both political parties, and therefore the government, have determined that the public interest is best served by a reduction of regulatory control; application of the invisible hand of marketplace competition is seen as the best path to the efficient provision of communication services. This idea has been codified in the historic Telecommunications Act of 1996. Details of the legislation are discussed in Chapter 7, but its major theme of deregulation and competition needs to be noted at the outset. By eliminating the barriers that keep these industries contained in separate business lines, the Telecommunications Act helped open a new era in information and communication services. It is the law referred to earlier that allows long-distance carriers and local telephone companies to compete for one another's customers; it is the law that opens local telephone service to cable operators and video service to telephone companies. It is rearranging the media landscape in a host of important ways that will be considered throughout the text.

Converging Markets

One of the important things to keep in mind is that deregulation, by pulling down the legal barriers, will allow previously disparate markets to implode and integrate. While technology and deregulation make possible new forms of telecommunications competition, the various industries would not plow that ground without some substantial market incentives. The most obvious is a rapidly expanding, multi-billion-dollar global market for information and communication services, including multichannel television. Each industry seeks to become the provider of multiple services to the consumer, even when those services are delivered over different technical platforms. BellSouth, for example, may provide video service over wireless cable and Internet access over its wired system, while TCI uses a combination of satellite delivery and cable to do the same thing. All the parties seek to play a role providing those services and reaping the potentially immense rewards of doing so. Beyond that, each of the major industries has its own set of more particular economic interests, although all of them are assuredly pegged to the bottom line.

DBS and DTH operators, for example, enjoy for the moment a technological advantage in their ability to market a national digital television service that will take years for wire-based companies to match on the ground. The market niche consisting of rural consumers without access to cable service has blossomed to include more and more people considering DBS competitive in quality and price to cable. For telephone companies, data services offer a new revenue stream. While residential telephone service is not a growing business, the demand for fax, wireless, and data telecommunication is mushrooming to the point that the country needs countless new area codes to support a proliferation of telephone numbers. RBOCs believe they can capture a significant percentage of the long distance traffic that originates in their territory. AT&T believes it can trade on its highly visible brand name to attract local telephone customers, and other long-distance providers will continue to compete on price. Interest in video services is driven by several factors. Telephone companies believe there is market share to be taken, and they look to the time when they have built high-capacity switched systems that will accommodate voice, data, and television, and it is in their interests to exploit to the fullest their investment in that technology. In addition, the telephone business itself has been long seen as a steady but unglamorous investment, the place where widows and schoolteachers put their retirement money. Entry into the arguably more exciting world of television and entertainment is seen as one way of increasing the value of the companies by serving new and lucrative profit centers.

Cable in particular has special capital incentives helping drive it to consider additional lines of business, including telephone and data communication. It has always been a highly leveraged business, acquiring significant debt to build its plant. Its strength has been cash flow and the spiraling value of its assets, with revenues typically plowed back into the purchase or construction of new systems. It is now faced with a fresh round of building necessary to upgrade its technology to provide for information superhighway services. At the same time, some analysts suggest cable penetration levels may have peaked and subscriber numbers may remain steady or even fall in the face of competition from the new multichannel competitors, especially DBS and wireless cable. Revenue streams from voice and data service are seen as one means to generate rising cash flow and to assure potential investors that the industry will remain a player in the twenty-first century. Developing these new businesses will not be an easy task, however, and, as we will see, many cable operators are moving cautiously.

Some Implications of the Emerging System

A variety of services, many already touched on, are envisioned in the developing system. They include multichannel television of the type most people are already familiar with, the programming networks like ESPN and Discovery. Additional specialty or "niche" programmers are waiting in the wings for the implementation of digital delivery technologies that will open up capacity and give them access to millions of U.S. homes. On-demand movies are especially seen as a significant source of new revenue, with subscribers ordering films at their leisure and controlling them, as described above, in ways indistinguishable from the control they have over their VCRs. Residential telephone service, business telephone service, fax, and data communication are part of the plan. Internet access has been an exploding market. The Internet promises all the interactive services once envisioned for cable— banking, shopping, education, games—but cable operators and others now see themselves as Internet providers.

The telephone and cable industries seek to use their wireline systems to provide services, but also look at wireless technologies. Wireless voice and data communication systems, including an advanced form of cellular telephone called Personal Communication Services, or PCS, are being built around the country. Systems already exist to deliver CNN news headlines over your pocket pager.

Eventually, futurists envision multimedia applications that give you remarkable control over your information environment. Advanced interactive software programs known as intelligent agents will allow you to send an electronic information collector out across the data libraries of the world to gather up to the minute details of any subject you fancy, from econometric analyses of welfare reform to recipes for brownies. The agents will analyze, synthesize, and package the information and have it all ready for you when you call it up, including written data, audio, and even video clips where appropriate. That kind of communication power and the provision of those kinds of services, along with showing you movies on HBO, is what contemporary cable and satellite industry development is all about.

These changes in technology, policy, and economics are also giving rise to a variety of issues involving the relationship between the new systems and consumers and citizens.

Control

One of the important policy debates involves the ownership and control of the developing infrastructure. Through the Telecommunications Act of 1996, Congress has endorsed a philosophy of government restraint in the regulation of media ownership. The law eliminates a variety of restrictions on broadcast and cable facility ownership. One of the consequences seems to have been a flurry of mergers and acquisitions among the companies in the affected industries. As form and function in the technology move toward convergence, industrial consolidation and concentration may follow, driven by economies of scale and scope and the market forces unleashed by deregulation. One method of generating the capital requirements to compete on a global scale is to join forces, creating ever larger companies. Such combinations involve horizontal and vertical integration, often both. Horizontal integration is the combination of companies across one level of business, manufacture or distribution, as when one cable system company acquires another. Vertical integration involves the merger of companies at different levels of the production–distribution process, as when a cable system operator buys a cable programming service. Such mergers and acquisitions are becoming more common across media industries, cable, satellites, and telecommunications.

Even before passage of the 1996 Act, the proposed merger of the country's largest cable company, TCI, with the RBOC Bell Atlantic sent shock waves through both industries. Many saw it as the first note in a symphony of coming combinations of cable and telephone concerns. The merger soon fell apart, but may have been only a short break in the trend toward industry consolidation. Shortly after passage of the 1996 law, another RBOC, U.S. West, announced the acquisition of Continental Cablevision, the nation's third largest cable company. In separate telephone company mergers, Bell Atlantic combined with Nynex, and the RBOCs SBC and Pacific Telesis joined. In cable, Time Warner purchased Turner Broadcasting, owner of CNN, TNT, and a stable of other cable properties, to create the world's largest media company (outside of the telephone industry). The nature and pace of concentration in the cable, satellite, and telco industries is of concern to many and is considered more closely in Chapter 5.

Globalization: Television without Borders

As the information superhighway is developing nationally, it is also expanding globally. The companies and industries discussed in this book are all very active internationally, the business of television and telecommunication is transnational. In

1996, British Telecommunications, Great Britain's principal telecommunications carrier, announced it would acquire MCI Communications, a major long-distance company based in the United States. For years, US West has had cable and telephone interests in Great Britain. Most of the major cable and satellite firms have operations around the globe and they are expanding steadily. MTV, CNN, and the Discovery networks, among others, have programming efforts in Europe, Asia, and South America. The hardware and software of the information age is increasingly oblivious to national borders, sometimes with the endorsement of sovereign governments, sometimes not.

Some governments have decided to privatize and liberalize their video programming marketplaces. The concept of Television without Borders typically means these governments agree that national security, sovereignty, cultural, and educational concerns no longer dictate that the government exclusively provide television service and that foreign broadcasts cannot be received. Having determined that private ventures in effect can compete with government outlets, nations, to varying degrees, permit competitors to import programming considered desirable by most consumers. Some government officials and members of the viewing public, on the other hand, have expressed concern about the social impact of imported programming. The concept of cultural imperialism stems from the view that such imported programming may make it harder for indigenous culture and video programming to survive. Currently, few nations fully embrace the concept of Television without Borders. Governments implicitly or expressly favor domestic content and some have imposed domestic content quotas.

Social Issues

Cable TV played a new role in the presidential elections of 1992 with candidates making appearances on everything from MTV to CNN's Larry King talk show. In the 1996 presidential elections, people turned to the Internet for information, and on election day Web operators reported up to five million "hits," or visits, per hour. Many of the most popular sites were those of cable and broadcast news operations. Multichannel television and the information superhighway have come to play an increasingly important role in our political, social, and cultural lives, and have been greeted with almost equal portions of hope and fear. Specialization of the media, for example, raises questions about the possible fragmentation of social organization, and the content of the media, especially violence on television, is a longstanding concern given new trajectory by cable and satellite TV.

Technological innovation raises broader questions of whether or not the coming "information age" signals a disjuncture from prior social epochs or is merely a continuation of existing social and technological trends. Likewise we will consider whether, in the broadest philosophical sense, we are better off with or without new communications technologies. Does the emerging system empower us to explore ourselves and our world more fully, or does it divide us into a world of information haves and have nots? Does it consign us to a media universe dominated by nothing more uplifting than sensational celebrity murder trials?

One of the interesting things about technological change, as the beginning of this chapter suggests, is that very often we do not know where it will lead. The inventiveness of the human imagination rarely fails to surpise us, and there are likely to be applications and consequences of the emerging system that no one dreams of today. As one might guess, then, there are a great many more questions than answers in this area.

SUMMARY

A guiding star for many of the early cable television operators, the cable pioneers, was the simple concept of choice. By bringing more channels of television to town, people had more TV choices, and it did not take long to discover that people were willing to pay for variety. It should not have been surprising. The concept of choice resonates deeply with a host of American cultural themes involving freedom, power, and the open marketplace of both goods and ideas.

Choices are now multiplying exponentially—choices in programming, choices in services, choices in providers. A shopping mall of electronic information and communications choices has opened up where once stood a handful of company stores. There remain important tensions surrounding the issue of who owns the new mall and questions about the relationship between the stores inside it; some are very competitive, many are controlled by the same interests. Some fear that, in time, the mall itself may revert to a company store. These remain open questions. One of the few certainties in the evolving media mix is that the system is currently in great flux. It is hoped that the following pages will help sort out some of the major themes and principal players in the fascinating story that is unfolding in television and telecommunications at home and around the world.

NOTES

[1]"Historic Telecast: Satellite Show Opens Cable TV Convention," *Los Angeles Times,* 19 June 1973, Orange County edition, 6.

[2]"Domsat show is high note of NCTA's all-stops-out convention," *Broadcasting,* 25 June 1973, 25.

[3]"Cable: The First Forty Years," *Broadcasting,* 21 November 1988, 42.

[4]Those that do, burn up in the atmosphere; others are sent out of orbit and into space. Some become useless "space junk" and a threat to other orbiting systems.

[5]WTBS, the original "superstation" (see Chapter 2), was scheduled to lose that status and become a basic cable service in 1998.

[6]Current estimates are that 97 percent or more of all homes are passed by cable (see Chapter 4), but the figure is debated by some, who suggest a slightly lower number.

[7]See John Pavlik, *New Media and the Information Superhighway* (Boston: Allyn and Bacon, 1996), 138–139.

[8]Ralph Lee Smith, *The Wired Nation, Cable TV: The Electronic Communications Highway.* (New York: Harper & Row, 1972).

2

A Brief History of Cable and Satellite Television

Consider what it might be like if today's system of delivering television to the home was owned and operated by the telephone company. As Chapter 1 points out, some telephone companies are interested in turning such a notion into reality and recent changes in the law have improved the prospects. But imagine growing up in an age when this was the norm, one in which your parents had always taken for granted the fact that AT&T brought them TV along with their telephone service.

Such a world, in fact, might have developed were it not for legal and policy decisions made by the Justice Department and the FCC in the 1950s and 1960s. The system we have today exists because particular business and regulatory actions were taken at certain times within specific technical and social contexts. At any point in the process, it is possible to say that it could have been different. The change in a political personality, a failure to advance in a technical field, or a different vote on the Supreme Court could have diverted the path of development. There are scenarios one could posit leading to the demise of the cable television industry in the late 1950s, or the blossoming of a wired infrastructure of multichannel national television in the early 1960s. The history of the cable and satellite industries is a story of staccato starts, stops, and changes of direction. Flashes of technological innovation, swings in the political climate, the ascension and downfall of industry leaders have all fed into the ever-changing stew of its creation.

Three main themes weave through the history: technology, economics, and policy. Technology has often been said to be the driving force in the development of cable and satellite television, but this is misleading. Technology itself is rarely motivational. The motivation of the individuals who built the industry has always been primarily economic. The search for business opportunities and profit lies behind the growth of the telecommunications system. A technology that does not promise to open new markets is a technology that will languish. Technology is better seen as an enabling force: It opens and makes possible opportunities that people seek to exploit. The nature of the technology will channel the system in a particular direction, but is not in itself causal. Regulatory decisions, meanwhile, exert a controlling, external force on development, promoting or retarding the evolution of the system. In theory, policy decisions counterbalance the potential excesses or deficiencies of a market-driven system. In practice, cable and satellite regulation has been an ever-changing kaleidoscope of philosophy and action.

The history, especially that of cable, has been organized in various ways. While all the expository schemes are moderately arbitrary, most follow similar lines. At the broadest level, they identify three epochs. The first, from cable's inception to 1975, characterizes cable television as a small-town retransmission service, a local business constrained by burdensome federal regulation; communication satellites for point-to-point signalling are launched in the 1960s. The second, from 1975 to 1996, sees the introduction of satellite distribution and the elimination of stifling regulation leading to the creation of today's cable–satellite distribution infrastructure. The third epoch has been heralded by the introduction of digital communication technologies and passage of the Telecommunications Act of 1996, which promoted competition by eliminating barriers to market entry. Within these broad classifications, moreover, one can distinguish finer historical demarcations. The following suggests eight stages in the growth of cable and satellite TV.

1. **Origins—1947: The "Pre-History."** The years during which the concept and the early technology of wire-based TV were set into place. This includes cable "protosystems" that presaged the creation of early contemporary cable operations.

2. **1947–1952: The "Pioneers" Phase.** The period when the first modern systems were established.

3. **1952–1964: The "Mom 'n' Pop" Phase.** The period when the business was characterized by systems emerging in small towns relatively free of regulatory interference. Complaints by broadcasters were turned aside by a free market FCC. In satellite communication, the United States launched its first orbiting repeater in the cold war "race for space."

4. **1964–1972: The "Freeze" Years.** The period when policymakers intent on protecting broadcasting placed numbing restrictions on cable that prevented it from penetrating larger cities and capped industry growth. At the same time, a concept of cable as an electronic town square gave rise to "Blue Sky" vision, foreshadowing the Information Superhighway, and a federal "open skies" policy paved the way for satellite operation by commercial interests.

5. **1972–1975: The "Thaw."** While business conditions and regulation still retarded cable, the rescission of FCC controls and the approval of domestic satellites sowed the seeds of a resurgence.

6. **1975–1984: Satellite Distribution.** The birth of a new national broadband system began with the launch of satellite distribution to cable systems, the reduction of regulatory restraints, and the dawn of cable–satellite programming, providing access to major markets with new products.

7. **1984–1992: Expansion.** Passage of federal legislation that had the effect of deregulating cable TV helped spark the rapid development of the industry, but was followed by a renewed pubic interest in controlling cable, especially subscriber rates.

8. **1992–1996: Control and Competition.** A period marked by the passage of two important pieces of legislation, the first controlling rates and slowing the industry's financial fortune, the second opening up all markets to new competition and ushering in the new era. Direct Broadcast Satellite services made real inroads in the market and telephone companies began testing broadband networks, largely free of regulation.

The following traces each of these stages. Throughout the journey it should be remembered that while great forces of technology, economics, culture, and politics have swept across the affected industries, in the end it has been people, individuals, who wrote the laws, made the business decisions, and strung the wire, and the story of cable and satellite TV is very much a story about people.

A PRE-HISTORY OF CABLE TV

The popular notion of the history of television sets the dawn of the medium in the early 1950s, at the start of TV's "Golden Age." The demand for TV was exploding, set sales were skyrocketing. Programming was epitomized by serious original drama and most of the stars of radio from the 1930s and 1940s had moved across the street and under the intense lights of the TV studios. Most of the country's television viewers had not heard of community antenna television in the 1950s. Many would not learn of CATV until the mid or late 1960s amid growing publicity about its potential as a "new communications technology," and even then, it would be something they read about rather than actually experienced. Television through a wire was not a reality for most people until the late 1970s. Television in 1955 was, as it had always been for the average viewer, a broadcast medium requiring some kind of antenna.

But seen through another lens, Community Antenna Television, CATV, was, from the beginning, an integral and in some ways inevitable component of a fully configured television system in the United States. CATV began almost at the very start of commercial television broadcasting; it was one of several methods America used in its rush to get TV. The first systems appeared in late 1950 and early 1951 (although earlier efforts are detailed below). In the early 1950s the number of cable systems doubled every year; by 1953 there were more community antenna systems

TABLE 2-1   Broadcaster and CATV Growth 1945–1955

Year	Stations	Cable Systems	% TV HH
1945	8		
1946	6		.02
1947	12		.04
1948	17		.4
1949	51	2–3	2.3
1950	98	10	9.0
1951	107	30–50	23.5
1952	108	70	34.2
1953	126	150	44.7
1954	354	300	55.7
1955	411	400	64.5

Sources: *Television and Cable Factbook* (Washington, D.C.: Warren Publishing, annual); *Broadcasting & Cable Yearbook* (New Providence, NJ: R. R. Bowker, annual); author's original research.

than there were broadcast television stations in the United States (see Table 2-1). In short, CATV accompanied, as much as followed, the development of broadcasting, although its trajectory was markedly different.

Insofar as cable constitutes communication by wire, its technological antecedents reach far back in history, predating even broadcasting.

Communication by Wire: Telegraph and Telephone

For centuries people have sought means of signalling across great distances. Flags, drums, trumpets, mirrors, smoke, cannon fire, and flares are only a few of the many ways in which we have tried to transmit information. The Roman Emperor Julius Caesar built a relay system in which messages were shouted from tower to tower for miles. One of the chief objects always has been speed, with the ultimate goal being instant communication. This was achieved only with the discovery of electricity and its application to communication.

Like so many other "firsts" in the history of communication, the first person to suggest the idea of using electricity for purposes of transmitting information is lost to us. The earliest published description of electric communication may have been contained in a letter appearing in *Scots Magazine,* in 1753. According to telegraph historian Alvin Harlow, the letter described a set of insulated wires, one for each letter in the alphabet, through which "electrical discharges should separately exhibit themselves by the diverging balls of an electroscope, or the striking of a bell by the attraction of a charged ball."[1]

A device of this type was demonstrated in 1774. It consisted of a bundle of twenty-four wires each representing one or two letters. As the operator on one end electrically "excited" the wire of a particular letter, its resonating partner at the far end of the device would be noted and a message spelled out. Similar devices became common in the late 1700s and early 1800s, and constituted the first telegraphs. These multiple and then single wire methods of communication were used in a variety of often imaginative forms. The most successful U.S. device was promoted by Samuel Morse, based on a magnetic transmission method and the code of dots and dashes that bears his name. By 1860 the first "wiring" of the United States was well underway as the telegraph line rolled out across the land.

Telephone Theater

Experiments with voice transmission by wire were also beginning in the mid 1800s. Alexander Graham Bell is credited with inventing, in 1876, the first practical apparatus for transmitting a live voice, beating a competitor, Elisha Gray, to the patent office by only a few hours. Interestingly enough, even in its earliest stages, the telephone had the capacity to provide many of the functions, in an audio format, now characteristic of cable television and in much the same manner. The telephone network that spread out across the world in the late 1800s had more flexibility to provide news and entertainment than we appreciate today. The telephone was used not just for a point-to-point method of interpersonal communication, but as an early form of mass media. Experiments with what was dubbed "theaterphone" or "electrophone" were conducted in Europe and the United States from the 1870s through the 1890s. By the end of the century, what media historian Carolyn Marvin describes as "performances by wire" were common.[2] Subscribers to telephone media services could listen to news, musicals, stock market reports, and even Sunday morning church services, from the comfort of their living rooms on these forerunners of pay-cable. In 1881 "wired broadcasting" carried concerts and plays from the Paris Electrical Exposition, and by the mid 1890s some European Opera Houses were equipped with telephone broadcast systems.[3]

Perhaps the most elaborate system of this type was built in Budapest, Hungary, and operated from about 1892 until World War I. Telefon-Hirmondo (Telephonic Newseller) began by delivering news programming, moving later into cultural fare, including plays, concerts, and even children's programming, all from the central telephone exchange. There was even a short-lived attempt in 1911 to import the Budapest system to the United States, although it succumbed to financial and legal difficulties.

These wire-based mass media systems were among the early predecessors of cable TV. Another important antecedent technology was the radio relay system.

Community Antenna Radio

Community antenna radio made its first appearance shortly after the start of radio broadcasting in the 1920s. These systems captured radio signals from the ether and retransmitted them over wire, usually for a fee. One of the first such systems in the United States was reported in the farming village of Dundee, Michigan, in 1923. *Radio Broadcast* magazine called it "municipal radio," a system in which radio was piped in "like gas or electricity" over lines operated by the local telephone company.[4] These systems never became widespread in the United States, but were commonplace in Europe by the start of World War II. The wire, usually a twisted copper telephone line,[5] carried amplified audio signals rather than radio frequency signals. They were quite popular in Great Britain for importing radio stations from the Continent.[6] In fact, by the time CATV was beginning in its modern form in the United States in the late 1940s, "radio rediffusion" had been a reality in England for more than twenty years.[7] Similar radio systems existed in Belgium, Sweden, Germany, Russia, Nigeria, and Malta.

Television by Wire and the Issue of Bandwidth

Television, like flight, is an ancient human dream. Its technical realization was first made possible in the 1870s by the discovery of selenium, a photosensitive material that varies its resistance to electricity under differing intensities of light, helping make possible the instantaneous transport of electric images.

One of the problems with images, however, especially moving ones, is that they contain an immense amount of information. The human eye is packed with thousands of receptors to decode visual data. Electrical and mechanical devices cannot replicate the sensitivity and capacity of the eye–brain processing connection. The conventional television picture tube in North America has 525 horizontal lines and 200,000 or more picture elements, small dots or squares each changing at a rate of 30 per second, but in some ways it is still barely adequate to convey what appears to be a moving image.

One of the challenges, therefore, of moving information instantly across vast distances has been the capacity of the replication and transport system. In every approach, the technology begins by dividing the original image into pieces, dissecting the picture and transmitting each small section separately. The smaller the pieces and the greater their number, the finer and more detailed the received image will be. Early attempts at signal transport used a kind of parallel processing in which the image would be divided by the camera and all the pieces sent simultaneously, each piece over its own circuit or wire to the receiver. Each circuit represented a separate sending and receiving cell, and a mosaic of cells built a full picture.[8]

An alternative to the multi-wire approach was to send the picture information sequentially, in a serial format, transmitting one picture element at a time over a single circuit. This involved scanning a picture, but doing it quickly enough that the eye's natural persistence of vision would see only the fully assembled image. The first reported scanning proposal appeared in the November 2, 1880, edition of *La Lumiere Electrique*. The more famous articulation of the scanning principle arrived several years later, when the German scientist Paul Nipkow filed a patent for a device to dissect the picture into its constituent parts using a disk perforated by a series of 24 holes set in a spiral pattern. Television historian Albert Abramson called the Nipkow disk the "master television patent."[9] Scanning remains a basic principal of television today. The challenge for television engineers since Nipkow has been to find ways to increase the number of lines that can be transmitted in a given time. The deserved fame attached to both Vladimir Zworykin and Philo Farnsworth—who worked independently and are each often credited with being the "father" of television—stems from the idea of taking Nipkow's mechanical concept and creating a method of scanning electronically, increasing the speed and capacity of the process. The amount of electronic space needed to transmit a given quantity of information is called bandwidth (see Chapter 4 for a detailed discussion). Pushing visual information through an electronic pipeline by either wire or broadcast, and finding ways to transmit ever more amounts by expanding available bandwidth or using it more efficiently, has been vital in the development of telecommunications.

AT&T and the Coaxial Cable

An early important example of efforts to increase transport bandwidth involved AT&T and the development of coaxial cable. As early as World War I, AT&T was working on what would become facsimile transmission, the electrical transmission of still pictures. It was interested in mining the market for the distribution of press association photography and had a viable fax machine by 1923. Encouraged by this success, the company started work, as early as 1925, on a similar technique for moving images. The company saw theatrical newsreels as the in-motion equivalent of newspaper still photos, and was keen to exploit its expertise in wire-based distribution.

Bell Labs claimed to have successfully televised, in the lab, its first motion pictures starting in June and July of 1925.[10] On April 7, 1927, it held the nation's first major public demonstration of television. AT&T linked its New York headquarters with the Bell Labs research facility in Whippany, New Jersey, and a studio in Washington, D.C. The transmission medium between New York and the capital was wire; the link to the Whippany site was by radio. The principal speaker in Washington was then-Secretary of Commerce Herbert Hoover whose image was seen on a tiny two-inch by two-and-a-half-inch receiver.

Even at this low level of visual resolution, the television information was more than could be accommodated by a standard telephone line. The company used separate circuits for voice, picture, and synchronizing data. Only by dividing the electronic stream and dedicating special paths for the different tributaries could the technology handle the necessary traffic.

The standard telephone cable was, and remains today, two copper strands twisted around one another and known as the twisted pair (see Chapter 3). To accommodate both television and the increasing amount of telephone traffic the AT&T system was experiencing, the company needed a new kind of wire.

The concept of coaxial cable was understood very early in the history of electrical communication; its first applications were in submarine telegraph lines. The electrical properties of coax, described more fully in Chapter 3, yield a significantly greater carrying capacity, or bandwidth, than does the copper twisted pair. In the 1920s Bell Labs began formulating plans, taking out patents, and testing coaxial cable. Happily, coax performed as well in the real world as theory said it would. By the mid 1930s AT&T had a coaxial circuit between New York and Philadelphia capable of carrying 240 telephone conversations or one 240-line television signal, a major achievement at the time. Successful testing led to eventual wide-scale deployment.

At the same time, AT&T abandoned plans to enter the television market as a theater distribution service, shifting its attention to interconnection services. It decided to provide transmission facilities for television networks in the same manner it served as the transmission backbone connecting the radio networks.

Bandwidth, Broadcasting, and the FCC

Meanwhile, radio broadcasters were also looking at the potential of television and facing similar issues. The government, through the offices of the Federal Radio Commission (FRC), forerunner of today's Federal Communications Commission (FCC), had to set aside spectrum space for television. In 1928 the FRC allocated several channels in the AM radio band for use by television experimenters. The selected channels were only 10 kHz wide, however, the same width as the standard radio channel and much too narrow to be of any real use to television. Over the course of the next nine years the Commission, responding to advances in TV transmission technology and broadcaster pressure, increased the amount of space for television and allocated new frequencies to provide more usable channels.[11]

In 1941 the Commission authorized the start of full commercial television service. About thirty stations quickly received permission to begin operations, but the plans of most were suspended within a year. The nation's deepening involvement in World War II meant its material and intellectual resources would be diverted to the war effort. Construction of television stations was halted. TV engineers turned their attention to radar and military communications and all but a half dozen television stations left the air.

The end of the war did not, however, signal the immediate resumption of commercial TV. The principle broadcast interests were engaged in a battle of standards. RCA had millions of dollars invested in VHF (very high frequency) transmission and in patents securing dominance in that technology. It wanted all television assigned to the VHF band (channels 2–13). CBS lacked the VHF patents and proposed moving television to the UHF spectrum (channels 14–82) where it was developing technology for color and high-definition black-and-white transmission. A 1945 decision by the FCC established thirteen channels in the VHF band, favoring RCA, but it left the door open to later development of UHF, especially for color. The apparent lack of a real decision stalled implementation of TV service nationwide. In March of 1947, the Commission finally seemed to settle the issue by denying a petition from CBS to develop a new UHF color format. The ruling, according to television historian William Boddy, "set off [an] explosion in television station licenses and receiver sales."[12] With the apparent resolution of standards, the television floodgates swung open, manufacturing plants readied themselves for mass production, and applications for television station licenses began once again to pour into the FCC. By the end of 1948 there were 78 different companies selling nearly 200 different models of television receivers. The affluent and the enthusiastic bought nearly 600,000 that year. An estimated 1,000 new sets were being installed every twenty-four hours.[13]

The land rush for TV licenses, however, especially for the larger, most promising markets, meant a landslide of paperwork for the FCC and raised important policy questions about the adequacy of the VHF allocation plan. The FCC, under increasing pressure to provide more outlets, reduced the permitted distance between co-located channels from its original 200 miles to 150 miles or less. Transmission theory at the time predicted stations on the same channel would not interfere with one another if they were kept 100 miles apart. But in practice, stations well over that distance were casting their signals into each other's markets and causing widespread interference. It was becoming clear that the VHF allocations alone would not be sufficient to satisfy demand or, given the interference problem, to establish a truly national system of broadcasting. The Commission also faced continuing pressure to address the problems of a standard for color television and to consider the needs of educational broadcasting.

On September 29, 1948, the FCC shut down the system. It needed time to sort out the increasingly tangled problems. The Commission issued a temporary ban on the allocation of television station licenses. The freeze was supposed to last six months; it lasted four years.

The 1948–1952 Freeze

The FCC, prior to World War II, had given commercial authorization to thirty-two stations. By the end of the war, only six stations were on the air. Between 1945 and the start of the FCC's freeze, more than forty new stations began operations and another fifty-five were granted construction permits. These were the only stations allowed to operate during the freeze, a total of about 108. During the freeze the FCC studied the various issues and in 1952 released its keystone Sixth Report and Order, assigning hundreds of new channels to the UHF band and apportioning those channels to towns and cities across the United States, typically on the basis of population with larger cities receiving more channels. The Commission also "intermixed" allocations so that many towns had both UHF and VHF channels.

For cable television, the freeze had two important consequences. First, community antenna operations began in earnest during this time, with many observers attributing the development of the small town CATV systems to the absence of local broadcast stations. The freeze was seen as a window of opportunity for CATV, but one that would evaporate when construction of broadcast stations resumed. Second, the FCC's allocation plan privileged a philosophy of broadcast localism, with a regulatory structure that attempted to insure that as many cities and towns as possible had access to at least one and preferably more broadcast outlets. As we will see shortly, however, the Commission failed to consider the economic requirements of broadcasting fully, and the resultant failure of the plan helped pave the way for the further spread of CATV.

The Problem of the Fringe

As television stood on the verge of becoming a consumer reality in the late 1940s, expectant viewers made ready. Even before the nearest television station was scheduled to go on the air, people were erecting all manner of antennas and antenna masts. Those who lived at the far edge of the signal and received just enough of it to get a faint picture often went to great lengths to seize the transmission. For a time, "DX-ing"—the reception of signals from hundreds of miles away on home-made equipment—was a popular pastime. Commercial manufacture of signal "boosters" was common. These were simple amplifiers inserted between the antenna and the TV set to increase signal strength.[14]

Community antenna television arose, along with technologies like set-top boosters, in the fringe areas where the new phenomenon of television was tantalizingly just out of reach. The booster, in fact, was one technical antecedent to CATV. Some of the earliest CATV efforts used modified or even off-the-shelf TV boosters strung together in long runs from the antenna site to the customer's home. Another technical precursor, and a model for some of the early pioneers, was the apartment house master antenna system.

Apartment master antennas were reported in New York City in the early 1940s, but didn't proliferate until after the war when renters, in reaction to the blossoming of TV, began installing private antennas on apartment rooftops. The possibility of a forest of antennas sprouting across the city, however, was of some concern to landlords, who had visions of lawsuits from fallen masts, tenant fights over the best spot on the roof, and an aesthetic nightmare of wires and metal. The obvious solution was a single antenna feeding all the flats in the building. By 1947 many landlords had banned individual aerials and were requiring master antenna systems.[15] Similar systems were produced for appliance store owners who needed to connect several showroom television sets to one antenna line. The basic concept behind community antenna television was so simple and in some ways so ubiquitous as to be, interestingly enough, unpatentable. At least one patent on something that resembled a CATV plan was registered in 1937,[16] but there has never been a record of an effort to protect it.

Shared antennas were not just a big city idea. The folklore of the mountainous coal country of eastern Pennsylvania, where the CATV industry first took root, suggests that it was common for individuals to run an antenna line down from the mountain, into their home and perhaps hook up a neighbor or two for good measure. The technical ability to capture, amplify, and distribute television signals moved to increasingly higher levels of sophistication as the systems advanced from storefront windows to apartment buildings to villages and towns. Cable was not, therefore, a technology that in any meaningful way was "invented." Rather, it was a logical extension of concepts and technology in existence at the time.

THE PIONEERS

With the above caveat in place, it is nonetheless possible to point to some of the first enterprises clearly recognizable as modern community antenna television systems.

L. E. Parsons.   The first business that included all the essential components of a contemporary CATV system and for which the historical record is undisputed is that of L. E. (Ed) Parsons of Astoria, Oregon.[17] Parsons began experimenting with distant reception of television signals after a trip to the National Association of Broadcasters (NAB) convention in Chicago in 1948 where his wife had seen a demonstration of television. According to Parsons, she had to have TV and told him he was the fellow who could make it possible.[18] Parsons had a background in electrical engineering and ran the local radio station, KAST. The nearest TV station, however, was KRSC in Seattle, 125 miles away. After some tinkering, Parsons was able to receive a usable KRSC signal off the air from an antenna on the roof of the Astoria Hotel, a short distance from his apartment house, and ran an antenna line to his flat. When KRSC officially went on the air Thanksgiving Day, 1948, Parsons and his wife Gracie were watching.[19] According to the story, the frequent visits by friends who wanted to see the only operating TV set within one hundred miles and even by strangers who stopped by unexpectedly, prompted Parsons to drop an extension line into the lobby of the Astoria Hotel.[20] When the lobby became too crowded with eager televiewers for the hotel manager, the antenna line was moved down the street to Cliff Pool's Music Store, where it was connected to a television set in the window. Finally, when the crowds in front of the window became too large for the comfort of the local authorities, the Chief of Police suggested to Parsons that he use the existing underground utility conduits to run the cable into the local bars. Soon most bars in downtown Astoria had a television set fed by Parsons's line. Demand drove the system from there.

Parsons had hoped to obtain permission from the FCC to set up a broadcast repeating station to relay the signals of the Seattle station via the airwaves, but his request was denied and he turned his attention to extending the cable system. People wanted the TV experience in their own homes, and soon they were asking, even demanding, that Parsons string his cable down their street. He had no city franchise and could not, initially, get permission from the telephone or the power and light companies to hang the line on their poles, so he tacked the cable to rooftops and trees. To cross a street he created low-power transmitting and receiving stations and actually broadcast the signal from one block to another. Within a few months, Astoria was wired with a patchwork system of coaxial cable running through underground conduits, through trees, across roofs, and occasionally being carried across the street by the low-power broadcasts.

Parsons charged a fee for his service and even began consulting on the construction of similar systems in nearby towns. National publicity led to letters from would-be TV fans around the country asking if they could set up a similar system.[21] Seeing the opportunity, Parsons established the Radio & Electronics Company of Astoria, with his business partner Byron Roman, to design, manufacture, and sell CATV equipment. From late 1949 until well into 1951 he responded to requests for information and orders for equipment. Within a few years he was physically exhausted, however, and the Astoria system was not faring well financially. In 1953 he piloted his small plane to Alaska on what was supposed to be a vacation, but he never returned to Oregon, and spent the rest of his years in and around Fairbanks, working on assorted radio and television projects. In the lower forty-eight, meanwhile, CATV was catching on.

Bob Tarlton.   Unlike Parsons, Bob Tarlton did not stumble into community antenna television. Along with other appliance dealers in Lansford, Pennsylvania, he had run a "twin-lead" line (a flat ribbon wire similar to those used to attach TV antennas today) down from the adjacent community of Summit Hill to feed TV signals into his shop. Lansford lies in a valley cleft between the ridges of the Appalachians, about seventy miles northwest of Philadelphia. The adjacent mountaintop community of Summit Hill could receive Phildelphia TV stations, but Lansford, shadowed by the steep ridge, could not. The bar owners on Summit Hill had been doing quite well, bringing in patrons by showing televised boxing and other sporting events, and it wasn't long before taverns in Lansford were running their own antenna wires down into town.[22] Tarlton, a radio and television dealer, helped install some of them. The technology was not complex and the appliance dealers regularly worked with antennas, boosters, and related equipment in the installation of home receivers. Tarlton also had experience installing apartment master antennas in the area. More importantly, Tarlton saw the business potential of a community system. He carefully recruited capital and well-connected partners from around Lansford. Together they founded Panther Valley Television.

Tarlton next needed equipment: cable, amplifiers, splitters, and similar material. In constructing master antenna systems for local apartment houses, he had used equipment from a Philadelphia company called Jerrold Electronics. Jerrold amplifiers were not designed for the demanding use to which Tarlton wanted them put, but he hoped to modify them for the job.

Jerrold was conveniently located for the cable pioneers of the coal region. It was a short trip to Philadelphia to pick up the equipment and one made by Tarlton frequently through 1949 and 1950 while he tinkered away. On one trip, the curious sales agent at Jerrold, Bud Green, asked Tarlton what he was up to. When Tarlton told him, Green, according to one story, asked Tarlton to sign a release pledging not to return the amplifiers in case they didn't work as Tarlton hoped. Green apparently was skeptical of the Tarlton plan, but he nonetheless told his boss, Milton J. Shapp, about it.[23] Shapp had founded Jerrold and was intrigued by Tarlton's scheme. In November of 1950, as Tarlton was busy with construction of his system, Shapp visited Lansford, grasped the potential of the idea and threw the support of the company behind the project.

Shapp and Tarlton began working together, and less than a month after Shapp's visit, the *New York Times* ran a small story on the Lansford cable television system.[24] About a week after that, a front page *Wall Street Journal* article, datelined Philadelphia, hailed the coming of the "community aerial."[25] The earlier trade press coverage of Parsons's system notwithstanding, this was the first real burst of national publicity for CATV.

Mahanoy City.   CATV systems quickly spread throughout the area. Shapp helped build a system in nearby Mahanoy City in late 1950, soon after Tarlton's system began operations. Mahanoy City may, in fact, have been the first city in the country to have competing commercial CATV operations. City TV Corp., founded by local businessmen and supplied by Jerrold, broke ground in September of 1950 and was operational by February of 1951. A second system was built and opened at about the same time by a local appliance dealer, John Walson, Sr.[26] Both systems offered two of the three available Philadelphia TV stations, but Walson was able to add the third station to his system in the summer of 1952, giving him a competitive advantage that City TV never overcame and the company eventually sold out to Walson's Service Electric Co.

In addition to operations in northeastern Pennsylvania, CATV systems were opening in northwestern Pennsylvania, picking up Pittsburgh television, in upstate New York and the hollows of West Virginia, pulling in signals from the Eastern Seaboard broadcasters. CATV pioneers, in addition to appliance dealers, included local broadcasters who saw CATV as a natural extension of their existing business. Department stores, which retailed TV sets, also were early providers of CATV service. A young man named John Rigas was running a movie theater in Coudersport, Pennsylvania, when he moved into CATV, acting on the advice of associates who warned him that the movie business would whither with the advent of TV. Eventually his company, Adelphia, would become one of the largest cable operators in the country.

The nearly insatiable demand for TV meant that as long as CATV could offer viewing opportunities beyond what was available over the air, people would sign up. The pioneers stepped in to fill a vacuum in local TV service. If it had not been Parsons, Tarlton, Walson, or Rigas, it would have been someone else. CATV was a business that, given the conditions of the time, almost had to happen.

By the beginning of 1951, community antenna television had taken root. Some thirty or more systems were operating by 1951, seventy by 1952. As new television stations went on the air following the lifting of the freeze, cable systems lit up at the edges of many broadcast signals. Some systems were the work of local business people. In the Pennsylvania communities of Franklin and Honesdale and Pine Grove, appliance dealers followed the lead of Tarlton, designing and building their own equipment. In other towns, cable was an idea imported by representatives of Milt Shapp as Jerrold fanned out looking for investment opportunities. There was only limited interest from established electronics companies. One of the significant exceptions was RCA. A Pottsville businessman, Marty Malarky, approached RCA about a system in his town and became the first to use the company's apartment master antenna equipment in a community system. RCA soon began producing antennas and amplifiers for the young industry, but it never matched the popularity of Jerrold Electronics, the undisputed king of early cable equipment.

Milton Shapp.   If anyone can lay a legitimate claim to being the "Father" of the cable television industry it may be Milton Shapp; at the very least he would be one of the first in line for the title. Shapp was an East Coast salesman and wholesaler of radio and electronics equipment. On a sales trip to Washington, D.C., after the War, he met a naval engineer named Don Kirk, who had designed a device to amplify the weak signals of television broadcasting, one of the early TV boosters. Kirk agreed to let Shapp manufacture and market the device as the Jerrold booster.[27] The Jerrold booster soon became the "Mul-TV" master antenna system, designed initially to be used by television dealerships to demonstrate their equipment. This system evolved into the Mul-TV Master Antenna system for apartment houses, the first one installed in an apartment house in Collingswood, New Jersey, in early 1950.[28] Shapp was soon wiring buildings in Atlantic City and elsewhere, and his efforts were heavily publicized, both by the industry press and by himself. By all accounts, he was a master of promotion and publicity. Following his 1950 trip to Lansford, Shapp directed his people to lend whatever assistance they could to Tarlton and made development of specialized equipment for the operation a company priority. Shapp, later in life, said, "I knew there was a pot of gold out there for Jerrold if we did things right."[29]

The equipment used in the early protosystems typically was handmade or modified from apartment systems and boosters, but those designs were not intended to carry a clean television signal for miles, and Shapp's engineers had to work out the special problems of a new technology. His products proved reliable and the market proved strong. Other companies soon followed Jerrold, most notably RCA and a company called Spencer–Kennedy Labs, but for years he remained the dominant supplier of equipment to the young industry.

Shapp applied his promotional talents as well as his engineering resources to CATV. There was very little money available to finance CATV in the early 1950s. It was a risky venture in the eyes of most banks. The people entering it were often untried, the technology was unknown, and there was a common assumption that once the freeze was lifted, demand would dry up. Shapp was one of the first to develop private capital for community antenna television, and was active in securing new franchises around the country. He would often recruit local businessmen to run the system and hold partial ownership for himself. He also set up a unique and controversial service contract that required operators who purchased his equipment to use Jerrold as the sole agent for maintenance and repairs. The price of the mandatory contract was twenty-five cents per subscriber and five dollars for each new hookup. Shapp saw it as a means of maintaining the integrity of his equipment; the government saw it as an illegal restraint of trade and filed an antitrust suit, eventually forcing him to end the practice. Nonetheless, by the late 1950s Jerrold Electronics was one of the largest suppliers in the industry and had interests in a number of cable systems.[30]

MOM 'N' POP: THE EARLY OPERATIONS

CATV grew rapidly from 1950 to 1955, expanding from fewer than a dozen systems to about 400. The vast majority of them were built by local entrepreneurs. Their business plans seem to have been solid since, by most accounts, nearly all of them began making money fairly quickly. The task of creating the business was not without its challenges, however. Some of the problems were similar to those of all start-up ventures, some were unique, including: finding capital, locating reliable suppliers, securing permission to use public and private rights of way, putting up an antenna, running wires, soliciting customers, and somehow keeping the whole thing from falling apart once it was built. Most of the operators were young, in their twenties, married, recently out of the armed forces, willing to take a risk and looking for an opportunity. One young couple was Bob and Betsy Magness who set up their first cable system in Memphis, Texas, in 1952. Magness had been a cottonseed salesman and part-time cattle rancher where he learned about a CATV system being built in a nearby town. The business sounded attractive and after some serious discussion, the Magnesses sold their cattle, mortgaged their home, and began what would eventually become Tele-Communications, Inc., the nation's largest cable company. At the start, however, the Magnesses, like the other pioneers, would find long hard hours ahead and more problems than they bargained for.

Financing came from local bank loans (sometimes secured with only the good name of the applicant), from family and friends, from second mortgages on homes, and occasionally from outside investors. While demand for service was often high, so was cost. Building a CATV system in the early 1950s took anywhere from $30,000 to $130,000, or more, depending on system size, with most of the money going toward the purchase of amplifiers and coaxial cable. Operators would string the cable themselves or, if they had the capital, hire crews from the local utility companies to work on weekends.

Operators charged $100 to S200 to install the service, a figure initially based on the equivalent price being charged to install a tall-mast television antenna. To assist new subscribers in finding the money for hookup (and build the business), operators were known to guarantee bank loans for new subscribers to cover the cost.

Relations with local officials were informal and though most operators obtained some form of franchise agreement, it was usually a simple device to indemnify the city from any problems or injuries associated with construction. Operators had to obtain access to power or telephone poles. Power companies proved more open to the idea than telephone companies. AT&T companies were especially resistant to having someone else's wire on their property. Eventually arrangements were made, with CATV operators typically paying a small fee for the use of each pole. In some instances, CATV operators found they could expedite pole attachment, franchise agreements, or a bank loan by taking on a utility official, city council member, or bank officer as a partner.

Maintaining the system once it was built had its own problems. In the earliest systems, power for the amplifiers was supplied by the subscribers themselves; a power cord was literally run from the pole into the home of the nearest customer, who in turn received the service free or at a discount. If the power went out in that house, or someone inadvertently pulled the plug, the entire CATV system from that point forward could go down. Operators also had to contend with weather. The co-axial system increased and decreased its resistance to the TV signal according to the temperature, and had to be manually adjusted as the sun rose and set. In the winter, snow and ice had to be knocked off wires and antenna lest the added weight pull down the equipment.

Over time, system-powered and self-adjusting amplifiers relieved many of the early problems, but the industry has always been labor intensive and the task of maintaining the system expensive and time-consuming.

The NCTA and the Birth of the Industry

The first commercial CATV systems began heavy construction in late 1950 and early 1951. By the fall of 1951, the Internal Revenue Service was knocking on their door. The IRS categorized CATV as a "communication by wire" similar to stock market quotation services and burglar alarms. As such it was subject to an 8 percent excise tax. The early operators, still struggling to establish their systems, were worried about the tax. Bob Tarlton, one of the first to be approached by the IRS called Marty Malarky. "Marty," he said, "we've got trouble."[31] Malarky began making phone calls, and on September 18, 1951, a small group of area CATV operators were sitting down in the dining room of the Neccho Allen Hotel in Pottsville, Pennsylvania, to consider their dilemma. The group decided the young industry needed a formal organization to represent it in matters such as the excise tax case, telephone company negotiations, and general information sharing. Initially calling itself the National Community Television Council, it soon changed its name to the National Community Television Association.

The tax problem was divided into two related legal issues and several cases. Operators were receiving revenue in two forms, the monthly fees for service and the installation charge. The industry split off the issue of the installation charge—then the largest portion of operator revenue—as a separate matter, arguing that it was not a charge at all but rather a subscriber "contribution in aid of construction," that is, a means of "bootstrapping" the creation of a system by taking the fees for next month's installation to buy the equipment for tomorrow's construction. Eventually the courts found against the industry on this issue, concluding that the money was indeed a charge for a private connection, not a contribution to a generally available public good.[32] The loss meant payment of a sizable back tax bill. But the case was not settled until 1958, giving many systems years of tax-free revenue. This grace period was helpful in freeing up the money necessary for establishment of early systems.

To combat the tax on subscription revenue, the industry argued that they were not in fact providing any form of active communication service, as with stock market quotes. They positioned CATV as a simple, passive extension of the customer's existing antenna. Operators, they argued, only provided a piece of equipment, they were not in any legal sense "carrying" a signal or engaging in any communicative activity. The position eventually proved successful, with an appellate court ruling CATV to be an extension of the customer's TV equipment, not a service subject to the excise tax.[32] Later, this technological–legal framework would protect cable from a much larger threat, that of copyright liability. In the meantime, the industry continued its steady growth.

Early Federal Activity and the FCC

The Federal Communications Commission knew about CATV through its contacts with Parsons and subsequently through the trade press. As public interest in the service grew, the Commission began receiving letters asking whether permission was required to start a system, and if so, what application forms might be necessary and what restrictions might apply. Broadcasters also were interested. Was CATV service subject to FCC oversight? If so, how would it be defined and regulated? Was it a common carrier, a retransmission service, a broadcaster? Under the Communications Act of 1934, the Commission was, broadly speaking, given the authority to regulate two kinds of services, the use of radio spectrum, e.g., broadcasting, and common carriage, whether by wire or radio. The former, under Title III of the Act, included services that used the airwaves (outside of military or governmental uses), especially commercial radio and television. The common carrier authority, Title II of the Act, primarily involved telephone and telegraph services. In order for the FCC to invoke authority, CATV might have to be declared a broadcasting service or a common carrier. Many people wanted to know which, if either, it would be.

To these requests, like the earliest ones sent by Parsons, Tarlton, and Walson, the FCC replied that it had, "as yet taken no position with respect to its jurisdiction over such systems, but that the matter (was) receiving attention, particularly with respect to the status of such operations under the provisions of Title II of the Communications Act, as amended, applicable to common carriers."[34] It was, in short, studying the issue.

There were several reasons for the FCC's lack of activity and perhaps lack of interest. Some of them involved the developing political philosophy of the Commission, which favored a free market approach to communications policy. More practically, the Commission at this time was still struggling with the much larger issue of the television freeze. It was putting together the pieces of the puzzle that would become the 1952 Report and Order, the master allocation plan for U.S. television. In the process of assembling this regulatory framework there was the aforementioned belief by some that CATV would vanish soon after the new allocation scheme was in place and broadcast television began lighting up the nation's towns and villages. Outside of a few internal memos on CATV, the Commission's only action came in response to specific complaints by broadcasters. Those complaints should also be seen in historical context. Overall, the CATV and broadcast industries had a reasonably good relationship through the early and mid 1950s. For many broadcasters,

CATV retransmission meant a larger audience on which to base advertising rates,[35] or at least broader exposure.

The allocation plan of the Sixth Report and Order, by privileging localism over diversity, created a situation ripe for exploitation by CATV. Because the FCC's scheme provided multiple broadcast signals for only the larger markets, many communities could get only one or two local broadcast signals. But the public wanted as much television as possible, and CATV offered one means of obtaining it, typically by importing a station from a distant town (a distant signal) into the local community. Broadcasters, and later the FCC, argued that such competition was a threat to the doctrine of localism on which the allocation plan was based. The genesis of the broadcasters' concern was much more practical, however.

There were several important dimensions to the problem. One involved property rights. CATV operators picked up a broadcaster's signal and charged a fee for redistributing that signal to customers. Broadcasters argued that the signal was their property and they ought to control who had access to it, or at least receive some form of compensation. In fact, section 325(a) of the Communications Act specifically prohibits unauthorized retransmission of broadcast signals. CATV operators were accused openly and repeatedly of being signal pirates and engaging in signal theft in violation of federal regulations. The property rights issue encompassed not just the physical broadcast signal but the intellectual property, the programming, as well. The programs, in legal theory, were protected by copyright laws that sought to assure the creators and owners of the material received fair compensation for their work. Broadcasters, through their network affiliations, helped pay copyright compensation; CATV operators did not.

The second major issue had to do with the potential competitive threat of CATV. Cable was accused of engaging in unfair competition. Broadcasters argued that because CATV received its signal, in essence its raw material, for free, broadcasters, who had to pay for programming, could not effectively compete for viewership against local CATV operations, especially in cases where the CATV operator allegedly would not carry that particular broadcaster on the system. At best, additional signals in a small community fragmented the audience base to the point that there was insufficient viewership to support local advertising. Advertising dried up and the broadcaster would be forced off the air.

This economic argument ultimately did not hold up. Through the 1950s only a handful of broadcast stations that failed blamed CATV for their troubles, and some studies suggested even those situations involved larger financial forces. The problem for most failed broadcasters was not CATV but rather that the FCC's 1952 allocation plan did not take into account the audience base necessary to run a successful commercial television station. Studies in the early 1950s predicted that network affiliated stations would need an unduplicated audience of between 25,000 and 50,000 to stay financially viable, a number far beyond what was possible for many small town broadcasters.[36] As policy historian Don LeDuc noted, the FCC's scheme provided the average applicant for a TV license in the entire state of Wyoming, for example, with an audience base of only about 3,600. There also was substantial confusion over the combination of both VHF and UHF stations in the same market. Few television sets at the time came equipped with UHF receivers. Viewers had to purchase an additional, and expensive, tuner to receive UHF signals and then switch back and forth between the UHF and VHF tuners to receive both signals. There was little public appetite to do so.

Belknap.   Several of these issues, which appeared practically on the heels of the industry's birth, would become the primary points of litigation for cable, in one form or another, over the next forty years. The FCC had an opportunity to address them as early as 1951 when a newly-formed business partnership, J. E. Belknap and Associates, in Poplar Bluff, Missouri, filed an application to import, via microwave, television signals from WMCT-TV in Memphis, Tennessee, about 150 miles to the south.[37] The partnership planned to operate the microwave relay as a common carrier, feeding CATV systems, at least one of them owned by Belknap. WMCT-TV protested the Belknap application, charging that it would represent an illegal retransmission of its signal. The Commission was additionally concerned about the common carrier status of the microwave system, which potentially had only itself as a customer. The issue never came to fruition, however. Belknap was reluctant to become a test case and separated its microwave and CATV activities, which was enough to satisfy the FCC. In May of 1954 the microwave application was approved.

Frontier Broadcasting.   The FCC's next opportunity to look at cable came in 1956, when a group of thirteen Western broadcasters, including a company called Frontier Broadcasting, filed suit against 288 CATV operators in thirty-six states.[38] The unserved and underserved markets of the West had long been a problem for television and the FCC. With an audience base insufficient to support a full compliment of stations, residents looked to other means for television. Cable was only one alternative. Local and regional TV enthusiasts and radio shop engineers installed broadcast repeaters and boosters to pick up the weak signals of distant stations and retransmit them into town, usually in flagrant disregard of the Communications Act ban on such activity. These nonprofit boosters and repeaters numbered in the thousands throughout the West and defied FCC attempts to shut them down. For several years cable operators saw competition from the illegal boosters as one of their primary concerns, after the excise tax. But while the booster activity helped lead to Congressional hearings on problems in television service in the West, they were never a serious competitive threat to CATV because there was no mechanism for turning them into a business. They survived on the goodwill and donations of local hobbyists, both of which lasted only until commercial broadcast or cable service came to town. The real clash was between the cable and broadcast industries.

The broadcasters who filed the 1956 complaint began by playing the common carrier card, arguing CATV ought to be regulated under Title II of the Communications Act and be subject to regulation of its rates and practices. Broadcasters claimed that CATV importation of large market signals into small towns would discourage advertisers from buying redundant time on the small-town stations. The local broadcast station, therefore, would eventually succumb to the CATV competitor, and the intent of the 1952 Report and Order would be frustrated. After nearly two years of consideration, the Commission responded to the complaint in April of 1958, issuing its first official pronouncement on the legal status of CATV. CATV, declared the FCC, was not a common carrier and did not fall within the jurisdiction of the Commission.[39]

The Commission also observed that CATV could not arguably be regulated as broadcasting since it used wires rather than radio transmission of signals.[41]

Beneath the surface logic of the FCC's decision was a deeper philosophical current, one that generally favored a market-based approach as opposed to government regulation. FCC Chairman John Doerfer was an Eisenhower appointee and an advocate of laissez-faire regulatory policy. He was keenly aware of the competitive threat of CATV in the smaller markets. For Doerfer, however, such competition was a natural and positive force in the marketplace.[42] It was the choice of the consumer as to which service would prosper and which would fail; the community would choose between the localism provided by the broadcaster or the variety provided by the CATV system.

Angered by the FCC's decision, broadcasters turned to Congress, which already was at odds with the Commission over allegations of corruption and malfeasance among some Commissioners (Commissioner Richard Mack was forced to resign in one influence peddling scandal). Sen. Mike Mansfield (D-Montana) announced he would call the FCC before his committee to explain its decision in *Frontier.* Bowing to the pressure, Commissioner Rosel Hyde announced at that year's convention of the National Association of Broadcasters that the FCC had already decided to begin a new study of the CATV "problem."

While the Commission was taking a second look at CATV, Senator Warren Magnuson held hearings on the issue of television service in smaller communities, with special interest in the role of cable.[43] After hearing from the Commission and representatives of both industries, the Senate Committee issued its report in December of 1958. Authored by committee counsel Kenneth Cox and immediately dubbed the Cox Report, it was generally hostile to the position of the FCC,[44] and it urged the Commission to expeditiously assert control over CATV. If the Commission failed to find it had authority to do so, it should immediately seek such power from Congress, stated the report.

The 1959 Report and Order.   Within a few months, the FCC issued its reply to Cox and the Senate Committee. Its April 1959 Report and Order was the most expansive and definitive statement yet by the FCC on its perception of the role of CATV in the national scheme of broadcasting.[45] The Commission either rejected or ignored much of the Senate's arguments and philosophy. The FCC could find no evidence that CATV presented an economic threat, and even if it did, the marketplace, it repeated, should be left free to operate. The FCC would restrict CATV or other competitive services when and only to the extent that a local broadcaster could demonstrate potential damage to the public interest, and the FCC would consider such complaints only on a case by case basis. It repeated its findings from *Frontier* that CATV was neither a common carrier nor a broadcast service. The Commission was sympathetic on the issue of retransmission consent, but found it had no authority to act and so recommended that Congress amend the Communications Act to extend the consent requirement to CATV. The Commission also saw merit in a provision that CATV systems be required to carry all local broadcast signals, although, again, the Commission felt it needed authorizing legislation from Congress. The decision was not a complete victory for CATV. The recommendation that Congress enact a retransmission consent law was especially unsettling.

S. 2653. Congress, driven by the political interests of Western Senators and their constituencies, as well as a concerned broadcast industry, was willing to draft legislation. Officials at the National Cable Television Association signaled their readiness to support a compromise, on the assumption that some legislation was inevitable and fearing the consequences of any new law that they could not influence. The bill that eventually emerged from committee, S. 2653, was a melding of prior proposals, one from the cable industry and one from broadcasting. Constructed primarily by Senate Communications Subcommittee Chairman John Pastore, the compromise defined CATV as a service subject to broadcast-like, rather than common carrier controls. It required all CATV systems to be licensed by the FCC under the public interest standard, with existing systems. It required carriage of local broadcast signals and provided for the development of rules to control duplication of programming. It did not require broadcaster consent for retransmission of the signal.

Broadcasters were rather quiescent on the proposal, perhaps in part because they got much of what they wanted, and what they didn't get—carriage consent—they were pursuing in the courts. The same was not true of the cable industry. Several major cable operators led by Milt Shapp and Henry Griffing, a cable TV and theater owner from Oklahoma, were opposed to the compromise and began a heavy assault on the legislation. In direct opposition to the advice of then-NCTA legal counsel E. Stratford Smith and Association Executive Director Edward Whitney, Shapp and Griffing conducted a mass mailing and telephone campaign to galvanize opposition to the proposed law. Whitney, Smith, and others argued that the compromise bill could be modified in the more cable-friendly House of Representatives and the NCTA had, in effect, reserved its right to oppose a bill that ultimately did not meet its criteria. The division led to a showdown within NCTA shortly before the bill was to come to the floor for a vote. Under pressure from Shapp and his allies, the NCTA changed its official position from one of qualified support for the legislation to unqualified opposition. Senators who had backed the compromise, especially Pastore, were shocked by what they saw as a cable industry betrayal. On the day the bill was brought to the floor of the Senate, cable operators from around the country crowded the Senate gallery while the legislation was hotly debated. With the cable industry in confused disarray, the bill lost its political steam. It failed by one vote and was sent back to committee where it died.

It was the end of serious Congressional consideration of cable legislation for nearly twenty-five years. Bills aimed at giving FCC authority over the medium were introduced in subsequent sessions, but none came to fruition. The FCC proceeded on its own, without the warrant of Congress, to rethink its position on cable and within a few years exert its authority.

Building the Business

Throughout the political upheavals of the latter 1950s and early 1960s, cable continued to grow. The technology was advancing, new money was being invested and operators were experimenting with programming, including early attempts at pay-TV.

Technologically, coaxial cable improved as companies began producing wires of differing gauges needed for specific applications in the system. Longer lengths of coax also were manufactured, making it easier to string miles of plant and improve reception. Broadcast signals need to be amplified at regular intervals along the coaxial line, but the earliest amplifiers were capable of carrying only one television channel at a time. To carry more than one station, a bundle of single "strip-band" amplifiers had to be assembled in bulky metal, or even wooden, containers. Even then, the amplifiers could not initially handle the "high-band" channels 7 through 13 (see Chapter 3). These higher frequency signals had to be converted to a lower channel. Broadcast channel 12, for example, might be converted to cable channel 3. The introduction of "split-band amplifiers" in the mid 1950s, capable of carrying both low band and high band signals, improved the situation. Eventually "broadband" amplifiers could read and amplify signals across the VHF television band.

Cable began to look a little less risky as a financial investment and lenders loosened their purse strings. Removal of AT&T as a potential provider of CATV services was helpful here. Many cable operators and some in the investment community had assumed that AT&T eventually would move into cable television, flexing its tremendous technical and marketing muscle and capitalizing on its established structure of poles and conduit into U.S. homes. The small entrepreneurs who had built the business would, according to this scenario, be quickly forced out. In 1956, however, AT&T signed a consent decree with the U.S. Justice Department following years of government investigation of the company's alleged monopolization of telecommunications equipment and services.[46] The negotiated settlement left the behemoth company intact, but under terms of the agreement, AT&T promised to stay out of any business other than common carrier communications. This included the provision of cable television service.

Cable pioneers like Shapp and Bill Daniels, one of the industry's first investment brokers, are among those credited with bringing new equity into the business, attracting investment from New York bankers and eventually some of the nation's largest insurance companies.

Cable systems, everyone soon found out, generated a great deal of cash from installation charges and monthly service fees. Very little was distributed in dividends. Most was plowed back into equipment and expansion. The high cash flow also meant the ability to service a great deal of debt. Early in its history, the industry found itself leveraging cash flow into new construction, acquiring more debt to build new systems. As the business expanded, total equity and stock value grew. The rapidly developing technology meant that existing equipment had to be replaced every five years, sometimes less. The accelerated depreciation on equipment kept taxes low and again made the business an attractive one. Consumer demand in communities that did not have three or four good broadcast stations remained high. As a result, the history books record exceptionally few failed CATV businesses.

Early Pay-TV

The idea of subscriber or pay-television dates back at least to AT&T's 1920s' vision of wired distribution of programming to theaters. In the 1930s Zenith began promoting what it called a Phonevision pay system that broadcast a scrambled signal that could be decoded and billed via a dedicated telephone line to the subscriber's home. Zenith actually tested the system in the 1950s in Chicago. International Telemeter Corp., a division of Paramount Pictures, experimented with a coin box service in the 1950s. A third company, Skiatron, was also active in promoting a pay-TV system. All three companies had to battle broadcasters and theater owners who reasonably saw the service as a serious threat. Lengthy FCC hearings were held throughout the1950s on the role pay-television would be allowed to play in the system.[47] In the end, massive political opposition coupled with unwieldy technology and consumer apathy killed early development of the service.

In cable, some operators experimented with local pay systems in the 1950s, only a few of them successfully. The first widely publicized cable trial of pay-TV was conducted on a small system in Bartlesville, Texas, in 1957 and 1958. The project was a joint venture of Shapp and Henry Griffing's Video Independent Theaters. Within a year, however, the Bartlesville project had folded. Area broadcast stations, responding to the pay-movie experiment, began airing scores of films and subscriptions never materialized in the numbers hoped for.

In 1963, a company called Subscription Television (STV), Inc., founded by a former Hollywood film executive, Matthew Fox, and run by Pat Weaver, previously the president of NBC television, made another attempt at pay-TV. The system, based on the licensed Skiatron decoder, used both wire and broadcast to distribute baseball games and movies to subscribers in San Francisco and Los Angeles. The possibility of STV's success was again perceived by theater owners as a serious threat to movie attendance and they launched a heavily funded publicity campaign to outlaw the service. Flying a "Save Free TV" political banner, the theater owners, supported by broadcasters, gained enough signatures to place a referendum on the 1964 California ballot that prohibited charging a fee for the delivery of a television signal to the home (referendum supporters were careful about the language because closed-circuit television events such as prizefights were shown in theaters). The measure passed. The courts overturned the law a year later, but by then STV had filed for bankruptcy.[48] For a time, pay-TV was dead. FCC regulations adopted in 1970 (see below) further restricted the potential of pay programming on cable. Only with the development of the satellite distribution system and the relaxation of regulatory controls did pay-TV start to play an important role in the business.

THE FROZEN 1960S

Despite its small-town success, cable's growth was limited by the nature of its product. The marketability of cable's only real commodity, retransmitted broadcast signals, was restricted to those communities without full access to broadcast television. As the number of broadcast channels increased, the demand for cable decreased. In cities with a full complement of network affiliates, cable could attract customers only by importing regional, independent stations (those stations not affiliated with a network). As cable entered the 1960s, federal regulations began to restrict cable's ability to import these signals and the industry was effectively locked out of the nation's larger cities.

Broadcasters had long argued that the FCC had authority to regulate cable operators who used licensed microwaves to import distant TV stations. When importation subjected the local broadcaster to competitive harm, claimed broadcasters, the public interest standard of the Communication Act, along with the FCC's doctrine of localism, were damaged. The use of microwave facilities for such purposes, therefore, could be prohibited or conditioned in such a way as to protect local broadcasting.

The Commission had responded to such arguments by declaring microwave transport to be a common carriage function and common carriers could not be restricted by the uses to which the signals were lawfully put. The Eisenhower FCC was unmoved by the argument that such importation might harm local broadcasting. In 1962 with new members, however, the Commission's interpretation of this point changed dramatically. In that year the FCC denied a request by the Carter Mountain Transmission Corporation to import via microwave a distant signal to a CATV system in Riverton, Wyoming,[49] a decision later upheld by the court. Turning the 1950s philosophy on its head, the Commission declared its intent to protect local broadcasters from competitive damage as a means of preserving local broadcast voices. Carter Mountain signaled the Commission's intention finally to bring cable under its jurisdiction. The Commission announced that cable operators would be denied microwave privileges unless they agreed not to bring in signals that duplicated existing local programming and guaranteed carriage of all local signals. Applications for microwave use would be considered on a case-by-case basis. These were the Commission's first formal restrictions on cable TV.

In 1965, the Commission extended the local carriage and nonduplication requirements of Carter Mountain to all cable systems that used microwave facilities. The FCC's First Report and Order imposed the "must carry" rules on all microwave-fed systems, and required carriage of any broadcast station within about sixty miles of the cable system. It also forbade duplication of local programming by imported stations, creating a window of protection fifteen days before and after a local program was aired.[50] More importantly, perhaps, a Notice of Inquiry and Proposed Rulemaking released with the First Report and Order declared that the Commission had authority to regulate even nonmicrowave affiliated cable systems and that it would hold further hearings to determine whether it should assert such authority.[51] Additionally, the notice erected a high barrier to cable expansion in large markets (those with four or more commercial channel assignments) by requiring any system wishing to import signals to demonstrate that the microwave grant would not threaten the development of UHF service in that area, a showing almost impossible to make.[52]

With its newfound adherence to a public interest standard that privileged local broadcasting, the Commission soon determined that cable television, whether or not it used microwave facilities, might pose a financial threat to the development of the national broadcasting system. In 1966 it released its Second Report and Order.[53] The pretense and limitation posed by the microwave linkage was abandoned. Reaffirming the language of the 1965 Notice of Inquiry, the Commission simply asserted that it had authority under the Communications Act of 1934 to regulate cable, whether or not the system was fed by microwave, and now had reason to apply that authority. Economic harm from CATV was assumed, and broadcasting was to be protected. Local carriage and nonduplication restrictions were extended to every CATV system, although the window of protection was reduced from thirty days to one. The Commission determined that it would not permit the importation of distant signals into any of the top one-hundred markets unless the cable operator could demonstrate that such importation would not threaten existing UHF broadcast stations. The rules were justified as a means of protecting the struggling UHF service that the FCC felt had a better chance of success in the larger markets. History, in fact, would demonstrate that cable eventually helped UHF gain parity with VHF stations and the 1966 rules served more to protect the interests of urban VHF stations than anyone else. FCC rulemaking throughout the 1960s, in fact, was designed primarily to protect big city broadcasters from the importation of distant signals that cable could provide. The rules, moreover, had greater potential to hurt small-town broadcasters more susceptible to competing, imported stations.

The FCC's Order effectively froze cable development in the nation's major markets and almost 90 percent of the country's television homes. In June of 1968, the United States Supreme Court upheld the FCC's authority ruling that cable constituted "interstate communication by wire," defined in section 152(a) of the Communications Act and therefore was subject to FCC regulation for the purposes of advancing the orderly development of the television system in the United States. In its decision in *U.S. v. Southwestern Cable Co.* the Court left ill-defined the limits of FCC authority, the only guidance coming in the admonition that such regulation be "reasonably ancillary" to the Commission's regulation of broadcasting.[54]

Copyright I

The disappointment felt by some in the industry following *Southwestern* was offset a few days later when the Supreme Court issued a second historic cable decision, this one on copyright. United Artists had sued two West Virginia cable systems, claiming they violated its copyright on certain programming. United Artists had secured the rights to a library of feature films it was then leasing to UHF stations, and the cable systems in question were carrying some of those UHF signals outside the broadcaster's licensed market. The case was one of cable's most critical. To lose the copyright battle would have meant that operators would have to begin paying for all the programming they took off the air, a multibillion-dollar prospect. Copyright liability would have meant the end of business for many and would have severely retarded the growth of the industry as a whole. Moreover, the record in the lower courts had not been promising. Cable had argued, along the lines of the 1950s tax cases, that it was not a communications service and did not "perform," in any sense, the copyrighted material. The performance distinction was central because liability for copyright was contingent on an unauthorized reperformance of the licensed work. Cable positioned itself as a passive retransmission device, an extension of the customer's home equipment. Both the District Court[55] and the Court of Appeals[56] ruled that cable carriage constituted a "performance" within the meaning of the law. But in a five to one decision, the Supreme Court sided with the industry.[57] Writing for the majority, Justice Potter Stewart explained: "Essentially, a CATV system no more than enhances the viewer's capacity to receive the broadcast signals; it provides a well-located antenna with an efficient connection to the viewer's set. . . ."[58]

Cable had won an important victory. It would not have to pay license fees for broadcast signal retransmission. The FCC, however, once again tightened the lid on industry development. In December of 1968 it announced it would no longer accept waiver requests from operators seeking to import signals into the top one-hundred markets and would deny those extant.[59] It stated that it was now satisfied that cable could pose a significant threat to UHF in major markets. It proposed regulations that would permit importation only when the cable operator gained permission from the originating station and further would entertain current requests for importation only from those operators already abiding by this proposed rule. A month later it clarified the ruling, in such a way as to make it virtually impossible for any cable operator to gain consent to import a signal. Instead of securing the permission of a station simply to retransmit its signal, a cable operator now was required to obtain permission for every program carried by that station and to obtain it from every party that had a property interest in every program, including the station, the network, the distributor, and the producer.[60] The retransmission consent orders, in practice, overturned the Supreme Court's copyright decision and ended any remaining hope for cable development in the top one hundred markets.

The Wired Nation

While the FCC was tightening the regulatory cords to fetter cable, a different force was at work exerting pressure to nudge industry evolution down a new path. Cable was becoming more widely known, especially among policy analysts and social observers, and was beginning to capture their imagination. The late 1960s saw the blossoming of what became known as the first "Blue Sky period," in which commentators saw cable as a technology pregnant with the promise of a broadband, interactive communication network that could help bind communities, deliver a wealth of human services from education to health care, and create a public forum for universal debate on the important issues of the day. It would displace the oligopoly held by the three major television networks and usher in a new era in television. New York City issued a report in 1968 praising cable technology and urging the construction of a citywide system that it saw as a potential solution of a variety of urban ills.[61] The same year the President's Task Force on Communication Policy released a paper calling for an enlarged role for cable in the national communications complex.[62] Similar studies, several of them produced in response to the FCC's request for comments on the future of cable, were published in the early 1970s.[63] Ralph Lee Smith turned a lengthy *New Yorker* magazine article into a book entitled *The Wired Nation,* a phrase and a vision that soon captured the public imagination.[64]

The period, in short, saw a dramatic change in the definition of cable television. Channel capacity had expanded and cable could now deliver, in most markets, a dozen channels, as opposed to the three or four that marked its debut fifteen or twenty years earlier. More important than the technology, however, was the new idea of cable. For purposes of copyright protection, the industry had labored to define itself as nothing more than an extension of the customer's antenna; the FCC had cast the service as little more than a adjunct or extension of the broadcaster's transmission tower. But what had earlier been a passive retransmission service was now being seen as an active participant in the communication process. In 1969 the FCC ordered all cable systems with 3,500 or more subscribers to develop a channel for local origination programming.[65] Part of the rationale was the value of cable as a means of local community expression, especially in service to minority interests. The origination rules were scheduled to take effect in 1971, but they were never implemented. Midwest Video won an injunction in district court blocking the order and a federal appeals court in St. Louis subsequently struck down the requirement.[66] On appeal, the Supreme Court reversed the appellate decision and affirmed the FCC's right to promulgate cable rules.[67] By then, however, the Commission had replaced its origination strategy with public access requirements. Those requirements, part of the FCC's 1972 rules (see below), required cable systems in the top one-hundred markets to provide at least three channels for public, government, and educational access and a fourth for commercial leased access (see Chapter 5 for details). Whether in the form of origination or access, the concept of cable television as a form of public service or a quasi-public utility, had begun to take hold. It would continue to play a role in policy thinking throughout the development of the industry.

The Telephone Companies

The Commission did help advance cable's cause in one area: its relationship with the telephone industry. While the 1956 Consent Decree had prevented AT&T from engaging directly in the provision of cable service, it left several loopholes for the Bell system and other local telephone companies. Bell companies were still permitted to build cable TV systems, then lease them back to cable operators who controlled the content. In this way, telephone companies managed to make some inroads into the business. Cable operators, however, complained that the Bell affiliates often demanded such high fees for rights to attach cable onto existing telephone poles that operators were forced to pay as part of the telephone lease-back option. By 1967 Bell System companies were leasing cable facilities in 178 communities. Moreover, the Consent Decree did not apply to independent telephone companies such as GTE or United Telecom, both of which set up cable subsidiaries to offer service in their areas. Concerned by their rising interest and market power, the FCC in 1966 ordered AT&T and GTE companies to seek Commission permission before constructing such systems,[68] and in 1970 issued an outright ban on the ownership of cable systems by telephone companies in their service area.[69] These regulations kept a powerful cable competitor at arm's length for more than two decades.

Despite the telephone rules, the overall effect of FCC activity through the latter 1960s was to position cable, to some extent, as a public service medium, but at the same time prevent it from growing as a commercial enterprise. It was prohibited from charging customers on a per-program basis, and was for most purposes cut off from the supply of content (imported signals) that would have allowed it to penetrate larger markets. It would take another change of Commission membership to crack the concrete the FCC had poured around cable.

Building the Companies

CATV in the 1950s has been called a "mom and pop" business, and for the most part this is an accurate description. Cable systems were locally run businesses in small towns. But as the business began to prove itself economically, larger interests gravitated toward it and ownership structures began to change. Some of the early pioneers built sizable holdings of their own. It was not until the 1960s, however, that the serious collection of cable systems and the early signs of industry consolidation began. The first large company to enter the industry as a new player was Irving Kahn's Teleprompter. Kahn, who began in the film industry, reportedly wanted to build a wire-based, pay-TV system to bring movies to homes on Long Island. He talked with AT&T about building the system, but the two could not come to terms so Kahn turned to cable. In 1960 he purchased a 750-subscriber system in Silver City, New Mexico, with the intent of testing his pay-TV concept there, but the system was so profitable as a retransmission service that the pay-TV idea was soon dropped and Teleprompter began buying cable properties. By the mid 1960s it was one of the largest MSOs in the country with fourteen systems, including a franchise in Manhattan, and more than 70,000 subscribers.

The largest multiple system operator in the United States, based on subscribers, was H&B Communications Corp. The company, then H&B American Corp., entered the CATV business in 1960. A manufacturing firm with no previous experience in cable, H&B purchased nine systems from Jerrold. By 1965 it had twenty-seven systems and more than 90,000 subscribers.[70] In 1964 entrepreneur and sportsman Jack Kent Cooke, one-time owner of the Los Angeles Lakers, ventured into cable television forming American Cablevision, and by 1965 controlled 70,000 subscribers across twenty systems. By the mid 1960s broadcasters were also moving into cable. Nearly 30 percent of all CATV systems were owned wholly or in part by broadcasters in 1966.[71] Cox Broadcasting and General Electric Broadcasting obtained franchises and began purchasing systems. NBC, Westinghouse Broadcasting, Gulf & Western, among others, bought cable properties or franchises. Time Life Broadcasting secured franchise rights to cities in Michigan and in the late 1960s and early 1970s began moving out of broadcasting and buying into cable. In 1970 H&B merged with Teleprompter, creating the nation's largest cable company. Compared to today's MSOs, which control hundreds of systems and millions of subscribers, these late 1950s and 1960s companies were quite modest, but they were the seeds that would grow into contemporary corporate giants.

In 1969, for example, Warner Bros. merged with a company called Kinney National Services, which owned an assortment of enterprises from car rental agencies and funeral parlors to National Periodical Publications, which published *Mad* magazine and DC comics. The company was headed by Steven J. Ross, who began restructuring the diverse holdings, selling off nonentertainment properties, and in 1972 investing in cable television. Warner soon became one of the nation's largest cable owners. In 1979 the American Express Company purchased half of the Warner cable properties and together they formed Warner Amex Cable Communications.[72] Warner Amex went on to develop a high-profile interactive cable system in Columbus, Ohio, called QUBE. While technologically primitive by today's standards, it allowed subscribers to order pay-movies and special events, look at stock quotes, and register votes and preferences during live, interactive TV programs. Warner Amex was also busy in program development, launching the Movie Channel (originally "Star Channel"), Nickelodeon, and MTV in the early 1980s. In 1989 Warner was acquired by Time, Inc. one of the nation's largest publishers and the owner of a chain of cable properties through its subsidiary, American Television and Communications Corp. (ATC). The combined company, Time Warner Inc., became the largest media company in the world at the time and the second largest cable MSO behind TCI.

TCI grew from the seeds planted by Bob Magness, who had built half a dozen cable systems by the mid 1960s and moved his company, Community Television, Inc., to Denver, Colorado. In 1968, Community Television merged with a small common carrier, Western Microwave, Inc., to form Tele-Communications, Inc. When the company went public in 1970 it was the country's tenth largest MSO. Two years later, Magness hired a young engineer-businessman named John Malone. Malone became President and CEO of TCI in 1973 and the company launched an aggressive campaign of acquisition and growth. By 1975 it was the second largest MSO with 149 systems in 32 states and in 1982 became the nation's largest cable provider with more than two million customers. TCI invested heavily in cable programmers throughout the 1980s, helping finance Black Entertainment Television, The Discovery Channel, and taking an equity interest in Ted Turner's programming services. The thick portfolio of programming assets was spun off into a separate company, Liberty Media Corp., in 1991. By the end of the decade, TCI was one of the most powerful forces in the industry. In 1970, however, those halcyon days were yet ahead.

THE EARLY 1970S: THAW AND RENEWAL

Policy analysts and historians Stanley Besen and Robert Crandall have offered a succinct description of cable's status at the beginning of the 1970s:

> Cable entered the 1970s as a small business relegated principally to rural areas and small communities and held hostage by television broadcasters to the Commission's hope for the development of UHF. The opportunity for cable to break these shackles occurred when Dean Burch replaced Rosel Hyde as Chairman of the FCC, several other Commissioners' terms expired,[73] and the Office of Telecommunications Policy (OTP) was established under Clay T. Whitehead.[74]

According to Besen and Crandall, Whitehead and Burch were more open to the possibilities of cable television and sought ways to ease its entry into larger markets. Other changes added weight to cable's position and set the stage for a slight easing of control. Expanding broadcast industry investment in cable was making it more difficult for broadcasters to take a monolithic position against cable development.[75] The cable industry itself continued to grow in small and medium-sized communities, from about one million subscribers in 1963 to 4.5 million in 1970, thereby accumulating a little more political influence in Washington. Cable operators also appeared more willing to compromise on the issue of copyright liability, a central concern for all parties. Economic studies conducted in conjunction with FCC proceedings on cable suggested that the dire consequences feared for broadcasters as a result of cable growth were not being realized.

The change of players and positions led to a negotiation process involving the affected industries, the FCC, Congress, and the White House. In the summer of 1970, the FCC issued wide ranging rules and proposals on cable TV. The rules included severely limiting the commercial possibilities of pay cable, especially the most attractive and profitable kinds of programming, movies, sports, and series. Meanwhile, Senator Pastore, Chairman of the Senate Subcommittee on Communications, and Representative Torbert MacDonald, Chairman of the House Communications Subcommittee, notified the Commission that no new rules should be promulgated without review by their subcommittees. In 1971 Burch sent a letter to Congress outlining the Commission's new proposals, most of which were again attacked by broadcasters, who took their case to the White House. Among the broadcasters' concerns were the long-standing issues of maintaining control of their own signals and the economic harm argument. The issue of copyright liability, however, was a problem only Congress could resolve and the parties agreed to move forward on new FCC rules while Capitol Hill worked out a solution to the intellectual property rights dilemma. President Nixon assigned Whitehead to act as arbiter in the dispute. Whitehead brought the parties together and forged what became known as the Whitehead Compromise, the foundation for a comprehensive rule set that the FCC released in 1972.[76]

The 1972 Rules

Under the new rules, cable systems were granted the right to import distant signals into major markets, but severe limitations were placed on the number and types of signals they could use. Systems were required to carry signals from all three networks and take them from the nearest network affiliate station. These "anti-leap-frogging" rules prevented a cable system from jumping over the nearest affiliate and importing a stronger station from farther away. Similar restrictions applied to importation of independent stations; if independent signals were imported from one of the top twenty-five markets, they had to come from one of the two largest markets closest to the system. The number of signals the system could import depended on the size of its market. Systems in the top fifty markets could carry three network and three independent stations. Systems in markets fifty-one through one hundred could import three network signals and two independents. Systems in markets below one hundred could carry three network signals but only one independent.

Broadcasters were protected by extensive nonduplication rules. Cable operators could not show a program from an imported station if a local broadcaster owned the exclusive rights in that market. Even if no such exclusivity contract existed, the retransmission of certain syndicated programs was prohibited in a complicated formula.

The new regulations required cable operators to file a Certificate of Compliance with the FCC before starting new operations or adding signals. They gave municipalities the right to control rates, but capped franchise fees at 3 percent. The FCC took control of rates for pay-TV. New systems were required to have at least twenty channels and two-way capacity, as well as one access channel if the system had more than 3,500 subscribers. Systems in the top one-hundred markets had to have four access channels (rules subsequently struck down by the courts).[77] Various technical standards also were applied.

For cable, the 1972 rules were a "half loaf" and subject to widely varying interpretations. Insofar as cable had been subject to an FCC freeze on development, the rules were characterized by many as a "thaw" and the Commission conceptualized the regulations as a liberalization. But while they lightened the burden for some operators, the restrictions remained stringent in the largest markets. Analyst Anne Branscomb wrote at the time that under the new regulations, cable could prosper in only seventeen of the nation's largest one hundred cities. Other observers agreed that cable was little better off under the new rules than the old[78] and some thought they were so restrictive as to signal the end of the industry.

The Economic Problem

While the wiring of many smaller markets continued, growth by other measures had stagnated in the early 1970s. The industry suffered a series of blows, some caused by a generally weak economy, some self-inflicted.

The cost of construction had skyrocketed, from $3,000 to $4,000 a mile in the 1960s to twice that for overhead construction and up to $50,000 a mile for urban underground installation. The recession made capital more difficult to obtain. Interest rates rose from around 6 percent in the late 1960s to 11 percent in 1973. Investors were hesitant. According to some observers, cable had failed to deliver on many of its earlier promises, making potential lenders cynical about the prospects for the industry. The public image of cable had taken a blow in 1971 when Teleprompter's Irving Kahn was found guilty of bribery and perjury in his attempt to obtain a franchise in Johnstown, Pennsylvania. Kahn admitted paying the mayor and a city councilman $15,000 to win the franchise, but claimed it was extortion. He served twenty-three months of a five-year sentence. Jack Kent Cooke, Teleprompter's largest shareholder, took control of the company in late 1972 but the following year the Securities and Exchange Commission suspended trading in the company's stock when it plummeted following a shockingly disappointing second quarter report and amid reports of an SEC investigation of possible financial improprieties (the MSO was later cleared of wrongdoing). Teleprompter, cable's largest MSO, slashed its operations and construction budget. Wall Street quivered and the value of most of the industry's firms plunged: ATC dropped from $39 to $9 a share; TCI went from $19 to $3; Cox from $31 to $4, and Teleprompter itself dropped $31 to $3 a share.

Cable continued to wire small communities around the country, but the regulatory barriers of the previous years had prevented it from penetrating the major markets and therefore most of the viewing public. Penetration in 1975 was only 13 percent. Through its pay-TV rules the FCC further had limited cable in its ability to develop a salable product beyond imported signals. With cable clearly bumping its head on the ceiling, investors became scarce.

Reregulation

The tide began turning for cable very soon after the 1972 regulations were released. The political philosophy of the 1970s was retreating from one of strong government regulation to a partially deregulatory view. By 1974 Congress had begun hearings on the deregulation of a number of industries, including airlines and trucking, and the White House had identified excess regulation as a source of higher prices and therefore inflation. After three years of study, a White House committee, headed by OTP's Whitehead, recommended a "separations policy" for cable that would deregulate the cable industry but at the cost of separating the content from the conduit and making cable a de facto common carrier on all but a few channels.[79] In 1975 President Gerald Ford made a commitment to deregulate the communications industry. The House Communications Subcommittee issued a report in 1976 severely critical of the 1972 cable rules,[80] and the President's Counsel of Economic Advisors attacked the FCC's restrictive policies. In the midst of this climate, the FCC in 1974 created the Cable Reregulation Task Force to review its policies.

The result was a series of small but telling modifications to the cable rules. The Commission, for example, decided that cable systems could begin importing an unlimited number of distant signals during periods when local stations were not on the air.[81] In 1976 it allowed the unrestricted importation of foreign language and religious programming.[82] Systems with fewer than 1,000 subscribers, about 40 percent of all the operations at the time, were exempted from all exclusivity and signal carriage rules in 1977.[83] The Commission cancelled its prior order mandating new construction and setting standards for minimum channel capacity, and it eased many restrictions on smaller cable systems. Significantly, it dropped its anti-leapfrogging rules, allowing systems to import signals from anywhere in the country,[84] paving the way for the development of the cable "superstations."

The major change in cable's fortunes did not result from the FCC's piecemeal elimination of terrestrial importation rules, however. The revolutionary change in regulation, technology and business revolved around the rise of the communications satellite.

LAUNCHING A NEW ERA IN TELEVISION

The United States launched the world's first active orbiting communications satellite in 1962. The AT&T-built Telstar operated in low earth orbit, thereby requiring very expensive and large earth stations that "tracked" the satellite as it sped overhead. Despite a limited start, Telstar represented a major part of a campaign by the

United States to regain supremacy in space, previously held by the Soviet Union, which had launched the first artificial satellite, Sputnik, in 1957. By the end of the 1960s, the FCC had articulated an "open skies" policy favoring competitive domestic satellite service and imposing a seven-year moratorium on AT&T's entry to forestall the potential for market domination.[85] Congress passed the Communications Satellite Act of 1962 that created a domestic enterprise, the Communications Satellite Corporation with a mandate to organize a single, global communications network. Comsat established and initially managed a global cooperative that became the International Telecommunications Satellite Organization (INTELSAT). The United States landed a man on the moon in 1969, and U.S. companies dominated all market segments in the construction and launch of non-Soviet commercial satellites.

While the U.S. initially may have been slow to realize the potential of space, it responded with vigor. U.S.-sponsored research and development made it possible to launch the Syncom 2 satellite into geostationary orbit in 1963 and the first international satellite, Early Bird, later relabeled Intelsat-1, provided 240 voice circuits or one television channel in 1965. This satellite carried the first memorable live international television events including an address to the United Nations by President Johnson, Pope Paul's visit to New York, and a concert by the Beatles.

U.S. broadcasters and satellite manufacturers quickly realized the commercial opportunities that satellites presented. In 1965 Hughes Aircraft Company teamed with ABC to propose that the FCC establish policies, rules, and regulations for domestic communication satellites. ABC sought to free itself from the costly and burdensome point-to-point microwave services provided by AT&T. A single domestic satellite could illuminate the entire continental United States, providing an instant and simultaneous connection to all of ABC's network affiliates.

The FCC started its inquiry into domestic satellite policy in 1965, but could not resolve the mostly political issues regarding the nature and scope of satellite competition until 1972. On one hand AT&T and Comsat had been instrumental in developing commercial satellite telecommunications. On the other hand, without regulatory safeguards, these companies could so dominate the incipient industry that competitive market entry might not occur. The Commission also expressed ambivalence at having private, noncommon carriers provide service, such as allowing ABC to construct and operate its own satellite in lieu of leasing capacity from an unaffiliated common carrier.

The FCC finally opted for a modified "open skies" policy whereby it would allow any financially, legally, and technically qualified applicant to provide service. The Commission qualified its open entry policy by limiting AT&T initially to service to the U.S. government, and by placing separate subsidiary requirements on Comsat in its provision of domestic services in addition to its key role in INTELSAT.

Western Union, RCA, and AT&T soon after applied for domestic licenses. By the time the FCC had established licensing policies, Canada had launched its own commercial communications satellite, "Anik." With relative speed, satellite transponder demand grew and a variety of new ventures sought licenses to provide domestic satellite service for fixed and broadcast services.

Home Box Office

With the opening of a communications network in the sky, the technology was in place for a new kind of cable television and it did not take long for someone to turn on the switch. Sterling Manhattan Cable was founded in the mid 1960s by Charles (Chuck) Dolan and was partly owned by Time, Inc. Time had poor luck with its cable properties and was selling them off. Sterling Manhattan was a prime candidate for the auction block. Most residents in its franchise area of lower Manhattan received reasonable reception with a standard TV antenna. There was little demand for cable and the company was a financial disappointment, so much so that Time was unable to find a willing buyer. In an effort to salvage the operation, Dolan proposed a plan to add a pay channel consisting of live sports events and old movies. To assist in the new venture, Dolan brought in a young attorney named Gerald Levin, who had ties with Madison Square Garden and experience in negotiating contracts for the distribution of sports events. Together they convinced Time management to support the project and the corporation created Home Box Office, with Dolan as president and Levin as vice president.

HBO's first client was John Walson's Wilkes-Barre, Pennsylvania, system, which debuted the service on November 8, 1972, showing a hockey game from Madison Square Garden followed by the film *Sometimes a Great Notion*. HBO's first original production, The Pennsylvania Polka Festival, originated from Allentown, Pennsylvania, on March 23, 1973.

It was a promising but not overwhelmingly lucrative enterprise. Sterling Manhattan Cable itself was not equipped to receive the HBO signal and fell into even deeper financial trouble. In 1973, Dolan left the company and Levin took over as president. HBO distributed its programming via microwave to the small systems in nearby Pennsylvania and upstate New York, but the cost and technical complexity of expanding the live microwave signal beyond the Northeast seemed to block further growth.

In 1973, however, the FCC, consistent with its Open Skies policy, approved applications for the construction and deployment of five domestic comsats, including Satcom 1, and Levin saw the opportunity for satellite-delivered cable programming. Teleprompter was already taking the lead in testing the viability of a satellite–cable distribution scheme. It had purchased a custom-made $100,000 receiving dish from Scientific Atlanta, which delivered the dish to the 1973 NCTA convention in Anaheim, California. As described in Chapter 1, HBO, in conjunction with Scientific Atlanta and Teleprompter, had arranged for one of the first demonstrations of the new technology. Cable executives gathered in the HBO suite at the Disneyland Hotel to watch the satellite-fed Ernie Shavers–Jimmy Ellis title fight. The bout lasted less than one round, ending with a quick knockout punch from Shavers, and many missed it entirely. The system, however, was a proven success.

In April of 1975 HBO and its affiliated systems unveiled plans at the NCTA convention in New Orleans for the new satellite distribution system. The operational debut was September 30, 1975. A UA–Columbia Cablevision System in Fort

Pierce–Vero Beach, Florida, and an ATC system in Jackson, Mississippi, were signed to receive the first transmission, the heavyweight title fight between Muhammad Ali and Joe Frazier, beamed from Manila. Teleprompter pledged over eighty systems to the new service and other operators soon followed.

HBO's efforts were initially hampered by the regulatory system. In 1970, the FCC had applied restrictions on the delivery of pay-cable programming to prevent "siphoning" of content away from broadcast TV.[86] In response to protests of those rules, the Commission opened a three-year rule-making proceeding that culminated in 1975 with the announcement of new guidelines, which continued to be heavily restrictive.[87] Cable could offer movies or pay services such as HBO only if the films were between three and ten years old and as long as films had not been broadcast in the last four years in the operator's market. The order permitted the use of television series that had not been aired on broadcast television, but unbelievably complex carriage restrictions discouraged use of sports programming.

Important legal victories subsequently opened the potential for pay-cable. In 1977 the Court of Appeals for the District of Columbia struck down the FCC rules on pay-cable, in a challenge to the regulations by HBO. In *HBO v. FCC,* the court ruled that the FCC had exceeded its authority and failed to present sufficient evidence to justify the regulations. The case ended federal limitations on the material HBO and others could purchase and distribute.[88] In late 1976 the Commission approved a request that cable operators be allowed to use smaller dish antennas to receive satellite signals.[89] Existing regulations required dishes of 10 meters (about 30 feet) across, but the cost of the receivers—about $100,000—was more than most small operators could afford. Permitting the use of dishes as small as 4.5 meters meant a significant reduction in cost to less than $25,000 and brought the satellite program distribution system within the means of most cable operators. As a consequence, the number of systems with earth stations rose from 829 in 1978 to more than 2,500 in 1980.

The HBO telecast of the "Thrilla in Manila" changed forever the economics of cable television. As HBO began signing up systems and customers for a regular schedule of uncut, uninterrupted films and sport events, it was raising the curtain on a new era in national telecommunications technology and business.

Copyright II

The copyright problem had plagued cable from the beginning. Because cable operators did not pay for the signals they retransmitted, they were considered by many to be taking unfair advantage of a loophole in the technology and, following *Fortnightly,* in the law. Through the 1960s, a number of efforts were made to revise the existing Copyright Act of 1909. In 1971, during the regulatory negotiations with cable, a bill was introduced in the Senate[90] to create a compulsory license, granting cable permission to take off-air distant signals without obtaining direct permission from the broadcaster or copyright holder. In return, the operator would pay a fee.[91] The bill, however, died on the vine.

Meanwhile, CBS had filed a copyright suit against Teleprompter. The broadcast network attempted to distinguish its case from *Fortnightly* by arguing that Teleprompter had used microwave hops to import the signals at issue, constituting a more active "performance" of the programming than was the case in *Fortnightly,* in which use of a simple antenna receiver was judged as a passive act of reception. CBS lost its argument in federal district court, but the Court of Appeals, in 1974, upheld the suit. The decision shook the cable industry, but the Supreme Court soon reversed the appellate decision, essentially on the same grounds it had used in *Fortnightly.*[92] Cable was again innoculated from copyright liability.

The decision, however, helped re-energize Congressional efforts to revise the ancient copyright law. As part of a wholesale revision of copyright, cable finally was held responsible for the use of broadcast programming. The compulsory license was adopted for all broadcast signals, local and imported. Cable operators would pay a royalty based on system size, market, and use of each imported signal (see Chapter 7 for details). A newly created Copyright Royalty Tribunal would be responsible for making adjustments in the fee schedule and the Library of Congress Copyright Office would collect the money and distribute it to the various claimants including broadcasters, film studios and producers, and sports interests. Liability under the act took effect January 1, 1978.

It was a new financial burden on the industry, but like many of the other regulatory reforms of the time, helped establish cable as an economically and legally more stable and therefore more viable business.

BLUE SKIES, REDUX

The settlement of the copyright problem, the elimination of restrictions on pay cable, the accelerating movement toward a free market regulatory philosophy, and the demonstrated success of the national satellite distribution system all combined to herald a new beginning for cable television. Among the first signs of renewed life were the stirrings of what would become the cable software industry—the new programming services.

In 1975, a young broadcaster and yachtsman who had inherited his father's outdoor billboard sign business and a struggling UHF independent in Atlanta, Georgia, heard about HBO. It sounded promising to Ted Turner. Before the end of the year Turner had launched WTCG (later renamed WTBS), joining HBO on Satcom 1 and servicing four cable systems. The simple plan of the country's first "superstation" was to expand to a national audience base and sell advertising at commensurate rates.

Pay providers and religious channels were first to follow in exploiting the satellite system. Madison Square Garden began using the satellite in 1977 to distribute sports programming and by 1980 it had evolved into the USA Network. In 1978 Viacom began satellite distribution of Showtime, shadowing the success of HBO; Pat Robertson's Christian Broadcasting Network ordered sixty Earth stations from

Scientific Atlanta and launched a twenty-four-hour cable feed; Chicago's WGN television followed Turner as the next cable superstation; and UA–Colombia announced plans for a children's channel called Calliope. In 1979, Brian Lamb, a one-time government official and trade press reporter, talked the industry into supporting a public affairs and information satellite service to cover Congress, opening the U.S. House of Representatives to the nation's television viewers; C-SPAN launched in March of that year. Among the first advertiser-supported networks to take to the satellite, along with USA, was ESPN. Backed by capital from Getty Oil, ESPN launched in September of 1979. Warner–Amex began Nickelodeon in 1979, and Turner announced plans for a twenty-four-hour all-news cable channel. The Cable News Network (CNN) began operations the following year, as did the Black Entertainment Network (BET).

Deregulation

At the FCC, Chairman Charles Ferris helped launched two economic studies to examine the relationship between local cable operators and broadcasters and the impact of Commission rules on the financial health of local broadcasting. Both studies, the Syndicated Exclusivity Report[93] and the Economic Inquiry Report,[94] were released in 1979 and both came to a similar conclusion: Cable television could not be shown to have a serious deleterious financial impact on local broadcasting. Cable constituted, at most, a minor threat to profitability and no threat to the public interest. The Commission determined that it no longer had any grounds on which to base its signal importation restrictions and syndicated exclusivity rules. Despite furious protests from broadcasters and some concerns by sympathetic Congressmen, the Commission repealed the rules in July of 1980, sweeping away the remaining principal components of the 1960–1970s rulemaking.[95]

Franchising Wars

The tumbling of the federal rules and the rise of new programming products meant that cable could at last move vigorously into the major markets, and it did, sometimes with unforeseen and unfortunate consequences. Cable broke into the urban markets, offering new packages of movies, sports, and broadcast signals imported from around the region and across the country, adding C-SPAN, CNN, and local access to the mix. The competition to acquire lucrative big city franchises, such as Pittsburgh, Boston, Chicago, and Denver, was intense. The situation was soon dubbed "the franchising wars." Cable operators competed among themselves for the exclusive rights to wire the metropolitan areas. They negotiated, pleaded, and sometimes clashed with city officials and local cable advisory boards over the nature of the system to be build and the service to be provided. Many systems ultimately promised much more than they could deliver in order to gain the franchise. As *Broadcasting & Cable* magazine later observed: "The attitude of the most aggressive operators was to promise anything to win the franchise and worry about fulfilling the promises later."[96]

City officials shared culpability for the excesses of the period. Driven by the utopian rhetoric of some social commentators and the very real needs of their local communities, city fathers and mothers demanded the most advanced forms of cable technology and perks that were at best only tangentially related to communications. Cities examined bidders for the most channels, the lowest rates, the greatest commitment to public access service, and the fanciest institutional networks. Cities typically privileged local interests in franchise negotiations. Applicants who could demonstrate local ownership, at least in part, had an advantage over those who did not. This led to a practice on the part of some operators of finding a prominent community member, preferably one with influence on the city council, and making him or her an investor in the system, even if it meant loaning them the money to do so. It was dubbed "rent-a-citizen."

The results were predictable. The franchising process became mired in unsavory publicity, winners often were unable to fulfill the franchise obligations and came back to the city council later to renegotiate. By then, of course, the incumbent system was entrenched, or becoming so, and many municipalities changed the original terms of the agreement. Losers in the franchise wars occasionally filed suit against both the winners and the city.

THE CABLE–SATELLITE EXPLOSION OF THE 1980S

In the absence of strong federal control of cable and in the turmoil of the franchising wars, the cable industry and the local municipalities tangled over issues of state and local regulation. In the vacuum caused by retreating federal oversight, the cities moved in to adopt local rules governing system size, programming content, subscriber rates, ownership, and other requirements. Cable, in turn, sought avenues of relief from the growing trend toward state and local control.

The Cable Communications Policy Act of 1984

Representatives of the cable industry sought repeal of such regulations through federal legislation aimed at abolishing the controls or at least limiting the power of the cities. The political lobbying group for the nation's municipalities, the National League of Cities, sought to repel these efforts and in return fight for a federal bill that would formalize and legitimize municipal regulation of cable. Legislation was introduced in 1982 and 1983 to establish, for the first time, a Congressional framework for federal cable policy. Representatives of the cable industry and the NLC met throughout early 1983 in negotiations over language that would satisfy both parties. Congress was looking for a compromise. The talks culminated in passage of

BOX 2-1   Summary of Provisions of Cable Communications Policy Act of 1984

- Cities were authorized to grant, and cable operators obligated to obtain, operating franchises.
- Cities were permitted to require Public, Educational, and Governmental (PEG) access channels.
- Systems with more than 36 channels had to assign 10 to 15 percent of capacity for commercial (leased access) use.
- Telephone companies were forbidden to own cable systems in their service area.
- Franchise fees were authorized, but capped at 5 percent.
- Federal and state regulation of basic and pay cable rates was prohibited.
- Local regulation of basic rates was allowed only in the absence of effective competition.
- The FCC's Equal Employment Opportunity (EEO) broadcast guidelines were extended to cable.
- Signal theft was made a crime subject to fine and imprisonment.
- Guidelines were established for the carriage of local public and commercial stations.

the Cable Communications Policy Act of 1984, the first federal legislation establishing general governmental authority over cable television (see Box 2-1).

The Act represented the product of a long and acerbic debate between the industry and the cities and, like most good compromises, made neither party especially happy, but held something of value for both. For the cities, it finally offered a statutory stamp of approval on the franchising processes, the core ability of cities to issue licenses and claim some level of legal oversight, a power the industry had challenged. The Act also sanctioned local franchise fees, allowing cities to maintain an auxiliary flow of revenue. The bill set limits on the fees of 5 percent of gross revenues, protecting the cable operator from subsequent increases and the cities from any effort by the FCC to reduce or eliminate them. The act also permitted cities to require access channels for public, educational, and governmental entities ("PEG" channels).

For cable, the act limited the types of control municipalities were allowed to exercise, preventing local authorities from interfering in programming decisions (such as requiring certain entertainment channels or prohibiting an adult service), or attempting to regulate cable as a common carrier. The law also gave less latitude to city officials in considering franchise renewals; renewal was nearly automatic unless the cable operator failed to abided by a specific list of basic service and legal requirements. Most importantly, it prohibited state and federal regulation of nearly all subscriber rates, authorizing local regulational of basic rates only in cases where "effective competition" did not exist. The Act then left it to the FCC to determine what constituted "effective competition" and the Commission did so in such a way as to insulate nearly all local systems from local control (see Chapter 6 for details). Cable had been subject to franchise agreements that specified rates for basic services, pay channels, installation fees, and services charges. For the most part, cable was now left free to charge whatever the market would bear.

The Surging Market

The 1984 legislation technically was not an act of deregulation, but rather a shifting of regulatory authority from the states and cities to the federal government. Nonetheless, it had the effect of loosening control and its passage was in some ways seen as a capstone in the deregulatory phase of the industry. By providing a single, federal framework for regulation, it gave the industry legal stability. Within that stability most of the primary controls perceived as onerous by cable and the investment community, including restrictions on programming and subscriber rates, were stripped away. Furthermore, laissez-faire regulatory philosophy was at high tide in Washington, D.C., and there was no reason to suspect the FCC or Congress would attempt to endrun the new regulations or revive the old. To the extent that the Carter administration and FCC Chairman Ferris had moved to reduce oversight of cable, the election of Ronald Reagan in 1980, and his subsequent selection of Mark Fowler to head the Commission in 1981, accelerated the process. Fowler, an enthusiastic free market champion, vowed to "unregulate" both cable and broadcasting and began a vigorous campaign to slash controls.

The policies and politics provided fertile ground for increased investment in cable and an unprecedented period of industry expansion both in programming and system construction. The same forces that drove the franchise frenzy in the major markets—a relaxed regulatory climate and increased programming—also drove expansion and amalgamation on a national scale. The recession of the early 1980s, with its soaring interest rates, dampened some forms of direct investment, but encouraged others. The cable industry began serious exploration of creative financing and acquisition; system trading, limited partnerships, and, above all, mergers, blossomed. Many of the largest MSOs joined to become even larger and new media entrants injected fresh capital into cable. In programming, Viacom's Showtime merged with the Warner–Amex Movie Channel to challenge the dominance of HBO and its sister service, Cinemax, and new programmers announced start-ups almost daily. From 1976 to 1987 the number of satellite-delivered programming services grew from four to over seventy, the number of systems increased from 3,681 to 7,900, penetration rose from 15 percent to over 50 percent, and revenues climbed from about $900 million to nearly $12 billion.[97]

The free market logic of Congress and the FCC rested on the assumption that cable service would grow and rates would be kept in check as a result of competition from broadcasters and, more importantly, from what were then seen as developing alternative multichannel delivery systems, including the burgeoning VCR and videotape rental market, MMDS, and DBS. The regulatory climate favored these market-based solutions and sought to support the development of new technologies and new businesses. In the mid 1980s, however, with the exception of the VCR market, the multichannel delivery systems envisioned by policymakers were not yet mature. Broadcasters did not offer the variety of content necessary to create widespread cross-elasticity of demand; the videotape rental market was cutting into premium service but did not have the same effect on basic cable; and technological and business conditions were not yet ripe for MMDS or DBS. The direct broadcast satellite industry, for example, was stutter-stepping through the decade.

Direct Broadcast Satellites: The False Start

From its rocky and tentative start in the 1960s, the domestic satellite market grew to become a profitable and dynamic industry in the 1970s and beyond. But the success enjoyed by AT&T, Comsat (in its international service), Hughes, and General Electric (which bought out RCA), was not shared by others. Many proposed ventures never became real and other venturers wished they never had attempted to become satellite operators. The failures provide insight on the importance of video programming, the technical limitations of satellites, the sovereignty of consumers, and the relentless efficiency of markets. By the end of the 1970s and early 1980s, it became quite clear that consumers would avoid satellite-delivered voice telephone service if given the chance.

A small but profitable industry grew up around home reception of video signals being distributed nationally by satellite. Using twelve-foot, or larger, dishes operating in the C-band (see Chapter 3), television enthusiasts could receive HBO, nationally distributed sports programming, in fact virtually anything on one of the satellites. More than 3 million such dishes were operating by the mid 1980s. The signals were not, at least initially, however, intended for home reception. With all the emphasis on video programming, it appeared quite reasonable to think that a business case could be made for dedicated Direct Broadcast Satellite service to homes. In the early 1980s, companies like United States Communications, Inc., (USCI) a subsidiary of Hubbard Broadcasting, and Satellite Television Corporation, (STC) a subsidiary of Comsat, attempted to serve the millions of households lacking access to cable television. But again most consumers voted with their dollars and opted for terrestrial options. Their decision making was sound and ironically other types of satellites supported the case for cable-delivered options. The companies attempting such service proposed to offer fewer than ten channels at rates at or above what cable operators offered for thirty or more channels.

The first generation DBS operators sorely underestimated the speed and scope of cable television market penetration and the importance of local broadcast television to consumers. The DBS operator could only offer a limited range of choices, without any provision for carriage of local broadcast stations. Until such time as satellite service could match cable's channel capacity, at a competitive price, satellite television would be restricted to rural areas where cable was not available.

In the case of first generation DBS, the pioneers failed to execute on a concept that made sense in a business plan, but that failed in the marketplace. The next generation of DBS, which evolved fully ten years later, would have the benefit of higher powered satellites, small, mass-produced, low-cost Earth stations, digitization, signal compression, and access to a rich source of programming.

CONTROL AND COMPETITION

Through the mid and late 1980s then, the hands-off approach of policymakers and the failure of alternative distribution industries left the multichannel video delivery business largely the sole domain of cable television. The industry took advantage of the opportunity to move aggressively into new markets both geographically and in terms of content. The growth was not, however, without its price, figuratively and literally. The cable industry faced significant pressure to increase its cash flow. It was highly leveraged, having secured massive financing for necessary expansion. It had to show reasonable return on investment if it was going to service its debt and continue to develop.

The result was what some critics characterized as an orgy of price gouging as operators nudged their subscriber rates up a bit more each year. The industry defended the rate increases, pointing to rising programming costs from the emerging programming services, inflation, construction costs, and the need for capital to continue expansion. In fact, programming costs were going up as program services began charging cable systems for content instead of paying operators for carriage. Some operators argued that their rates on a per-channel basis had remained stable or even decreased, if inflation and increased program channels were figured in. Nonetheless, angry consumers faced with what they perceived as spiraling cable bills were not persuaded and their concerns reached back to Congress.

In 1989, Congress's General Accounting Office issued a report finding that basic cable rates had risen about 29 percent over two years. Overall subscriber rates (including pay channels) had risen 14 percent.[98] Moreover, in presenting the study to Congress, the GAO spokesman declared that cable was probably a monopoly in need of regulation.[99]

The Cable Television Consumer Protection and Competition Act of 1992

The political mood in Washington had swung once again, this time away from the Reagan–Fowler cry of caveat emptor. Cable was now perceived as a flinty monopolist, weak on service and strong on pricing. Congress enacted the Cable Television Consumer Protection and Competition Act of 1992. It contained a number of items fiercely opposed by the cable industry. President George Bush, along with others, saw it as overly regulatory and burdensome and vetoed the legislation, but Congress overrode the veto (shortly before the President lost his bid for reelection).

Among the provisions of the bill were requirements that the cable industry adhere to certain service standards, such as answering telephone calls in a timely manner and installing new service expeditiously. It also required program providers to make their content available to alternative distribution services, such as wireless cable. Rules governing the ownership of home wiring, restricting indecent programming over access channels, and expanding job categories for purposes of Equal Employment Opportunity reports also were enacted. Ownership limits on cable were adopted but later struck down by the courts.[100] The most far-reaching provisions, however, dealt with rate regulation and the carriage of local broadcast signals. In the case of the former, the FCC was vested with the responsibility of controlling subscriber fees and launched a series of complex, even confusing proceedings and rules that rolled back cable rates for several years. Details of the rate regulation are discussed in Chapter 6; for the industry, it meant a significant drop in cash flow, revenue, and the ability to obtain capital. The act also had a profound impact on the relationship between the cable and broadcast industries.

Must Carry and Retransmission Consent

While the 1984 Act culminated a period of deregulation for the industry, it left one long-standing requirement in place, the obligation of cable systems to carry local television stations. While cable operators, for obvious business reasons, carried most local stations, especially network affiliates and popular independents, the requirement had created some problems. Carriage of all available local signals, including the weaker independents, ate up channel capacity and occasionally prevented operators from adding new networks. Cable owners also argued that the rules interfered with their ability to choose the content they wished to carry and therefore constituted a violation of their First Amendment rights. In 1986 and again in 1988, a federal appeals court struck down the FCC's must carry rules primarily on these constitutional grounds.[101]

Broadcasters, however, rode the wave of public dissatisfaction with cable rate increases into the 1992 Cable Act, and successfully lobbied to reinstate the must carry regulations. The new law required systems with more than twelve channels to set aside up to one-third of their capacity for local signals. Broadcasters argued that cable had abused its power, dropping or denying carriage to local stations. Cable operators countered that many of the reporting systems were dropped to comply with reimposed syndicated exclusivity rules or from fringe systems, and paid carriage typically came from shopping channels. They argued that the FCC report largely overstated the nature of the problem.

Broadcasters, nonetheless, won the right to negotiate to be paid for their signal. In effect, the Act gave powerful local broadcasters (i.e., ones with highly desirable content) the ability to demand payment for their signal and weak operators the right to demand carriage. They could not have both—one could not demand carriage and payment—but they could choose either. It was intended to give the broadcaster significant market power over cable operators.

The cable industry again appealed the rule, but this time a specially convened three-judge federal panel upheld the law. Their decision was split and ambiguous, with one jurist holding the rules constitutional, one unconstitutional, and a third expressing some doubt about the requirements but, to avoid a judicial stalemate, privileging Congressional authority. In an initial look at the question, the high court upheld the economic theory behind the law but sent it back to the lower panel for a final consideration.[102]

In the meantime, broadcasters were given an opportunity to bargain with local operators for carriage. While visions of dollar signs danced in the heads of network executives, the cable industry, led by some of the larger MSOs, drew an economic line in the sand. They declared they would not pay and would be willing to drop network affiliates if necessary. Networks desperately wanted the second revenue stream and a tense period of broadcast–cable negotiations ensued. In the end, it was the broadcasters who blinked. Broadcasters failed to negotiate direct payments as a result of the 1992 Act. Instead, they settled for something that may prove more lucrative in the long run: channel space. When they could not get money, they used the law to leverage a guaranteed channel on most cable systems, giving them the opportunity to start their own new cable networks. From this strategy ABC launched ESPN-2, and NBC started the CNBC spin-off *America's Talking* (which later was transformed into MSNBC). Fox began the fX network. Independent broadcasters and station groups struck deals with new networks, as in the Scripps Howard–Home and Garden TV combination. Other independents worked out agreements for carriage of possible future programming, looking forward to a time when digital transmission would give local broadcasters multiple channels (see Chapter 3), or simply settled for local cross-promotions, ad sales alliances, or coproduction efforts.

CBS, which had held out for direct payment and refused to bargain with the cable industry for channel space, was left holding an empty bag at the end of the negotiation period. The system operators refused to pay and CBS had to offer carriage without compensation. In 1996, when broadcasters were given an opportunity to renegotiate following the first mandated three-year agreement cycle, CBS, under new Westinghouse management, was ready with a proposed new service, "Eye on People." Eventually, the law worked its way back up to the Supreme Court which, in a 1997 decision, finally upheld the must-carry rules on a five-to-four vote.

EPILOGUE

Within a few years of the passage of the 1992 Act, DBS had begun national service and digital technologies were opening up the potential for wireless cable to offer the kind of service previously available only through a wire. The Internet and the Information Superhighway were making daily headlines and the pendulum of politics was moving again. The Telecommunications Act of 1996 (detailed in Chapter 7) repainted the landscape.

Whether it was an evolution or a revolution, cable had changed the face of television. It initially extended television's reach. Later, with the expansion of carriage capacity and the introduction of satellite distribution, it extended television's scope. Because of its ability to provide more channels, more information, and more entertainment, and because of the growing demand in society for increasing amounts of each, wire-based transmission technology probably was inevitable; broadcasting alone, even digital broadcast platforms, cannot provide the speed and capacity necessary for the requirements of the information society. The infrastructure of broadcast was, historically, cheaper and easier to build and by virtue of broadcasting "getting there first" it could leverage its entrenched economic dominance into political power, thereby delaying the full deployment of cable technology. However, as deployment was achieved and use of the wired system began to outpace that of broadcast, one could start to recast the life history of television. Cable or cable-like transmission systems were moving from an ancillary service to a dominant distribution mode. Analog broadcasting, in the long run, may even be seen as the transitional technology.

NOTES

[1]Alvin Fay Harlow, *Old Wires and New Waves: The History of the Telegraph, Telephone and Wireless* (New York: Appleton-Century Company, 1936), 39.

[2]Carolyn Marvin, *When Old Technologies Were New, Thinking About Electric Communication in the Late 19th Century* (New York: Oxford University Press, 1988), 209.

[3]Elliot Sivowitch, "A Technological Survey of Broadcasting's 'Pre-History,' 1876–1920," *Journal of Broadcasting* 15:1 (1970–71): 1–19.

[4]Grayson Kirk, "Supplying Broadcasts Like Gas or Electricity," *Radio Broadcast,* May 1923, 35–7.

[5]Or a double twisted pair, or "star quad" formation, in post-war years.

[6]Ralph Negrine, "From Radio Relay to Cable Television: The British Experience," *The Historical Journal of Film, Radio and Television,* 4:1(1984): 28–48.

[7]Kenneth Easton, *Thirty Years in Cable TV: Reminiscences of A Pioneer* (Mississauga, Ontario: Pioneer Publications, 1980), 15.

[8]See, e.g., description of a multi-wire "mosaic" device using small separate squares of selenium. *Nature,* 21 April 1880, 10.

[9]Albert Abramson, *The History of Television, 1880 to 1941* (London: McFarland & Company, 1987), 13.

[10]Abramson, 78.

[11]In October, 1937 the FCC moved TV out of the short-wave band and gave it nineteen new channels, seven of them in the lower 44–108 MHz region and twelve in the higher but as yet technically unexploitable 156–300 MHz range. The channels were 6 MHz wide, enough bandwidth to carry the new electronic TV signals.

[12]William Boddy, "Launching Television: RCA, the FCC and the Battle for Frequency allocations, 1940–1947," *Historical Journal of Film, Radio and Television,* 9:1(1989): 54.

[13]"Young Monster," *Time,* 3 January 1949, 31.

[14]Technically the fringe was defined as the area in which the over-the-air signal dropped below a strength of 100 microvolts and the boosters would hike the signal to a usable level.

[15]"Television Antennas for Apartments," *Electronics,* May 1947, 96.

[16]Louis H. Crook filed a patent in 1937 for a method of delivering television to the home via telephone cable. The patent was granted in 1940 (Application #2,222,606).

[17]No relation to coauthor.

[18]Oral History with L. E. Parsons, National Cable Television Center and Museum, Pennsylvania State University and University of Denver.

[19]The station ran experimental transmissions prior to its formal inuaguration and Parsons obtained written permission to intercept the test signals. Oral History, L. E. Parsons.

[20]Mary Alice Mayer Phillips, *CATV: A History of Community Antenna Television* (Evanston, IL: Northwestern University Press, 1972).

[21]*Sylvania News,* November, 1949.

[22]Ed Gildea, *Valley Gazette,* March 1988; Oral History with Robert Tarlton, National Cable Television Musem and Center, Pennsylvania State University and University of Denver.

[23]Shapp's company derived its title from his middle name, Jerrold.

[24]Jack Gould, "TV Aerial on Hill Aids Valley Town," *New York Times,* 22 December 1950, 30 LT.

[25]Michael Saada, "Stretching Television: New 'Utilities' Deliver TV to Towns Outside Usual Reception Range," *Wall Street Journal,* 3 January 1951, 1.

[26]The popular press and even some academic writers have credited Walson with starting a system in 1948 and even founding CATV. The historical evidence, however, does not support this legend. See, Patrick Parsons, "Two Tales of a City," *Journal of Broadcasting & Electronic Media,* 40:3 (Summer 1996): 354–365.

[27]"My View: Milton Jerrold Shapp 1912–1994, *CED: Communication Engineering & Design,* February 1995, 78.

[28]Phillips, 35.

[29]Milton Shapp, Unfinished draft of autobiography, National Cable Television Museum and Center, Pennsylvania State University and University of Denver.

[30]Shapp sold the business in 1966 and went into politics, becoming a two-term governor of Pennsylvania in the 1970s.

[31]Tarlton, Oral History.

[32]*Teleservice Company of Wyoming Valley v. Commissioner of Internal Revenue,* Tax Court (27 T.C. 722), and Federal Appellate Court (254 F.2d 105).

[33]*Lilly v. United States,* 238 F.2d 584 (4th Cir. 1956); and *Pahoulis v. United States,* 242 F.2d. 345 (3rd Cir. 1957), reversing 143 F.Supp. 917 (W.D., Pa. 1956).

[34]See, U.S. Senate, Committee on Interstate and Foreign Commerce. *Television Inquiry Part 6: Review of Allocations Problems, Special Problems of TV Service to Small Communities.* 85th Cong. 2d Sess., 1958, p. 3490, (1952 FCC memo).

[35]Although the idea did not always work out that well in practice because local advertisers were not interested in distant customers.

[36]Don Le Duc, *Cable Television and the FCC: A Crisis in Media Control* (Philadelphia: Temple University Press, 1973), 65.

[37]Belknap and Associates filed applications with the FCC for two experimental microwave relay stations, one in Osceola, Arkansas across the Mississippi River and about forty-five miles from Memphis and another in Kennett. The Belknap relay would be a common carrier feeding the Poplar Bluff CATV system, also owned by the Belknap partnership, and a proposed CATV system in Kennett, operated by a separate company, the Kennet Distributing Co. See, U.S. Senate, Committee on Interstate and Foreign Commerce, *Television Inquiry Part 6: Review of Allocations Problems, Special Problems of TV Service to Small Communities.* 85th Cong. 2d Sess., 1958, pp. 4120–4127.

[38]*Frontier Broadcasting v. Collier,* 24 FCC 251 (1958).

[39]*Frontier,* ibid.

[40]*Frontier,* 254.

[41]*Frontier,* 256.

[42]John Doerfer, "Community Antenna Television Systems," *Journal of the Federal Communications Bar Association,* 14 (1955): 13.

[43]U.S. Senate, *Television Inquiry Part 6,* 4120–4127.

[44]Kenneth Cox, Special Counsel on Television Inquiry. "The Television Inquiry: The Problem of Television Service for Smaller Communities." Staff Report prepared for the Comm. on Interstate and Foreign Commerce, U.S. Senate. Committee Print. 85th Cong. 2d sess. Dec. 26, 1958.

[45]Inquiry into the Impact of Community Antenna Systems, Report and Order, 26 FCC 403 (1959).

[46]*United States v. Western Electric, Co.,* 1956 Trade Case (CCH) 68,246 (D.N.J., 1956).

[47]Richard Gershon, "Pay Cable Television: A Regulatory History," *Communications and the Law,* June 1990, 3–26.

[48]See, David Ostroff, "A History of STV, Inc. and the 1964 California Vote Against Pay Television," *Journal of Broadcasting,* 27:4 (Fall 1983), 371–386.

[49]Carter Mountain Transmission Corp., 32 FCC 459 (1962); aff'd *Carter Mountain Transmission v. FCC,* 321 F 2d 359 (D.C. Cir. 1963) cert. denied 375 U.S. 951(1963).

[50]First Report and Order in Dockets 14895 and 15233, 38 FCC 683 (1965, April 23).

[51]Notice of Inquiry and Proposed Rulemaking, 1 FCC 2d 453 (1965).

[52]Notice of Inquiry, 500.

[53]Second Report and Order in Dockets 14895, 15233 and 15971, 2 FCC 2d 725 (1966).

[54]*U.S. v. Southwestern Cable Co.,* 392 U.S. 157 (1968).

[55]*United Artists Television, Inc. v. Fortnightly Corp.,* 255 F.Supp. 177 (S.D.N.Y. 1966).

[56]377 F.2d 872 (1967).

[57]*Fortnightly Corp. v. United Artists Television,* 392 U.S. 390 (1968).

[58]*Fortnightly,* 399.

[59]Notice of Inquiry and Notice of Proposed Rulemaking in Docket 18397, 15 FCC 2d 417 (1968).

[60]Amendment in Docket 18397, FCC 69-54, 17 January 1969.

[61]New York City, Mayor's Advisory Task Force on CATV and Telecommunications. *A Report on Cable Television and Cable Telecommunications In New York City,* 1968.

[62]President's Task Force on Communications Policy. *Final Report* (Washington, DC: Government Printing Office, 1968).

[63]See, e.g., The Sloan Commission on Cable Communications, *On the Cable: The Television of Abundance* (New York: McGraw-Hill, 1971); Walter Baer "Interactive Television: Prospects for Two-Way Services on Cable," Memorandum R-888-MF, Santa Monica, Ca., Rand Corp., 1972.

[64]Smith, Ralph Lee, *The Wired Nation* (New York: Harper & Row, 1972).

[65]First Report and Order, 20 FCC 2d 201 (1969).

[66]*Midwest Video Corp. v. United States,* 441 F.2d 1322 (8th Cir. 1971).

[67]*United States v. Midwest Video Corp,* 406 U.S. 649 (1972).

[68]Common Carrier Tariffs for CATV Systems, 4 FCC 2d 257 (1966); in 1968 it extended the requirement to all telephone companies (General Tel. Co., 13 FCC 2d 448).

[69]21 FCC 2d 307.

[70]"CATV Industry Cites New 'Firsts,'" *Sponsor,* 15 March 1965, 16.

[71]*Television Magazine,* March 1967, 3.

[72]Warner bought out the American Express interest in the company in 1985.

[73]Ken Cox stepped down in 1970, James Wadsworth in 1969.

[74]Stanley Besen and Robert Crandall, "The Deregulation of Cable Television," *Law and Contemporary Problems,* 44(1981): 77–124, 94.

[75]Mark Seiden, *Cable Television U.S.A.: An Analysis of Government Policy.* (New York: Praeger, 1972), 7.

[76]Cable Television Report and Order, 36 FCC 2 143 (1972).

[77]*Midwest Video Corp. v. FCC,* 571 F.2d 1025 (1978), affd, 99 S.Ct. 1435 (1979).

[78]Smith, *The Wired Nation,* 62–63.

[79]Cabinet Committee of Cable Communication, "Cable: Report to the President" (1974), (The Whitehead Report).

[80]Staff of the Subcommittee on Communications of the House Committee on Interstate and Foreign Commerce, Cable Television: Promise Versus Regulatory Performance, 94th Cong., 2d Sess. (Subcomm. Print, 1976).

[81]Report and Order, 48 FCC 2d 699 (1974), and Memorandum Opinion and Order, 54 FCC 2d 1182 (1975).

[82]First Report and Order, 58 FCC 2d 442 (1976).

[83]63 FCC 2d 956 (1977), but see *Clearview TV Cable of Enumclaw, Inc.* 68 FCC 2d 1179 (1978).

[84]Report and Order in Docket 20487, 57 FCC 2d 625 (1976).

[85]47 U.S.C. sect. 701 et seq. (1993).

[86]Second Report and Order, 23 FCC 2d 825 (1970).

[87]First Report and Order, 52 FCC 2d 1 (1975).

[88]*HBO v. FCC,* 567 F. 2d 9 (1977).

[89]In re. American Broadcasting Co., 62 FCC 2d 901 (1977).

[90]S. 644, 92nd Cong., 1st Sess. (1971).

[91]See Stanley Besen, et al., "Copyright Liability for Cable Television: Compulsory Licensing and the Coase Theorem," *Journal of Law and Economics,* 21(1978): 67.

[92]*CBS v. Teleprompter,* 415 U.S. 394 (1974).

[93]Report and Order in docket 20988, 71 FCC 2d 951 (1979).

[94]Report in docket 21284, 71 FCC 2d 632 (1979).

[95]Cable television Syndicated Program Exclusivity Rules and Inquiry into the Economic Relationship Between Broadcasting and Cable Television, 79 FCC 2d 663 (1980). The repeal was subsequently upheld by the court, *Malrite TV. v. FCC,* 652 F.2d 1140 (2d Cir. 1981), cert denied, 454 U.S.1143 (1982).

[96]21 November 1988, 44.

[97]NCTA, *Cable Television Developments,* May 1992.

[98]U.S. General Accounting Office, *Telecommunications: National Survey of Cable Television Rates and Services* (1989).

[99]"GAO on Cable," *Broadcasting,* 7 August 1989, 30.

[100]*Daniels Cablevision, Inc. v. U.S.,* 835 F.Supp. 1 (D.DC 1993).

[101]*Quincy TV, Inc. v. FCC,* 768 F. 2d 1434 (D.C. Cir. 1986), and *Century Communications v. FCC,* 835 F.2d 292 (D.C. Cir. 1987), cert. denied, 486 U.S. 1032 (1988).

[102]*Turner Broadcasting System, Inc. v. FCC,* 114 S.Ct. 2445 (1994).

3

How It Works:
The Technology

When you slide down into your easy chair at the end of a hard day and turn on the local news, weather, or even an old movie, chances are very good that you are not thinking about electrons and Hertzian waves, satellite look angles, asynchronous digital subscriber lines, or tree-and-branch architectures. And yet without some of these things, you would be staring at a blank screen. Most people do not consider the universe of electronics behind and beyond the box, and quite reasonably so. For most of us it is sufficient that the channels change obediently when we click the remote and that the pictures do not have too much snow or too many ghosts. To achieve an understanding of the cable and telecommunications industry, however, one must acquire some familiarity with the vast, intricate, and expensive electronic network that makes up the business.

This chapter explores the technology of cable, satellite, and telco television. It looks in detail at the changes that constitute the much-heralded technological convergence. These include the movement from distribution systems based on telephone lines and coaxial cables to those based on fiber optics. It also includes the critical evolution from analog to digital communications. We also will look at the important issues of system architecture and which configuration of wires and computers is most likely to deliver the interactive, full-service system of the next century.

TRANSMISSION PATHWAYS

The Electromagnetic Spectrum

Every television viewer, remote control and popcorn in hand, sits at the end of an electronic pipeline that has captured, condensed, stored, switched, transmitted, and reconstituted sound, images, and even data over thousands of miles. It is a network made possible by a sophisticated and complex harnessing of the electromagnetic spectrum. This spectrum is the foundation of the system, the ground on which the pipeline is constructed.

The analogy of the electromagnetic spectrum to land is a useful one. The spectrum shares qualities with some of the classical elements, earth, air, and water. Like land, the spectrum is, for practical purposes, a finite and useful natural resource. It shares many of the same economic attributes as well. Some rather large parts of it have been claimed by the government for public purposes, while other parts have been licensed by lottery or competitive hearing. Recently, the FCC auctioned off a few slivers of quite usable spectrum to private interests. Some locations within the spectrum are more valuable than others and new technologies make it possible to expand or make more efficient use of it everyday. Even small parts can be economically precious; as with land, more is almost always better and location is critical. It is the tangible lifeblood of modern mass communications generally, and cable and satellites, specifically.

Physically, the spectrum is electromagnetic energy. More like the air than land in this respect, it is the medium through which and within which television and radio signals are carried; it is an invisible part of our natural environment. Television programs travel pathways created by the harnessing of discrete and narrow portions of the spectrum. When you turn on your set and surf over to channel five or channel six, you are skimming across and accessing particular pieces of the electromagnetic spectrum, specified amounts of space set aside to create each channel.

Finally, like water, electromagnetic energy moves in waves. The waves can be long and slow, like the swells of calm sea, or they can be short and quick, like the chop of waves on a windy lake. The length and frequency of the waves give electromagnetic energy its flexibility. The differing characteristics make possible the separation of signals moving through the "ether," so channel five's signals have different wave characteristics than those of channel 25.

Light itself is part of the electromagnetic spectrum. The colors in visible light are nothing more than the different speeds at which light waves travel. The slower light waves make up color in the warmer palette, the reds and yellows; higher frequency waves create the cooler colors, the blues and greens. Above and below our range of visual perception are light waves traveling at even faster and slower speeds, the ultraviolets and infrareds, respectively. Below the range of visible light are radio waves: along with light, the stuff of electronic communication (see Figure 3-1).

Radio Waves	Infrared	Visible Light	Ultra-violet	X-Rays	Gamma Rays	Cosmic Rays
3 kHz–300 GHz	10^{13} Hz	10^{14} Hz	10^{16} Hz	10^{19} Hz	10^{21} Hz	10^{23} Hz

FIGURE 3-1   The Electromagnetic Spectrum

Electromagnetic energy is measured and expressed by the length and frequency of its waves. One full wave, from its highest to lowest point, is said to constitute one full cycle and waves are measured in cycles per second, or in the language of electronics, one *Hertz,* named after the German physicist Heinrich Hertz, who first detected and measured radio energy in the 1880s. Because the range of frequencies typically used in radio communications is greater than a few cycles per second, 1,000 Hertz is expressed as one kilohertz (kHz); one million Hertz is one megahertz (MHz), and one billion Hertz is one giga Hertz (GHz). When you tune to 1390 on your AM radio, or 91.5 on your FM dial, you are tuning to the specific frequency, in Hertz, at which those signals are being transmitted. While the range of frequencies at which these waves can and do move is quite broad, our ability to exploit them is finite and so the usable portion of the spectrum is always restricted by how well our existing technology can distinguish between a desired signal versus undesired signals transmitted on nearby frequencies.

The frequency or channel of the signal is typically called the *carrier wave.* The actual information, the intelligence or the television programming, is imposed onto the carrier wave in one of several ways. You can vary, or modulate, the height of the wave—its amplitude—as in AM (amplitude modulation) radio, or you can hold the amplitude constant and vary the frequency of the wave, as in FM (frequency modulation) radio. The latter is less prone to interference and produces a higher quality signal, although it typically requires more spectrum space. In television, the video portion of the program is transmitted with an AM signal while the audio is carried separately by FM.

Hertz not only is the measure of the frequency of a signal—its location, so to speak, in the radio band—it is also used to measure how much bandwidth a particular kind of channel uses. Some types of signals require more of the valuable territory of the spectrum than do others, depending on the amount of information one wishes to send and how one wishes to send it. Radio, for example, carries only an audio signal, involving relatively little raw information and so very little spectrum space is required. An AM radio signal uses only 10 kHz of bandwidth, while an FM signal takes up 200 kHz, in order to achieve two-channel stereo, high fidelity and to carry additional information like the electronic trigger for the stereo light on your receiver. Visual images have a much greater amount of information, so television requires significantly more spectrum space than do audio radio services. A standard

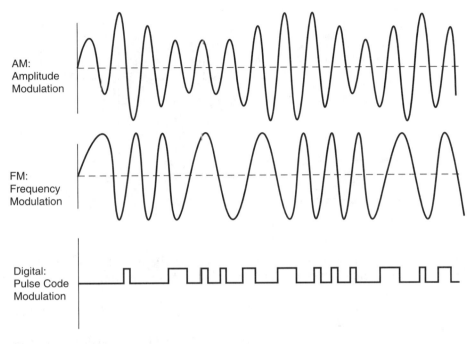

FIGURE 3-2   Wave Forms

analog television signal needs 6 MHz of spectrum, about 600 times that of a single AM radio channel.

Traditional broadcasting and broadcasting by satellite use the open spectrum, the "airwaves." While the amount of usable spectrum grows larger with every leap in transmission technology, the usable natural spectrum remains limited and so demand for this scarce resource is heavy. It is subject to a staggering array of services—commercial broadcasting, cellular telephone, military communications, wireless paging systems, children's walkie-talkies, CB radio, radar, garage door openers, even the keyless remote entry fobs on today's cars. The important broadcasting services for our purposes are primarily those that offer multichannel video programming, and wireless voice and data transmission. Among the services we will examine are wireless cable, direct broadcast satellite, and personal communications services (PCS).

Historically, the spectrum has been owned by the public and its allocation, including recent auctions of spectrum space, controlled by the government (see Chapter 7). One of the important roles of the Federal Communications Commission (FCC) is oversight of that part of the spectrum devoted to public and commercial services. Figure 3-3 shows the usable bandwidth as it relates to the full electromagnetic spectrum, and how the government has apportioned services within it. AM radio is positioned in the medium frequency band, FM in the VHF (very high

Very Low Freq. (VLF)	Low Freq. (LF)	Medium Freq. (MF)	High Freq. (HF)	Very High Freq. (VHF)	Ultrahigh Freq. (UHF)	Super High Freq. (SHF)	Extremely High Freq. (EHF)
Time Signals Military Comm	Navigation	AM Radio Marine Comm CB	Shortwave Civil Air Patrol	TV Ch. 2–13 FM Radio	TV Ch. 14–69 PCS MMDS Adv. Digital TV	Ku & C band Sat. DBS PCS	Military & Future use

3 kHz   30 kHz   300 kHz   3 MHz   30 MHz   300 MHz   3 GHz   30 GHz   300 GHz

FIGURE 3-3   Broadcast Frequencies and Services

ferquency) band, terrestrial broadcast TV in the VHF and UHF (ultrahigh frequency) bands, and satellite television in the C-band (4 to 6 GHz), Ku-band (11 to 14 GHz), and Ka-band (20 to 30 GHz).

The competition for spectrum space historically has been fierce and accounts, in part, for the limited number of over-the-air television channels.[1] Its quality as a desirable "natural resource," and one for which demand has usually exceeded supply, helps give rise to its economic value along with debates over state-controlled allocation and assignment. There are long-standing arguments about whether the spectrum is a finite resource in some way distinguishable from other goods, and whether the spectrum ought to be held in trust for the public or sold in pieces to the highest bidder. In recent years, policymakers have been more receptive to market-based forms of spectrum distribution. In 1995 and 1996, for example, FCC auctions of spectrum space for commercial communication, such as DBS and wireless telephone, generated over $20 billion for the government.

Wire-Based or Closed-Circuit Systems

Broadcasters and satellite services transmit over the open spectrum. Telephone and cable companies use open-air transmission for a number of important purposes, but the bulk of their infrastructure is in closed-circuit, wired systems. In contrast to broadcasting, one of the key advantages of wire-based systems is the relative abundance of spectrum space. Wired systems, including cable and telephone, in effect replicate, in an isolated and controlled environment, the natural spectrum. Wired systems vary in their bandwidth capacities, but some can provide an exceptional amount of spectrum space. Unlike the open spectrum, wired systems are also less hampered by the problems of adjacent channel interference. Over-the-air broadcasters operating on adjacent channels (such as channels two and three) can interfere with each other's signals if their transmitting towers are located too close together. The FCC requires a geographic spacing of about sixty miles between transmitters in such situations. Not all channels are technically adjacent in the natural spectrum even though their numbers are consecutive. For example, channels six and seven operate in widely separate parts of the spectrum. As a result, the FCC has set up a system of allocating television frequencies in towns and cities around the country so that stations on the same channel or adjacent channels are not situated so close together as to interfere with each other. That is why you'll rarely see a broadcast channel 9 and broadcast channel 10, for example, in the same market and why the "re-use" of channel 9 can occur only in another city at least one hundred miles away.[2] While you can get interference and bleedthrough of one channel to another on cable, generally the wired spectrum suffers less from this problem because of the differing magnitudes of power and the differing transmission methods used in broadcast versus cable.

In addition, where the open airwaves are used for all the services, and more, mentioned previously, wired systems can dedicate their full capacity to a limited number of select services. Traditional cable TV uses nearly all of its available enclosed spectrum space for programming, which is why it can offer fifty, one hundred, or more channels, depending on the technical sophistication of its transmission equipment.

While wireline systems have important advantages over the open spectrum, not all wires are created equal. Three types of wired systems are used in modern telecommunications: the "twisted pair," the "coaxial" cable, and the "fiber optic" cable.

Twisted Pair

The twisted copper pair is the most technically limited of today's wired media. This is the familiar telephone line and the wire that carries the bulk of our collective global conversation. Little more sophisticated than an electric lamp cord, it is, at least in principle, two twisted strands of copper.[3] As with its predecessor, the single-line telegraph wire, the electrical information flows physically through the copper. Twisted pair is a "narrowband" medium. That is, spectrum space by contemporary standards is tiny, just over 4 kHz when used as the "first" and "last mile" of the telephone network. It is sufficient to carry acceptable quality voice conversations and computer data over moderate distances but if it does not provide enough bandwidth to offer even acceptable high fidelity music, and in its traditional form cannot come close to generating the 6 MHz necessary to transmit a single conventional television channel. The wire itself, in fact, can carry more information, and techniques are available today, as we will see, to greatly expand its bandwidth, at least over short distances. It is the electronics of the system, in conjunction with the wire, that limit its capacity.

Coaxial Cable

The cable television industry derives its name, its technological prowess, and its sociocultural prominence from the coaxial cable. It is the wire that delivers your cable television. Coaxial refers to the two axes of the cable, a solid center wire (the first axis) surrounded by a metal sheath or tube (the second axis).

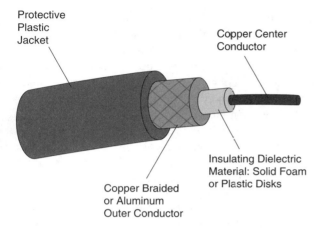

Protective Plastic Jacket

Copper Center Conductor

Copper Braided or Aluminum Outer Conductor

Insulating Dielectric Material: Solid Foam or Plastic Disks

FIGURE 3-4   Coaxial Cable

The two axes are separated with donut-shaped spacers or a solid "dielectric" material transparent to radio waves. A durable, outer plastic covering completes the cable. Instead of current moving physically through the wires, as in a twisted pair, the electronic information rides primarily along the surface and between the axes in the electronically hollow space of the tube. The advantage is a dramatic, in fact theoretically almost infinite, expansion of bandwidth, again in an environment isolated from the outside ether. Cable, therefore, is a "broadband" medium.

Coaxial Amplifiers.   While infinite in theory, the actual exploitable bandwidth of the cable is contingent on the capacity of the signal amplifiers. In all wired systems, the line itself presents a resistance to the signal, which thereby loses its strength, or attenuates, over the course of its travel through the conduit. To maintain their strength, the signals have to be amplified. In modern cable systems amplifiers are placed about every 2,000 feet, and a series of amplifiers on a given line is called a *cascade*. As suggested in Chapter 2, much of the work of cable television engineers since the inception of the industry has been aimed at finding ways to increase the bandwidth capacity of the amplifiers, thereby creating space for more television channels. While early amplifiers could carry only one channel at a time, and a three-channel cable system had to have a separate set of amplifiers for each channel, today's broadband amplifiers carry scores of channels simultaneously. The practical state of the art in bandwidth capacity in the mid-1990s was 750 MHz, or about 110 channels. More powerful 860 MHz and 1 GHz amplifiers are available, but their increased cost and technical complexity have prevented widespread adoption. Today, less than 10 percent of the country's cable plant, most of it older, has a bandwidth of 220 MHz or less, about 12 to 22 channels. Systems of 330 MHz to 400 MHz, 40 to 50 channels, make up about 75 percent of the nation's cable plant. High-capacity systems account for about 15 percent of all cable miles, but that figure is increasing steadily as the industry upgrades its capacity. These are systems of 450 MHz, delivering up to about 60 channels, 550 MHz and 750 MHz systems, with 80 to 110 channels. The latter tend to be in larger urban systems.[5]

In the late 1970s and early 1980s, some companies constructed double and even triple cable systems, in which two or three cables were strung side-by-side, boosting capacities to over 100 channels, but high cost and low demand led to a decline in interest in those architectures. By one estimate, up to 95 percent of all the new cable systems or rebuilds being constructed today are single-cable architectures running at 750 MHz or higher.[6]

The Cable Spectrum and Set-Top Boxes.   Because the coaxial spectrum is a closed universe, cable operators are largely freed from the interference–avoidance requirements that have limited the transmission power and number of over-the-air broadcasters. They can place their channels on almost any frequency they want, and do so to make the most efficient use of the space and technology. Traditionally, this has meant that the broadcast VHF channels 2 through 13 have been carried in their "normal" place on the cable, but the UHF channels 14 through 69, which in the open spectrum are higher than and separate from the VHF channels, have been moved downward, in part because of the attenuation problem mentioned earlier.[7] The cable spectrum universe is divided into bands. As Figure 3-5 shows, channels 2 through 6 are carried in the low band, channels 7 through 13 in the high band, and other cable network programming is distributed across the midband, superband, and hyperband channels. Note that part of the low band, the 0 to 50 MHz range, is often used for upstream or interactive communication that allows the viewer to send information back to the cable operator.

While this scheme makes efficient use of the cable spectrum, it presented early problems for the viewer and the consumer electronics industry as CATV grew in popularity. Prior to the advent of "cable-ready" television sets, TV tuners could receive only standard UHF and VHF signals. They were not equipped to receive the midband or superband cable frequencies that carried much of the programming. The solution was the set-top cable TV box. The set-top box translated the converted UHF

Sub Band	Low Band	Mid Band	High Band	Super Band	Hyper Band
Reverse Path & Guard Band	Channels 2–6 & FM Radio	Channels 14–21 98, 99	Channels 7–13	Channels 23–36	Channels 37 and up & (Reverse Path)

6 MHz   48 MHz   108 MHz   174 MHz   216 MHz   300 MHz   459 MHz–
                                                                                                                                 1 GHz

FIGURE 3-5   Cable Frequencies and Channels

signals and subsequently all the new cable-only programming services, until the cable-ready TV was introduced.

The set-top boxes also provided a technical location for the scrambling of pay-TV signals. While cable-ready TV sets have taken over most of the simple functions of signal reception in modern systems, converters remain a staple of the industry for the provision of more advanced services like the delivery of premium programming and "pay-per-view" services.

Fiber Optics

Fiber deployment has been called the fourth wiring of America. The first wiring of the United States was the telegraph, the golden thread that spun out from the East Coast, across the West following the railroad, and for the first time in history provided instantaneous communication. The second wiring of America was the telephone, with its twisted pair cable and extension of cross-country conversation to every citizen. The third wiring was cable television's broadband pipe, the coaxial cable, which revolutionized the television world. The fourth wiring, with fiber-optic cable, has the same potential as the telephone and coaxial cable to revolutionize the way we communicate, receive news and entertainment, and acquire information and education.

Fiber-optic lines are the most advanced and capacious carrier available. Fiber is the carrier of choice for many if not most telecommunications applications. The worldwide fiber optics market was estimated at $7.1 billion in 1996 and was expected to reach $17.38 billion by the end of the decade.[8] A sizable portion of those expenditures was destined for cable and telecommunications systems. Telephone and cable companies began replacing their old "copper" plants with fiber starting in the 1980s. Projections call for virtually the entire national telecommunications infrastructure, except for feeds into individual homes and businesses, to be fiber sometime early in the next century, 2005 to 2015 by various projections. Someday, even the last few feet of wire into the home will be fiber-optic cable.

The fiber itself is a thin glass thread, about the thickness of a human hair (50 to 125 microns). Instead of carrying the information via electromagnetic radio waves, voice, data, and video are carried on beams of light, which are contained in and channeled through the transparent fiber. The glass fiber is often "doped" with a mineral compound like bromide to better reflect the laser signal off the fiber walls.

Fiber is superior to twisted pair and coaxial cable in almost every way. It is a more powerful and efficient medium, it is cheaper to make, less subject to interference, and the raw materials are readily available. Light itself, again a part of the electromagnetic spectrum, exists at such high frequencies that the available bandwidth for communication is expanded dramatically. Fiber optics provides hundreds of times the channel capacity of coaxial cable.

Fibers come in multimode and single-mode capacities. When the diameter of the fiber is as small as the wavelength of the light—single-mode fiber—the light propagates down the pipe with less attenuation and so is the favored format in most communications applications. A single fiber is capable in experimental situations of

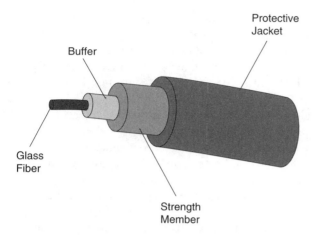

FIGURE 3-6   Optical Fiber

bandwidths measured in teraHertz, or trillions of cycles per second. Moreover, the normal industrial application of fiber involves cables comprised of scores, sometimes hundreds, of individual fibers bundled together. In cable television applications, a typical high-capacity optical cable may have 16 or 24 fiber pairs.

While the optical signal in fiber does attenuate over distance, due to the absorption and scattering of light in the pipe, it does so much more slowly than coaxial cable. A fiber-optical signal may travel thirty miles or more before it has to be regenerated in the pipeline, although the distance can vary greatly depending on a number of factors including the source and strength of the signal and the purity and size of the glass fiber.[10] Given the architecture of many cable systems, this means much of the fiber used in the system may not need any amplification at all. In contemporary cable television, the optical signal is generated by tiny but powerful semiconductor chip laser.

The other principle advantage of fiber optics is cost. Very simply, copper is expensive and glass—made out of silica or pure sand—is cheap. The cable industry has found that fiber can be more expensive to install, because it requires greater care in handling, especially in splicing, than coaxial cable. Once in place, however, the actual purchase costs and maintenance over time make it a bargain, especially when you consider it from a dollar per MHz standpoint. While fragile for some purposes, fiber is lighter and in other ways easier to work with than cable, and, unlike a coaxial system, which can "leak" radio signals, fiber optics poses no threat of interference to other radio devices.

Fiber is not without some drawbacks. Its principle problem is that you can not run the electricity needed to power amplifers through glass. Coaxial cable carries electricity that supplies the amplifiers along the line. The telephone companies' twisted pair runs its own 48-volt, direct-current power, which is one reason your telephone works even when the lights in your house go out. Solutions to the problem have included embedding copper in a cable with the fiber, running power through a metal shield around the fiber or even stringing twisted pair or coax along with fiber.

Other challenges have included trying to find cheap and easy ways to splice together fiber lines and to switch optical signals in the system. Most of these problems were being solved and prices continued to drop through the mid 1990s.

Deployment.   As a result of fiber's cost and performance advantage, the telephone and cable industries spent billions of dollars in the 1980s and early 1990s to replace much of their metal. Long-distance telephone companies had installed 102,000 route miles of fiber by 1992 and Regional Bell Operating companies 258,000 miles.[11] Local telephone companies have replaced most of the metal between their central offices and between the central and remote offices, and are beginning to spin fiber out from the remote offices toward homes. By 1995 the cable industry had strung more than 81,000 route miles of fiber, accelerating its rate of deployment rapidly from the beginning of the decade.[12]

None of this is to say that there is a focused program to get fiber into the consumer's home as quickly as possible. Such a prospect is financially infeasible. As we will see, the vast majority of the wire in all networks is tied up in the last few yards that go the home and replacing that on any accelerated schedule is beyond the means of even the largest companies. At the same time, existing wires do wear out and market pressure demands the continual upgrading of equipment. Cable systems must replace their aging plants on a regular basis and the telephone companies replace about 5 percent of their lines every year as a matter of course.[13] A growing percentage of the replacement is fiber, and over time, it will dominate the system.

Fiber is one of the two most important technological developments in television and telecommunications in the last twenty years. The second is the rise of the digital bit.

BEING DIGITAL

The information superhighway is about the global movement of weightless bits at the speed of light. As one industry after another looks at itself in the mirror and asks about its future in a digital world, that future is driven almost 100 percent by the ability of that company's product or services to be rendered in digital form.[14]

Analog Signals

Cable television, like all forms of electronic communication, has been moving steadily toward a digital universe, the conversion from the use of analog frequencies to digital bit streams. The progress has been characterized by frequent stops, starts, and deadends, but it has been nonetheless inexorable, and the implications for consumer services, industry structure, and financial survival can hardly be overstated. It is the single most important technical force pushing the industry away from a service that simply provides traditional or niched television programs, whether it's four channels or forty, and toward an interactive video and communication service that gives the viewer the power to choose programming and information almost at will and then manipulate it in ways we can only speculate on today. It is a linking of computers with telecommunications that represents the fundamental paradigm shift in modern media.

Traditional means of delivering television, either over the airwaves or by wire, involve the propagation of radio waves described in the earlier section. This is the "analog" method of broadcasting and cablecasting and still the dominant approach in the world. The term *analog* derives from the idea that the carrier wave resembles in some way, or is analogous to, the audio wave that it carries, in the same sense that a phonograph record is an analog copy of the original music because the pressure of the original sound waves were converted directly into electronic waves that were then physically embedded in the vinyl disk. All home television sets, traditional broadcasting outlets, and traditional cable systems use analog technologies and techniques, in which video and audio information are superimposed on the 6 MHz-wide radio frequency carrier wave. (The video portion of the signal uses 4 MHz, the remainder is used for audio and technical information.) Through the late 1990s and into the early part of the next century, this will all be changing, however.

Digital Signals

Imagine watching a television program on African lions and halfway through the show you start to wonder whether lions can see in the dark. You take the TV "mouse," run the television pointer toward the lion, click to stop the action of the show, then click on the lion's eye. A pulldown menu appears on your screen with various selections involving the eyesight of the big cat. You click on night vision and you get a textual description, long or short depending on your mood, of the lion's ability to see at night. You also can look at more video of lions hunting at night. Clicking back to the main show you start to think about a trip to Africa and you click on the main menu to call up information on travel to the continent, the tourist attractions in different countries, accommodations, currency, political climate, and airfares. You may decide to order travel brochures from one or two places, or perhaps even book your trip right then.

All the information at your fingertips is mixed together, video interacts with audio, audio with text, text with interactive shopping. It is possible because, to the television set and the telecommunications system, all the information and programming is the same: It is a sequence of pulses representing the ones and zeros in a stream of bits.

Digital communication is the language of computers. It is the conversion of all information into the zeros and ones of machine language, the on–off switches of micro circuits. All the intelligent activity in your computer is conducted in this "binary" code, and the single binary unit, the bit (for "Binary digIT"), is the building block of the digital world. For a number of years, the cable television industry has committed vast sums of money, time, and talent to convert its delivery platform from the horse-and-buggy world of analog technology to jet-age digital.

In practice, this has involved developing techniques and technologies to convert analog signals into digital bits. The process, in theory, is straightforward. It involves sampling a given audio or video signal at regular intervals. The variation or frequency of the signal at a given point in time is assigned a numerical value. The run of values across time represents the curve of the wave, and so the numbers themselves become the video and audio information. It is the same principle used in the production of compact discs in the music industry. The details, of course, are more complicated and schemes for sampling and encoding the information can vary.

In cable, the numerical value, like any number, becomes the raw material of the digital delivery system. Instead of sending out analog waves of television programs on the cable system, the operator sends out streams, or more accurately torrents, of numbers, that are translated back into viewable analog signals somewhere near the end-user. Through the 1990s most television programs will continue to be shot on analog videotape and subsequently converted to digital. Eventually, however, most professional audio and video production will be mastered directly onto some form of digital storage, with the conversion process done in the camera or original recorder.

Advantages

The world's electronics and communications industries have spent billions of dollars to develop and implement digital technologies. Why bother? Because digital communications has a number of strategic advantages over analog.

Digital storage and transmission allows the original signal to maintain its integrity, its "first copy" quality, across both time and distance. In traditional cable-casting and broadcasting analog signals erode and weaken as they move out across the system. Resistance and impurities, or variations in the wire, introduce noise into the signal, the power of the signal itself diminishes as it pushes through the coaxial cable and the amplifiers increase the inherent noise along with the signal. On the home set, the results can be ghosts, snow, interference, or distortion. Similar losses in picture and sound quality are typical when you copy a video- or audiotape for storage or distribution. Each new generation, or copy, of the tape is significantly inferior to its predecessor.

When it is working properly, digital storage and transmission suffer none of these weakness. A given set of numbers, representing specific picture elements, is replicated unerringly from the source to the receiver. The cable household closest to the source of the program or channel gets exactly the same signal as the home farthest away from the cable headend, or main office. The signal maintains its original quality throughout the system and, in theory, it is the same quality as that available at the source of the program's production. Similarly, copies made in a digital medium are replicated in the smallest detail and with the same vividness as the original tape.

Another advantage of the digital signal is its malleability. Once the signal is digitized it can be altered and manipulated in countless ways and toward innumerable ends. Because digitization translates television signals into the same language as computer data, it allows the mixing of the two. This opens the door to new services that combine video and data at higher levels of consumer interactivity than is possible with analog techniques. It is what makes possible the scenario painted earlier involving the program on African lions. This kind of high-end interactivity is available today in the form of computer-based CD-ROM (computer disk, read only memory) multimedia applications. Interactive CD-ROM software lets you explore the New World with Christopher Columbus, build your own cities, or probe imaginary lairs of dragons and wizards. This capacity is becoming available on the computer Internet system and the World Wide Web.

It will be a few years before the same level of digital interactivity is available in the cable and telco TV system, because these infrastructures are only now starting to build their digital capacity. In the long term, however, the technical differences between the computer and the television set in your living room will start to vanish. You may use them for different purposes and in different social settings, but the electronics behind them will become increasingly indistinguishable.

Digital Bandwidth and Compression

The biggest drawback to digital transmission is its voracious appetite for bandwidth. Absent bandwidth conservation techniques, a digitized television signal consumes at least five times as much bandwidth as an analog signal. In other words, it would take five or more "normal" television channels to carry one channel of digital television. This is due to the immense complexity of the video signal.

The U.S. standard for television transmission is called NTSC (National Television System Committee) after the government–industry committee that developed the color norms in 1953. The NTSC standard is 525 lines of horizontal resolution and, if you look closely at your TV screen sometime, you can actually see these lines of colored dots that make up the picture. A given set of 525 lines constitutes one frame. A scanning beam paints the lines in a sequential pattern, illuminating the colored dots to an appropriate intensity as it passes. In fact, the beam only paints half the picture with each pass, scanning every other line. This pass is called a field and two fields make up a frame. By alternately painting the odd and even lines, the annoying phenomenon of picture "flicker," the kind you see in old movies, is eliminated and the motion smoothed out. A new field is drawn every 60th of a second (following the 60-cycle-per-second rhythm of our electric power system). A new frame, therefore, is presented every 30th of a second.

This practice of drawing only every other line with each pass is called "interlacing." It is important because computer monitors use a different method for creating images, called *progressive scanning*. It is a noninterlaced format that can create a much higher resolution picture, drawing more lines and more dots. The number of lines and dots is contingent on the hardware and software of the computer. One of the issues in the convergence of television and computer technologies are the standards to be used in monitors, including whether interlaced or noninterlaced methods will prevail. As we will see, this was a serious sticking point in the debate about how to implement digital broadcast television in the United States. Whether it is done by progressive or interlaced means, however, hundreds of picture lines changing thirty times or more per second means a huge amount of data bits.

To digitize and distribute a full-motion NTSC television signal requires a transmission speed of 100 million bits per second (100 Mbps), and increased data speeds require increased bandwidth. By comparison, a typical uncompressed digitized telephone voice conversation runs at 64,000 bits per second (64 Kbps), a fraction of the speed and bandwidth of video.

One solution has been to increase the speed at which data can be sent continually, and thereby expand the bandwidth. In experiments in 1995, the most advanced experimental "erbium-doped" fiber-optic cable transmitted one trillion bits of information a second. That was two-and-a-half times faster than the previous record of 400 Gbps and hundreds of times faster than the fastest commercial systems, which run at 10 to 20 Gbps.[15]

An even more important step in harnessing the power of digital technology has been digital compression. In video, this means squeezing, or compressing, the digital signal into a narrower bandwidth, to reduce the amount of information necessary to transmit an acceptable picture. A number of techniques have been developed to accomplish this, but most share the common theme of eliminating unnecessary picture information and processing only that material necessary to maintain and advance the image. The process takes advantage of the fact that, like film, television is really nothing more than a progressive series of still pictures, those thirty frames per second mentioned above. In the analog universe, all the information in every still frame is transmitted. But in a simple shot of a person standing against a blue sky, for example, the picture of the sky may not appreciably change for several seconds, or even minutes. Digital compression exploits the unchanging image. Instead of assigning and sending a code number for every single picture element, or pixel, of blue sky in each frame, it may send only the first frame of blue sky and an electronic note directing the receiving device to maintain the blue sky image until further notice. In this way, millions of bits of data need not be sent. Compression digitally refreshes the picture elements only when necessary.

There is a point at which so much information is deleted that a visible degradation of picture quality can be seen, and the technical–economic trick is to balance the loss in picture quality against the gain in bandwidth. Luckily the technology has advanced enough to allow high levels of compression without noticeable loss in picture quality at the consumer level. Compression can bring down the necessary data speed from 100 Mbps to 4 to10 Mbps while still maintaining an acceptable

image. Transmission rates of about 1.5 Mbps create a VHS quality picture acceptable for some applications.

Compression is usually expressed as the ratio of the number of compressed
digital signals to one traditional analog signal. A five-to-one compression ratio
means the ability to squeeze five digitally compressed signals into 6 MHz of bandwidth, or one analog channel. Compression ratios of 10-to-1, 20-to-1, and more are
now feasible. In practice, different kinds of video information are amenable to different levels of compression. A televised news conference, for example, in which
there is little action or picture detail can be subject to high levels of compression
because the need to refresh the data continually is low. A football or hockey game
with constant action and the minute detail of cheering crowds requires more updat-
ing and so lower compression rates. Software in a transmission system can sense the
need for varying levels of compression and allocate bandwidth as necessary, creating variable or dynamic compression rates.

Digitizing the Process: Production and Servers

The digital format is displacing analog at every level of television, from the capture
of images to editing to storage to transmission. Through the early 1990s most video
had to be shot, or captured, in traditional ways, on analog film or videotape, and
converted into digital form later. But major electronics manufacturers such as
Panasonic and Sony are producing equipment to capture video directly to digital
formats, either in tape or on disc. Television production already has adopted digital,
or "nonlinear" editing, using videotape shot in analog and converted to digital. Digital cameras are now even available for the home consumer market, although at premium prices.

Cable operators also have been moving to all-digital production formats. When
the neophyte Golf Channel built its new studio and production complex, it went all-
digital (providing digital-ready capacity where it had to remain analog). In one of
the most expansive efforts, TCI built its National Digital Television Center near
Denver, Colorado. The facility is designed to use digital as much as the state of the
art will allow, from original production through satellite distribution, and is being
used by a number of cable programming services.

All the DBS services broadcast in compressed digital formats, as do the emerging digital wireless cable services. As we will see, cable system operators are also
spending handsomely to deploy compressed digital services.

Servers

For most of the cable industry, the digital storage of programming is more important than digital production. While digital signals can be, and in some applications are, stored on tape, the tape medium is much too slow and inflexible to meet
the demands of an interactive network. Most interactive digital programming systems require disc-based storage systems similar to the ones used on home comput-

ers, but with much greater capacity. These digital "servers" contain the actual programming that subscribers tap into. The advantage is that more than one customer can access the same material and then have some control over that material in a way that would be impossible, or at least impractical, using videotape. For example, one digitized movie on a computer server at the main office of a cable company can be watched by many different subscribers at once. Moreover, with sufficiently sophisticated equipment, each subscriber can start watching when they please, stop the movie to take a break, back it up and watch something again, or fast-forward to the end, all without disturbing the viewing of any other subscriber.

Servers are also useful in some of the more mundane cable operations. They are increasingly used to insert local advertising at preprogrammed spots in various channels on the system (see Chapter 6). It is easier, faster, and more efficient than handling videotape.

Servers will become a critical component of the interactive media system as multichannel providers move toward "video on demand" services. The system that allows viewers to select reruns of old television shows, news clips, and historic sports events, called up instantly and tailored for and by each subscriber, is based on servers that can store billions of bits and efficiently route hundreds of requests in and out of the database.

While servers are being used increasingly in broadcasting and cable, engineers continue to work to expand available memory and extend the number of users that a given server can accommodate. The industry meanwhile has begun the laborious and expensive process of digitizing decades of films and television shows.

Optical Storage

Optical storage technologies like the CD-ROM on your home computer hold significantly more information than magnetic floppy or hard discs, but the massive amount of data contained in a typical two-hour Hollywood movie constitutes more than even a standard computer CD-ROM can hold. A new form of CD-ROM, however, will aleviate this problem. In 1995 two warring electronics groups compromised on a standard for "digital versatile discs" (DVD). The two groups, one led by Sony Corporation and Phillips Electronics, the other by Toshiba Corporation and Time Warner, fought for months in an attempt to make their technology the international standard. With eventual replacement of all commercial and home videotape by the new disc as the prize, each group was seeking to control a multibillion-dollar industry. The settlement, brokered in part by IBM, ended with the adoption of a double-sided disc, the size of a normal computer CD-ROM but capable of holding seven times the information, over 9 gigabytes (9 billion bytes) per disc, enough for a digitally compressed two-hour movie with "CD" quality stereo sound and room left over for extras like voice tracks in multiple languages.[16]

Advances in technology are also making it possible to record and erase CD-ROMS in ways functionally similar to magnetic discs. "WORM" discs (write once, read many) have been available for several years and newer "rewritable," or "CD-RW," discs increase the flexibility of the technology. In time, optical storage will be integrated into server technology and advances like DVD, WORM, and CD-RW discs will give cable operators new options in creating quick-response interactive systems that eventually will become essential elements in the system.

HDTV

Digital compression is also a necessary part of the potential transition to "High Definition Television" (HDTV). HDTV substantially increases the amount of picture information over the existing 525-line NTSC standard. Under one proposal, HDTV would provide 1080 lines of resolution and a wider screen aspect ratio than existing television. But the dramatic improvement in picture quality costs dearly in bandwidth. An analog HDTV signal requires about ten times as much bandwidth as a traditional analog signal, and a digitized HDTV signal can require transmission rates of a full gigabyte per second. A compressed HDTV signal can be distributed in one standard 6 MHz TV channel.

Standards

Overcoming the technical challenges of television transmission, be it analog or digital, has never been the only, or even the most, vexing problem in bringing a new service to market. Business and regulatory difficulties are nearly always present, but a related problem that is not widely recognized by the public involves the selection of technical standards.

The goals of standard-setting are essential to the smooth operation of the telecommunications system. You want to make sure that your rental video will play on a VCR made by Sony as well as it will on one made by RCA, and on a TV set made by Mitsubishi and by Phillips, and in Chicago as well as Tampa. In fact, your tape will not play on a European VCR or television set, because they operate on different standards than U.S. machines. Interoperability is the key phrase: All the components of the system must be able to talk with one another.

Determining a particular version of a technology or a specific protocol from among many possibilities has been an issue worth fighting over since the introduction of television itself. CBS and NBC, for example, both had their own version of color TV in the 1940s and fought bitterly over which would prevail as the industry standard. NBC eventually won, but the fight delayed the introduction of color by several years.

Through the early and mid 1990s, the industry struggled to agree on a uniform standard for digital compression, one that would allow the various parts of the telecommunication system to speak the same digital language. While General Instruments introduced a proprietary "DigiCipher" system, others sought an open uniform standard. The Motion Picture Experts Group (MPEG) was formed under the supervision of the International Standards Organization (ISO) and the International Electrotechnical Commission (IEC) and charged with the task of formulating an industry-wide compression protocol. Its initial effort resulted in the MPEG-1 standard. But with a transmission rate of only about 1.5 Mbps, the industry balked at adopting it as a commercial broadcast–cablecast norm, because of the marginal picture quality.[17] A second effort led to the MPEG-2 standard for broadcast quality video at variable transmission rates of up to 15 Mbps. (Broadcast quality video can be achieved at transmission rates of around 3 to 6 Mbps.) Industry-wide adoption of the MPEG-2 benchmark was accepted in principle in November of 1994 and real-world application was accelerated when the DBS services DirecTV and USSB implemented it in 1995.

Compression standards are farther along than some other technical issues. For example, cable television, direct broadcast satellites, and digital broadcast television have chosen separate methods for modulating their digital signals.[18] While the effect on the consumer market is unclear, it will not make it any easier to develop interoperability for set-top boxes or digital television sets.

Clearly, the universe of video and telecommunications is becoming increasingly more complex. Competing technologies and protocols will continue to emerge and the question of interoperability will likely become more difficult before it becomes easier. This is especially true as cable attempts to move into the telephone business and vice versa. It also will become more complicated as consumer electronics manufacturers create products that seek to match and take advantage of the digital power of the new delivery systems.

Digital Boxes

Someday, probably early in the twenty-first century, when cable operators, broadcasters, and television set manufacturers have agreed on standards, all television sets will be able to decode digital signals on their own. But there were more than 200 million television sets in U.S. homes in 1997 and very few could make sense out of a stream of zeros and ones. Until deployment of digital TV sets de-encrypted, digitized cable television programming will require a set-top decoder box, similar in some ways to the better-known analog set-top boxes described earlier.

Many in the industry had anticipated the roll-out of a digital system, and the plethora of profit-enhancing services that the 500-channel future would present, in the early 1990s, but that hope crashed on the rocks of political, technical, and economic reality. Squabbles over adopting a proprietary versus open transmission standard were part of the problem, but failure to create a set-top box at a cost-effective price constituted a large part of the delay.

Ultimately, however, most agree that the future is digital. Hybrid analog–digital systems will be an interim step. In the fall of 1996 major suppliers such as General Instruments began shipping thousands of digital set-top boxes, at about $400 to $450 each, to the major MSO's, and systems began the conversion process. Other alterations to the system are required. Digital modulators cost several thousand dollars for each 6 MHz channel, but on a system-wide, per subscriber basis, it is not a heavy price. Existing lasers and standard coaxial amplifiers can handle the digital streams because they are carried via special amplitude modulated processes (quadrature amplitude modulation, or QAM).

In practice, digital applications, at least initially, will take up only part of the bandwidth of those cable system offering the service. The bulk of bandwidth capacity, up to 450 or 550 MHz, will be used for conventional analog programming services. Capacity above this, in the 550 to 750 MHz range, will be dedicated to compressed digital services and largely used to deliver movies. Several hundred channels will be made available; the precise number will depend on the amount of space set aside and the compression levels used. Time Warner, for example, was planning 750 MHz systems with 80 channels of analog programming and 180 to 250 channels of digital services. For cable systems that do not have sufficient capacity and lack the capital to upgrade, a hybrid system that combines the cable with satellite delivery may be used. The existing coaxial system will continue to carry analog programming while digital signals are delivered via one of the DBS services and the two signals mixed in the customer's set-top box.

Many questions about the boxes remain. Will they eventually be available in retail stores? Will they be sufficiently standardized that they can be used from one system to another? How far down will mass production drive the price? How soon will they be replaced by "digital ready" television sets? Even the people in the industry can only speculate on the diffusion of digital. Whatever the timing, the basic transmission pathways are, through fiber and digital expansion, developing tremendous capacity, flexibility, and interactivity.

DISTRIBUTION SYSTEMS

The evolution from analog to digital transmission is only one part of the sweeping technological change that lies at the heart of the emerging media infrastructure and the developing industries that will constitute the information sector in the next century. Digital technologies are being applied to broadband fiber systems that, at the same time, are evolving from classic cable television "tree and branch" topologies to switched systems more closely resembling traditional telephone architectures. These are the systems that, as they mature into the next century, will provide the foundation for converging news, entertainment, telephone, and data businesses now characterized simply as cable television and telephone. The following sections will examine telecommunications architectures and techniques, the topology of multichannel television distribution. The national distribution system begins at the site of a program or channel producer, who beams material by satellite to local carriers around the country, or, in the case of direct broadcast satellites, straight into the consumer's home. We will look first at the satellite system and then at the evolving local wired systems, starting with the classic "tree and branch" cable system that serves most cable homes.

Satellite Systems

As noted in Chapter 2, satellites radically changed the structure of the cable television business and the nature of the service. CATV evolved from a conduit for retransmitting broadcast signals into a video programming platform providing access to originally produced, nonbroadcast television programming and retransmitted broadcast signals. Satellites make it possible to reach a prospective audience large enough to support profitable operation of both general and specialized cable channels. Satellites can deliver usable signals to a geographical space equal to approximately one-third of the world, because the signal "footprint" expands in coverage in the thousands of miles it travels to illuminate the surface of the earth.

Satellites as a "Bent Pipe"

Communications satellites receive and retransmit signals much like very tall radio towers. In 1945 science writer Arthur C. Clarke predicted that three strategically located space stations could provide service to most of the world. Clarke speculated that there existed a particular orbital location where satellites would appear stationary relative to the earth, thereby presenting a fixed, "geostationary" location for sending and receiving signals. If the satellite hovered over a particular point on earth, then signals could travel up to the known location occupied by a stationary receiver/transmitter and then downward to Earth. The satellite could operate as a bent pipe: receiving signals and bending them back to earth much like what portions of the ionosphere do to propagate "skywave" radio signals over long distances.

Clarke correctly predicted that objects sent into a particular orbital location could operate in synchronicity with the earth's orbit, that is, the satellite would rotate about the earth at the same rate that the earth revolves on its axis. In other words, both communication satellites and the earth rotate at a velocity of one revolution per twenty-four hours. At 22,300 miles (35,800 kilometers) satellites appear to hover in a stable location, even though they travel at 6,879 miles per hour in a circular orbit with a circumference of 165,000 miles.[19] Satellites operate in geostationary orbits when they are positioned above the equator and thereby have no tilt (also known as 0 degree inclination) relative to a horizontal line. Put another way, a satellite with no inclination operates in a perfectly circular orbit relative to earth, with no deviations in its orbital plane. Other satellites, operating in inclined orbits, lack perfect circularity and thereby have orbits with a high point ("apogee") farthest from Earth and a low point ("perigee") closest to Earth.

Large Footprints and Point-to-Multipoint Services

Satellites have made a substantial impact on cable television because of two fundamental characteristics:

1. With an orbital location so far from earth, satellites transmit a weak, but usable signal over a broad footprint;
2. Large geographical coverage makes it possible to serve thousands, if not millions, of different locations from a single satellite. The incremental cost of each

new point of communication typically stems primarily from the additional receiving equipment and is borne by the receiving party.

One can visualize the concept of a satellite footprint and point-to-multipoint service by using a flashlight on a globe or even a flat surface. A flashlight quite close to the globe illuminates a small area, but provides a strong (bright) signal. Consider the area illuminated as the footprint. As you pull the flashlight farther from the globe, the coverage area, or footprint, increases, but the signal strength (light intensity) decreases. Point-to-multipoint service means that a single flashlight beam can provide signals to any location it illuminates. A single signal transmitted upward ("uplinked") to the satellite can be received ("downlinked") by users anywhere within the footprint.

Point-to-multipoint transmission capabilities change the calculus and economics of video program distribution. In lieu of a single cable system distributing a movie over an unused channel, a company can package a series of movies and other sorts of premium entertainment for distribution over the same unused channel. The programmer can aggregate audiences throughout the nation, while the cable operator can participate in a new profit center, without the labor and logistical effort involved in physically receiving videotape or film. Widespread coverage also means that the cost of satellite service can be spread over a number of different routes of different length and traffic density.

Basic Components in Satellite Systems
Satellite systems divide into five basic components:

1. The transmitting earth station(s)
2. The uplink
3. The satellite
4. The downlink
5. The receiving earth station(s)

In simple terms, a communications satellite is a radio relay operating in space for ten or more years without the possibility of on-site servicing, repair, adjustment, lubrication, parts replacement, or replenishment of exhaustible components like station-keeping fuel, which keeps the satellite in proper orbit. Satellites contain numerous transceivers that receive and transmit signals, including video programming, telephone calls, and data. They must operate in a vacuum at a location exposed to extreme changes in temperature, and varying solar conditions, including the temporary absence of sunlight needed for power.

Shapes
Satellites come in two primary designs, reflecting different methods for keeping the satellite in proper orbit and oriented to receive and transmit signals. A satellite's entire body can spin like a child's top to achieve gyroscopic stability. Alternatively

it can rely on internal flywheels that spin inside a stationary body. The former method is called spin-stabilization and the latter is called body stabilization. You can visualize spin-stabilized satellites, called a *spinner* in the vernacular, as a large spinning can with solar cells on the outside and antennas situated on top and bottom. A body stabilized satellite, frequently called a three-axis stabilized satellite, looks like a large box with wings containing the solar cells needed to power the satellite.

Satellite shape affects the major criteria used to evaluate performance:

Stability—The ability of the satellite to maintain the desired orbit without resorting to a finite amount of onboard fuel to maintain it. Spin-stabilized satellites have a stability advantage until requirements of power generation and transponder capacity necessitate increasing the height of the drum. Higher drum size and the interaction between spinning and nonspinning parts of the satellite contribute to destabilization and "nutation" anomalies in how the spinning occurs. Three-axis (yaw, pitch, and roll) satellites require a more complex attitude (pointing direction) and orbital control that translates into higher power requirements.

Power—Satellites require electricity to operate the payload and other systems that keep the satellite in orbit and in contact with tracking, telemetry, and network control facilities. Spin-stabilized satellites have limits on the amount of power they can generate as solar cells attach only to the surface area of the drum. Three-axis stabilized satellites can contain larger solar cell surface as the solar wings can be folded and subsequently released in orbit. Both kinds of satellites must have onboard batteries—the heaviest component in a satellite payload—to operate during solar eclipses near the spring and autumn equinoxes when the earth stands between the satellite and the sun.

Thermal—Satellite design must manage the heat generated by solar cells as well as the operation of the station situated 22,300 miles closer to the sun. The larger solar cell surface of a three-axis satellite requires more heat pipes to radiate the heat away from the satellite and heat-sensitive components.

Propulsion—Spinner satellites can use centrifugal force to pulse thrusters on and off to provide any desired torque. A three-axis satellite requires a more complex thruster array, because units are needed to operate in all three axes. Station-keeping fuel represents 25 percent of a satellite's total weight, and is the single most likely component to become depleted, resulting in the end of a satellite's useful life.

Communications Payload—The communications payload represents the electronics needed to provide the relay function: the reception, amplification, and retransmission of signals. Spinner satellites limit the number and size of antennas, because they all must be de-spun, that is, situated on a part of the satellite that does not spin like the top and bottom of the satellite. Three-axis satellites provide ample locations for antenna mounting.

Designers make every effort to reduce the weight of a satellite in view of the approximately $45,000 per kilogram it costs to launch a satellite into GSO. In addition to using aluminum honeycomb panels, composite materials, and lighter components, designers have to make trade-offs affecting such key factors as power, usable life, and back-up system availability. As a rule of thumb, one kilogram of satellite weight corresponds to one watt of power consumption. Designers could reduce power levels, but the prevailing trend has been to increase power output to make it possible for smaller Earth stations to access satellite services. Satellites could operate with less onboard station-keeping fuel, but that would reduce their usable life. Satellites could be stripped of redundant electronics and subassemblies, but these devices provide an insurance policy against premature failures of primary systems.

Some new weight savings opportunities have evolved. For example, a new generation of electronic components physically requires less power and weight. Developments in battery technology have improved efficiency ratings. Propulsion systems have migrated to lighter fuels like xenon that can be ionized when blended with electricity. New composite materials and graphite also can be used to reduce the antenna weight while promoting greater size and flexibility.

Components of an Earth Station

Satellite signals are received by Earth stations, large and small dishes of the type described at the beginning of this book. While the dish itself is the largest component, it is only part of the complex receiver.

The Dish.   The antenna represents the most visible element in an Earth station. It physically concentrates and reflects signals to a single focal point. A satellite antenna operates like a parabola in that signals arriving at various parts of the dish are collected and funneled to one conduit. The aggregation of signals helps concentrate signals with sufficient energy to make it possible for the receiver portion of the earth station to detect, process, and amplify a signal. This function parallels that of the mirror in a reflecting telescope, concentrating the desirable input, like the light from a distant star. Satellite antennas are made of solid or perforated aluminum, wire mesh, or fiberglass.

The Mount.   The mount is a pipe or pole attached to the dish antenna in such a way as to permit the antenna to move and reorient to any satellite scattered across the sky. The most common type is called a *polar mount,* so named because it replicates the earth's axis, making it easier to track a satellite.

The Positioner Arm (Actuator).   The actuator is a device, typically motorized, that moves the dish antenna from one horizon to the other as it points to different satellites. Adjacent satellites may locate as close as two degrees together, a distance of 800 miles. The dish pointing process requires some skill to orient the antenna to the desired satellite.

The Feed Assembly.   After the parabolic antenna concentrates signals from the satellite, the feedhorn funnels the radio energy into the electronic components. The feedhorn is situated away from the surface of the satellite dish at a point in a line from the center of the dish.

The Low Noise Block Converter.   The Low Noise Block Converter (LNB) amplifies the weak, very high frequency signals received from the satellite and converts them to lower frequencies that can be more easily processed and transformed into television channels. It typically converts both C-band (4–6 GHz) and Ku-band satellite frequencies (11–14 GHz) to a standard block of intermediate frequencies from 950–1450 MHz.

The Receiver.   Earth stations require a receiver to take the LNB intermediate frequency, process it, and produce a television signal along with associated audio and subcarrier signals that may add a second language track or other types of text or audio programming. Because of the value in satellite-delivered television, programming operators scramble the signal to ensure that only paying customers have access. As part of the signal processing, receivers may have a descrambler, known as an Integrated Receiver Descrambler ("IRD"), to convert a scrambled signal. A descrambler generally works as a gate that opens and allows the receiver to descramble only if it receives a signal containing the same unique identification code or address as the identification code for the descrambler.

There is a large illegal market for the interfaces needed to make it possible for a receiver to unscramble the satellite signal. Because of this black market, satellite programmers must develop increasingly more sophisticated scrambling systems. The most recent system has an encryption technology like that used by the military. It involves the use of a dual decryption key that triggers the receiver's descrambling capabilities. The first key originates from the satellite operator's authorization center, as part of a digital code containing the serial numbers of all authorized decoders. This signal becomes part of the digital audio transmission, and is combined with "seed keys" contained in the receiver. If the seed key matches with the authorization center's code sequence, they combine to create a master key that decodes the audio and triggers the descrambling function.

Signal pirates have created clones of integrated circuit chips containing the digital code sequence of a paying customer. They then acquire unscrambling circuit boards and install the clone chip, making it appear as though the receiver with the board is operated by a paying customer. Operators have needed to change subscriber codes and engage in other Electronic Counter Measures to frustrate the pirates and their customers (see Chapter 6).

Physics and Electronics of
Satellite Transmission and Reception

The great distance traveled by satellite signals requires both electronic amplification and the natural concentration of signal strength. The FCC authorizes two types of satellite service for direct-to-home television programming: Broadcast Satellite Service (BSS) and Fixed Satellite Service (FSS). The former operates at high-power (120 to 240 watts per channel) in the Ku-band, the latter includes medium-power (20 to 100 watts per channel) service in the Ku-band and C-band. Both are used in digital DTH service, but the high-powered satellites permit smaller receiving dish sizes, down to eighteen inches or less.

Satellites operate at extremely high frequencies where the wavelength approaches the infrared and visible light spectrum. In the 1980s carriers began to use the Ku-band (14 GHz "uplink" and 11 GHz "downlink") in addition to the C-band (6 GHz uplink and 4 GHz downlink). In the latter part of the 1990s, operators will continue up the spectrum to the Ka-band (30 GHz uplink and 20 GHz downlink), frequencies currently used for terrestrial microwave services and satellite links primarily oriented to tracking and controlling satellite orbits. Some carriers also may stake claims to other less cluttered frequency bands, such as the S (2 GHz) and X (7–8 GHz) bands.

At these high frequencies, signals have many of the same characteristics as light. Satellite beams travel in a straight "line-of-sight" manner. Scientists exploit this characteristic by using the principles of physics to concentrate beams and thereby increase signal strength, commonly referred to as gain.[20] By analogy, with nothing more than a magnifying lens, a sunny day, and a piece of paper or wood, one can carve initials in wood or even ignite a fire. The glass in the magnifying lens concentrates solar energy onto a single fixed point thereby increasing the temperature of the solar beam. In the same way, satellite transmitting and receiving dishes have a parabolic design that aggregates and concentrates signals.

Most receiving dishes have a parabola design that concentrates signals from the dish to a small point at the center above the dish. Satellite manufacturers achieve further beam concentration by configuring the parabolic antennas on the satellite in such a manner as to concentrate signal strength. This reduces the size of the signal footprint, but increases the signal strength in the smaller area served. Footprint sizes are categorized by the scope of geographic coverage. An unshrunk footprint is commonly called a "global beam." This beam can be shaped so that a stronger signal illuminated only highly populated terrestrial, as opposed to maritime or Arctic, locations. Beam concentration runs a continuum from global to zone to hemispheric to spot beams.

Zone beams can cover an entire continent, while hemisphere beams cover portions of a continent, such as North or South America. Spot beams are narrowed to portions of a region, such as Western Europe with Ka-band "pencil" spot beams as small as a single metropolitan area. Spot beams have become increasingly important, because of the physical trade-off between beam size and signal strength: the more concentrated the beam, the smaller the earth station receiving dish size needed to receive an adequate signal. Geographical areas served by spot beams may receive an adequate signal using dishes the size of a large pizza. Such small Earth station dish sizes makes it possible for installation of unobtrusive, lightweight terminals at homes and businesses.

The developing Direct Broadcast Satellite (DBS) industry needs receiving dishes that are low-cost, lightweight, and easy to install. These three characteristics make it possible for the technology required in DBS to become consumer electronic items rather than complex, costly, and heavy components of use only to a relatively few hobbyists, rural residents desperate for any source of video programming, and operators of cable television and Satellite Master Antenna Television (SMATV) services (see Chapter 4). Rather than deploy several spot beams, DBS operators have launched high-powered satellites capable of delivering a usable signal to one meter, or smaller, dishes

Scientists have solved the problem of achieving adequate signal strength, despite the signal attenuation resulting from the long transmission path through a dusty, smoggy, ionized, often rainy or snowy, and sometimes obscured atmosphere. However, they cannot make the signals travel faster than the 250 milliseconds it takes for uplinking and downlinking. Despite advances in echo suppression, consumers do not like using geostationary satellites for voice communications. Without the uncharacteristic discipline of sequential and uninterrupted speaking, satellite-carried calls will result in breakups in the transition from one speaker to the other. As a result, satellite operators have lost most of the voice communications traffic that can be loaded onto terrestrial and underwater cables.

Interference-Free Operation

Interference-free operation of satellites requires coordination on the use of radio frequencies and the geostationary orbital arc. That is, nations must agree on which frequencies different types of satellites will operate and how they will register orbital slot usage. Likewise, the satellite and associated receiving Earth stations must operate with sufficient signal strength to override potential interference resulting from other terrestrial transmissions, like microwave relays.

Again physics plays a primary role. The receiving Earth station must have an unobstructed "look angle," or a direct visual link to the satellite unblocked by trees, terrain, and buildings and at an angle sufficiently above the plane of the earth so that the link extends above the horizon. As look angles increase to 90 degrees, directly overhead, the path to the satellite becomes more direct, meaning that the signals sent or received travel more directly through the earth's atmosphere. Lower look angles require longer transit through the earth's atmosphere, leading to greater signal attenuation.

The physics of satellite telecommunication also affects the vulnerability of Earth stations to interference. As Earth stations move farther from the centerpoint of a transmission, where signal strength is highest, signal quality from the intended source deteriorates even as other signals from adjacent satellites increase in strength, particularly if they operate on the same frequency. Signal strength typically degrades in concentric circles or contours. The farther from the satellite's "boresight," the weaker the signal becomes with signal roll-off (degradation) accelerating as the distance from the boresight increases.

Frequency Reuse

Satellites also promote the efficient use of spectrum by reusing frequencies. A satellite can reuse spectrum by transmitting a footprint into two separate geographical regions. This is known as *geographical discrimination.* Additionally, a satellite can use different polarization of the same spectrum. Such "cross-polarization" means that the same spectrum can be used by transmitting signals in both vertical and horizontal polarization or by left and right circular polarization, i.e., the direction of the transmitted radio waves from the satellite.

Transmission Formats

SCPC: The most common high speed digital transmission method for satellite networks is Single Channel Per Carrier (SCPC). SCPC is used for economical distribution of broadcast data, digital audio and video, as well as for full-duplex or two-way data, audio or video communications. In an SCPC system, information is transmitted to the satellite continuously on a single satellite carrier. The satellite signal is received at a single location, in the case of a point-to-point system, or at many locations in a broadcast application. Full-duplex "leased line" applications employ two satellite uplinks that transmit to each other on two carriers—one per uplink location—to provide the equivalent of a "4-wire" data circuit, meaning that parties on both ends of a link can transmit and receive simultaneously.

SCPC got its name from older analog transmission technology, when a single satellite channel could carry only one data carrier. With today's technology, SCPC can actually operate in a MCPC (Multiple Channel Per Carrier) mode, with several data carriers multiplexed into a single digital circuit. For example, two Earth stations transmitting 64 kbps circuits to each other can actually provide several compressed digital telephone channels as well as full-time low-speed data channels if proper multiplexing equipment is added to each basic system.

DAMA: For applications in which high-speed transmission is required, but not all the time, it may be more cost-efficient to employ a Demand Assigned Multiple Access network topology rather than a full-time SCPC system. DAMA networks allow for the dynamic allocation and reallocation of satellite power and bandwidth based on the communications needs of network users. It can provide a 500 percent improvement in spectrum efficiency. Therefore, if a network has multiple sites with voice and data requirements, but doesn't have a twenty-four-hour-a-day need for all sites to be in communication with other sites, a smaller amount of satellite power and bandwidth can be shared by all users. This will lower the recurring monthly segment costs.

TDMA: Satellite users can serve more points and generate greater capacity through a network architecture known as Time Division Multiple Access

(TDMA). This technology allocates a sequence of time to each service point, making it possible to provide low-speed (300 bps to 19,200 bps) data communications to multiple points via the same, shared transmission link. Such low-speed links can provide rural and remote locales with the type of information processing services typically available in urban areas. These include credit card processing and verification, point-of-sale inventory control, and general business data communications. A typical TDMA network employs a large satellite hub system that manages all network terminal access and routing. Data is transmitted to and from the hub in short bursts on satellite channels that are shared with thirty to forty other terminals (depending on network loading parameters). The hub communicates with very small aperature terminals (VSAT) over a higher-speed "outbound" satellite carrier in a conventional time division multiplexing (TDM) format.

TDMA networks can be very cost efficient when large numbers of sites require low to moderate data rate communications with a central point, or with each other, as traffic can be routed through the hub from one VSAT terminal to another. Since network deployment costs can be high, smaller operators (less than one-hundred sites) often take advantage of shared-hub systems. Low-cost VSAT terminals are installed on and operated by a third-party hub provider for a fixed monthly fee, allowing smaller operators the luxury of reliable satellite communications without the high start-up cost of a hub installation. Newer TDMA technologies are available that use conventional "TCP/IP" Internet Protocol routing and higher throughputs than older (X.25) networks.[21]

CDMA: An alternative to TDMA is Code Division Multiple Access (CDMA) a wireless transmission scheme derived from military spread spectrum techniques. Rather than divide an available channel into time slots, CDMA transmits a relatively weak signal spread across the entire allocated bandwidth. Over this spread spectrum platform individual voice and data channels are derived by creating a unique code sequence to each user. Only the extended call recipient will have the key for decoding the particular call with all other channels considered low-level noise that can be filtered out.

The primary benefit of CDMA lies in the ability to expand the number of simultaneous channels that can be carried for any amount of available bandwidth. While TDMA has a circuit multiplication capability of about four, CDMA promises more like eight to ten channels. Both digital technologies promise clear reception, fewer dropped calls, better privacy protection, the ability to carry both voice and data traffic and greater capacity. Both CDMA and TDMA also are being used in the digital, wireless PCS telephone systems discussed in Chapter 5.

Satellite distribution of multichannel programming increasingly will require advanced, high bandwidth techniques as digital distribution of materials becomes the norm and demand for services grows. Similarly, the ground architectures of terrestrial systems have been changing to meet the requirements of the information age.

Terrestrial Multichannel Broadcasting

Most people are familiar with traditional analog television broadcasting. Depending on the size of your town, you are likely to have one or more local broadcast stations, some of them probably affiliated with one of the major TV networks, NBC, CBS, ABC, or Fox. They transmit their signals using the open spectrum on frequencies assigned to them, as described earlier, in the VHF band, channels 2 through 13, or the UHF band, channels 14 through 69.[22] Broadcasters, however, have the ability to create a multichannel delivery system using existing and emerging technologies, some of which are in place today.

Digital Broadcasting

Digital compression technology allows traditional analog broadcasters to transmit several program services over one 6 MHz channel, that is, squeeze five or more channels into a space that previously could only accommodate one. While the technology has been available for some time, a fight over the technical standards has held up implementation. The debate began as a question of standards relating to High Definition TV. An attempt by the Japanese to establish a worldwide standard for HDTV transmission failed in 1986 when European countries rejected the proposal. The FCC subsequently established an Advisory Committee on Advanced Television Service to assist in the creation of a national HDTV standard. A number of companies submitted analog-based proposals for high definition broadcasting, but in 1990 General Instruments introduced a digital format that eventually forced competing companies to follow suit. As differences in the proposals were ironed out, the Advisory Committee announced a compromise dubbed the "Grand Alliance" standard, which it presented to the FCC in late 1995. Several problems arose, however.

First, broadcasters realized that digital distribution would allow them to use the expanded transmission capacity not just to deliver HDTV but also to deliver multiple NTSC channels. As we will see in Chapter 5, there are economic incentives for broadcasters to favor multichannel broadcasting over single-channel HDTV transmission. Questions arose over how much flexibility broadcasters would be given in the use of the new technology. Secondly, interests in Congress, and elsewhere, questioned the process by which the FCC would assign new frequencies for digital broadcasting: Would broadcasters receive a "free" second channel? Would they get to keep their old analog channel? Should they be required to pay compensation for either one? The FCC set aside channels in the UHF band for the new service, but spectrum allocation issues lingered (see further discussion in Chapter 4). Finally, opposition to the Grand Alliance standard gathered steam in late 1996, especially from the computer and film industries. The Grand Alliance standard called for a flexible set of 18 digital formats, including a 1080-line resolution format and 16:9 picture aspect ratio. It also called for NTSC-type interlaced scanning. Computer interests opposed interlaced scanning as both incompatible with and inferior to the progressive scanning method used in computer monitors. The film industry was also uneasy, and advocated a system that would show televised films in their original

movie-screen aspect ratio. In late 1996, the broadcast, computer, and consumer electronics industries settled on a compromise that eliminated the proposed digital formats and dropped interlacing as a requirement. The compromise permitted the
market to determine preferred formats, opening the way for the FCC to approve
flexible standards and make possible the commercial implementation of digital
broadcast television.

MMDS

For microwave broadcasters, multichannel digital distribution is available now.
Multichannel, Multipoint Distribution Systems (MMDS) use microwave broadcast
methods. Because of their ability to organize more than thirty analog microwave
channels into one service, MMDS has been labelled "wireless cable." MMDS beams
programs from a central transmitter to homes in a given geographic area. The microwaves travel a "line of sight" path and so the transmitter is often mounted on a tall
building or high ground in order to cover as wide an area as possible, usually no
more than twenty or thirty miles. Subscribers receive the signals on small dish antennas and convert them using special set-top boxes. Wireless cable can create up to
thirty-three analog channels by tapping into several services in the 2 GHz frequency
band including MMDS, its predecessor, Multipoint Distribution Service (MDS), the
Instructional Fixed Services band (ITFS), and Operational Fixed Services (OFS), a
private microwave service that includes video delivery.[23] Digital compression provides the possibility of converting these thirty-plus channels into hundreds of digital
signals, giving digital MMDS significant potential as a distribution platform for
multichannel television and affiliated services. Close technical cousins to MMDS,
Local Multipoint Distribution Service (LMDS) and Interactive Video Distribution
Systems (IVDS) use similar high-frequency transmission methods and may offer
alternative, albeit unproven, video and telecommunications distribution options.
The commercial application of these digital wireless platforms, especially the use of
MMDS by some telephone companies, is discussed more fully in Chapter 4.

While broadcast multichannel technologies can be divided into satellite and terrestrial platforms, wireline technologies also have two major divisions, one based on
architectures evolving out of the cable industry, the other based on a system arising
out of telephone technology, although many suggest the two approaches will eventually merge.

Cable Architectures

Most of the multichannel programming distributed by satellite still goes to the
headends of analog cable television systems characterized by a classic "tree and
branch" topology. While this architecture will continue its dominance through the
end of the century, it is being replaced by more advanced configurations. This section will look at the tree and branch as well as the basic telephone "star" architecture,
and consider transitional measures to deliver video services over twisted pair. As

both systems evolve, their competing successors will include the "hybrid fiber coax" (HFC) and, eventually, "fiber-to-the-curb" (FTTC) architectures.

Tree and Branch

The basic architecture of the cable television system has been changing, in a number of ways, over the last ten to fifteen years. The industry has been deploying fiber, increasing the interactive capacity of the system, and considering plans for the integration of switched services. A full understanding of the changes is best begun with a review of the classic structure of the community antenna television system.

From the earliest CATV operations in the late 1940s to some of the most advanced systems of the 1980s, the technical configuration of the systems—how the cables are laid out across town and through the neighborhoods—has been the same, a so-called "tree and branch" architecture.

The cable television wire that brings programming to everyone's home begins at a local main office, or "headend," where all the signals are assembled and modulated onto the coaxial system. The signals themselves originate from several sources. Many, as noted above, are received by satellite, as in the case of most cable television networks, such as CNN and MTV. Local commercial or public broadcast stations are received using conventional antennas, or in some cases are sent directly to the headend over coaxial or fiber lines. There are videotape players, and increasingly, digital servers, at the headend that insert local commercials and play back public access programming. Many cable systems have the capacity to transmit programming live from remote sites around town or from studios, if they have them, at the headend.

Each signal is imposed on a separate carrier wave, or channel, and the combined radio frequency package transmitted "downstream" through the system. The signal leaves the headend over high-capacity "trunk lines," which snake their way through the main arteries of the community, down boulevards and city streets and into the local neighborhoods. From there a second level of lines, the "feeder" or distribution cables, branch off to feed specific areas of hundreds, sometimes thousands of homes. Finally, smaller gauge lines, or cable "drops," sprout off the feeder cable to service individual homes. These lines—trunk, feeder, and drops—are strung along poles typically rented from the local telephone company or power utility, or they are buried underground. Buried cable may be required by local ordinance and is aesthetically preferred, but is also more expensive and so accounts for only about 20 percent of total U.S. plant. Coaxial cable strung on poles cannot support its own weight and must be lashed to strong steel cable called "strand," which also supports the amplifiers.

Most of the actual cable in the system resides in the cable drops, between 45 and 50 percent depending on penetration levels; feeder lines account for about 40 percent, and trunk lines take up 10 to 15 percent. In the 1980s systems operators began replacing the coaxial cable in the trunk, and in many cases the feeder lines, with fiber. The drop lines, the final jump into the home, however, are likely to remain coaxial for several years.

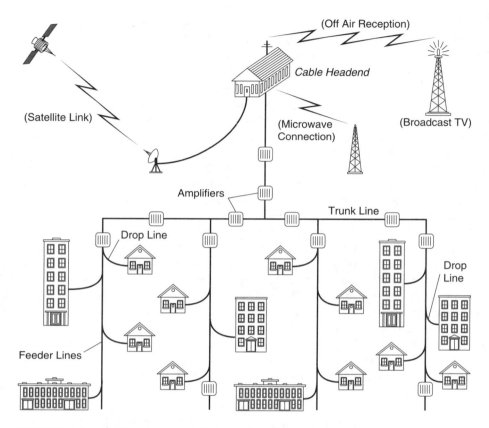

FIGURE 3-7   Cable Tree and Branch Architecture

As noted previously, each amplifier in the system introduces a small amount of noise or interference, and so the total number of amplifiers is limited by the gradual build up of distortion. The actual number of amplifiers used and the spacing between them is dependent on the system bandwidth and the medium, coaxial or fiber. A high-bandwidth coaxial system may have a cascade of twenty or thirty amplifiers in the trunk, while an older system with fewer channels may have up to sixty.[24]

A given cable system, then, can have hundreds, even thousands of miles of fiber and coax and hundreds of amplifiers. The system in San Antonio, Texas, for example, passes more than 400,000 homes and has 4,000 miles of coax with 2,000 trunk amplifiers and more than 11,000 distribution amplifiers.[25]

The total cost of constructing a cable system varies widely, depending on the number of subscribers, kind of technology used, the local geography, and regulatory constraints. According to industry experts, a 35-channel system serving a town of

50,000 with a penetration rate of 53 percent and 75 homes passed per mile could cost between $600 and $1,200 per subscriber to build, depending on local conditions.[26]

Regional Interconnections

Cable companies frequently transmit programming from a distant site to the headend, from one headend to another in the same region, or from a central headend to a remote hub. This feed may originate as the incoming signal from a satellite reception dish or the full slate of system programming transmitted to the hub of an affiliated mini-system. The most popular means of sending these signals has been microwave, but increasingly the industry is using fiber optics. Microwave has a long and distinguished history in the cable industry, providing most of the transport for imported distant signals. Amplitude modulated microwave links (AML) and amplitude modulated coaxial "supertrunks," high-capacity coaxial lines, have been standard techniques for moving special or bulk signals in and out of the headend.

Microwave signals, however, are subject to fading and interference in rainstorms. Fiber offers greater signal integrity and capacity and is being used more frequently. As we will discuss in Chapter 5, cable companies are becoming more regionally consolidated. Autonomous systems that had, for example, served the differing contiguous suburbs of a large city, are being brought under the same ownership and subsequently being tied together in regional networks. An important new technology for the provision of interconnected facilities has been introduced and is gaining widespread acceptance as the transport vehicle of choice. Called SONET, for Synchronous Optical Network, it is a family of optical transmission rates and interface standards allowing the simultaneous broadband carriage of many divergent services. It promises to be used heavily in the telecommunications architectures of the next century. SONET, laid out in a fiber-optic "ring" topology, with sources and users strung out all along the rim, insures a large measure of system redundancy. If there's a break or signal interruption at one point in the ring, traffic can be directed to destination points by moving it in the other direction. Additionally, it can provide a dedicated fiber path for upstream traffic, improving interactive capability (see Figure 3-8).

As cable–telecommunications infrastructures become increasingly regionalized, interactive SONET rings may carry most of the video, voice, and data traffic from large, centralized regional offices to smaller remote headends and hubs.

Interactivity and Addressability

Because the amplifiers in a classic cable system usually push signals in only one direction, in the tree-and-branch topology programming flows in a one-way cascade from the headend, down the city streets and into consumers' homes. Everyone gets the same signals at the same time in the same manner. As early as the 1960s, cable systems began offering the technical ability to send simple signals back up the system, from the subscriber's home to the headend, but for most of cable's history that capacity was used sparingly.

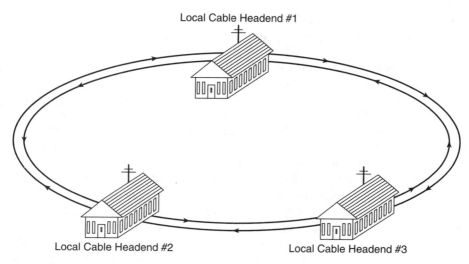

FIGURE 3-8 Fiber Ring Network

In order to deliver special or premium services, such as pay-TV, to select homes, cable systems have relied on set-top boxes and simple filters, or "traps." Positive traps generate a distorting signal that scrambles the premium channel; negative traps, inserted in the drop line, simply block the premium channel. Positive traps are most economical when fewer than half the subscribers take the premium service; negative traps are more efficient when more than half subscribe.[27] Specially equipped converter boxes also have been used to decode scrambled signals. Traps and set-top boxes, however, must be physically added, removed, or modified by the cable operator to alter the reception of the premium service. Boxes and traps, even when attached to poles outside the customer's home, also have been prone to widespread tampering and blackmarketeering. It has been relatively easy to "steal" the cable signal. "Addressability" is the capacity of the cable company to code and identify each customer's home, either through the set-top converter or electronics on the drop pole, and thereby turn signals on and off from the headend. The cable company, for example, can send a scrambled pay-per-view signal out through the system, but activate only those addressable homes that have ordered the program. It has helped reduce the problem of piracy, although not eliminate it (see more on signal theft in Chapter 6).

Addressablility, still, is not the same as interactivity. Cable's often-heralded capacity for interactivity remained little more than a hazy promise through the mid 1990s. Most pay-per-view services required customers to pick up their telephones and call an 800 number to order the movie. But the industry was working furiously to create a delivery system that would increase its existing bandwidth and provide a level of interactivity that would permit it to provide a host of new services once regulatory barriers fell. Many of the goals of the advanced system will be met through the use of digital compression and increased dependence on fiber.

Hybrid Fiber Coax (HFC)

When cable systems began replacing their coaxial cable with fiber, they started with the trunk lines. Because these lines constitute the smallest proportion of the system, it was the most cost-effective approach. Installation of this "fiber backbone" also helped dramatically reduce the number of amplifiers through which the signal had to pass and thereby improved its quality. Instead of passing through a cascade of dozens of trunk amplifiers, the signal now moves through only a few repeaters, or none at all, before being converted back into a coaxial signal near the subscriber's home. This also reduces problems associated with occasional amplifier failure.

The obvious advantages in bandwidth, cost, and performance drove the rewiring process. Also spurring construction was the need to meet the competitive threat from the telephone companies, DBS services, and wireless cable operators. The cable industry needed to move briskly toward a system that increased channel capacity by three- and fourfold and provided a platform for advanced interactive services. The tree-and-branch system was not up to those tasks.

Therefore, as companies began tearing down their coax and installing fiber, moving out from the headend, replacing first the trunk lines, then the feeder lines, and driving the fiber deeper into each neighborhood, they developed a new architecture, one that combined fiber and coaxial in what came to be know as the "Hybrid Fiber Coax" (HFC) system (see Figure 3-9).

Unlike the tree-and-branch architecture, HFC sends several fiber lines directly from the headend into local neighborhoods. In the early fiber installations, the fiber cables terminated at neighborhood "hubs." Mini tree-and-branch coaxial networks feed off the fiber hub, delivering programming to up to 2,000 homes. This "fiber-to-the-feeder" or FTTF configuration later moved more deeply into the system, with fiber lines extending from the hub to fiber "nodes," with each node serving 500 to 2,000 subscribers, or in advanced systems as few as 125 homes. As the number of coaxial amplifiers servicing each home is reduced, the signal quality is proportionally enhanced. As the number of homes at each node decreases, the amount of bandwidth available to each customer increases because overall system bandwidth is divided among fewer people (an important consideration for interactive services, as will be seen).

As with the tree-and-branch architecture, the full complement of programming is continuously fed downstream and is available at every drop or home. Interactivity through an upstream path from the viewer's home is available, but in most architectures restricted to the 0–50 MHz band. Critics of the HFC platform argue that this relatively narrow return path is insufficient to provide interactive services customers will soon expect. Others contend that consumers will require less upstream than downstream bandwidth as most instructions from the subscriber will be used simply to access and return data and video to the home. The debate over how much two-way

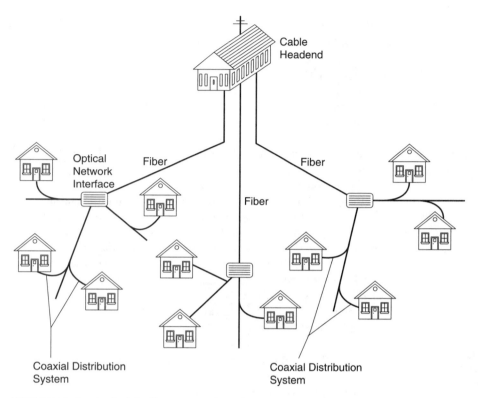

FIGURE 3-9 Hybrid Fiber Coax (HFC) Architecture

capacity is necessary will likely continue for several years. Meanwhile, the telcos are exploring an alternative architecture that arguably provides greater interactivity, albeit at a higher price.

Telephone Architectures

The phenomenon of technological convergence centers, in part, on the mating of the unique characteristics of cable technology with those of the telephone system. While cable, historically, has had a relative abundance of bandwidth, it has had little real interactive capability. Conversely, the telephone companies have been restrained by a very small information conduit, the twisted pair, but one, unlike cable, that can be switched, making it possible for each subscriber to communicate with every other subscriber.

In the 1970s and 1980s, addressability gave cable operators interactive power only to the extent that an individual subscriber could communicate with the headend. The standard cable system did not allow one subscriber to directly contact another. This critical, but taken-for-granted capacity has been, until recently, the exclusive province of the telephone company. This power is embedded in switching capability. The simple switch, first an electromechanical device, now a highly sophisticated computer, directly connects any subscriber with any other subscriber or, more to the point in the information age, any subscriber with any database, information server, web site or voice mail box, public, private, or commercial.

This is the telephone companies' classic "star" system architecture (see Figure 3-10). Unlike the traditional cable television topology that pushes information downstream in ever smaller rivulets, the star system clusters homes around switched hubs, connecting these hubs globally and in effect creating a temporary, hardwired, single-channel, two-way path between users every time a telephone call is placed. This is the public switched telephone network, or PSTN, that we all use everyday.

The philosophy of the emerging switched digital video system arises as much from the switchable legacy of the telephone system as it does from cable's bandwidth. The challenge taken on by both the cable industry and the telephone industry, in short, has been the adoption of the strengths of the competing system. As cable has sought to penetrate the telephone business and enhance its interactive services capacity, it has moved to create or link with systems with greater switching ability. The telephone industry, concurrently, has been searching for ways to increase the

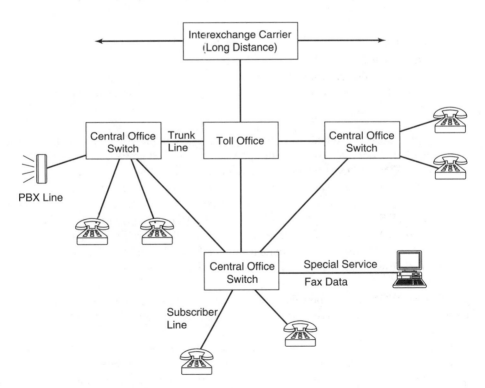

FIGURE 3-10   Telephone Star Architecture

bandwidth it can make available to individual homes in order to offer video and data services in competition with the cable system operators.

Toward this end, the telephone industry, like the cable industry, has been up-grading its system with fiber for years. Most of the long-distance lines today are fiber, as is much of the regional transport. Coaxial cable, microwave links, and other broadband technologies also make up significant parts of the telco infrastructure. The telephone companies therefore have broadband capacity in much of their system. But that capacity stops a short distance from the customer, the important "last mile" of plant. The connection between the consumer's home or office and a neighborhood pedestal or junction box is twisted copper pair. This part of the "local loop" constitutes the last remaining bottleneck in the telco broadband pipeline. As with cable's topology, however, it also constitutes the largest percentage of the total wired plant and an immense capital investment.

This is the technical hurdle that the telephone companies are struggling to clear in preparation for entrance into the broadband market. In order to deliver fully interactive video, as well as voice and data, the telephone industry will have to adapt or replace the ubiquitous twisted pair. In the first instance, the telephone industry has been developing transmission methods to increase the carrying capacity of its existing system, in the second instance, it has been looking at new or enhanced architectures. Each will be considered in turn.

ISDN and ADSL

ISDN and ADSL are transmission techniques designed to expand the capacity of the current telco system and thereby create greater opportunities in markets such as Internet access.

ISDN. Some of the earliest attempts by the telephone companies to provide switched digital service involved an approach called Integrated Services Digital Network (ISDN). ISDN is a technique that combines existing telephone circuits to increase bandwidth and data transmission speed. Standard analog telephone lines, which can support a bit rate of 51 Kbps, can be converted into digital lines of 64 Kbps, or one DSO circuit. A basic rate interface ISDN circuit provides 144 Kbps by joining two 64 Kbps lines and a third 16 Kbps signalling circuit.[28] A primary rate interface melds 24 DSO lines to create a switched circuit of up to 1.5 Mbps. This is enough for a low-level, MPEG-1 video channel, but insufficient for widescale television delivery.

One of ISDN's most promising applications is in the provision of wideband data communications; it gives consumers and business greater access to the Internet, for example, than that available over the standard telephone line and has been heavily marketed by some telephone companies (see Chapter 5). Use of ISDN in fully-switched video network, however, has been dependent on the development of broadband ISDN, or B-ISDN. B-ISDN increases the circuit capaicty from 1.5 Mbps to around 150 Mbps and eventually may reach 600 Mbps. B-ISDN may become an important component of a full-service network, but the evolution of alternative transmission protocols has clouded the future of B-ISDN application in video.

ADSL.   One approach has been experimentation with a form of digital transmission called *asymmetrical digital subscriber line,* or ADSL. The basic idea behind ADSL is to deliver full-motion video, or any broadband service, over a standard twisted pair copper wire. Developed by Bell Communications Research, Stanford University and British Telecommunications,[29] standard ADSL technology can deliver up to 8 Mbps of data per second, far beyond the normal 51 Kbps speed of a normal residential telephone line. The capacity of the ADSL link decreases as the length of the twisted pair line increases, but at 12,000 feet between a residence and local switching facility—well within the range of a majority of homes—it can send 6 Mbps downstream and 64 to 640 Kbps upstream. That's enough for four simultaneous, compressed television signals and a telephone conversation.

Bell Atlantic used an early version of ADSL (1.5 Mbps) in a video delivery trial in Northern Virginia in 1994, and by the mid 1990s, advanced editions of ADSL had attracted the attention of several regional Bell operating companies as methods for providing high-speed Internet services (see Chapter 5).

There are cost questions associated with ADSL. While it turns twisted pair into an avenue for acceptable broadband services, it is seen by some as an expensive approach. Costs of the equipment needed to generate and decode the ADSL signals were initially estimated at up to $4,000 per line[30] and weren't expected to come down into an acceptable target range of $500 to $600 a line for several years, and then only if there was sufficient interest from the industry. Much of the existing copper in the telephone system is aged and "weak" and unable to support the high-demand ADSL service.

xDSL.   Close technical cousins to ADSL are being developed in an effort to overcome some of these shortcomings. Rate-adaptive, or RADSL, varies speeds depending on line quality. Specialty use "high-bit-rate" HDSL requires two, twisted pair lines. "Single-line" SDSL offers high speeds but has a limited reach. Similarly, VDSL, very high-bit-rate digital subscriber line, provides speeds of 12 to 51 Mbps downstream but only over stretches of 1,000 to 4,500 feet. Together, the family of technologies is known as xDSL.

ADSL was being implemented more fully internationally and the surge in interest in Internet services (see Chapter 5) has boosted domestic enthusiasm for the technology. ADSL and the xDSL group are seen as methods of high-speed data delivery, as opposed to video service. While the return path for interactive services would likely have to remain the standard phone line, ADSL was seen as one possibility for increasing the bandwidth for data service to the home. For video programming, however, most telephone companies appear to be moving toward coaxial and or fiber solutions, some of them working on prototype HFC systems.

Fiber-to-the-Curb (FTTC) and
Switched Digital Video (SDV)

ISDN and xDSL techniques utilize, to the extent possible, the existing infrastructure. Advanced architectures require substantially more original construction. They cost more to build but also offer powerful and flexible operating environments. They combine sophisticated digital switching technologies with substantial bandwidth. An architecture called Fiber-to-the-Curb (FTTC) is one such design. By providing switched service for broadband applications, including digital voice and video, it can create a system sometimes labelled Switched Digital Video (SDV). SDV differs from tree-and-branch and HFC cable systems by creating switched, dedicated paths between the program source and the customer. In contrast with an addressable cable system, for example, the SDV approach sends a program only to the home requesting it instead of throughout the sytem (with specified homes given addressable access to the signal).

The SDV system is designed to meet the predicted, increasing demand for integrated voice, data, and video services. Even some advocates of HFC architectures concede that all systems eventually may involve into something like an SDV network.

One of the core characteristics of currently evolving FTTC architectures includes heavier reliance on fiber lines and the use of very sophisticated switching technologies. The distinctions, for example, between Hybrid Fiber Coax systems and FTTC begin with a blueprint that brings the broadband fiber closer to each customer's home. In FTTC, fiber runs directly from the local switching station to neighborhood nodes or pedestals, which may serve as few as a half dozen homes. Here the signals are converted and sent the last few hundred feet by coaxial cable, twisted pair, or a combination of the two. In the dizzying universe of telecommunications acronyms, these neighborhood conversion units are sometimes dubbed network interface units (NIU) or optical network units (ONU) (see Figure 3-11).

The system combines regular telephone voice functions with computer data transport and television carriage. As with HFC, customers can order movies and other TV programming through their remote control, the request is sent back to a local or even regional office where the material, stored on high-capacity digital servers, is retrieved and directed to that particular customer's home. Billing is processed automatically along with the programming order. System capacity is sufficient that other members of the family can be talking on the telephone, playing on-line videogames, or accessing distant data bases, all over the same network.

Part of what makes this all possible is that, unlike the HFC architecture, advanced SDV does not constantly flood the system with the full menu of available programming; 500 channels do not continuously flow past every home on the system. In fact, there need not be channels in the conventional sense of the term on the SDV system. Each home is sent only that material it requests; each home, in effect, has one dedicated channel or as many channels as it needs at the time.

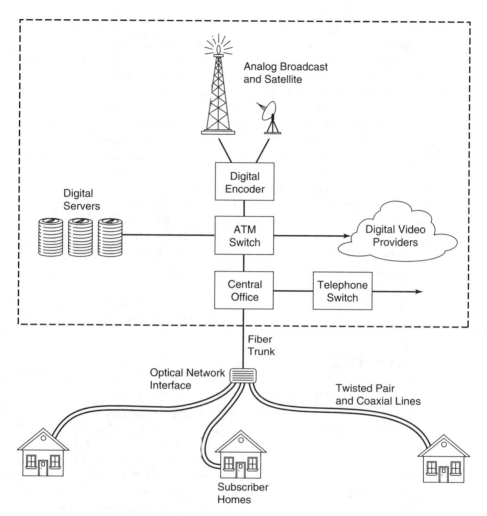

FIGURE 3-11   Fiber-to-the-Curb (FTTC)

ATM

Both cable and telco industries look to the day they can fully (or largely) enjoy broadband digital capacity. The long-term plans for both envision integrated, interactive, video, voice, and data services. One of the technical keys to this digital flexibility, for both FTTC and HFC, is the concept of breaking each signal into discrete packets that can be tagged, switched, delivered, and reassembled in the subscriber's home. Asynchronous transfer mode, or ATM, is increasingly the dominant form of this technology and is being used in conjunction with a variety of delivery techniques. ATM breaks all digital information—video, data, voice—into packets of 53 bytes each. Five bytes are used to give the packet an address, the remainder carry the substantive information. (If there is too little information to fill a transmission cell, ATM inserts empty bytes to fill the packet.) Computerized switches read the address and send each packet to its appropriate location. A given line may be carrying packets for a host of users, bits of a software program or movie, or voice mail message. No one signal or channel monopolizes the line and each line's capacity can be fully exploited. Instead of pouring all the available video signals downstream, high-speed ATM switches route the packaged signals to individual addresses.

ATM switches have other advantages. They are relatively cheap: A typical telephone switch costs about $100 per 64 Kbps line or $1,500 per Mbps; a high-speed, 10 Gbps ATM switch costs $100,000 or about $10 per Mbps.[31] The ATM protocol accommodates MPEG-2 compressed video, and it provides "bandwidth on demand" by varying packet speeds appropriate to the required service. In other words, it opens "virtual channels" throughout the system, creating and destroying them as necessary, making the system highly efficient.[32]

Again, ATM is not restricted to FTTC architectures. ATM packets can be used in conjunction with ADSL delivery systems and HFC systems.

DUELING SYSTEMS

Dueling Systems #1: HFC or FTTC?

FTTC is not without its drawbacks. It is expensive, at least initially. Estimates vary widely and costs are expected to fall each year, but as of 1995 the price of new construction for a FTTC system ranged from about $800 to $1000 per home at 15 percent penetration levels, as much as twice the cost of an HFC system. FTTC is more expensive in part because of labor costs associated with installing additional fiber and coax. Building FTTC only makes sense when the construction costs are spread out over enough households to generate self-sustaining total revenues. In other words, the costs of building the competing systems are contingent on penetration levels. Building fiber nodes designed to serve twenty people that end up with only two or three subscribers means a lot of stranded investment.

But as penetration climbs, the cost of HFC increases, according to some analysts. HFC may cost as little as $500 per subscriber for new construction, at 15 percent penetration levels, but FTTC proponents say HFC becomes more expensive than FTTC when penetration passes 15 percent.[33] Others figure the cost at closer to 25 percent or even 50 percent, but the point is the same. The increasing costs of HFC are attributed to the heavier demand that interactive services place on the system. As subscriber use goes up, the system becomes congested and the company has to increase bandwidth. That means splitting each HFC node to serve fewer homes, which in turn means additional nodes, lines, and amplifiers.

These costs are for original construction, however. By building on its existing plant, cable companies can upgrade their systems to HFC for only $45 per subscriber, according to one study.[34] Although the same study noted that the cable industry would have to spend $415 per subscriber to initiate telephone services, and none of the figures included the cost of the digital set-top boxes required for each home; these were estimated at initial prices of between $300 and $500.

Technical limitations in each system contribute to their costs. In HFC, the normal return path used for interactive services is narrow and noisy. Signals are sent upstream to the headend using the 5 to 40 MHz band. As noted, this band can become quickly crowded if interactive services gain popularity in a given node, although most upstream traffic is "bursty," that is, it is sent in short bursts of bitstreams. Still, this band always has been prone to electrical interference, especially in "leaky" cable systems, those with loose connections that permit interference ingress on the line or in the home. This noise can come from CB and amateur radio operators, lightening flashes, neon signs, hair dryers, garbage disposals, or even vacuum cleaners.[35] In addition to splitting nodes, compensation techniques include tighter maintenance and monitoring standards and even shifting the return path to higher frequencies.[36] Lack of a clean and efficient return path could hamper chances for successful development of a cable-delivered telephone business as well as wider-ranging interactive services.

It appears that cable companies will move incrementally into enhanced and then full-service networks, expanding their fiber lines and offering interactive services as consumer demand warrants. Hybrid fiber coax architectures will likely dominate the cable industry for the near term, when fiber deployment is so extensive and nodes so small that the switch to SDV becomes economically viable. In the meantime, for telephone companies that must build video systems essentially from scratch, the choice is not as obvious. As one industry observer has phrased it, the contest between FTTC and HFC is the telecommunications version of "less filling, tastes great."[37]

The choice for a specific company rests on the perceived cost versus functionality and its long-term business goals and philosophy. Several telephone companies have chosen HFC architectures, including Ameritech. US West has experimented with both HFC and FTTC. Bell South and Southwestern Bell (SBC) also were considering SDV. Bell Atlantic, one of the more aggressive of the regional Bell companies in video, ran trials of all the possible delivery systems in the early 1990s, including HFC, FTTC, and ADSL, and appeared to have committed to SDV for the long run (see Chapter 4).

Dueling Systems #2:
Satellites versus Terrestrial Options

Given the emphasis on fiber-optic cables as the preferred medium for deploying broadband information superhighways, satellites may seem to have been relegated to subordinate status. Many consider wireless options as inferior to wireline services in view of the latter's broader bandwidth and interference-free operations. Yet wireless options will likely play a significant role in the National Information Infrastructure development, and they possess a comparative advantage in some respects.

Recently launched satellites have digital transmission capabilities that match that available from fiber-optic terrestrial networks. The satellites operate with higher power thereby reducing the size of receiving dishes. Satellite systems generate digital signals that can be compressed, coded, packetized, and transmitted to multiple users. More selective earth stations promote higher performance and the ability to derive more channels.

Mobility and Ease in Reconfiguration. Electronic component miniaturization on integrated circuits and microprocessors, higher powered satellites, more sensitive receiving terminals, and orbiting satellites closer to Earth make it possible to support diverse mobile, "wireless" applications. Information service providers cannot use fiber-optic cables access to users in vehicles, ships, aircraft, and sparsely populated locales. Likewise, they cannot easily add and subtract service areas and users by reconfiguring their networks. The wide satellite footprint makes it possible to add another service point simply by installing a transceiver, a process that typically takes only a few minutes.

One-Stop Shopping. Satellite carriers recognize the potential for footprints to traverse national boundaries and the service territories of different cable television operators and broadcasters. They can package programming in such a manner that the retailer simply plucks programming from the satellite for distribution to end-users.

New satellite networks will increasingly convert all traffic into a digital bit stream and next generation satellites will likely have onboard processing capabilities to switch traffic to the appropriate downlink beam or link to another satellite in an operating constellation. Satellites operating as part of the information superhighway look less like simple, unintelligent bent pipes that only relay signals and more like complex airborne analogs to terrestrial, switched fiber-optic telecommunications networks.

A CONCLUDING NOTE

Delivery technologies and architectures will continue to evolve and new techniques will blossom, displacing old ones. It is impossible to predict which of the existing or proposed systems will come to dominate telecommunications delivery in the coming decades. The vision of some engineers and futurists is a system that takes the optical fiber right into the home, and even into the back of the television set and the computer. Others see a greater role for wireless transmission paths as the last step to the consumer. The best guess is that HFC architectures will proliferate and constitute the greatest number or proportion of total systems, but eventually most will move toward more interactive configurations such as those provided by SDV. While the mix of wired and wireless will continue to evolve, the functional characteristics of the emerging system seem clear: a broadband, digital, truly interactive platform that combines voice, data, and video.

NOTES

[1]Twelve in the VHF band and 55 in the UHF band.

[2]You will see channels 4 and 5 and channels 6 and 7 in some large cities because FCC spectrum allocations created ample separation.

[3]Four wires (two pair) in standard home loop.

[5]Walter Ciciora, *Cable Television in the United States: An Overview* (Louisville, CO: Cable Television Laboratories, Inc., 1995), 21–22.

[6]C. David Chaffee, "Cable TV—Fiber-rich," *Communications Technology,* January 1996, 32.

[7]The frequencies between 88 and 100 are reserved for FM, and frequencies from 108 to 137 and 225 to 400 MHz, which are used in the open spectrum for, among other things, aviation communication and navigation information, are governed by FCC rules designed to prevent interference.

[8]Chaffee, 34.

[9]Leslie Coffee, "Fiber Optics and Switched Broadband Networks," in *Communication Technology Update,* 4th ed., August Grant, ed. (Boston: Focal Press, 1995), 344.

[10]Eugene Bartlett, *Cable Communications* (New York: McGraw-Hill, 1995), 130.

[11]"The Handbook for the Competitive Market, Blue Book Vol. III," *Cablevision,* 1996, 18.

[12]*Telecommunications and Advanced Services Provided by the Cable Television Industry* (Washington, DC: National Cable Television Association, 1996), 5.

[13]Nicholas, Negroponte. *Being Digital* (New York: Alfred A. Knopf, 1995), 26.

[14]Negroponte, 12.

[15]Andrew Pollack, "Speed Record: One Trillion Bits a Second," *New York Times,* 1 March 1996, D2.

[16]Andrew Pollack, "After the Digital Videodisc War," *New York Times,* 18 September 1995, D-1.

[17]The MPEG-1 standard is used for compression in CD-ROM applications.

[18]Quadrature Amplitude Modulation (QAM), Quadrature Phase Shift Keying (QPSK), and Vestigial Sideband modulation (VSB), respectively.

[19]See, Donald M. Jansky and Michel C. Jeruchim, *Communications Satellites in the Geostationary Orbit* (Boston: Artech House, 1987).

[20]Typically, satellite signal strength is measured in decibels, a unit of measure that is 10 times the logarithm to the base 10 of a number. Using decibels makes it easier to measure very small and large values associated with measuring signal strength and the associated gain or loss resulting from amplification and the use of signal concentrating technologies as well as the loss resulting from transmitting a signal through the atmosphere. For comprehensive

coverage on satellite technology topics, see Gary Gordon and Walter Morgan, *Principles of Communications Satellites* (Boston: John Wiley & Sons, 1993) and Morgan and Gordon, *Communications Satellite Handbook* (Boston: John Wiley & Sons, 1989).

[21]Frame relay VSAT networks are also available within the TDMA architecture model.

[22]The FCC has considered reallocating, through auction, channels 60–69 to new services (see Chapter 4).

[23]Thirty-three channels in the top fifty markets, thirty-two in markets below fifty, and wireless operators must lease ITFS channels from educational institutions.

[24]Ciciora, 22.

[25]Ciciora, 24.

[26]Ciciora, 19.

[27]Ciciora, 40–41.

[28]T. Aaron Choate, "Integrated Services Digital Network," in *Communication Technology Update,* 4th ed., August Grant, Ed. (Boston: Focal Press, 1995).

[29]Barry Fox, "Can Telephone Kill the Video Shop?" *New Scientists,* 27 November 1993, 22.

[30]Fred Dawson, "Technology Race Tightens for MSO's, Telcos," *CED,* September 1995, 88–94.

[31]Michael Adams, "ATM and MPEG-2—Part 1," *Communications Technology,* December 1995, 36.

[32]Ibid.

[33]Carl Weinschenk, "The HFC—vs.-FTTC Debate Rages On," *Cable World,* 23 October 1995, 36.

[34]Leslie Ellis, "HFC, SDV Cost Differential Still Muddy," *CED,* September 1995, 50.

[35]Ron Hranac, "Two-Way or Not Two-Way," *Communications Technology,* February 1996, 16.

[36]Michael Smith, "The Challenge of the Return Path," *Communications Technology,* February 1996, 34–35.

[37]Weinschenk.

4

Distribution, Competition, and Convergence: "The Waltz of the Elephants"

Companies of size will be the ones that survive. It's going to be the waltz of the elephants, and you want to be sure you don't get stepped on.
—AMOS HOSTETTER[1]

Amos Hostetter was chairman and CEO of Continental Cablevision, the country's third largest cable television operator. In late February, 1996, he stood at a podium during a news conference to proclaim that his company was not going to get stepped on in the coming information age. He took his place before the reporters with Chuck Lillis, President of US West Media Group, to announce the acquisition of Continental by the parent company of US West Media Group, US West Inc., the Regional Bell Operating Company serving much of the Western United States. The combination of the cable and telephone giants was worth more than $11 billion. US West Media group already had a 25 percent equity stake in Time Warner Entertainment, the second largest cable operator in the country. With the addition of Continental (later renamed Media One), US West now had ready access to more than 14 million subscribers. US West provides telephone service for customers in fourteen states; now it would also be the cable company for cities from New England to California.[2]

Hostetter's allusion to dancing elephants was apt. The arena for the delivery of video programming and broadband services was expanding rapidly, thanks both to the leaps in the power of the delivery technology and to the relaxation of regulatory constraints on potential players. But that arena was very large and the price of entry was steep. It was widely observed that only the biggest and most heavily financed companies could compete in the emerging telecommunications environment. Through the early 1990s small cable companies sought buyers while large companies sought partnerships and alliances. Mergers, acquisitions, and joint ventures proliferated among cable companies, between cable companies and programmers, and between cable companies, programmers, and a host of interested parties from allied fields such as telephone, computer, film, and even the electric utility industry. The elephants were dancing; sometimes it was a waltz, sometimes a jitterbug, but everyone, it seemed, was looking for a partner.

Competition and Convergence

Convergence became the watchword of the telecommunications industry in the 1980s. Initially it described the convergence of communications technologies, the melding of the computer, the television, the telephone, and satellites into a unified system of information acquisition, delivery, and control. Held together by the global network of satellite dishes, copper, coaxial, and fiber wires and the accelerating flow of digital bits and bytes, convergence was a foundation concept for the National Information Infrastructure and the Information Superhighway. It was, and is, an engaging and accurate metaphor for the changes taking place in the technology of personal and mass media in the remaining years of the twentieth century. It soon became apparent, however, that the term had an additional meaning. Convergence described not just the technological changes taking place, but changes in business and ownership structure of the media as well. Convergence characterized the evolving consolidation of heretofore disparate industries and firms.

Critics such as Ben Bagdikian have argued that the media—print, broadcast, and film—have for decades been in the process of accelerating consolidation, the ownership of more and more outlets by fewer and fewer companies.[3] The notion of convergence, in this economic sense, rephrases Bagdikian's argument and draws attention to the cable television industry in its internal structure and to the relationship of the cable industry to all other communications sectors, including broadcast, telephone, and data processing. It envisions not just a technologically unified (or at least correlated) information–entertainment utility, but an economically integrated megaindustry, as well. To achieve favorable economies of scale (see Chapter 5), companies have vertically integrated into all market segments up and down the food chain, from production to exhibition. To achieve economies of scope, these ventures have diversified into adjacent markets, with broadcasters like NBC exploiting existing personnel and resources to create their own cable networks, such as CNBC and MSNBC.

Given these observations about economic convergence, therefore, it is in some ways counterintuitive that there is also great fanfare about the competitive open market that technology and deregulation have reportedly forged. How is it, one can fairly ask, that intense competition and convergence can be taking place simultaneously?

Two points must be kept in mind. First, we are in some ways in the very early stages of convergence, at the beginning of a process. The technology of the distribution systems, as well as their industrial organization, retain significant distinctions despite their trajectory toward convergence. The structure and operation of the local telephone company is not identical to that of the local cable company or DBS service. Their technology, ownership structures, and business histories, while related, are not the same. One day the industries that had been known as cable and telephone may, in fact, merge and synthesize into a new system. That day may be decades away, however. For the near term, the cable, broadcast, telco, and other distribution providers will approach various markets with differing levels of interest and energy.

This then raises the second important point—that is, distribution platforms are not the same as programming and services. Satellites, cable companies, and telephone companies, technically, can all provide you with your telephone and your video service. This is the sea change that deregulation and technical innovation have brought about; similar but distinct distribution systems, and the industries they have spawned, are now capable of providing customers with a similar set of products and services. In other words, technology and deregulation have *redefined the relevant markets* for this host of industries by collapsing consumer markets that had earlier constituted separate businesses.

Prior to these changes, the telephone companies' switched, narrowband system delivered local and long-distance voice communications and data, and legal barriers in place since the early 1980s kept the local Bell Operating Companies separate from long-distance companies. Broadcasters and cable companies provided television entertainment. Satellite services were primarily middlemen in the communications transport business, invisible to all but those consumers with ten-foot wide dishes in their backyards.

Fiber-optics, digital technology, and deregulation pulled down the walls between these industries, some of them very large, that had not heretofore faced each other in the competitive arena. AT&T's system has faced off against Time Warner's, while General Motors, through its DirecTV DBS business, has taken on the cable industry. The question, in short, is quickly becoming, do you want to buy your Internet and television service—a package deal—from BellSouth or from TCI?

This idea is also at the heart of Hostetter's elephants' waltz: companies that were giants in their own, previously separate, industries clashing in a newly created, combined market for content and services. The early results have been predictable. Some firms, as we will see, have gone head-to-head in the new multiservice market, competing vigorously in television, data, and voice telephony. Some people have chosen, like Hostetter, to sell out rather than attempt a competitive struggle that would cost millions if not billions of dollars and the outcome of which was very uncertain. The extent to which this new and contested market will remain competitive and afford consumers lower prices and better services or, alternatively, lead over time to yet another cabal of regional communications monopolists, is yet to be seen. In his news conference, Hostetter prophesied the consolidation of the nation's cable companies into six or eight regional monopolies, following the pattern of the local telephone companies.[4] Others see a more competitive and open market.

Distribution and Programming

This chapter and the next will look at the general structure of the multichannel television and telecommunications industries. They will describe the major players in Hostetter's dance, both the traditional competitors and the new entrants, as well as the programming and services they provide. The arena is populated by several different categories of players. As suggested above, the broadest distinction one can make is between companies that: (1) serve as the transport structure, those that distribute content to the home, and (2) those that create or provide the content and services. The first category includes, for example, your local cable system, while the second category includes programming networks such as Cable News Network and Home Box Office. It is not a perfect dichotomy. Distributors, in fact, provide many services and often fashion their own programming content, and, as we will see, there are deeply intertwined ownership ties connecting the two. In practice, the lines between them are increasingly blurred. Nonetheless, as a beginning point, it is a useful way to think about industry structure. The first category provides the hardware or distribution technology, the wire-based or broadcast infrastructure; the second category provides what some have described as the software of the industry, the programming and the services carried by the distribution network (see Table 4-1).

The present chapter will consider the structure of and recent developments in the distribution networks of multichannel telecommunications and the nature and control of the competitive delivery systems that bring the services to market. Chapter 5 examines the programming and services that the broadband platforms will deliver and, where appropriate, industry structures in programming distinct from those of distribution. In addition, Chapter 5 will further look at the question of ownership and control as it is evolving across all of these industries and sectors including distribution, programming, and services. It will consider, for example, arguments surrounding the issue of whether the cable television industry constitutes a "natural" monopoly. It will look at the complex web of interlocking business relationships that has come to epitomize the cable, satellite, and telecommunications businesses in all of their varied activities.

The Distribution Landscape

By distribution, we mean the manner in which technologies have been organized into coherent systems. The emerging distribution infrastructure can, at least for pur-

TABLE 4-1

Distribution	Programs and Services
Wireline	*Video*
Cable Television	*Programming Networks and Services*
Telephone	Basic Networks
Utilities	Premium or Pay Networks
	Pay-Per-View
Broadcast	Near Video-on-Demand and Video-on-Demand
Terrestrial	*Broadcast Retransmission*
Traditional VHF & UHF Broadcast Television	Local Stations
Emerging Multichannel VHF & UHF Television	Regional, Imported Stations
Multipoint, Multichannel Distribution Systems (MMDS)	Superstations
	Local Cable
Local Multipoint Distribution Systems (LMDS)	Local Cable Origination
Satellite	Cable Access Channels: Leased, Public, Educational and Government (PEG)
Satellite Carriers	
Fixed Service Satellites (FSS)	
Direct to Home satellites (DTH)	*Telephone*
Direct Broadcast satellites (DBS)	POTS, Plain Old Telephone Service
Television Receive Only (TRVO)	CAPS, Competitive Access Providers
Satellite Master Antenna TV (SMATV)	PCS, Personal Communications Services
	Data
	Internet and WWW Access
	(E-mail, information, entertainment, games, shopping, banking, and so on)
	Telemetry: Fire and burglar alarms
	Distance Education
	Telecommuting
	Paging and Positioning

poses of exposition, be divided initially between wireline and broadcast platforms. The former includes the cable television and telephone industries along with a smaller player, the utilities industry. Broadcasting includes terrestrial broadcast systems such as the traditional local television broadcaster and wireless cable systems, among others. Satellite broadcasting platforms include DBS and TVRO.

In practice, the nationally and internationally integrated system that brings you television, telephone, and data service uses a combination of wire and broadcasting paths. A given television signal, for example, might travel the airwaves via satellite and terrestrial microwave before reaching the cable company for final wired delivery. Computer data may run through narrowband and broadband conduits, wired and broadcast. The organization of distribution systems presented here speaks more to the nature of the platform in its final stage or stages, the local system that distributes signals in a given community (although in the case of DBS it is clearly a national "neighborhood"). This organizational scheme reflects not just the technical reality of the difference between distribution systems but also the structure of ownership and control. Distribution systems have related but differing histories and organizations. The discussion below is about how distribution technologies have been ordered into rational systems, and also about how and by whom these systems are controlled.

WIRELINE INDUSTRIES

Cable Television

The traditional cable industry is composed primarily of thousands of local cable systems and scores of national Multiple System Operators (MSOs). Local systems are the individual cable systems that serve a particular town or community. Classic cable systems have the tree-and-branch architecture described in Chapter 3, with a main office, or headend, fiber or coaxial trunk lines, feeder lines, and drops. There are about 11,660 systems in the United States. The number of systems grew slowly but steadily through the 1960s and 1970s then, as Figure 4-1 illustrates, exploded in the early 1980s following deregulation and the rise of satellite-delivered cable networks.

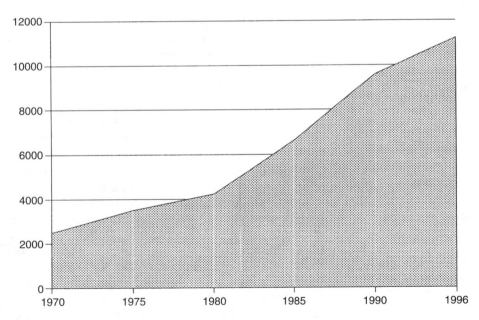

FIGURE 4-1   Cable System Growth 1970–1996

Source: © 1997 Warren Publishing, Inc., from *Television and Cable Factbook* (2115 Ward Ct. N.W., Washington, D.C., 20037), F-2.

TABLE 4-2   Systems and Subscribers by Channel Capacity

Channels	Systems	% Systems	Basic Subs	% Subs
54+	1,558	14	27.7 m	46.71
30–53	6,376	57.31	28.5 m	48.16
20–29	1,104	9.92	1.19 m	02.01
13–19	353	3.17	.125 m	0.21
6–12	588	5.28	.219 m	0.37
5	10	0.09	2,732	0.005
<5	4	0.04	517	0.001
NA	1,133	10.18	1.49 m	2.518

Source: © 1997 Warren Publishing, Inc., from *Television and Cable Factbook* (2115 Ward Ct. N.W., Washington, D.C., 20037), F-3.

The typical system has between thirty and fifty-three channels, with capacity growing steadily as systems rebuild and increase their bandwidth. The introduction of digital delivery technologies in the late 1990s will dramatically expand capacity as compression multiplies the number of available channels. Systems with fewer than thirty channels tend to be older and located in smaller communities. Cable operations with more than thirty channels account for about 70 percent of all systems and serve more than 95 percent of all cable subscribers (see Table 4-2).

While two-way capacity for cable is critical to its success in competing with the telephone companies and multichannel broadcast services, nationwide the industry is at best only partway through the installation of the equipment necessary for true interactive services. As Table 4-3 shows, the top five MSOs, which lead the industry in modernization of their architecture, have on average less than 50 percent of their total plant at two-way capacity.

Nationwide, cable system wires pass about 97 percent of all television households, and about 66 percent of all TV households in the country, about 64 million, subscribe (see Table 4-4).

TABLE 4-3   MSO Two-Way Capability

	1996	1997	1998
TCI	20%	35.0%	60.0%
Time Warner	24%	65.0%	90.0%
US West	22%	33.0%	67.0%
Comcast	20%	51.9%	71.2%
Cox	37%	42.0%	64.0%

Sources: *CableWorld,* 26 February 1996, 1; *Broadcasting & Cable,* 29 April 1996, 12.

TABLE 4-4   Basic Cable Subscription 1975–1995

	Cable Subs (millions)	TV Homes (millions)	Cable Penetration
1996	64.8	97.0	66.8%
1995	63.7	95.4	66.8
1990	55.8	92.1	60.6
1987	44.1	87.5	50.4
1985	41.5	84.9	48.9
1983	34.1	83.3	40.5
1980	17.6	76.3	23.0
1975	9.2	68.5	13.4

Sources: *Cable TV Facts* (New York: Cable Television Advertising Bureau, 1996), 5; *Cable Television Developments* (Washington, D.C., 1996), 2; *Television and Cable Factbook* (Washington, D.C.: Warren Publishing, 1997); Paul Kagan Associates, Inc., Carmel, Calif.; U.S. Bureau of the Census, *Statistical Abstract of the United States,* vol. 101 (Washington, D.C.: Government Printing Office, 1980), 589; *Broadcasting & Cable,* July 21, 1997, 111.

While the total number of cable systems is large, the vast majority of those systems are tiny operations serving only a few hundred customers. Most of the nation's cable customers are concentrated in a relatively small handful of large systems in major markets. About 42 percent of all subscribers are served by only 2 percent (about 250) of all cable systems; these are systems with more than 50,000 customers each (see Table 4-5). The top 10 percent of all cable systems serve more than 79 percent of the nation's subscribers. About 56 percent, or 8,239 systems, divide up less than 4 percent of the total subscriber base, and some 3,272 systems serve fewer than 250 customers each.

TABLE 4-5   Systems and Subscribers by Number of Subcribers in System

Subs	Systems	% of Systems	Basic Subs	% Total Subs
50,000 +	256	2.3	26.6 M	44.9
20,000–49,999	437	3.93	13.4 M	22.7
10,000–19,999	512	4.6	7.2 M	12.1
5,000–9,999	658	5.9	4.5 M	7.6
3,500–4,999	421	3.7	1.7 M	2.9
1,000–3,499	1968	17.69	3.7 M	6.3
500–900	1458	13.1	1 M	1.7
250–499	1513	13.6	0.5 M	0.9
249 or less	3272	29.41	0.4 M	0.6
N.A.	631	5.67	—	0
Total	11126	100.0	59.2 M	100.0

Source: © 1997 Warren Publishing, Inc., from *Television and Cable Factbook* (2115 Ward Ct. N.W.,Washington, D.C., 20037), F-3.

Despite the multitude of small systems, the day of the "mom and pop" cable operation is long over. Most cable systems are owned by large companies that operate groups of systems. These MSOs comprise the dominant ownership structure in the industry. There are more than 600 MSOs in the United States controlling over 90 percent of all cable systems.[5] The bulk of all local subscribers, however, is held by only the top ten or twenty companies. Concentration in the industry is examined more extensively in Chapter 5, although it is worth noting here that two MSOs in particular exercise special influence on the business by virtue of their massive size, relative to other MSOs, and through their partnerships with, and equity interests in, other ventures operating in adjacent markets such as programming. They are Tele-Communications, Inc. (TCI), based in Denver, and Time Warner, Inc., out of New York. As Table 4-6 illustrates, they dwarf other MSOs in terms of their overall subscriber base.

TCI is the nation's sixth largest media company (not counting the telcos) behind Time Warner, Disney, Viacom, News Corp., and Sony (based on annual revenues). It has assets estimated at more than $20 billion and serves more than 14 million subscribers, 12.5 million through wholly owned subsidiaries, the rest through equity

TABLE 4-6   Top 20 MSOs in the United States

Rank	Company	N of Subs (in millions)
1.	TCI	13.9
2.	Time Warner	12.1
3.	US West Media Group	5.2
4.	Comcast Corp.	4.2
5.	Cox Communications, Inc.	3.2
6.	Cablevision Systems Corp.	2.8
7.	Adelphia Communications	1.8
8.	Jones Intercable, Inc.	1.4
9.	Marcus Cable	1.3
10.	Falcon Cable TV	1.17*
11.	Century Comms Corp.	1.1*
12.	Charter Comms.	1.07*
13.	Lenfest/Suburban Cable	1.0*
14.	Prime Cable	0.85
15.	InterMedia Partners	0.82
16.	TCA Cable	0.7
17.	Post-Newsweek/Cable One	0.63
18.	Fanch	0.5
19.	Multimedia Cablevision	0.47
20.	Triax	0.45

Sources: Paul Kagan, Associates, Inc. (Carmel, Calif.) in *Cable Television Developments* (Washington, D.C., Spring, 1996); "Databank," *Cable World,* 9 December 1996, 34; "Cable Television's Top 10 MSOs," *Broadcasting & Cable,* 9 December 1996, 79–84; *Broadcasting & Cable,* 16 June 1997, 36–42.
*Subscription figures for Falcon, Century, Charter, and Lenfest are close to one another and vary by source, so rankings may shift.

interests in other cable systems, and through the acquisition of Viacom's cable operations. TCI systems pass about 22.5 million homes. Its revenues, including income from its affiliated programming arm, Liberty Media, grew from $4.9 billion in 1994 to $6.9 billion in 1995.[6] It spent S980 million on system upgrades in 1995 and $260 million on maintenance with a goal of bringing most of its systems up to 550 MHz before 2000. TCI's operating cash flow was $1.8 billion in 1994 and $2.0 billion in 1995, although it posted a loss of $171 million in 1995 and its stock had been stagnant for several years.

As we will explore in the next chapter, TCI has an impressive array of ownership interests, partnerships, and joint ventures. Through Liberty Media, it has full or partial ownership of many leading cable networks, including Encore, the Discovery Channel, BET, QVC and all the Turner channels, including CNN and TNT, and, through Turner, an ownership interest in Time Warner. It owns broadcast properties, clothing stores, and a major interest in McNeil–Lehrer Productions.

Time Warner is similarly situated, although, unlike TCI, cable and telecommunications is not its only nor its primary media business. This much larger corporation has its roots in publishing, recording, and film, with major subsidiaries in these areas as well as others. Time Warner, following its acquisition of Turner Broadcasting, became the world's largest media conglomerate. A partial list of its holdings includes Time-Life Publishing, the WB Television Network, Warner Bros. films and Warner records, and Turner Broadcasting Systems. More will be said about both corporations throughout the next two chapters. The next tier of MSOs includes prominent and typically long-standing companies such as US West–Media One, Comcast, Cablevision, and Adelphia.

The business philosophies governing the relationships between the MSOs and their individual systems vary, but MSOs typically exercise tight control over the local franchise, managing, often on a regional basis, the hiring and firing of system heads, promotional campaigns, technological innovation, financing and construction, and, most importantly, programming. Large MSOs are in a strong position to negotiate with programmers when they are considering additional channels or services. In the cable television industry, power is concentrated in the corporate headquarters.

Cable Competition

Until the early 1990s the only serious competitor to cable in the area of television programming was the local over-the-air broadcast station, although videotape rental did hinder the development of pay services such as HBO. While deregulation and advances in technology were fundamental in opening the doors to new entrants, these forces were not the only ones at work. Some of the cable industry's own activities nudged the opening for competitors a little wider. The increase in subscriber rates following the 1984 deregulation (see Chapter 2), the industry's reputation for weak customer service, and the failure to made good on blue sky promises all plowed fertile ground for new entrants. In 1992, for example, TCI President and CEO John Malone announced the dawn of the 500-channel universe. Cable, he declared, would use digital compression to turn on a gusher of new programming, and TCI would deliver the new technology by the end of 1994. Unfortunately, the technology and the programming failed to materialize.

The results were public disillusionment and the failure of cable stocks, including TCI's, to keep pace with a surging market in 1995 and 1996. It made it all the easier for potential competitors to attract consumers. Direct broadcast satellites and wireless cable operators were among the first to begin providing multichannel television to consumers (although C-band satellite services had enjoyed moderate success in some markets previously). While critics claimed DBS would be limited to rural areas where cable was unavailable, the service soon demonstrated it could attract subscribers from urban cable systems. And these services were only the first to demonstrate the competitive reality of the new marketplace. Waiting in the wings were the broadcasters and telephone companies. The task for the traditional cable operators in the latter half of the 1990s seemed to be to successfully roll out digital capacity and begin offering the programming and services long promised. TCI began offering digital services in a few markets in 1997 under the label "ALL TV," and Time Warner was preparing similar digital implementation. The roll-out was hampered, however, by high capital costs and technical challenges. Through recent court decisions and deregulation, cable lost much of its legal market protection; the doors were flung open to new players. The following looks more closely at some of them.

The Telephone Companies

> *My worst nightmare has to do with Ameritech*
> *saying that they're ready to rock 'n' roll and*
> *that their next concert is in Massillon, Ohio.*
> *—BOB GESSNER, MASSILLON CABLE*[7]

Massillon Cable is a family-owned business serving a small town about half an hour south of Akron. Ameritech is one of five multibillion-dollar Regional Bell Operating Companies (RBOC); it provides telephone service to five Midwestern states. Gessner was worried because Ameritech had determined that it was going into the cable television business. By the time Ameritech reached Ohio in early 1996 it already had acquired franchises to build cable systems in a dozen cities. Its first franchise in Ohio was in Hilliard, about one-hundred miles from Massillon and it soon acquired operating rights to Columbus and the suburbs around Cleveland. If Gessner was nervous, he probably had a right to be. The elephants were dancing in his direction.

The entry of the telephone industry into television in the mid 1990s was potentially one of the more important communication business developments of the decade. With the RBOCs and some long-distance carriers entering or considering the video market, cable television faced what some saw as the most serious long-term threat to its historic dominance of the multichannel television business, DBS notwithstanding. Telephone industry competition was not a surprise; in many ways it wasn't even a new event. As noted in Chapter 2, AT&T was delivering television pictures over coaxial wire before cable television was a gleam in any entrepreneur's eye, and the telephone industry had toyed with various ways of getting into the entertainment business as early as the 1920s. The telephone company had been kept standing enviously on the sidelines of the cable business for decades, prevented from entering the game by the courts and the federal government. As the Berlin Wall of regulatory restraint fell, the two industries prepared for incursions into each other's territory. The telephone industry had to overcome the technological challenges described in the previous chapter in order to deliver broadband services over its narrowband pipe. But innovations such as digital compression, ADSL, ATM, and the simple willingness to spend lavishly to rebuild its infrastructure made real the possibility that the telephone companies would eventually come knocking on consumers' doors with packages full of CNN and HBO.

Of greatest concern to cable operators was the sheer size of the competitive threat. The telephone industry dwarfs the cable industry in almost every measure. It has more wire, more people, and a lot more money, more than $140 billion in annual revenues compared to about $26 billion for cable. The telephone industry has very deep pockets and can afford to use some of that money to explore ways to develop its video enterprises, of which there are many. The telephone companies were engaged, by the mid 1990s, in scores of experiments, test beds, and joint ventures around the country, exploring new technologies, cultivating programming streams, and testing marketing approaches in video and data services. And the trials were not limited to investigating the possibilities of their existing or even expanded fiber and copper network. Telephone companies were looking at alternative delivery systems including DBS, MMDS, and plain old cable systems.

Telco Basics

The major companies in the telephone industry include AT&T, the five RBOCs, the largest independent local operator, GTE, competitive long-distance carriers such as MCI and Sprint, and a host of smaller local and regional companies, including an affiliate of Sprint, Altel, and Continental (not affiliated with the cable company). Basic local telephone service, or POTS (plain old telephone service) is provided by a local exchange carrier (LEC), usually one of the RBOCs or a local independent such as GTE. Long-distance service is provided by AT&T, MCI, Sprint, or one of the smaller long-distance carriers.

It is a world much more complicated and competitive than before the breakup of the Bell system in 1982. Prior to that there was really only one major telephone company, AT&T, the Bell System. A host of medium and small independent companies swarmed around this communications behemoth like flies at a picnic, annoying it, but little more. The forced divestiture broke up the Bell picnic; AT&T was spun off along with seven RBOCs. These "Baby Bells" would continue, as separate companies, to serve as local exchange carriers, while the AT&T long-lines division stayed in long-distance and opened other ventures.

Even before the breakup, MCI took advantage of regulatory opportunities created by the FCC, and frequent and successful litigation, to challenge the almost mythic dominance of AT&T. MCI had been one of many smaller microwave common carriers, which, headed by Bill McGowan, led the way in developing a high-capacity fiber-based national infrastructure and then sank millions of dollars into marketing and promotion. Sprint Telecommunications later followed and by the mid-1980s no family could sit down to a quiet dinner without a telemarketing phone call interrupting the meal while a salesman tried to convince them that they ought to switch their long-distance service. It may be some testimony to the strength of AT&T's name recognition and its advertising that, despite the monumental change that the 1982 divestiture brought to the industry and despite the millions of dollars local companies have poured into television advertising, direct-mail marketing and annoying sales calls at home, polls have shown that anywhere from 30 to 60 percent of the population still thinks that AT&T is their local phone company.[8]

In fact, for some people, reality may catch up to their mistaken perception. As tangled as the competitive universe of common carriage is, the 1996 Telecommunications Act will increase the number of knots and intersections by deregulating the business even further. Under the Act, long-distance carriers such as AT&T will be allowed to offer local service and the RBOCs can try their hand at the long distance business,[9] all of this in addition to and concurrent with telco efforts to penetrate the video services sector (see Chapter 5 for more on interconnections between incumbent and competitive providers). A host of very large telecommunications companies that once fed only on carefully limited common carrier services have been freed to dine from an expansive menu of à la carte items, including home television. The timetable for execution of these market plays is uncertain. A host of legal, technical, and business issues will need to be resolved, but the phone companies are working on several fronts to expand their traditional offerings.

The original seven Baby Bells were reduced to five in early 1996 when Texas-based SBC Communications (formerly Southwestern Bell) acquired Pacific Telesis, and two weeks later Bell Atlantic announced its intention to merge with Nynex. The newly formed SBC serves the Central Southern states, PacTel serves California and Nevada. The new Bell Atlantic (Nynex intended to give up its name while corporate headquarters moved to New York) covers the northeastern seaboard. The other RBOCs include BellSouth in the Southeast, Ameritech in the Midwest, and US West, serving the western and northwestern states.[10] GTE is the largest of the non-Bell LECs. As Table 4-7 shows, each company is a multibillion-dollar enterprise and controls millions of telephone lines. The long-distance carrier AT&T is the largest of the phone companies, and one of the largest companies in the world, with annual revenues of nearly $80 billion.

POTS to PANS.   While much of the telephone industry's history and profitability is grounded in plain old telephone service, the simple call you place to your neighbor is not where the future of the business lies. The POTS segment of the business has been relatively flat for some time and is not expected to grow more than

TABLE 4-7 U.S. Telephone Companies

Company	Revenues	Customer Lines
AT&T	$79.6 bill	
MCI	$15.2 bill	
Sprint	$13.6 bill	
SBC/PacTel	$21.0 bill	30.1 mill
Bell South	$17.8 bill	20.9 mill
Nynex	$13.3 bill	17.0 mill
Bell Atlantic	$13.4 bill	19.7 mill
Ameritech	$ 9.6 bill	18.8 mill
US West	$ 8.2 bill	14.7 mill
GTE	$20.2 bill	18.0 mill

Sources: *Financial World,* 22 April 1996, 44; *New York Times,* 2 April 1996, D-9; *Cable World,* 7 September 1992, 1; *Cable World,* 8 April 1996.

4 or 5 percent annually. In contrast to POTS, the telcos have been seeking to deliver enhanced services, or what some called PANS, "pretty amazing new stuff." Simple augmented customer services like call-waiting and call-forwarding are seen as helping lift the bottom line, but the serious growth markets are linked to business service and wireless and data communications. The explosion of cellular telephones, fax machines, and computer modems has been so pronounced that the decreasing supply of available telephone numbers has become a serious problem for the industry, and an expanded, more complex dialing regime has evolved, including a proliferation of area codes and a new toll-free dialing prefix (888).

The multichannel video business, therefore, is only one part of the larger picture that the telephone companies are trying to assemble. The ultimate goal is to be a full-service provider, bundling voice, data, and video over one wire and sending you one bill at the end of the month. It is not, however, a new vision.

The Long and Winding Road

The floodgates of telco entry into the video business really opened with passage of the Telecommunications Act of 1996. It gave the telephone industry not just formal legal approval to expand its business, but it was the final crescendo of what had been a building chorus of political philosophy that almost uniformly endorsed competition in the telecommunication sector over government control and separation of industries. The FCC, the White House, and both parties in Congress were, to a greater or lesser extent, embracing the ideology of the open marketplace and committing themselves to the notion that competition was better for the consumer than regulation.

It was not always so. As described in Chapter 2, the Justice Department, through its consent decree with AT&T, had effectively blocked the telephone company from entering the cable business and other information services in 1956. As the telephone industry, and especially AT&T, eyed cable TV in the 1960s, the fear then, as today, was that the telco would use the river of revenues from its protected monopoly telephone business to deliberately underprice new competitive ventures like the cable business with an eye toward driving out the competition. There was even concern that the telephone company would raise residential rates above normal levels in order to fund construction of competitive cable systems. This cross-subsidization would give the company an unfair advantage over almost everyone else by providing access to huge amounts of interest-free capital and giving it the ability to offer below-cost service, undercutting competitors' rates and driving them out of business. Cable companies were at an additional disadvantage because of their dependence on the telephone companies for pole space to string their wires. A telephone company attempting to offer competitive cable service could, by raising pole attachment fees or imposing burdensome technical requirements, force the local cable company off the poles, as the telephone industry in fact tried to do in the mid-1960s.[11] Those efforts, aimed at forcing local cable companies to lease telephone company facilities for the provision of TV service, are again what led the FCC in 1970 to tighten the restrictions on the Bell System and the independent phone companies.[12]

The FCC 1970 prohibitions on telco-delivered television were codified in the Cable Communications Policy Act of 1984. With some minor exceptions (e.g., rural services) the phone companies now were prevented both by Congress and the FCC from entering the video business. Finally, the provisions of the Modification of the Final Judgment (MFJ), which split up AT&T in 1982, additionally frustrated any RBOC efforts to enter cable service. But the winds of political change were blowing strong in the 1980s. The doctrine of deregulation, then un-regulation, that began under the Carter administration expanded during President Reagan's eight years in office.

In 1987 the Reagan Justice Department released a report on the status of the MFJ, recommending that the RBOCs be released from their restrictions. While lifting many of the constraints imposed on the companies, the court initially declined to allow them into the information services business and only did so following the directive of a higher court.[13] By 1991, therefore, the Baby Bell companies had cut one of the cords that bound them. (The MFJ was formally rescinded in April of 1996, quietly vanishing after more than ten years of momentous and controversial life.)

Meanwhile, the FCC began a series of proceedings designed to loosen their restraints on the RBOCs. In 1988, Alfred Sikes, then head of the National Telecommunications and Information Administration (NTIA), presented a report calling for the creation of what would become a Video Dial Tone service.[14] Under Video Dial Tone (VDT), the telephone companies would be able to provide video services in their territories on a common carrier basis, that is they could be access providers but could not hold ownership interests in the content. When Sikes was named Chairman of the FCC in 1989, he took the idea with him. The Commission's declaration in

1988 that the cross-ownership ban should be lifted set the stage for the 1992 FCC decision to implement VDT and recommend to Congress that the 1984 Cable Act be amended to permit telephone companies even greater control over programming "subject to appropriate safeguards."[15]

The RBOCs did not wait around for Congressional action but won a series of court fights that struck down, on First Amendment grounds, the statutory ban on the provision of video service. Bell Atlantic's victory on this issue in 1993 was only the first in a series of judicial decisions that struck down the Cable Act prohibition for RBOCs nationally. And while the cable industry and others appealed those rulings, passage of the Telecommuncations Act of 1996 made the issue moot by giving the telephone industry even wider latitude to diversify into new communications fields. The Act replaced VDT, under which the telephone companies were prevented from programming the local system themselves, with a concept called "Open Video Systems" or OVS.

Under OVS, telcos are permitted to offer their own programming, up to one-third of their channel capacity if demand exceeds supply. Moreover, operating under OVS rules, they are insulated from most of the state and local regulations that typically have attached to cable, including local franchising requirements and rate regulation. They do, at the same time, have to lease the remaining portion of their system to other programmers on a nondiscriminatory basis.

Although implementation of the OVS guidelines meant somewhat clearer sailing for the telephone industry as it moved into television, most of the Baby Bells had already stepped into those waters by the time the FCC formalized its rules. In fact, by mid-1996 some of the Bell companies had months and even years of experimentation in home delivery of television. The following is an overview of the major efforts in telco TV.

US West

This Denver-based company provides local phone service to 25 million customers in fourteen states. When it purchased Hostetter's Continental Cable, it became the country's third largest cable television operator. The acquisition was not, however, the company's first foray into cable. US West owns a 20 percent stake in Great Britain's largest cable operator, Telewest Communications. Jointly owned with TCI, Inc. and SBC, Telewest provides a combined cable and telephone service to 4.1 million subscribers (see Chapter 8).[16] In 1993, US West also bought 25.5 percent of Time Warner, Inc.'s Time Warner Entertainment Co., the holding company for Time Warner's cable properties and film studio. It was noted during the acquisition of Continental that US West, through its additional affiliation with Time Warner, had access to more cable television homes in the United States than any other company.[17]

As early as 1992, US West announced its intention to rewire some of the major markets in its service area, including Denver, Minneapolis, Phoenix, Seattle, and Portland. US West began in Omaha with a hybrid analog-digital FTTC system featuring seventy-seven basic cable channels and digital video-on-demand services. It attracted 13,000 customers to its system, but found the digital traffic more complicated and demanding, as well as more expensive, than it had expected and by mid-1996 had postponed its plans for rolling out high-end systems beyond Omaha. The company's plans seemed to refocus on the development of traditional cable systems in the near term.

SBC/Pacific Telesis

Of the two partners in the SBC–PacTel combination, PacTel has been the more aggressive in moving into video services. It announced ambitious plans in late 1993 to rewire the entire state of California, but backed away from those plans and began looking at alternative delivery systems, including wireless cable (MMDS) and conventional cable franchises.

As will be discussed below, MMDS is one cost-effective way to get digitally compressed television into the home. Some RBOCs are looking at MMDS as an interim technology offering a number of benefits. Constructing wire-based systems or converting existing plant is expensive and time-consuming. It also may give the Baby Bells a chance to learn more about running multichannel television companies, a business in which they had very little expertise. Because of its limited interactivity, few saw it as the foundation for a fully integrated switched digital network, but as a shoe in the door of the cable customer's home, it is attractive in some situations. Part of the PacTel plan therefore was to enter the Southern California video market through the air. In 1995 it bought Cross Country Wireless for $175 million and was planning MMDS service to 4 million potential customers in Los Angeles and Orange counties in 1997. The company also launched cable service in San Jose in 1996 in competition with the incumbent provider, TCI.

While getting off to a quick start, SBC has been generally slower than some of the other RBOCs in venturing into broadband services. It was the first RBOC to purchase a cable company, buying two cable systems in the Washington, D.C. area from Hauser Communications, for $650 million, in 1993. (It sold the systems in 1977.) A subsequent effort to merge with Cox Cable, one of the country's leading MSOs, fell apart, however. By 1997, SBC had decided to reduce its activities in video, halting the PacTel cable operations in San Jose and San Diego, as well as its own SDV experiment in Richardson, Texas, and putting the Los Angeles MMDS initiative in doubt.

Bell Atlantic/Nynex. In April of 1996, Bell Atlantic CEO Ray Smith and Nynex CEO Ivan Seidenberg announced the $21.4 billion merger of the two firms. It was the single biggest telecommunications merger in history. It joined two contiguous Baby Bells and created a telecom empire that stretched from Maine to Virginia, encompassing the entire northeastern seaboard and the huge metropolitan profit centers of Boston, New York, Philadelphia, Washington, D.C., Newark, and Richmond.

The new company had a stock market value close to $51 billion, 127,000 employees, and 36 million customers in twelve states.[18] Fundamental to the merger were the possibilities opened up by the large geographic spread of the new company and the long-distance market that it created. The Telecommunications Act of 1996, which made it possible for the Baby Bells to compete in long-distance, was credited as an important factor in the merger. Bell Atlantic now could be the local and long-distance carrier for all calls made within its region.

The attraction of the easy and lucrative long-distance market distracted the new company from its interests in video and may have slowed the pace of the telco's activities in the area. Video could wait while it established its local prominence in the long-distance market. But a flagging concern with video did not mean abandonment. Bell Atlantic maintained a healthy interest in telco television.

Of the two pre-merger companies, the original Bell Atlantic was the most active in television. Some observers marked the aborted merger of Bell Atlantic and TCI as the beginning of serious telco interest in cable. While the deal sank amongst the whitecaps of business and regulatory uncertainty, it nonetheless showed that the telcos were sailing. In fact, however, Bell Atlantic had been underway for some time. In 1992 the company joined with Sammons Cable to announce an experimental broadband full-service network in northern New Jersey to provide telephone and cable service to several towns in the area. Initially intended as a VDT network, Bell Atlantic subsequently dropped those plans and opened two new trials.

In the northern suburbs of Washington, D.C., it conducted a lengthy experiment with ADSL technological, supplying full Video On Demand to 1,000 customers. The VOD service, called "Stargazer," provided one of the first peeks at what a fully interactive pay-per-view system might look like. The Stargazer platform used high-capacity digital servers to store a library of more than 655 programs, including 200 films, 120 TV shows, and 120 children's programs. Prices for each program varied: A motion picture might cost $3 to $4, while a twenty-minute cartoon or a news feature clip from ABC's *Nightline* might run $1 or less. Some titles were sold for as little as 49 cents.[19]

A much more ambitious project in both technology and programming was conducted by Bell Atlantic in Dover Township, New Jersey. Bell Atlantic began commercial service over a 384-channel, digital FTTC system in early 1996, offering voice, data, and video. Originally devised as VDT system, Bell Atlantic already had contracted with a third-party programmer, FutureVision, to supply a 77-channel menu of cable and broadcast channels, but other programmers also rented space on the system. Bell Atlantic subsequently purchased FutureVision, taking full operational control and obtaining OVS status from the FCC.

For Bell Atlantic, however, Dover was just a start. Its next big step was the announced deployment of a full-service SDV system in its original home city of Philadelphia.[20] With Bell Atlantic's bold philosophy in video programming, the City of Brotherly Love was likely to become the first major metropolitan area in the country to measure the feasibility and potential of the new technology.

In the exploration of the possibilities of multichannel video, Nynex was as timid as Bell Atlantic was bold. While it does have extensive cable–telco holdings in the

United Kingdom, its domestic wire-based television trials were restricted to relatively small-scale projects.

Bell Atlantic and Nynex also looked at MMDS delivery technologies, investing $100 million in CAI wireless in 1995 and announcing plans for digital wireless services in Boston and Hampton Roads, Virginia, beginning in 1997. Tests with the digital MMDS technology proved disappointing, however, as foliage from trees interferred with the digital signal. In late 1996 the telcos suspended plans for the service and were reportedly considering DBS opportunities.

Ameritech

About the only avenue Bell Atlantic did not pursue in its television activities was the outright creation of traditionally franchised, HFC cable systems. This was the primary strategy of Ameritech, however, which eschewed the more expensive switched digital video approach. The Chicago-based company declared in 1993 that it would get into the switched broadband video business, but withdrew its Video Dial Tone applications in mid-1995, citing a cumbersome and time-consuming approval process. Instead, it sought and won local cable TV franchises throughout the Midwest, gaining permission to overbuild and compete with entrenched cable operators. Ameritech offered local municipalities a 5 percent franchise fee, a 750 MHz, HFC system featuring interactive banking and shopping services and a $1-per-year local government channel that could be used to generate revenue through advertising and infomercials.[21] It became the first Baby Bell to win its own local franchise in 1995 when it was granted the right to wire the Detroit suburb of Plymouth, Michigan. It went on from there to gain building rights in Ohio, Wisconsin, and Illinois.[22]

BellSouth

BellSouth has, in some ways, maintained a lower profile in telco television than some of its RBOC brethren, but its has not been inactive. The company began experimenting with fiber and ISDN-based delivery systems in Florida as early as 1986. Like Ameritech, it has secured franchises for traditional cable systems in South Carolina, Alabama, and Florida. It has explored interactive HFC architectures for possible deployment in its top thirty Southern markets, and has been moving into MMDS systems and experimenting with LMDS.

GTE

With 18 million access lines in twenty-eight states, GTE is the largest non-Bell telecommunications company. It began a highly publicized trial of interactive video services in Cerritos, California, in 1989, but the results proved disappointing, in part because of the undeveloped technology. The pre-digital test offered twenty on-demand movies but required employees at the GTE central office to scurry around and load videotapes into twenty VCRs. GTE announced its intention to build OVS networks in sixty-six markets by 2005,[23] and was negotiating for cable overbuild franchises in Florida and California where it planned to build 750 MHz HFC systems.[24]

AT&T

With the deregulation of the industry, AT&T began moving enthusiastically into the local loop business, winning regulatory approval to offer local services and securing deals with competitive access providers (see Chapter 5) that gave it a toehold in more than half the states for the joint provision of local and long-distance service. Whether this eventually would permit AT&T to offer local video services, by itself or in concert with the local providers, was not immediately clear.[25] In early 1996 AT&T announced it was purchasing a 2.5 percent equity stake in DirecTV, with an option to buy 30 percent of the company. The move suggested the telephone company's intention to enter the video delivery business at least intially using a DBS platform. AT&T, however, had taken a position against the outright purchase or construction of traditional cable systems, and may not venture beyond its broadcast and equipment services in the immediate future.

AT&T also divided itself into three separate companies to pursue more focused business interests. In the "tri-vestiture" AT&T spun off its computer interests, the manufacturing arm that had been Western Electric and its Bell Labs research component. The new AT&T would concentrate on telecommunications sectors, while the computer firm, recapturing its former NCR logo, tried to recover from disappointing results in that market. Through its newly spun-off and renamed equipment manufacturing company, Lucent Technologies, AT&T shareholders sought to become major turnkey equipment suppliers for the emerging full-service industry. The SBC trial in Richardson, Texas, was conducted on a high-end SDV system supplied by AT&T in conjunction with Broadband Technologies, Inc. The company also sold a full-service digital system to Walt Disney Co., which intended to make it part of its Disneyworld-like planned community, "Celebration, Florida," near the Orlando theme park.

Some observers felt the telephone companies, in their multibillion-dollar efforts to get into television, were driven in part by the popular frenzy of new technology and the glitter of Hollywood; utiltities such as telephone companies were seen on Wall Street as steady but boring investments. Entry into television and data services was seen as a vehicle for moving the companies toward a more attractive, perhaps even exciting, position as growth stocks. Interest also was driven by the real possibility that the telephone industry could effectively compete in new markets in the next century with attractively priced, bundled information and communication services tailored to individual homes. Whatever the causes, the voice/data/video mantra was spreading from the RBOCs and long-distance companies down to the second tier telcos. Southern New England Telephone, for example, sought a cable television franchise for the entire state of Connecticut, and Carolina Telephone, in conjunction with Sprint, was building a VDT platform in Wake Forest, Georgia, challenging the existing Time Warner system.

The Utilities

Public utilities are interesting contenders in the contest for wireline television customers. The same deregulatory philosophy that affected telecommunications has also been opening the market for electric utilities. While still a minor player in the communications distribution game, the possibilities for the nation's power companies are beginning to open up, and they could become significant niche providers in the next century. In fact, if you live in Glasgow, Kentucky, or Lariat, Texas, you currently get your cable television, local telephone service, Internet access, and electric power all from the same company, the "power" company. Electric utilities were initially drawn to coaxial and fiber communication networks because they provided a means to monitor and control electrical usage and because utilities already had engineered a right-of-way conduit and wire path to all residences and businesses. Meter reading, connections and disconnections, immediate diagnoses of outages, load management, and even customer control of usage are all made possible by a telecommunications overlay using the company's existing network. Of course, these energy management functions take up only a fraction of the capacity of the broadband system. There's plenty of room left for MTV, CNN, fax, and voice traffic.

Only a handful of such operations currently exist. The Glasgow Electric Plant Board, noted above, began a pioneering effort in 1989. CSW Corp., a Texas utility, built a pilot system in Lariat in 1995 and was constructing a $300 million HFC system in Austin.[26] Deregulation, however, has touched the power industry in ways similar to the telecommunications field and utilities are looking at a variety of ways to leverage their existing and planned infrastructures into new business ventures. The Telecommunications Act of 1996 amends prior legislation to make it easier for a utility's subsidiary to enter the telecommunications market.

Utility companies have little experience in telephone or video service, but are willing to contract out much of the expertise while providing the fiber backbone. Still, while the regulatory and technological changes of the last few years have made it easier for utilities to consider such systems, the likelihood of the industry becoming a major player in video and data services is uncertain.

BROADCASTING

Traditional Broadcasters

There are about 1,190 commercial broadcast television stations in the United States, 559 VHF stations (channels 2–13) and 635 UHF stations (channels 14–69). Most are owned by groups, although historically the number of stations any company can own, including the networks, has been limited by law. The Telecommunications Act of 1996 loosened these restrictions somewhat and an individual or group can now own any number of stations as long as their total audience reach does not exceed 35 percent of the national market.[27] The three major networks, ABC, NBC, and CBS, therefore, historically have controlled programming, but have been restricted in the number of stations they can actually own. In 1996, under the loosened regulations, CBS owned about seventeen television stations, ABC ten, and NBC six.[28] Most of the stations that run network programming are "affiliates" of the network, that is they have contractual arrangements for the carriage of the network schedules. Through the affiliates, the major networks reach nearly all the television homes in the United States. This extended reach allows them to sell advertising on a national scale and generate the millions of dollars necessary for the production and acquisition of high quality programming. Only a national network system (in both broadcast and cable television) makes possible the generation of revenue sufficient for the costly development of modern television programs.[29] Nonaffiliate stations, or "independents," typically subsist on a program diet of network reruns, old movies, talk shows, and game shows.

The FCC, as noted in Chapter 2, assigns station licenses across the country, in part, on the basis of market size. The larger the market, the more broadcast licenses have been allotted by the FCC, albeit with an eye toward reserving enough channels for smaller communities to support localism. The largest cities in the United State have ten or more stations, including all the major networks; smaller towns or cities may have only two or three stations, some only have one. Many towns in the United States have no assigned TV stations.

Cable has always had a competitive but symbiotic relationship with the broadcasting industry, because broadcasting represents not just a principle historic competitor to cable but also its chief source of programming. The long debate over "must carry" and "retransmission consent" regulations illustrates the roller-coaster relationship between the industries. Cable, initially, was dependent on the broadcast signal for its survival, but as cable penetration grew, broadcasters found they needed to be carried by the local system if they were going to be seen by a majority of their audience.

As noted in Chapter 2, some broadcasters began battling cable operators almost as soon as the first CATV antenna sprouted on the neighboring mountaintop. Broadcasters feared the competitive power of cable's multichannel technology, and with good cause. Cable television ultimately stole viewers and broke the national oligopoly of the three dominant television networks by fragmenting audiences. Cable's web of wires spread out through the towns and neighborhoods of the United States, and cable-only networks proliferated through the 1980s. As access to cable service increased, viewers voted with their remote controls; ratings and "share" increased for cable and decreased for the broadcast networks. (*Ratings* are the percentage of viewers watching out of the universe of people with TV sets; *share* is the percentage watching a particular program or network out of all those with their sets turned on at that time.) From 1979 through 1995, the combined prime time share for ABC, NBC, and CBS fell from above 90 percent to 53 percent.[30] The combined share of all basic cable, meanwhile rose, from less than 10 percent to more than 30 percent in all TV households and up to 42 percent in cable households. And these trends showed no signs of abatement.[31]

Cable and the New Broadcast Networks

Cable's basic programming services accounted for much of the viewer migration but not all of it. While cable was extending its reach, the networks also were challenged by the rise of independent television stations. In 1964 television set manufacturers were required to include UHF tuners in all sets so viewers would no longer have to buy separate devices. A change in FCC regulations made it easier to buy and sell stations and increased the number of stations a given company could own. Carriage by cable also made available UHF channel allotments more attractive and helped lead to an increase in the number of these stations around the country. While the new stations competed directly against existing network affiliates, they had an even greater impact by providing the base from which to build new networks. The first to do so was media mogul Rupert Murdoch, owner of News Corporation and 20th Century Fox movie studio. Murdoch began in the publishing business with a chain of Australian newspapers. expanding into British and U.S. publishing largely with sensationalist tabloids. In 1985 he entered the broadcasting business buying a group of U.S. television stations and half of the Fox studio (later acquiring the entire company), using them as the base to build his broadcast and cable programming networks. Murdoch relied heavily on independent television stations and exercised a keen marketing savvy that targeted younger audiences to create the "fourth" television network. Fox Broadcasting aired hits shows such as *Married with Children, The Simpsons,* and *Beverly Hills 90210.*

Cable's role in the development of the new network was twofold. First, carriage by cable of the local independent stations helped to give them greater visibility to the home viewer. Cable carriage, in many instances, improved the reception of the UHF signal, brought it into the homes of people who might not have been able to receive it over the air, and, most importantly, moved it off its "over-the-air" channel of, say, forty-eight, and brought it down on the subscriber's television dial to a channel below 13 and next to the network channels the viewer was used to watching. It helped establish a kind of home-viewing parity for the new independents. In addition, cable in some cases carried the new Fox network even when there was no local broadcast affiliate.[32] TCI struck a deal with Murdoch to carry the Fox network in markets that did not have an independent station to align with Fox.

Murdoch's success led to the launching of other broadcast networks. In 1993 both Warner Brothers and a partnership between Paramount and Chris Craft Broadcasting announced the start of broadcast networks. Warner Brothers began the WB network in 1994, and Paramount–Chris Craft started the UPN network in 1995, anchored by Paramount's hugely successful *Star Trek* franchise in its latest iteration, *Star Trek: Voyager.* While neither network generated large ratings, they did add to the general fragmentation of audiences and the continuing slide in the viewership of the previously dominant big three networks.

At the same time, it is important to note that although the ABC, NBC, and CBS networks are no longer the only players in the television universe, they are still the biggest. The combined prime time ratings of the top twenty basic cable networks in 1995 was only 22.4, less than half that of the combined ratings for the three broadcast networks.[33] The viewership of the USA network, consistently one of the most watched cable channels, is only about 2.3 ratings points, a fraction of that of any one of the broadcasters; only CNN, during the occurrence of important news events, generates ratings comparable to the broadcasters. Network broadcasting will likely remain a significant force in television, both as a delivery system and as a source for programming. In fact, as we will explore in detail later, much of the programming run on cable television remains old network material sold into syndication. Cable networks such as Nickelodeon, with its "Nick at Night" and "TV Land" schedules, has thrived almost exclusively on broadcast sitcoms from decades ago, featuring such pop cultural icons as *Bewitched* and *Mr. Ed*. ABC, CBS, and NBC will continue to be a dominant force in programming for many years because, more than anyone else, they require and generate an unending supply of original shows. "Nick at Night" can succeed on a steady diet of black-and-white reruns, NBC and CBS, obviously, cannot. The supply of original programming from the broadcast industry not only will continue, but will likely increase.

The New Broadcast Industry

The switch from analog to digital broadcasting described in Chapter 3 will open up new program delivery possibilities for local and network broadcasters. As noted, while digital compression was once conceived of largely as a way to allow broadcasters to provide High Definition Television, the industry quickly realized that the same digital transmission techniques would allow them to broadcast several digitally compressed conventional television channels instead of one HDTV signal. It additionally offers the potential for providing nontraditional broadcast services such as paging and data delivery. Four or five channels of conventional television equate to equivalent multiples of advertising time and constitute a much more lucrative prospect than one channel of HDTV. Broadcasters began an intense and bruising political campaign in the early 1990s to allow them to use the new technology for delivery of multiple services. The FCC had set aside frequencies in the existing UHF band for the new digital broadcasting, but some in Congress felt broadcasters should be require to pay, up front, for the right to use that space. Many saw spectrum sales or auctions as one vehicle for helping balance the federal budget. The spectrum in question has been valued at anywhere between $12 billion and $70 billion and broadcasters were predictably chagrined at the prospect of having to pay for it. Broadcasters have not yet had to pay for their digital or analog frequencies, however. Stations throughout the nation's top 10 markets planned to begin digital broadcasting before the end of 1998 using the UHF channels granted them by the FCC. At the same time, they will not have to relinquish their existing analog frequencies until 85 percent of the viewers in their market can receive digital signals. The FCC has authority to then auction off the returned analog channels.

Traditional broadcasters, therefore, are likely to become multichannel video and service providers using digital broadcast technologies within a few years. In some isolated cases this may make them more directly competitive with the local wire-based service. More likely, it will mean additional programming retransmitted by the local cable operator as the broadcaster places several channels, rather than just one, on the system.

In the long run it is unlikely that cable television will trigger the demise of broadcasting or the end of existing broadcast networks. Over-the-air television will continue to serve those who cannot, or choose not, to subscribe to cable TV or other paid, multichannel program services. Moreover, broadcasters will remain important content providers and, with additional channels made available to them, will increase their production of programming and their development of new telecommunications services. While maintaining their multichannel delivery systems they will likely concentrate their talents and energy in the development of programming, and so increasingly move to the software side of the business.

Wireless Cable

MMDS

The broadcasters' vision of being able to provide multiple channels of digital terrestrial broadcast programming is, as noted in Chapter 3, available in one sense today. MMDS has been around in some form for decades. The FCC initially envisioned a service providing spectrum access for specialized programming by school districts, religious organizations, and similar groups. For such organizations, the opportunity to transmit video programming proved attractive despite the cost of installing special antennas and converters at each receiving location. Because such organizations did not expect to transmit to the general public, the number of costly installations appeared manageable. Wireless cable when used in this way represented the FCC service category called Instructional Television Fixed Service (ITFS). Most ITFS licensees needed only one channel and typically did not operate continuously. The Commission subsequently recognized that it may have allocated too much spectrum for such a narrow application. ITFS licensees persuaded the FCC to allow sharing of their facilities and authorizations with commercial ventures as a way to secure needed funds. In time, commercial video services proliferated and their bandwidth requirements grew. The FCC accommodated such wireless cable service by allocating dedicated MMDS spectrum contiguous to the ITFS frequency band.

Initially, even MMDS lacked the kind of channel capacity sufficient to constitute the functional equivalent of cable television. Lacking compression technologies, the MMDS operator primarily operated where cable television was unavailable, including urban areas where the politics of franchising and other factors delayed the construction of coaxial systems. The operator simply provided a handful of premium channels and was content to carve out a profitable and unobtrusive niche. Home Box Office, for example, used a single-channel MDS (multipoint distribution service) in the late 1970s and early 1980s to penetrate markets that were not yet wired for cable.

As an alternative to cable, MMDS has a number of advantages, chief among them being cost. Compared to cable, MMDS is very cheap, about $400 to $450 per subscriber, according to the industry. You do not have to build an expensive infrastructure nor maintain hundreds of miles of coax, fiber, amplifiers, and taps. The transmitter costs about a million dollars and the only other facilities expenses are subscriber dishes and converters. MMDS operators do not have to pay local franchise fees, nor are they subject to rate regulation. It is a very cost-effective business.

As long as MMDS was restricted to a few dozen channels, it never represented much of a competitive threat to cable, and was more typically used in large cities that had no cable service. As with other transport technologies, regulatory relief and digital technology are changing the picture, however. With digitally compressed signals, it is estimated that MMDS can deliver up to 250 channels. With its relative ease of installation, MMDS can quickly bring digital television and 200-plus channel service to market and at a relatively low operating cost. It is, in short, a way to get into the high-capacity transport business quickly and cheaply.

But MMDS also has its limits. Even with 250 channels, its capacity is dwarfed by the potential of a truly broadband wired network, which, as we have seen, can provide, in its interactive form, a virtually unlimited number of program choices. In addition, MMDS is largely a one-way transmission path. Its interactivity is generally restricted to using conventional telephone lines as a return path. That is, a subscriber can select pay-movies and other services, but must place a telephone call to initiate the service. This is likely to prove awkward and overly burdensome to an audience raised on the instant gratification of the remote control and computer mouse. Importantly, MMDS is also prone to interference by physical objects, such as tall trees and buildings, which has limited its utility in some communities and is one the reasons some proponents have backed away from it. In 1996 there were about 200 systems and one million MMDS subscribers in the country; revenues were about $272 million.[34]

The long-term potential for MMDS is unclear. Its most likely role is as an interim transport technology in locations where it is technically effective. It could be useful to cable companies as a way to extend their reach into more scarcely populated areas where sending a line is not cost effective. It may also be used by some telephone companies as a means of testing the multichannel video business. Some industry experts see a window of opportunity for MMDS to move in with digital services before wire-based systems can get up to full digital speed, but fade as wired systems mature.

LMDS and IVDS

The FCC also has allocated spectrum for a close cousin to MMDS, Local Multipoint Distribution Service (LMDS). This service operates in the 28 GHz band and will provide broadband video and wireless telephony services. Unlike MMDS, LMDS breaks its service area into small cells, each with a low-power transmitter covering a local area of two to six miles in radius. The shorter distance between sender and receiver means a smaller receiving dish than DBS or MMDS, from six to twelve inches across. Interactivity is possible using laptop-sized home transmitters to feed signals back to the system, and the cellular nature makes it possible to deliver different content in different cells, tailoring programming to the interests of a particular neighborhood. A digital LMDS system could provide several hundred channels of programming. In 1996, the FCC established a spectrum allocation plan that balanced the requirements of prospective LMDS and low Earth-orbiting satellite operators with existing satellite operators who use a portion of the band to transmit traffic and network control signals.

Interactive Video Distribution Systems (IVDS) present a yet to be proven narrowband (500 kHz) wireless option. With such limited spectrum, the services involve "bursty" digital data commands from subscriber terminals, rather than broadband downloading of content Yet even a narrowband link into the home presents some promise for polling and interactive applications.

THE SATELLITE INDUSTRY

Industry Structure

Consumers using very large dishes have been watching satellite-delivered television for many years, and satellites will continue to be central to the distribution of national cable and broadcast programming. But only recently have higher powered satellite services made serious competitive inroads against cable television. Moreover, satellites have been expanding their base of consumer and business services, from international paging to position determination and navigation to interactive data. Satellites can distribute digital movies, but increasingly will supply your data and telephone needs as well. This section looks at the structure of the satellite industry, which is comprised of a number of specialized business segments, including satellite manufacturers, carriers, and program distributors.

Satellite Manufacturers

The domestic U.S. satellite manufacturing industry has consolidated into a tight oligopoly dominated by Hughes Space and Communications Company, with lesser market shares held by Lockheed Martin Astro Space and Space Systems/Loral. Heretofore, satellite manufacturing has involved an expensive, time-consuming development of a product line that is customized on a per-satellite basis to the particular requirements of an operator. Each satellite is one of a kind in the sense that satellite manufacturers do not establish and maintain an ongoing assembly line. The best a manufacturer can expect under current market conditions is the development of a uniform "bus" onto which different payload configurations attach.

Think of current satellite manufacturing as "designer" clothing: A relatively small number of any designer's creations reach the market. Satellite manufacturing began as a project-oriented, government-contracted project. Even now, the few satellites ordered in any year supports a "designer" satellite operation that can result in a two-year manufacturing timetable. The specificity of design and configuration means that the manufacturer cannot fully capture the kinds of economies of scale that might be available in cases where several different customers were ordering the same satellite model and technology could be standardized and applied across the manufacturing process.

Large constellations of satellites, such as low Earth-orbiting (LEO) satellites providing mobile services (see Chapter 5), present opportunities for the manufacture of "off-the-rack" or "ready-to-wear" satellites; a constellation of 66 Iridium and 228 Teledesic LEOs, for example, requires efficient, assembly line manufacturing of at least several satellites per month. Slashing production times makes the satellite construction business more like short-cycle automobile production, in which standard components can be installed on a number of modules that fit onto a single bus model.

Hughes Space and Communications Company. Hughes Space and Communications (HSC) is a wholly owned subsidiary of General Motors and the principal owner of one of the two dominant DBS services, DirecTV. Since 1961, the company has manufactured over 150 spacecraft including more than 166 commercial communications satellites. HSC is engaged in the development and production of state-of-the-art space and communications systems for military, commercial, and scientific uses, including meteorological observations. The company designed and built the world's first geosynchronous communications satellite, Syncom, launched in 1963. It has manufactured more than 50 percent of the satellites now in commercial service worldwide.

Lockheed Martin Astro Space. Lockheed Martin Astro Space has perennially run second in satellite sales to Hughes Space and Communications and has undertaken an aggressive campaign to bolster its manufacturing capability. The company has invested over $1 billion to close facilities in New Jersey and Pennsylvania and to construct a state-of-the-art production facility in California. It also has announced plans to construct a $4 billion constellation of nine Ka-band communications satellites for service commencing in the year 2000.

Space Systems Loral. Space Systems Loral is a joint venture of Loral Space and Communications (itself the consolidated the satellite manufacturing capabilities of Ford Aerospace and Loral) and the European manufacturers Aerospatiale,

Alcatel, Alenia, and Daimler–Benz Aerospace. The company has diversified into several different types of satellite product lines, including large general purpose satellites used by INTELSAT, and ones used for mobile telephony, DBS, air traffic control/weather observation and high-powered regional services, including video program delivery. The company also has agreed to provide a communications payload for a new line of Russian satellites.

In early 1996 Lockheed Martin Company and Loral Corporation announced a $10 billion strategic alliance. Primarily as a result of the slowdown in defense contracting in view of the Soviet Union's collapse, Lockheed Martin acquired Loral's defense electronics and systems integration businesses for approximately $9.1 billion. Additionally the companies will share in the ownership of a new venture, to be known as Loral Space and Communications Corp., that will own Space Systems/ Loral and its telecommunication interests, including Globalstar.

Conversion from "Designer" to "Off-the-Rack" Manufacturing

The Global Information Infrastructure will stimulate a proliferation of services, frequencies, orbits, operators, and low Earth-orbiting satellite constellations containing dozens of space stations. The commercial communications satellite marketplace will continue to diversify in terms of products and markets. This industry no longer just supports the one-by-one manufacture of a few dozen satellites a year, with services provided by a few predominantly government-owned carriers participating in global or regional cooperatives. Instead, a variety of developing markets present the prospect for service diversity and perhaps even greater price competition. The option of procuring satellites, available in-orbit or for quick launch, has accelerated the development of a more diversified and maturing marketplace.

What an "off-the-rack" manufacturing process loses in terms of design flexibility, it gains in speedy deployment and economies of scale. Diverse markets and satellite roles require quicker turnaround in the manufacturing process, particularly when market opportunities occur within a "window" caused by short-term capacity shortages. Likewise, market opportunities will require different types of satellites, some containing less than the standard of twenty-four to thirty-six transponders, each with 36 MHz of bandwidth. "Lightsats" will operate in LEO satellite constellations by the dozens and as well can meet short-term capacity requirements while operating from geostationary orbital locations already occupied by a heavysat.

The Launch Industry

Very few companies launch satellites, primarily because of the substantial market entry costs and risk. The launch of a typical communications satellite into geostationary orbit costs $85 to $100 million. Until the decision to partially commercialize the industry, a few national governments or government-backed consortia monopolized the market. Even with a commitment by some nations to commercialize space, government enterprises still dominate. The pervasive and ongoing influence of government on this sector results because taxpayers have underwritten research and development of this essential component of modern intelligence-gathering. It persists now because incumbent operators like Araianespace and recent commercial market entrants in Russia and China are government-owned and governments in other nations worry that without quotas and price floors, government underwritten ventures will predatorially price launches and drive out private competitors.

Beginning in 1958 and running to the early 1980s, the United States government exclusively provided launch services for itself and for all civilian ventures. The decision to commercialize space resulted from an overall change in political philosophy as well a pragmatic recognition that the government could not handle the entire demand for space shuttle and expendable launch vehicles. In quick order, the companies that had contracted with the U.S. Government became commercial operators.

The lead companies now involved in launching include Lockheed Martin and McDonnell Douglas (which merged with Boeing in late 1996). In the near future, launch operators will need to respond to diversifying satellite product lines. Most launches now insert one or two satellites into orbit. The LEO mobile satellite constellations will require launches of six or more space stations at a time, and the quick deployment of replacement lightsats.

Launch Insurance.   A satellite typically costs about $250 million to $275 million to construct and launch, and the technology of transporting several thousand pounds into a particular orbit 22,300 miles above earth has yet to become a routine endeavor. Launches also involve the ignition of highly combustible materials and the propulsion of large and heavy equipment that potentially could kill people and destroy property if a rocket were to go out of control. Because of the expense and risk in launching a satellite, most operators seek insurance rather than attempt to beat the odds. Launch insurance tracks historical launch failure rates and can vary from a low of about 7 to10 percent of total cost to a high of about 25 percent. Because so many factors can adversely affect a launch, the matter of an insurance payout can trigger disputes over who is liable when a launch fails. The launch provider may claim that the satellite manufacturer erred in the construction or installation of the satellite onboard the rocket. Likewise, the launch provider may blame a subcontractor, particularly one responsible for the construction of one of the several stages in a launch sequence that must ignite and successfully propel the satellite to a particular intermediate location en route to its final orbital slot.

Insurance typically pays for construction and launch of a replacement satellite but not lost revenues and profits. A satellite operator that has suffered a launch failure may have to scramble if it has not negotiated with the initial launch provider for an early replacement launch. Even if an operator has such a commitment, the launch operator may have to delay a relaunch until such time as it can determine what went wrong. Such delays have triggered litigation over expenses and lost profits.

Satellite Carriers

Satellite carriers managed the construction, launch, and operation of commercial satellites. They lease transponders for the life of the bird, as well as for shorter fixed terms and on an occassional use basis. The number of domestic U.S. satellite operators also has declined with mergers and acquisitions distilling the industry into three major operators: Hughes Communications, Inc. (HCI), GE Americom, and Loral Space and Communications Ltd.

HCI. HCI, a subsidiary of General Motors, has the dominant market share with seventeen satellites owned, or individually managed on behalf of international customers. The company all but created the commercial satellite manufacturing business as prime contractor for the INTELSAT-1 (Early Bird) satellite. HCI operates ten satellites for domestic service and other subsidiaries of the company have a major market share in satellite manufacturing, and direct broadcast satellite service (DirecTV) in the United States with strategic joint ventures for DBS in other regions, including Latin America and Japan. In 1996 Hughes agreed to pay $3 billion to acquire PanAmSat Corp., the first private satellite operator to have operational facilities in each of the three major ocean regions.

GE Americom. GE Americom now operates a business previously served by affiliates of RCA, Contel, GE, and American Satellite, Inc. The company has plans to diversify by increasing the number of communication satellites, acquiring 80 percent of a "little LEO" system, Starsys (see Chapter 5), that will provide data, position determination, and messaging services.

Loral Space and Communiations. In 1996 Loral Space and Communications acquired AT&T's Skynet system for $712.5 million. AT&T had operated four Telstar domestic satellites, primarily for video program distribution, but also for other business applications including teleconferencing and data transmission. Loral Space plans to invest an additional $700 million to expand Skynet with an eye toward more aggressively competing with Hughes.

Teleport Operators

Satellite users may own their own ground facilities for sending and receiving satellite transmissions. Teleports, however, provide this relay function for those who prefer to delegate it to a full-time professional organization, or whose service requirements do not justify the capital outlay in Earth stations and other facilities. Teleports provide more than simple uplinking and downlinking, they are more than just "antenna farms." The successful teleport operator provides a number of sophisticated multimedia services, including the processing of signals originating on terrestrial wireline networks to make them optimized for satellite transmission. This processing may involve digital compression, signal encryption, the addition of foreign language tracks, inserting advertisements, and coordinating with other satellite carriers abroad. Teleport customers include universities, programmers, radio and television stations, government agencies, and corporations.

Network Externalities in Satellite Telecommunications

Satellite-delivered telecommunications can enhance consumer welfare by generating higher value as a satellite serves increasing numbers of users and points of communication.[35] Satellites can provide such expanded access without increased costs and often without higher user rates.[36] Once a carrier incurs the substantial sunk cost to make its footprint available, the incremental cost for it to serve an additional point of communication and additional users via another Earth station approaches zero. An additional point of access requires users to install or interconnect with an Earth station, acquire domestic facilities to link their premises with the Earth station, and pay space segment charges.

The value of satellite service accruing to users therefore can increase as the satellite serves more Earth stations and more users, often without higher charges to reflect the increased utility.[37] The concept of direct network externalities reflects this enhanced value.[38] The benefit is considered an externality, because standard economic analysis and the pricing of service may not take into account this outcome. Indirect network externalities result when increasing coverage and market penetration result in more plentiful, lower costing complementary goods. For example, consensus on technical standards for Earth stations accessing INTELSAT and Inmarsat satellites can promote industry-wide equipment compatibility and help manufacturers achieve economies of scale by having to support fewer product lines with different technical standards.[39]

Hot Birds and Hot Slots

Massive startup costs and the large inventory of transponder capacity in new generations of satellites also create incentives for satellite operators to compete for the business of video program distributors. Video programming occupies a large portion of satellite capacity as compared to voice and data traffic. A satellite operator can achieve certain financial success by convincing video programmers that a particular satellite will become the preferred target for the Earth stations operated by cable and broadcast television operators. Because a single satellite Earth station typically can receive programming from only one satellite, broadcasters and cablecasters have a financial incentive to limit the number of satellite sources of video programs. The "Hot Bird" concept reflects the interest in pointing a single Earth station to one satellite for all video programming.

Satellites become Hot Birds when their operator has the good marketing fortune of attracting a key video programmer who can serve as an "anchor tenant." Once an operator attracts a key video programmer, whose content viewers expect to receive, other programmers follow suit. These follow-on programmers join the bandwagon with the expectation that once a broadcaster or cablecaster points an Earth station to a particular satellite to access the key anchor tenant, they will become more likely to contract to carry somewhat less desirable programs that happen to occupy transponders on the Hot Bird. In effect, providers of somewhat less desirable programming can ride the coattails of the most desirable program simply by occupying space on the "right" satellite. A programmer occupying transponders on a less desirable satellite may find cablecasters reluctant to install yet another Earth station simply to receive its programming.

Hot Birds help make certain satellite orbital slots the preferred location to which Earth stations point. A satellite operator who succeeds in loading a satellite with video programming also typically succeeds in making the orbital slot that the satellite occupies an essential point. Cablecasters lock in Earth stations to that orbital slot. Simple inertia and the cost of repositioning the Earth station would tend to keep them pointed to that particular orbital slot. But additionally the Hot Bird operator works to institutionalize that orbital slot as one of the key "Hot Slots" for access to cable television programming.

The Hot Slot concept has another characteristic in the DTH/DBS marketplace. DTH/DBS operators in Europe have launched more than one satellite into the same orbital slot to provide an even larger inventory of programs via a single Earth station. These operators deploy satellites that operate on adjacent frequencies. Rather than interfering with one another, the satellites operate much like a number of different television stations all serving the same locality but transmitting on different channels. The satellites collectively provide a larger bandwidth of frequencies with each satellite's operating frequencies segueing into the other to create a continuous range of transponders.

Digital Television Distribution

Satellites, which have distributed analog television signals to broadcasters and cablecasters for years, are now providing similar links for distribution of digital television signals. Many program providers, such as HBO and Showtime, send fully digitized signals to local and national home providers. DBS services and digital MMDS platforms maintain a digital signal to the subscriber; most cable systems translate the digital signal to conventional analog form before putting it on the system (conversion to full digital cable delivery will be a gradual process).

Some programmers choose to use a digital distribution service instead of digitizing the signal themselves. TCI has invested substantially in satellite distribution as part of the company's vision of a digital future. TCI's "Headend in the Sky" (HITS) service is part of its National Digital Television Center near Denver. Originally slated to begin operation with the delivery of digital set-top boxes in 1994, operations were delayed along with arrival of the decoders until late 1996. The HITS service uses digitization and compression technology to feed its own headends, and the headends of any other companies that wish to purchase the programming, with a plethora of cable networks and pay-per-view entertainment options. Programming services using this distribution option can feed HITS a digital signal or have HITS convert their analog feed.

Even DBS operators can play a role as distribution "middlemen." In addition to direct-to-home service, DBS services, along with such businesses as HITS, can deliver bundled digital feeds to local providers such as MMDS and satellite master antenna systems serving apartment houses (see more on SMATV systems below). Such a delivery scheme can save digital MMDS operators a substantial amount of money that would otherwise be necessary to encode the signals.

Direct-to-Home Satellite Television

Subscribers to DirecTV, PrimeStar, or one of the several other DBS/DTH services take part directly in satellite television. After failing in the early 1980s, DBS operators, providing service to dishes less than one meter in diameter, achieved a successful debut in 1995 with 1.4 million new subscribers. With a collective annual advertising budget of more than $400 million, DirecTV, United States Satellite Broadcasting, PrimeStar, and EchoStar succeeded in converting satellite-delivered television into a mass market and one of the success stories of the mid 1990s. By 1997, satellite television services had more than 5 million subscibers.

Previously, most satellite television reception occurred in rural locales unserved by cable television. The expense, complexity, and size of the television receive-only (TVRO) terminals operating at C-band meant that hobbyists with some technical know-how dominated the market. The medium-powered DTH and high-powered DBS satellites opened the market with smaller, cheaper dishes and cablelike packages of programming networks. The service particularly thrives where consumers have endured years of limited channel choices and where terrestrial options, like cable television, have been slow to materialize. DBS use of digital technology also meant crisper pictures on the home receiver and digital compression made it possible to increase the capacity of each transponder many times over, providing DBS distributors hundreds of available channels.

True DBS, as opposed to the use of satellites licensed to provide Fixed Satellite Service, operates in orbital slots optimized for full continental U.S. coverage, and separated from another DBS satellite by 9 degrees. The three primary DBS slots in the United States are at 101, 110, and 119 degrees West Longitude. The newly recognized value of these slots is evidenced by the fact that MCI bid $682.5 million dollars in an auction to obtain the 110 degrees West Longitude (W.L.) slot. The following looks at the current major DBS distributors.

DirecTV/USSB.   Hughes Communications, Inc., operates DirecTV in a shared satellite access arrangement with United States Satellite Broadcasting, an affiliate of Hubbard Broadcasting. Hughes has two DBS satellites operating at 101 degrees W.L. The number of channels it can offer depends on FCC frequency assignments, not simply the number of transponders it has available from dedicated satellites. DirecTV has twenty-seven available frequencies at 101 W.L. and USSB has five. Both DirecTV and USSB provide service to compact, pizza-sized 18-inch Ku-band satellite terminals.

Hughes has invested about $1 billion in DirecTV. By 1997 it had 2.6 million subscribers and expected to reach a breakeven operational point with three million. As noted, AT&T also has an equity interest in the company. The service provides access to over 150 channels of programming, 60 channels of which are allocated to pay-per-view. Service packages are priced from $6 to $30 and offer most cable, movie, broadcast, and sports networks, with some programming, such as NFL football, available on an à la carte basis. USSB, with fewer channel offerings than DirecTV, has emphasized access to premium movie channels. It reported about 850,000 subscribers in early 1997.

PrimeStar/Tempo.   PrimeStar Partners, a venture owned by several cable MSOs—including TCI, Time Warner, Continental, Comcast, Cox, Newhouse, and Viacom—operates medium (DTH) and high-powered (DBS) services. The company serves about 1.9 million subscribers and uses compression technology to provide more than 150 video and audio channels to satellite terminals with 13.5-inch (high-powered service) to 48-inch (medium-powered service) dishes.

Under the name Tempo, TCI also holds DBS licenses in the 110 and 119 degree W.L. slots and had sought to develop its own independent DBS service. In 1996, Tempo tried to acquire the Construction Permit of Advanced Communications, Corp., which had failed to meet due diligence deadlines for constructing, launching, and operating a DBS service. Rather than permit the transfer of the Permit, the FCC offered the license to the highest bidder, which turned out to be MCI. Tempo then executed a sale–lease back agreement with Telesat Canada, whereby Telesat would have acquired two Tempo satellites in exchange for the rights to use two Canadian DBS satellite orbital slots and the lease of twenty-seven of the available frequency channels. The FCC ultimately rejected the proposal, however, because it concluded that Canadian content restrictions denied effective competitive opportunities to U.S. programmers. TCI subsequently decided to launch a high-powered satellite into its 119 degree W.L. slot and provide high-powered service as an adjunct to Primestar.

TCI, through PrimeStar, had plans to use the high-powered service to offer a DBS "overlay" for cable subscribers. The overlay would give customers of analog cable systems an additional DBS-fed digital capacity that would be used largely for premium services, pay-per-view movies, and sports.

Echostar.   Marketing itself as "The Dish Network," Echostar offers the standard menu of basic services and premium channels plus pay-per-view options, for an additional charge, on a 160-channel service. It began operations in the Spring of 1996 with a cut-rate package of cable channels designed to appeal to cost-conscious consumers. In 1997 it had about 590,000 subscribers. The high-powered service has two satellites at 119 degrees W.L., each with sixteen transponders, although it has long-term licenses for only twenty-one of the thirty-two frequencies it currently uses. It also holds licenses for frequencies in the 61.5 degree W.L. and 175 degree

W.L. slots. In addition to its consumer operation, EchoStar offers a twelve-channel business service used in corporate training.

Through the late 1990s, Rupert Murdoch, head of News Corp., attempted to enter the DBS business via several avenues, initially proposing a separate DBS service, ASkyB, along the same lines as his BSkyB British satellite television operation. This idea was replaced by a failed effort to merge with EchoStar. Subsequently, Murdoch bought into PrimeStar, trading an orbital slot and two satellites for an equity interes in the company. Meanwhile, another fledgling DBS service, AlphaStar, declared bankruptcy in 1997 after only a few months of operation.

Some DBS services have been developing plans to carry local broadcast signals in some markets. The proposal appeared to require government approval on copyright issues. If approved it would help neutralize the advantage held by MMDS and cable in the provision of local broadcast channels.

Shrinking Satellite Dishes

DBS is only one of a number of services that satellite distribution is making possible. As these services proliferate, businesses and households may have multiple Earth stations, or Earth stations configured for different uses, including video programming, real-time position determination and navigation, cellular radio-like telephone service, digital audio radio, Internet access, distance learning and teleconferencing, and data communications. More will be said about each of these in the next chapter. DBS service received a boost from the FCC in 1996 when the Commission limited the ability of local authorities to restrict homeowners from setting up dishes on their property. Some cities have used zoning ordinances to control satellite dish proliferation. At the same time, the price and complexity of home reception equipment has had to drop to a level equivalent with other consumer electronic devices, before homeowners were willing to purchase them. They must be widely available and require little technical know-how to install and operate.

In fact, satellite Earth stations have shrunk in size and cost. Part of the reduction in size results from the migration upwards in power and frequency, from C-band to Ku-band and now onward to the Ka-band. As we have seen, as satellite power increases, dish size can decrease. Lower costs also have resulted from scale economies brought on by mass production. Thomson Consumer Electronics, using the RCA logo and the trade name Digital Satellite System (DSS), introduced a retail, ready-to-install DBS receiving package for less than $1,000 in 1995. With increased production and the onset of competition from Sony, Toshiba, Uniden, and Hughes Network Systems, the cost to the consumer dropped to below $200 in early 1997. PrimeStar provides customers with the option of not having to purchase the receiving equipment by paying a somewhat higher monthly subscription rate, although they do levy an installation fee of from $100 to $200, and as with the other DBS service, outlets for additional television sets in the home cost extra. Competition among the providers continues to drive down dish and installation prices, which are absorbed into the monthly service fees, and may soon be near zero.

Even more complex, special-purpose terminals will follow the size and cost reduction trend. The next chapter describes satellite data communications services using "Very Small Aperature Terminals" or VSATs. Currently a VSAT terminal costs about $15,000 and requires installation by skilled technicians. By the year 2000, the terminal should cost less than $2,000 and become a more user-friendly, ubiquitous business tool. The more diversified Earth station makes it possible to convert a home, bank teller machine, and mobile personal computer into a Local Area Network service site no different than if a wire had provided access to the network.

TVRO and SMATV

While DBS is an industry in ascension, at least for the next few years, TVRO and analog SMATV are competitive providers in decline. TVRO is "television receive only," satellite receivers operating in the C-band. The large dishes, up to ten feet or more across, that dot the country's rural landscape are used to pick up the hundreds of channels directed at Earth by the various kinds of communications satellites. TVRO became popular in the late 1970s and early 1980s, initially with hobbyists who could peek at television signals not meant for home consumption, including network feeds to local stations, sports programs in the network distribution system, and even movies being fed nationally to local cable systems. The equipment was cumbersome and expensive. In addition to the dish, owners needed expensive electronic tuners and the more enthusiastic would purchase motorized mounts that allowed the dish to swivel and point to different satellites. As cable networks proliferated and equipment costs came down, TVRO became a common means of getting multichannel programming by people outside the reach of a city cable television system.[40]

In the mid to late 1980s, the TVRO industry counted up to 3 million dish owners. Interest in the technology began to wane when the cable industry started scrambling and charging for its signals. Prior to about 1985, TVRO owners could get most of their programming unscrambled and for free, although many in the cable industry considered it signal theft. While initial industry efforts to scramble their signals were met as much with pirated decoder boxes and blackmarket descramblers as they were with stoic compliance, eventually most dish owners that continued the service paid monthly fees just like local cable subscribers, and subscriber counts increased. The rise of dedicated DBS further suppressed the interest in TVRO again, however. For rural television consumers who simply wanted the convenience of cablelike service, the small dish and relatively low cost of DTH made more sense than the large TVRO dishes. At its height in 1985, there were about 4.5 million C-band subscribers, but that number had dropped to about 2.2 million by 1997. TVRO use is likely to continue, but recede to its roots as a pastime for hobbyists and serious television fans.

SMATV, or Satellite Master Antenna Television, is related to TVRO in that it is a satellite-based system. It can be conveniently described as a mini-cable system that serves an apartment building, "retirement village," condominium complex, or similar multidwelling structure or set of contiguous structures. The architecture is simple and cheap, consisting of little more than a TVRO dish to pick up the common cable channels and a set of wires to carry the signals through the complex. The roots of SMATV trace back to before the advent of community antenna television. The pre- and post-war apartment master antenna systems described in Chapter 2 are functionally equivalent, although SMATV developed as a contemporary business in the early 1980s. SMATVs were a means to bring cable service to apartment houses before a full city-wide cable system was deployed. Even after cable was available, the SMATV service was often cheaper because of its lower operating costs.

Cable fought SMATV on legal and economic fronts, challenging the SMATV operators' right to operate without a franchise in the first instance and offering expanded services at attractive prices in the second. By 1990 there were only about 250,000 SMATV customers in the United states. Existing analog SMATV operations are attractive marketing targets for DBS and MMDS services. There are 6 million apartment units in the United States (in buildings with 200 or more units) and both satellite and MMDS providers seek to replace the analog C-band dishes with digital multichannel service, sharing revenue with the SMATV operator.

DANCING IN THE DARK

If Hostetter's elephants' waltz was a dance contest, the winner was far from certain, and in many ways the contestants were just stepping out onto the floor. There are a number of considerations in handicapping the dancers. Working for the cable industry and providing a hopeful note, perhaps, for Massillon Cable is the fact that following the 1996 Telecommunications Act, the attention of the RBOCs was drawn away from television and toward the much more lucrative long-distance market. Bell Atlantic, for example, can generate more than a billion dollars in annual revenue simply by picking off 10 percent of the long-distance traffic that originates in its region. RBOCs are much more readily equipped to enter this line of business both technologically and in terms of expertise. Because the equipment and experience already is in place, the long-distance market can be tapped more quickly and more cheaply than the broadband services. The Baby Bells, therefore, have turned their interest in television down to a slow simmer while bringing long-distance activities up to a rolling boil. The RBOCs could be expected to build high-end wired systems in some of the major markets over the next few years, but not venture far beyond them before 2000.

Meanwhile, cable and DBS services will continuing expanding their digital capacity, although it is unlikely that digital service from cable providers will reach a national critical mass for several years. The digital boxes that began shipping in late 1996 were being installed in a handful of cable systems around the country. By the estimate of one set-top chip manufacturer, there will be 20 million customers taking digital service by the end of 2000, about 20 percent of all television households (see Figure 4-2).

Despite the inroads of digital DTH, it could be well beyond 2000 before the 500-plus channel universe is a reality for most consumers. In the meantime, the public will, probably, as a result of intense advertising and marketing by all providers, begin thinking about which kind of company they will trust to deliver bundled services. Some in the cable industry once predicted that basic cable penetration would eventually reach 80 percent, citing studies that show 80 percent of today's high school students say they will sign up when they're adults. By the time they are adults, however, the other providers will be knocking on their door and, cable's public image is not strong. One recent survey showed that only 4 percent of those polled would trust their local cable operator with an integrated service of voice, data, and television; 21 percent said they would buy such a package from their local Bell operator, and 50 percent said they would trust the service to AT&T.[41] The group that conducted the study suggested that cable companies partner with firms that had better public relations records.

The price of service appears to make a difference, but even then the public currently privileges the telcos over cable. Another consumer poll reported that 36 percent of those asked would switch their telephone service from their current phone

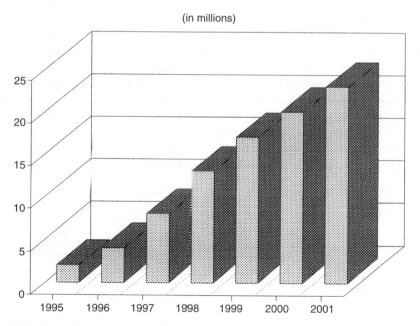

(in millions)

FIGURE 4-2   Predicted Worldwide Digital Set-Top Box Deployment

Source: "C-Cube Bites Back," *Cable World,* 8 April 1996, 22.

company to a cable provider if it saved them $2 a month. But 59 percent would drop their cable company and take television service from the phone company for the same $2 savings.

One result of this looming competition are forecasts that show the new distribution services pulling viewers away from cable television. Several independent predictions call for basic cable subscription to peak at around 64 million in 1999, under 70 percent penetration, even accounting for an expanded TV universe, and then begin to fall, with viewers lured away principally by DBS and wireless cable. Industry analysts from Kagan Associates predict total basic cable viewership will then drop to 60.8 million by 2005 as viewers migrate to the program offerings of these digital broadcast services.[42]

The combined market for entertainment, data and Internet access, voice, and assorted other interactive services is expected to expand dramatically over the next few decades, but the pie will remain nonetheless finite, and one of the questions is how much erosion can cable or any of the alternatives stand. MMDS or telco wire-based providers do not have to siphon off all the cable subscribers in a given town, only enough to drive penetration levels below a certain margin. At some point, the dwindling subscriber base will be insufficient to maintain a cash flow that makes the business worthwhile. Important market questions include how much erosion can a given system take from the combined competition of DBS, wireless cable, and telco overbuilders and, additionally, how much revenue loss can be offset by income streams from new services such as cable telephone and Internet access. These are some of the issues we will look at in the next chapter.

While technology deployment, service, consumer loyalty, pricing, and cash flow will all figure in the resolution of the competition, the only thing sure about the outcome is that it will take at least several years to start to reveal itself. There are many questions yet to be resolved about the number and nature of competitive services the market can support. There are, however, some issues on which most observers and participants agree. Two of them are the move to digital transmission and the convergence of technologies and media functions discussed here. Two others are examined more closely in Chapter 5: the centrality of programming and services in the emerging industry, and the gravitational strength of ownership integration and convergence.

NOTES

[1]Kim Mitchell and Vince Vittore, "Hostetter: 'Companies of Size Will Survive,'" *Cable World,* 4 March 1996, 1.
[2]Rich Brown, "US West Buys Continental," *Broadcasting & Cable,* 4 March 1996, 12–13.
[3]Ben Bagdikian, *The Media Monopoly,* 4th ed. (Boston: Beacon Press, 1992).
[4]Brown, "US West," 13.
[5]As of November 1995, there were 11,586 systems; 973 of them independents and the rest held by 645 MSOs.

[6]Liberty is held as a separate tracking stock by TCI shareholders.

[7]Kim Mitchell, "Telco–Cable Crunch Time," *Cable World,* 19 February 1996, 56.

[8]Pablo Galarza, "Happy Independence Day," *Financial World,* 22 April 1996, 40.

[9]On satisfying a fourteen-point FCC checklist designed to ensure fair interconnection and competition.

[10]Service Areas: **SBC/PacTel:** California, Nevada, Texas, Oklahoma, Missouri, Alaska, Kansas; **Bell Atlantic/Nynex:** New York, New Hampshire, Rhode Island, Maine, Connecticut, Massachusetts, Vermont, Pennsylvania, Maryland, New Jersey, Virginia, West Virginia, Delaware; **Bell South:** Kentucky, North Carolina, South Carolina, Georgia, Mississippi, Alabama, Louisiana, Florida, Tennssee; **Ameritech:** Wisconsin, Michigan, Illinois, Indiana, Ohio; **US West:** Montana, Washington, Oregon, Utah, Wyoming, North Dakota, South Dakota, Nebraska, Minnesota, Iowa, Colorado, Idaho, New Mexico, Arizona.

[11]See Thomas Hart, "The Evolution of Telco-Constructed Broadband Services for CATV Operators," *Catholic University Law Review,* 34: (1985): 697.

[12]Report & Order, 21 FCC 2nd 307.

[13]See *United States v. Western Electric Co.,* 767 F. Supp. 308 (D.D.C. 1991) and 900 F.2d 283 (D.C. Cir. 1990).

[14]Anita Wallgren, "Video Program Distribution and Cable Distribution: Current Policy Issues and Recommendations," National Telecommunications and Information Agency. U.S. Dept. of Commerce, June 1988.

[15]Second Report and Order, Recommendation to Congress and Second Further Notice of Proposed Rulemaking, 7 FCC Rcd, 5781, 5784 (1992).

[16]Landler, Mark, "Rivals Yawn at US West Cable Deal," *New York Times,* 29 January 1996, D-1.

[17]Landler, "Rivals Yawn."

[18]Mark Landler, "Nynex and Bell Atlantic Reach Accord on Merger," *New York Times,* 22 April 1996, 1.

[19]Richard Tedesco, "Bell Atlantic Blows Its VOD Horn," *Broadcasting & Cable,* 25 March 1996, 69.

[20]Glen Dickson, "Tele-TV Due for Digital MMDS in Fall," *Broadcasting & Cable,* 11 March 1996, 80.

[21]Carl Weinschenk, "Ameritech Scores a Telco First in Landing Cable Franchise," *Cable World,* 3 July 1995, 1.

[22]Ameritech ran into anticipated resistance from the local cable companies, especially Continental Cablevision, which held existing franchises in several of the towns, and had to back away from some areas because Continental owned exclusive local rights to Home Box Office and Cinemax through a system-wide, and legally controversial, arrangement with Time Warner.

[23]"GTE Expands Reach of Disney," *Telecommunication Reports,* 14 August 1995, 31.

[24]"GTE Close to Florida Cable Deals," *Broadcasting & Cable,* 6 May 1996, 9.

[25]Vince Cittore, "AT&T's Local Telephony Push," *Cable World,* 22 April 1996, 33.

[26]Jim McConville, "Utility Looks to Be Cable Player," *Broadcasting & Cable,* 15 April 1996, 70.

[27]Telecom Act. sect. 202.

[28]*Broadcasting & Cable Yearbook, 1996* (New Providence, NJ: R. R. Bowker, 1996).

[29]See, Bruce Owen and Steven Wildman, *Video Economics* (Cambridge: Harvard University Press, 1992).

[30]"The Drop Continues," *Broadcasting & Cable,* 25 March 1996, 10.

[31]National Cable Television Association, *Cable Television Developments,* Spring 1996, 5.

[32]Laurie Thomas and Barry Litman, "Fox Broadcasting Company, Why Now?" *Journal of Broadcasting & EM,* 35 (Spring 1991): 139–157.

[33]"USA Makes It Six in a Row," *Broadcasting & Cable,* 1 January 1996, 39.

[34]"The Handbook for the Competitive Market, Blue Book Vol. III," *Cablevision,* 1996, 4.

[35]For an introduction on satellite technology see: Andrew F. Inglis, *Satellite Technology: An Introduction* (Boston: Focal Press, 1991); Donald M. Jansky and Michel C. Jeruchim, *Communications Satellites in the Geostationary Orbit* (Norwood, MA: Artech House, 1987).

[36]See Michael L. Katz and Carl Shapiro, "Technology Adoption in the Presence of Network Externalities," *Journal of Political Economy* 94 (1986): 822; Michael L. Katz and Carl Shapiro, "Network Externalities, Competition, and Compatibility," *American Economics Review* 75 (1985): 424.

[37]INTELSAT typically does not engage in price discrimination on the basis of demand elasticity and user desire to lease capacity on a particular satellite. Private operators typically do. The "Hot Bird" concept reflects the added value and commensurately higher lease prices for satellites that become home to the most desirable video programs and networks. Because users have a financial incentive in limiting the number of Earth stations they need to install and maintain, they prefer to access only a few satellites for their complete inventory of video programming. Private satellite operators who have executed transponder leases with programmers having the most desirable video product find that other programmers, perhaps offering less attractive fare, want to lease capacity and possibly exploit the benefits of being more widely accessible.

[38]"There are many products for which the utility that a user derives from consumption of the good increases with the number of other agents consuming the good." Katz and Shapiro, "Network Externalities."

[39]See Carmen Matutes and Pierre Regibeau, "'Mix and Match': Product Compatibility Without Network Externalities," *Rand Journal of Economics,* 19 (1988): 221.

[40]Homeowners in the cities who wanted the additional channels TVRO offered were sometimes frustrated by local codes and ordinances that prohibited the large and unsightly dishes in residential neighborhoods.

[41]Alan Breznick, "Time to Buddy Up?" *Cable World,* 29 April 1996, 8.

[42]Alan Breznick, "Some Sobering Predictions," *Cable World,* 15 April 1996, 4.

5

Content and Control: "It's the Programming (and Services)"

In the 1992 Presidential elections, then-candidate Bill Clinton's campaign manager, James Carville, led his political troops with the now famous slogan: "It's the economy, stupid!" His intent was to keep everyone focused on what the campaign perceived to be the most important issue of the day and not to get distracted by electoral sideshows. In the sizzle and sparks of the telecommunications industry's technological wizardry, some observers are continually reminding everyone, in like fashion, that "it's the content, stupid!" Their point is that consumers do not buy ATMs, MPEGs, HFCs, and SDVs. They buy CNN, ESPN, USA, and telephone service. Early skeptics of the high-tech, high-priced information infostructures observed that industry planners often seemed guided by a philosophy of "if we build it, they will come." That is, telephone and cable industry leaders were approving multibillion-dollar business plans for broadband networks without really knowing whether consumers had any interest in buying the services that those networks could provide. Telephone companies especially came under attack for proposing a rewiring of the United States, at costs estimated as high as $500 billion, without any convincing evidence that the plans could be justified on the basis of consumers' needs or interests.

At the point of purchase, in the living rooms and dens of families across the United States, the ultimate market question is whether or not people are interested in buying the programs and services the information highway offers, and if they are interested, what price will they pay. Clearly the development of the broadband network has important implications for our cultural and political life (explored in Chapter 9), but the extent and nature of that network will, in the first instance, be heavily influenced, if not determined, by consumer support.

This chapter is about content, defined as both programming and services. It is also about the relationship between content and distribution. The first part of this chapter looks at the various types of traditional and emerging services in the cable–telecommunications industry. These include the basic programming networks such as CNN and USA, local broadcast channels and superstations, public access, pay-per-view channels and, video-on-demand, among others. It also includes basic telephone service, the advanced digital cellular telephone service known as personal communication services, and data communications that range from Internet access to electronic banking. The second part of this chapter looks at the ownership structure of the industry. It considers not just the ties between the owners of the distribution systems and the owners of the content, but also the increasingly complex and interconnected web of relationships between all the players in the industry. It looks at the forces of vertical and horizontal integration that characterize much of the recent activity in the cable, satellite, and telco business.

SOFTWARE: PROGRAMMING AND SERVICES

There are two points about programming and services that, while implied in earlier chapters, need to be moved to the foreground here. First, there are three primary market segments involved: video (and audio) entertainment, voice telephony, and data communications. Second, the competing providers are looking to capture significant portions of all three segments, often by bundling them in discounted packages. This is the home market manifestation of converging services and it will be measured in the hundreds of billions of dollars by 2005, if not before. Economic projections call for global expansion in all three areas, although the splintering of the provider market and the accelerating development of the data segment will mean differential growth across categories. Cable, for example, as a result of the migration of subscribers to DBS and other competing services, is expected see a proportional decline in revenue from basic cable, but an increase in a variety of other categories including pay-per-view movies and data communications (see Table 5-1). According to projections by Kagan Associates, total cable industry revenues could grow from about $27 billion in 1997 to $60 billion by 2004, but income streams will change as cash flow from telephony and other service increase and the percentage of total revenue from basic cable drops from 67 percent to 45 percent. Similarly, while residential voice telephony in the United States is not a growth area, various forms of data communications are expanding rapidly. Competing industries, therefore, are looking to expand into new markets as one means to spur company growth.

More inclusively, the content or software side of the broadband business can be broken into a variety of categories and subcategories, outlined in Figure 5-1.

TABLE 5-1   Estimated Cable Revenue Breakdown (in billions)

	1995	2004
Basic cable	$15.6	$27
Advertising	3.3	7
Telephony	0.76	9
PPV/NVOD/VOD	0.28	6.6
Pay TV	5.3	5.4
On-Line Services	.005	3.8
Videogames	0.1	1.2
Miscellaneous	0.76	5.4
Total Revenue	$26.1	$65.4

Sources: "The Handbook for the Competitive Market, Blue Book Vol. III," *Cablevision,* 1996, 6; Paul Kagan Associates, Inc. (Carmel, Calif.), "Data Bank," *Cable World,* 19 February 1996, 46; "Data Bank," *CableWorld,* 9 December 1996, 13".

This chapter looks more closely at each of these segments, as they have traditionally existed in cable and satellite television, and as they appear to be evolving in the new broadband environment.

PROGRAMMING

Programming Networks

As we've seen, cable, satellite, and telco delivery systems will soon be capable of a vast array of interactive video services. But for most people, for the last twenty years, television has not meant high definition, interactive multimedia, and it has not meant computer interfaces, digital architectures, or network interface units. Few care about ownership structure, finances, or technology. Viewers know CNN and MTV and C-SPAN. They know Larry King and Beavis and Butthead, not Amos Hostetter or Ray Smith (although they may know Ted Turner). People watch programs.

For the average viewer, cable or satellite television is the programming. Some have even suggested that cable television has come to be known more as a body of programming, "cable channels," than as a distribution system. But while cable may, for some, have become synonymous with programming networks, it should be stressed that programming networks are more than just cable. To underscore this we will shy away from the commonly used term "cable networks" in favor of the broader "programming networks." This usage reflects acknowledgment of the changing industry structure. CNN and MTV are delivered via DBS, MMDS, and even telco SDV systems.

Video Services

Programming Networks and Services
Basic Networks
Premium or Pay Networks
Pay-Per-View
Near Video-on-Demand and Video-on-Demand
Telco Program Packagers

Broadcast Retransmission
Local Stations
Regional, Imported Stations
Superstations

Local Cable
Local Cable Origination
Cable Access Channels
Leased, Public, Educational, and Government (PEG)

Telephone Services

Local POTS, Plain Old Telephone Service
CAPS, Competitive Access Providers
PCS, Personal Communications Services

Data Communications

Internet and WWW Access
Proprietary On-Line services
(E-mail, information, entertainment, games, shopping, banking, and so on)
Telemetry: Fire, burglar alarms, metering
Distance Education
Telecommunting
Paging and Positioning

FIGURE 5-1

No matter what distribution system the services come through, however, people have a broad array of choices. There are existing or planned programming services for all manner of tastes and demographic groups. There are channels for sports enthusiasts, car collectors, military buffs, women, children, shoppers, nature lovers, bookworms, and computer hackers. Select a topic or an ethnic group and the odds are good that someone has started or proposed a cable channel just for it. Some channels are almost household words, like CNN and MTV, some are highly focused or esoteric, like proposals for Chop TV: The Karate Channel or the Opera Channel. They can have the backing of some of the world's largest corporations, like Time Warner and Disney/Cap Cities, or they can be the hopeful products of venture capitalists. There are audio or radio cable services and text-only channels, each again with a wide range of niched programming options. There are more than one hundred programming services planned or in operation today, although the precise number fluctuates with the birth and death of new services ideas (see Appendix A). Most of them are full video programming services, and about two dozen provide audio channels or text, including channel guides.

Performance

Basic cable television channels have done well in competition with the broadcast networks, especially in recent years. The cumulative ratings and share for these services have steadily increased since their inception (see Table 5-2).

The successful emergence of DBS distribution and the addition of new cable subscribers made possible by the FCC's "going forward" rules (see Chapter 6) also helped expand the reach of most of the larger services beginning in 1995. The fastest growing networks have included the Cartoon Channel, The Learning Channel, ESPN2, the Sci-Fi Channel, and Court TV.

The Nature and Types of Programming Networks

Broadband programming services can be divided into several major categories and subcategories, starting with classifications based loosely on how the subscriber pays for the channel. These include:

Basic and Expanded Basic Services: This is the largest category of programming networks and refers primarily to those channels supported by advertising, although shopping channels and religious networks, which generate revenue in other forms, are also typically included, as is C-SPAN. These channels are usually part of a cable system's basic and expanded, or extended, tier (see Chapter 6). They include channels such as CNBC, MTV, Discovery, Lifetime, ESPN, and BET.

Premium or Pay Services: Broadly speaking, these are channels that do not include advertising. Consumers pay separately for them, either individually or

TABLE 5-2 Full Day Shares for Basic Cable and Broadcast Network Affiliates

	Basic Cable in Cable HH	Basic Cable in All TV HH	Broadcast Affl's in All TV HH
1995	42	30	47
1993	36	25	53
1991	35	24	53
1988	25	15	61
1985	19	11	66

Sources: *Cable TV Facts* (New York: Cable Television Advertising Bureau, 1996), 13–21; *Cable Television Developments* (Washington, D.C., National Cable Television Association, 1996), 5.

TABLE 5-3   Selected 1997 Program Service Ratings

Programmer	Full Day Rating	Prime Time Rating (Mon.–Sun, 8–11 p.m.)
Nickelodeon	1.6	1.9
WTBS	1.0	1.8
TNT	1.0	2.4
USA	0.8	1.8
Cartoon Channel	0.8	1.3
Lifetime	0.8	1.5
A&E	0.8	1.3
ESPN	0.7	1.4
Discovery	0.6	1.3
WGN	0.6	1.0
TNN	0.5	0.9
CNN	0.4	0.8
Family Channel	0.4	1.0
MTV	0.4	0.6
The Learning Channel	0.4	0.7
fX	0.4	0.6
TV Land	0.4	0.5
The Weather Channel	0.3	0.3
Headline News	0.3	0.3
Sci-Fi Channel	0.3	0.7
ESPN2	0.3	0.5

Source: *Broadcasting & Cable,* 30 June 1997, 73; and individual networks.

bundled as small "premium" tiers of two to four channels. The staple programming is recent films and special events, and the best-known examples include cable's first nationally distributed programming service, Home Box Office, and its sister service, Cinemax. Their chief competitors have been the Viacom services, Showtime and The Movie Channel, and more recently, TCI's Starz channel.

Pay-Per-View (PPV): While viewers pay for premium service on a monthly basis, Pay-Per-View, as the name suggests, charges customers for every program selected, with prices ranging from a few dollars for a recent movie to $30 or more for a major sports or entertainment event. The primary program categories for PPV include recent films; sports, especially boxing matches and staged wrestling shows; and adult channels. Request Television and Viewer's Choice TV are among the major PPV programmers.

Near Video-on-Demand (NVOD): This is the next technological step up from PPV. Its focus is on current movies but it offers greater choice to the viewer both in terms of the selection of films and flexibility of viewing time. It requires significant bandwidth because it uses dozens, even hundreds, of channels. It works by running a given film, say *Gone With the Wind,* on three or four channels, but staggering the start times of each showing so that a viewer doesn't have to wait for more than a few minutes before the film begins. Pricing is on a per-program basis. DBS services have been running limited versions of this service for several years and if it proves out financially, it may become more common in cable systems as they move further into a digital environment.

Video-on-Demand (VOD): In its most advanced form, this is the fully interactive system described at various points in this text. It requires, in practice, a switched digital system that connects the viewer to a server containing the film or program of choice. It gives individual subscribers VCR-like control over the program, which could be a movie, news clip, or old television show. It will be several years before VOD is widely available and pricing structures are still uncertain, but much of it will certainly be on a per-program basis.

Network Niches
Within each of these categories, but most typically and widely in the basic, advertiser-supported domain, networks are also characterized by their target markets, or market niches. These are generally defined along interacting lines of content and demographics. They include: news and public affairs; sports; general interest; specialty entertainment, such as comedy or science fiction; education and information; improvement; shopping; religion; women, children, and ethnic channels. This list is not exhaustive. There is a broad variety of programming types, philosophies, ownership structures, and audiences. To understand programming today one needs a familiarity with some of the major players and their histories in this kaleidoscope of choice.

General Entertainment. It is interesting that in the multichannel world of micro-targeted content, where twenty-four hours of programming can be dedicated to horses, or golf, or antiques, the most watched networks continue to be aimed at the broadest audiences, channels that mimic the broadcast networks in their mix of movies, sports, and serials.

For much of the early 1990s, the number one programming network was USA, often followed by TNT and TBS. The USA Network also has the distinction of arguably being the first advertiser-supported basic channel. Launched originally as the Madison Square Garden Network (MSG) in 1977, it became USA in 1980 in a partnership between Madison Square Garden and United Artists/Columbia Cablevision. It was subsequently purchased by a partnership that included Time, Inc., Paramount Pictures, and MCA, although Time sold its interest in 1987. With its heritage in MSG, USA relied heavily on sports programming in its early years, being the first cable network to carry Thursday night Major League Baseball, the first to sign the National Hockey League and the National Basketball Association to game-of-the-week contracts, and the first to carry live college football.

Over time it expanded its offerings, running game shows in the afternoon, buying major off-network programming like *Miami Vice,* and developing a full slate of original programming. While its breadth has been one of its chief assets, it did prompt a legal fight with Jones InterCable in the late 1980s when Chairman Glenn Jones dropped it from his systems, complaining that it looked too much like the broadcast networks and relied too heavily on network reruns. The move temporarily cost USA some one million Jones' subscribers, but the network was restored to the systems in 1991 following the out-of-court settlement of a breach of contract suit brought by USA. USA expanded its offerings in 1992 with the purchase of the Sci-Fi Channel.[1]

TNT, Turner Network Television, debuted in 1988 and was intended from the start as a direct competitor to the established broadcast networks. It features a mix of films, major league sports (including the National Football League), and children's programming. When Ted Turner purchased MGM/UA Entertainment Co., in 1986, the chief prize was the MGM film library of more than 2,000 titles including *Ben Hur, Dr. Zhivago,* and *Gone with the Wind.* TNT became a primary distribution outlet for this treasure trove of movies and its heavily-promoted *Gone with the Wind* showings helped launch the network.[2]

Other mixed programming networks include the Fox Television channel, fX, and The Family Channel, although the latter is discussed below with religious networks.

News and Current Affairs.   Turner, again, is a dominant player in this category. Cable News Network (CNN) was one of the earliest and has been one of the most socially and politically influential of all the cable networks. An audacious brainchild of Ted Turner, CNN launched on June 1, 1980, to some skepticism from the broadcast industry and various critics. Since then it has grown to become an international first source of breaking news for millions. It has spawned several sister networks, including CNN Headline News (or CNN 2); CNN International, a major source of domestic news for citizens abroad; and CNNFn, a financial news competitor to the market leader, NBC broadcasting's CNBC. The latter does economic and market news in the day and consumer news and talk shows at night.[3]

Other channels worth noting in this category include C-SPAN I and C-SPAN II. The creation of former journalist and political press secretary Brian Lamb, these channels carry live coverage of the U.S. House of Representatives and the U.S. Senate, respectively, along with quietly thoughtful, bi-partisan public affairs programming. C-SPAN, the Cable-Satellite Public Affairs Network, launched in 1979 after Lamb convinced several executives in the cable industry of the need and usefulness of such a service. Beginning with less than a half-million dollars in funding and no equipment, the operation grew to two channels, with more being planned, and multimillion-dollar funding by the cable industry through subscriber fees.

One of the big surprises in cable television programming was the success of the Weather Channel. Few thought that a twenty-four-hour forecast would generate the intense interest that it has. Launched in 1982, the Weather Channel, with its revolving format of local forecasts, national maps, weather features and, best of all, live radar, has by many popular accounts turned thousands of people into weather junkies.[4] It is one of the few of the highly popular channels owned by a company generally outside the cable industry, although its owner, Landmark Communications, Inc., has interests in the newspaper industry as well as broadcast television and radio stations.

While other channels have come and gone in this area—including the Financial News Network (FNN) and the Satellite News Channel (SNC), a failed attempt by ABC and Westinghouse to compete with CNN—new entrants are again knocking on CNN's door. In 1996, NBC and Fox began twenty-four-hour news channels of their own. NBC teamed with computer software giant Microsoft to begin MSNBC, combining a CNN-like video channel with an on-line news service. Fox and TCI partnered to begin FoxNews. Ted Turner, reacting to the Fox–TCI announcement, made trade press headlines, declaring, "I'm looking forward to squishing Rupert (Murdoch) like a bug."[5] Fox and MSNBC have been obtaining distribution over cable systems, however, and the competitive struggle between the various services was being closely watched by the industry.

Finally, systems in some major markets offer regional or local twenty-four-hour news channels, often in partnership with other local media. Examples include: New York 1 News; ChicagoLand Television News; New England Cable News; Newschannel 8, in Washington D.C.; and Orange County News Channel, in Southern California.

Sports.   Like news, this is a category that until recently has been dominated by one network. ESPN, the Entertainment and Sports Programming Network, is regularly one of the highest rated of the basic networks. Disney/Cap Cities owns 80 percent of ESPN, which was the only full-time national sports network until 1993, when ESPN2 was launched. When the idea of a twenty-four-hour sports network was announced in 1978, many observers thought it absurd, but within a few years it was obvious that the appeal of sports, especially among American males, was compelling, and fan loyalty was so great that it helped ESPN begin an industry-wide policy of charging systems for each subscriber (see Chapter 6). It helped create an essential new revenue stream for programmers. As Charles Warner and Michael Wirth note in their history of ESPN:

> *By the end of 1991, ESPN had become the most widely viewed cable network (especially among men), the most widely distributed cable network in the US, and the one the cable network viewers said they valued most. Virtually no major male-oriented national advertiser could afford to ignore it.[6]*

In 1996, Turner teamed with *Sports Illustrated* (both of them Time Warner properties) to create CNNSI, a sports news network, TCI was working with Fox on the Fox Sports channel, and ESPN created a sports news service, ESPNews. Classic Sports Network specializes in running historic sports events. The Golf channel is often offered as a premium service. In addition to the national services, there are a host of smaller, regional cable sports networks with such names as PrimeSport Northwest, Sports Channel New England, Sports Channel Chicago, and Empire Sports Network. Some fifteen regional "Prime Sports" networks are owned by Liberty Media, the programming arm of TCI, although the company has used most of them in the development of Fox Sports.

Demographics.   Right behind ESPN in recent prime-time ratings have been Nickelodeon and Lifetime TV. Nickelodeon, in fact, is often ranked first of all the niched services in ratings that take into account a full day's viewing (as opposed to just prime time). Nickelodeon is targeted for children during the day, and Lifetime promotes itself as the only network programmed specifically for women.

Nickelodeon began as a children's service over the experimental QUBE system run by Warner–Amex in Columbus, Ohio, in the early 1980s. It was subsequently offered to cable systems as a means of convincing parents of the value of a cable subscription. Initially an advertiser-free channel, it began accepting commercials in 1983 and expanded to twenty-four hours in 1985, although the children's programming component stayed in the daytime block while the "Nick at Night" programming of 1960s and 1970s TV sitcoms took up the evening. Sold to Viacom, along with the MTV networks in 1985, it blossomed along with increasing cable penetration in the late 1980s.

Lifetime, the channel for women, is owned in partnership by Disney/CapCities and Hearst Entertainment. It grew out of the merging of Daytime TV and the Cable Health Network in 1983; the former offered women's programming for only a few hours a day over satellite. Through the late 1980s and early 1990s it developed a lineup of off-network programming it hoped would appeal primarily, although not exclusively, to women, including prior network hits like *L.A. Law, Cagney & Lacey,* and *China Beach.* With its continuing success it began development of original material in the early 1990s, like many of the other large programmers (see Chapter 6).

Black Entertainment Television (BET) was organized in 1980 by Robert Johnson, who held positions at the National Urban League, the Corporation for Public Broadcasting, and the National Cable Television Association. With his vision of a network programmed for the African American community, he approached the contacts he had made in the cable industry, beginning with TCI. TCI, then Warner Cable, ATC, and Teleprompter bought into the idea and the company, and BET launched in early 1980.[7] While encountering some initial financial difficulties, additional support from the cable industry helped propel BET into the growth phase of the industry in the late 1980s and established it as one of the important networks, culturally and financially, in cable.

BET, Lifetime, and Nickelodeon were among the earliest and most successful of the networks in this category, but others followed and more are promised as channel space opens up. At least two networks, GalaVision and Univision, program for the Spanish-speaking market, and the more specialized GEMS International television targets Hispanic women. Others either operating or in the planning stages include: CelticVision: The Irish Channel; Jewish Television Network and The National Jewish Television Network; Gay Entertainment Television; Asian American Satellite TV; KALEIDOSCOPE: America's Disability Channel; The Filipino Channel; The Parents Channel; The Singles Network; and combining sports and demographics, The Women's Sports and Entertainment Network.

Specialty Entertainment.   By specialty entertainment we mean those channels programming in a particular genre, such as music, comedy, science fiction, or westerns. The dominant subcategory here is music, with a number of closely targeted channels. The biggest name in this category is MTV, or, more formally, Music Television.

Like CNN, MTV is one of those standout services that has had an impact far beyond the cable industry. Its role as a cultural, even political force, is explored more fully in Chapter 9. It is enough to note here that, in addition to creating a new form of popular music—the music video—MTV has influenced the style of at least one and maybe more generations. Given its influence, MTV's development and effect on the music and cable business is worth a brief examination. The concept for MTV was developed by John Lack, then Vice President of Warner–Amex Satellite Entertainment. In 1980 he pitched his idea for a cable channel that targeted the late baby boomers and the children of the baby boomers (the "echo") to executives at Warner Communications and American Express. With a corporate green light, Lack brought in radio programmer Robert Pittman, who headed the effort to develop the MTV concept. The idea was to run videos, originally designed as promotional vehicles for records, in the same way that top 40 radio stations aired records.[8] MTV launched on August 1, 1981, and quickly accomplished two important things: First, it attracted a new and younger audience to popular music, a generation that had been raised on television, and second it introduced to this audience a new set of artists and new kinds of music. In 1986, Warner sold MTV—along with its spin-off channel VH-1 and Warner–Amex's Nickelodeon—to Viacom for about $550 million.

While perhaps dominant in music television, MTV is not the only music network. TNN, The Nashville Network, and Country Music Television, CMT, cater to the C&W market; MTV's VH-1 targets the baby boomer demographic and Z TV provides a Christian version of MTV. The Box is a low-level interactive music service, and there are jazz (BET on Jazz) and classical (Classical Music Channel) networks.

Other genre programmers include the Science Fiction (Sci-Fi) Channel (USA Networks), which programs a heavy schedule of off-network material such as the original *Star Trek* series and *The Outer Limits;* Comedy Central; The Game Show Network; and one of the most successful launches in network history, Ted Turner's Cartoon Network, which catapulted into the top 20 cable networks within a year of its launch in 1992.

On a somewhat more elevated plane, there are several networks serving the classical arts or simply dedicated to a higher quality product. These include the well-established Arts and Entertainment, A&E, (owned jointly by Hearst, Disney/Cap Cities, and NBC), Bravo, and the embryonic Ovation: The Fine Arts Network.

Information and Education.   Nonfiction programming has proven very popular with cable audiences. The genre was inaugurated in 1985 with the debut of the Discovery Channel, the idea of John Hendricks, a former University of Maryland fundraiser and media relations consultant. He saw a market for the vast libraries of educational and nonfiction audio–video materials available in schools, colleges, and private collections around the country. Hendrick's original business plan failed and the network almost folded, but in 1986 TCI purchased an equity interest and other MSOs followed suit. With a new business plan and a cash infusion from the major cable operators, Discovery built a programming mix of nature shows, history, adventure, science and technology, and a reasonable measure of original material. By the mid 1990s it was on systems that passed more than 65 million homes and was one of the largest cable networks.[9]

In 1991, Discovery purchased the Learning Channel for $30 million and began repositioning the two channels to more clearly distinguish between them, although both continued to offer nonfiction material. Mind Extension University began operations in 1987, offering extended education and college credit programming in cooperation with colleges and universities around the country. In 1995, A&E Networks launched a more targeted service, the History Channel.

Improvement.   Closely related to the information networks are a host of new channels devoted to self-improvement or home improvement. Perhaps stirred by the success of the how-to shows on Discovery and the Learning Channel, audiences now have access to Home and Garden Television, the Food Network, and potential channels such as FAD TV (Fashion and Design Television), the Fashion Network, and Home Improvement TV Network. There are several health and fitness channels in operation or proposed, including Fit TV, America's Health Network, the Health and Fitness Network, The Health Channel, and the Recovery Network.

Religious.   The use of broadcasting by organized religion is as old as broadcasting itself, and it is well represented in cable. The most successful religious channel has arguably made the transition to a general interest basic service. The Family Channel, in some ways like USA and TBS, programs an eclectic mix of news, movies, and off-network shows, although, unlike some of the programs on USA, it maintains a firm line on wholesome, family-oriented material, featuring series such as *Little House on the Prairie,* and *The Waltons.* The Family Channel began life as the Christian Broadcasting Network (CBN), the media ministry of evangelist Pat Robertson. The channel suffered financially when Robertson launched his presidential campaign in 1987, but began recovering with his return and a reconceptualization of the service in 1988. As the network became more secular and more profitable, it separated from the Robertson ministry in 1990 to become the Family Channel. While the channel moved more to the mainstream in the early 1990s, it retained some of its conservative religious emphasis, most pointedly in the form of its nightly news–talk program, *The 700 Club*. In 1997, Robertson sold the channel's holding company, International Family Entertainment, to Rupert Murdoch's News Corp. for $1.9 billion.

The Catholic church also offers a popular network, EWTN: Global Catholic Network. Other religious programmers include Odyssey (formerly the Faith and Values Channel), which joined two earlier networks, ACTS and the VISN Network, into a service that programs for a wide range of faiths, and the nondenominational Trinity Broadcasting Network, one of the largest religious programmers. The smaller Inspirational Network started life as PTL, the television voice of evangelical ministers Jerry Falwell and Jim and Tammy Bakker. The network was renamed in 1987, following the Bakker's financial scandal and the jailing of Jim Bakker.

Shopping.   The shopping channels can be considered in a separate category because of their unique financing. Unlike advertiser-supported or pay channels, the shoppers make money like any retailer: they take a percentage of the revenue generated in the on-air sale of the products. Most of the money goes to the network. Local systems and MSOs usually receive about 5 percent of the revenue generated by sales in their area. While initially lampooned as the "zirconium networks," for the imitation diamond jewelry and other low-end items hawked by these services, they have proven highly profitable. The two dominant services are Home Shopping Network and QVC (formerly Quality Value Network), each of which program two domestic channels. The Home Shopping Network originated the format in 1985 and its success was quickly imitated by QVC, its chief rival. Other shopping services include Shop at Home, ValueVision, and the Video Catalog Channel. Additional networks are planned, some of them with an eye toward exploiting the greater interactivity promised by the emerging distribution systems.

Special Interest.   Finally, there are scores of special interest channels, either in operation or in the planning stages, that defy clear classification. They cover topics from pets to politics, aviation to antiques, and include: interactive gambling channels; military channels; arts and antique channels; NASA Select television; The Pet Television Network; C/Net–The Computer Network; the Crime Channel; DRAGnet (an infomercial channel); Jones Computer Network; NET, Political NewsTalk Network; The Outdoor Channel; The Auto Channel; The Love Network; Hobbycraft Network; and Sewing and Needle Arts Network, to name just a few.

Premium Channels.   While premium and PPV services are categories of service based primarily on economic structures, they can also fairly be considered niche services as well. Their staple is recently released theatrical films, although they also feature comedy specials and original series that often contain material that would be considered too risqué for network broadcast or even basic services. The premium services have been increasing their proportion of originally produced programming (see Chapter 6).

Premium services were very popular in the 1980s, helping power cable penetration into larger markets. Beginning in the early 1990s, however, the introduction of VCRs and home video rentals dramatically reduced gross revenue in premium providers. Initial industry reaction was to develop nonfilm content. In addition, premium services introduced "multiplexing" strategies. Multiplexing is the creation of additional channels. HBO developed HBO 1, 2, and 3 and HBO Ole, for example. Multiplexing was designed in part to preempt shelf space on systems and keep competitors out of the market. It was also a recognition of the need to offer greater variety and convenience to compete with rentals. In some cases, each of the channels was thematically niched. TCI began a mini-pay service, Encore, in 1991, featuring a $1 per month fee, in part to drive down the price of other premium services. It soon developed a fleet of multiplexed Encore movie channels, each with a specific theme: romance, westerns, mysteries, action, even a young people's Encore (Encore-7, WAM!). Each multiplexed channel establishes its own, albeit linked, identity and is offered on a monthly fee basis.

An interesting exception to this general classification is the Disney Channel. While it is often offered as a premium service, many cable operators also use it as a loss leader on their extended basic tier. While it costs the operator more to package it this way, the channel can attract new families to the overall service and more than make up for the loss. Disney has also began multiplexing and offers at least two signals. Also, unlike most premium services, it runs the full spectrum of Disney fare rather relying on just its films.

Pay-Per-View (PPV) and Near Video-on-Demand (NVOD).   Pay-per-view and NVOD are the next steps up from premium, multiplexed services. PPV began with special events programming, primarily boxing and wrestling. In the early days, cable technicians would sometimes have to go to each house and change a trap to enable reception of a PPV prizefight. Addressable converters made PPV more practical and more lucrative; there are more than 27 million cable addressable homes in the United States, and the number is growing. Addressability did not dramatically change the nature of the progamming, however. Boxing still accounts for more than half of all PPV revenue.[10] Expectations are that this will change over the next several years, however, for several reasons.

As Table 5-1 illustrates, revenues from premium are likely to decline and PPV/NVOD/VOD to climb. PPV revenues were estimated at more than $600 million in 1996, about 45 percent of which came from special events, primarily boxing. By the end of the century PPV could generate over $3 billion with 60 percent coming from films.[11] The increase will be driven by the changing technology and the changing content.

The move away from special events and toward recently released films will require additional bandwidth. Where delivery platforms have been limited to one or two channels, start times for PPV films are too widely spaced to mirror the convenience of a VCR rental film. Increased channels means services can run the films (or even the same film) on several channels, staggering start times so a viewer need only wait a few minutes to see it. Some PPV services offer "anytime" viewing by allowing subscribers to activate one channel, in effect one movie, for a full day so they can watch it at any time in its cycle.

Classic PPV services run a limited number films on a given channel and most cable systems have dedicated only a few channels to PPV. In 1996 the average number of analog cable PPV channels nationally was about 3.2 per household.[12] This number was expected to increase, however, with the implementation of digital distribution. MSOs such as Jones Intercable and Continental have been building capacity for ten to twenty PPV analog channel systems, and the major PPV services, which were operating five to six channels, are doubling and tripling their feeds. As channel capacity increases, buy rates (the number of PPV purchases per addressable household per month) increases. Kagan Associates reported 1995 cable movie buys rates at 26.8 percent; DirectTV, the DBS service with fifty PPV channels, reported a 200 percent buy rate, and full VOD Bell Atlantic experiments reported buy rates of 300 percent or more (although they included inexpensive, nonfilm programming).

Other factors will increase NVOD revenue even in a transitional analog universe. The spread of addressable converters will give more homes the ability to access PPV and NVOD. Digital deployment is expected to help spur growth over the next few years. Ordering movies will become easier. Services are increasingly using automated telephone ordering systems, or ANI (automatic number identification), in which the viewer places an 800-number call to a computer that acknowledges the order, activates the viewer's channel, and records the billing information. Even more convenient are two-way systems that permit "impulse" ordering via the remote control and converter box. DBS set-top boxes, for example, are attached to the home telephone line and a movie order entered using the remote control is relayed via the telephone system.

The current principal PPV services include Request, Viewer's Choice, and Action PPV. TCI and News Corp. (Fox) are joint owners of Request, along with the company founder Reiss Media Enterprises. Viewer's Choice is an MSO-owned company with partners that include Time Warner, Continental, Cox, Comcast, and Viacom. A merger of the two PPV companies was pending in late 1997. Action PPV, operated by BET, features current action/adventure and mature theme "B" movies.

Graff pay-per-view operates a smaller service, Cable Video Store, and runs one of the two primary adult PPV services, Spice. The larger player in adult PPV is The Playboy Channel. Both feature soft-core "adult" programming; Spice relies more heavily on films and Playboy promotes its original programming. Playboy began as a premium service and switched to a PPV format in 1989, although, unlike other services, it charges for blocks of time instead of on a per-program basis. Six dollars for a twelve-hour block at night is typical. Even without strong promotion, adult channels have done relatively well in the PPV universe, with total revenues in 1996 estimated at more than $100 million. Finally, major league and college sports are making greater use of PPV outlets with the NFL, NBA, and NHL signing contracts with different providers to carry individual games and packages of games.

Neither PPV nor NVOD have the VCR functionality that will earmark full digital VOD. One the challenges of the broadband TV industry will be the development of pricing and marketing strageties for VOD services.

Audio Channels.   There are several types of broadband audio programming, or cable radio services. The most basic involves distribution by a cable or MMDS operator of locally available radio signals pulled off the air and retransmitted over the system. More often, local and regional signals are mixed with satellite-distributed audio feeds that include a mix of proprietary programming and national or international radio. A service might, for example, distribute a classical format FM station, or an international service, such as BBC broadcasting. SuperAudio Cable Radio service offers a blend of FM music formats plus the Business Radio Network and a reading service for the vision impaired.

The early 1990s saw the start of digital music services that distributed satellite-fed, CD-quality programming. While earlier cable audio services were normally included in the subscriber's monthly bill and, in a sense, invisible, the digital services provided by cable, DBS, and MMDS operators require a special set-top box and sometimes charge an additional monthly fee. The advantages of the service include more than one-hundred channels of music in nearly every conceivable format and CD-quality sound. Two of the leaders in this area, Digital Music Express (DMX) and Music Choice, were able to eliminate announcers by encoding all the information about the music into the digital system. The listener can display, either on the set-top box or on a remote control, a song's title, artist, and composer. The services also anticipate the ability to purchase the original CD by including a special "order" button on the audio remote, one touch and the CD will be shipped to your house and your credit card or cable bill charged.

Every year literally dozens of new programming services are announced. Each must secure financing, programming, and distribution, none of them easy tasks. The problems associated with getting space on cable systems is discussed more fully below, and the broader financial problems of starting new channels generally is explored in Chapter 6.

Telco Program Packagers

When telephone companies first began public discussion of entry into the video market, there was considerable skepticism about the ability of the historically heavily regulated common carriage business to obtain or develop television programming and compete effectively in the freewheeling world of broadcasting and cable. But the telcos quickly demonstrated the power of their deep pockets by simply buying the experience and personnel they initially lacked. Two new companies were formed in 1995, both designed to create programming networks for Telco TV. One consortium of companies, including Ameritech, SBC, BellSouth, Southern

New England Telephone, and GTE announced as early as 1994 that it was engaging the Walt Disney Co. to help lead them into television. After a slow start, the newly formed "Americast" company hired Steven Weiswasser, former president of the Cap Cities/ABC multimedia group, to take the helm. Meanwhile, Bell Atlantic, Nynex, and Pacific Telesis jointly formed "Tele-TV," hiring Howard Stringer, previously president of CBS Broadcasting, to lead the company. The phone companies committed war chests of $500 million to Americast and $300 million to Tele-TV and were soon seen on the floor of the national conventions of television program producers, cutting deals and signing sales agreements like veterans. Within months, both companies had acquired rights to most of the major cable programmers, including the various Turner channels. By late 1996, however, the telco interest in Tele-TV had cooled considerably as attention turned to development of long-distance and other services. As noted, Bell Atlantic and Nynex suspended their plans to launch MMDS service. Funding to Tele-TV was cut back and it soon withered away. Meanwhile Americast continued operations albeit on a reduced scale.

Broadcasting

For decades local television broadcasters and cable operators have had a tense and interdependent relationship. As the history of cable reveals, cable's initial raison d'être was carriage of broadcast signals, and for some broadcasters (although not for all) this was a welcome extension of their local audience. Eventually they became competitors, often antagonistic ones, for audience attention, but with 65 percent of all homes attached to the cable and homeowners reluctant to install A-B switches and antennas, broadcasters today must go through the wire to reach their audience. The traditional broadcasting networks still supply most of the programming that America watches. As noted in Chapter 4, viewing of all the basic programming services combined accounted for about 30 percent of the viewing in all television households (a 30 share) in 1995 and 42 percent in cable households. By contrast broadcast network affiliates accounted for 47 percent of all viewing (a 47 share in TV households) and independent TV stations, incuding Fox stations, claimed a 22 share.[13] (see Table 5-2). Multichannel operators, in short, are dependent on broadcasting for a significant portion of their most heavily viewed programming.

Local Broadcast Stations

DBS services are only beginning to explore the possibility of carrying local television stations, but local stations have always been fundamental "anchors" of most cable channel lineups. Cable operators usually carry all the local network affiliates along with the commercial independent stations. There are some local specialty stations that cable would prefer not to have to carry, but as previously noted, under the "must carry" rules, operators are obligated to set aside channel capacity for local signals, (the rules do not apply to wireless cable). These include financially marginal stations that may rely on a steady diet of infomercials (program-length commercials, see Chapter 6) or religious programming. It also includes home shopping channels, which the FCC ruled in 1993 were local stations for purposes of the must carry regulations. Cable operators have long argued that the requirement to carry such signals forces them to drop other, more popular and even substantive cable programming services. C-SPAN, for example, claimed that it lost millions of subscribers when implementation of the must carry rules forced some operators to replace it with local broadcast programming.

Distant Signals

Cable operators import regional signals not available over the air in their community. Regional imported stations are likely to be independent stations or affiliates of Fox, the WB Network, or the Paramount Network, when there is no local affiliate. Existing syndicated exclusivity and network nonduplication rules prevent local operators from importing programming that would violate the exclusivity agreements that local broadcasters have with their programmers.[14]

Superstations

Ted Turner's WTBS pioneered the idea of superstations, independent broadcast stations fed to cable, DBS, and MMDS homes around the country. Other superstations include WGN in Chicago, WWOR and WPIX in New York, KTLA in Los Angeles, and WSBK, Boston. Superstations initially programmed a mix of old movies, local or regional sports, and network reruns. Importation of these and some regional broadcast signals by cable systems often replicated programming, especially syndicated material, being broadcast by local stations, however. The FCC had, as part of deregulation, eliminated its syndicated exclusivity rules in 1980. But complaints from programmers about widespread violation of local exclusivity agreements prompted the Commission to reimpose the rules, effective in 1990.[15] The rules forced some systems to drop regional imports that duplicated local programming. WTBS and other superstations acted quickly to remove programming that might cause duplication problems. They limited their programming to material for which they held exclusive national distribution rights and made themselves "blackout proof." In 1998, WTBS planned to move to basic cable status.

Cable Access and Local Origination

Local cable systems do a limited amount of original programming and open their systems to other companies and agencies to program specified access channels. The earliest form of local original was often an inexpensive camera pointed at a set of dials that told subscribers the temperature, time, and barometric preassure. As previously noted, the FCC instituted in 1969, then rescinded, local origination requirements for cable operators. Since then, voluntary, commercial local origination has taken a number of forms. There are both live and automatic originations. The tradition of the time–weather ticker has continued, often supplemented with news, stock, and sports information, all in automated, text form. These typically advertiser-supported text services are often operated in conjunction with a local newspaper or broadcast station. Some local real estate companies are banding together to program a channel that promotes local homes sales as well. Community bulletin board and channel guides may also be used.

Popular in larger systems is a channel devoted to classified advertising and public service announcements. Live programming is less common. The expanding success of local and regional news channels in major metropolitan areas, mentioned above, is one of the most substantive examples. Often operated in conjunction with an area newspaper or broadcast station, they can be profitable and provide an important public service. Some operators are also looking to expand local programming as a means of keeping existing subscribers and attracting new ones in the more competitive environment. Programmers such as CourtTV and ESPN, for example, are developing local material to compliment their national feeds.

Local origination, either automated or nonautomated, is common in larger systems but again, most cable operations are small. Origination of any type is available on only about 4,700 of the country's 11,000 systems. Local live programming is seen on only about 1,100 systems; time–weather channel, the most popular automated origination, is available on about 2,600 systems.[16]

PEG Channels

PEG channels are public, government, and educational access channels. They are usually franchise requirements established by local government and designed to promote local expression and foster a diversity of editorial voices. Historically, they are acknowledgment of the ownership bottleneck created by monopoply cable systems in most communities. A governmental access channel typically carries city council meetings, planning commission hearings, and like activities. Educational access channels provide area colleges and high schools with outlets for student-produced work. Public access provides any citizen an opportunity to get on the cable, with some restrictions. Availability of access channels and access centers has sparked the development of hundreds of public access groups around the country. These grassroots production organizations generate more than 15,000 hours of access programming every week.[17] Unlike local origination channels, the cable operator has no control over the content or administration of the channels, although the operator is liabile for any obscene or indecent material run on the channel.

Nationwide there are about 2,000 systems with public access, 1,500 with educational access, and 1,300 with governmental access. While these represent a minority of all systems, they are typically larger systems and constitute a large portion of overall penetration. Atkin and LaRose, in a 1991 survey, reported that upwards of 60 percent of all cable subscribers received at least one access channel.[18] Not many of them watch, however. In the Atkin–LaRose study, 16 percent of those surveyed reported viewing an access channel the previous week. By some estimates viewership of all public access channels put together accounts for well under 1 percent of all viewing time. Exceptions include the R-rated public access sex programming that has been a part of New York cable for years and, more importantly, the occasional city council meeting in which a topic of intense local interest draws viewers who cannot or do not go to the meeting. None of this is to suggest access channels are without value. Even though they are not heavily viewed, people report liking the idea that they exist, that the outlet is there when it is needed.

Digital technologies will loosen the choke-hold on channel capacity and likely increase the availability of access channels. The Telecommunications Act of 1996 extends the PEG channel requirement to Open Video System platforms, a hybrid between telephone company common carriage and cable television (see Chapter 7).

Leased Access

The 1984 Cable Act also required system operators to make available channels for leased access. That is, a company can arrange to lease a channel from the cable operator and then is responsible for the programming and administration of that channel. To encourage program diversity and prevent monopoly editorial control, the law provides that systems with thirty-six or more channels must set aside 10 percent of system capacity for leased access; systems with fifty-five or more channels must dedicate 15 percent of capacity to leased access.[19]

In practice, leased channels are likely to be religious programmers or home shopping channels that cannot obtain scarce channel capacity in any other way. Such services are distributed nationally via satellite to participating cable systems. Locally and regionally, a leased channel might offer sports programming on a pay-per-event or a monthly fee basis.

Program Guides and Navigators

One of the challenges for both viewers and programmers in a world of multiplying channels is keeping track of everything. Twenty years ago you could look at the television listings in your local newspaper or turn to a TV guide to find out what was on that evening. The system worked well with ten or even twenty channels. Printed guides with forty or fifty channels start to become too bulky and awkward to use conveniently and will not replicate the special functions being prepared for today's interactive program guides (IPGs). On-screen electronic guides in their basic, analog form use a narrow bandwidth data channel to send simple text material and graphics to a specified channel on the viewer's set. They are little more than video versions of printed guides with scrolling program times and titles. Sophisticated, interactive on-screen guides are available today and will become increasingly necessary to sort through the torrent of program choices coming with digital distribution.

Interactive program guides, or program navigators, offer a variety of high-powered features. They can display a full week's programming on all available channels on their program grid. A viewer can scan across all programs and use pop-up windows to get more information about a particular show, anything from a plot summary to a list of actors, the time remaining in the program, even sample clips of a movie. The viewer can click directly from the guide to the program. Navigators feature one-button VCR recording: the viewer simply highlights any program that coming week and clicks; the guide does the rest. Parents can use it to lock out programs or channels they don't want their children to watch. The screen can be customized, channels never watched can be dropped, and favorite channels placed ahead of less frequently viewed listings. Programs can be sorted by theme, with news, sports, children's shows, or movies grouped together and then subcategorized, with sports, for example, divided into football and golf listings. PPV films or shopping channel merchandise can be impulse ordered with the touch of a button.

TELEPHONE SERVICES

While not as glamorous perhaps as mass (and specialized) video programming, point-to-point voice service, plain old telephone service, is the second primary use to which today's electronic network is being put, and in pure dollar terms it easily predominates. The local telephone business alone generates $90 to $100 billion a year, more than three times the size of the total revenues of the cable industry. The cable industry has long hungered to use its plant to sell telephone service, and the satellite industry with international coverage has extensive plans of its own. Both would very much like to take even a small percentage of existing telco revenues.

Cable Telephone Service

Some cable operators have, since the mid-1980s, been offering telephone services to the business community as "competitive access providers" or CAPS, primarily as a link to and from a long-distance carrier's switching and transmission facilities, referred to as its "point of presence." In addition, cable operators have been running limited tests on cable phone service to the home, and with passage of the Telecommunications Act of 1996, have been given legal clearance to start offering local loop service when their technology is in place. Cable operators also have been working to develop the advanced wireless telephone service, PCS.

CAPS
Competitive access providers offer telephone services primarily to local businesses and other organizations in large urban markets, providing high-capacity access to local and long-distance carriers. Customers are attracted by the typically lower rates that the CAPS offer in comparison with those of the incumbent local exchange carrier (LEC). CAPs service started as a discount conduit to inter-exchange carriers and long-distance services. It has since expanded to include interconnection with providers of local telephone service and may constitute the platform for some CAPS operations to become more widely deployed competitive local providers of POTS and other services (see below). Cable operators have been reasonably successful at developing these services. Kagan Associates predict that by 2004, 17 percent of all businesses will use cable phone service, generating $3.3 billion annually.[20]

Provision of competitive access service has been technically less problematic than fully switched home service because it normally uses a dedicated two-way broadband line (typically fiber) to join the customer to the switch of the local telephone company. It does not require switching capacity of its own (although some CAPS have it) or a heavy upgrade of the entire local cable plant.

POTS

Cable operators have been experimenting with local home service for some time. TCI has been running a trial with "friendly" users in Arlington Heights, Illinois, and West Hartford, Connecticut. Jones Intercable has provided service to apartment buildings in Alexandria, Virginia. As of 1996, however, there were only two operational cable phone local exchange networks, one run by Cablevision Systems Corp. on New York's Long Island and one by Time Warner in Rochester, New York.[21] The Rochester situation was one of the industry's most interesting. There, three different companies were competing for the customer's telephone dollar, including the incumbent provider, Rochester Telephone, Time Warner, and AT&T. Initial results suggested that many people preferred the company they knew best, the incumbent LEC. An AT&T executive described attempts to penetrate the market as "extraordinarily difficult."[22]

Cable companies remain interested in POTS, nonetheless, because local service, especially local business service, constitutes a very large market; some suggest that cable phones could capture as much as 20 percent of that market by 2004.[23] But local service also presents substantially greater technical and business challenges to the cable industry. The costs of providing cable phone service are estimated at $750 to $1,000 a line.[24] As has already been pointed out, cable's real interactive capabilities are still being developed. Preparing the upstream path necessary for POTS requires time, money, and significant attention to plant integrity. Cable engineers are battling problems with signal ingress and interference that could hamper cable phone service.

Physically installing the expensive and complicated computer switches that are at the heart of the local loop poses a challenge. Thousands of individual, physical connections need to be planned and executed. Emergency power to run the telephone network when local power fails must be supplied as well. And there are business challenges. In the same manner that the telephone companies have little experience in the home entertainment industry, cable companies must develop expertise in a completely new line. The nature of the service, the technology, and the regulatory environment are all very different. Billing systems must be created, customer service representatives must be trained, and government relations and legal departments must be enhanced.

Under the 1996 Telecomunications Act, telcos must allow access to businesses like cable that wish to interconnect their networks. But the technical and financial details of interconnection are complex and subject to interpretation, negotiation, even disputation. Some of the decision making over these details has been vested in the state public utilities commissions, where cable and telco companies have been slowly hammering out agreements on a state-by-state basis. One of the many issues involves terms and conditions under which cable companies must pay the LEC to interconnect. A ruling by the FCC to set national standards for some of the access, unbundling, and pricing issues was overturned by a federal court in 1997. The FCC action would have made it easier for competitive entrants to interconnect with local exchange providers, a decision the local providers strongly opposed.

Other issues involve such things as whether the cable company will establish its own 911 emergency number and its own parallel signalling system (which helps manage the voice network), and number portability that allows customers to keep their telephone number even if they change providers.[25] Similar issues plague cable operators' attempts to connect PCS operations to LECs. While these issues eventually will be settled, some of them perhaps in the courts, it will take time and add to the delays in cable getting fully into the business.

There are alternatives for the cable industry. Under the 1996 Telecommunications Act, cable (and others) can offer "facilities-based service" in which the company owns its own lines and switches, as in the situations discussed above, or they can offer "service-based" POTS on a resale basis. Service-based provision involves buying carriage and switching capacity from the incumbent LEC, at a discounted price, and reselling the service to the local customer. Under the 1996 Act, RBOCs and other LECs are required to sell capacity for this purpose to competitive providers. This resale approach provides low-cost entry into the market, but potential providers have voiced concerns that entrenched telcos will drag their feet in essential negotiations just as in facilities-based access. Some operators are looking at resale, however; Continental, for example, is looking to enter the resale market in ten California counties. Some cable operators might prefer to use their own lines, but may consider resale options as a means of getting their feet wet.

Finally there are, once again, marketing questions that may impact cable no matter which route it chooses. Surveys suggest the cable industry may not yet have established a high degree of customer loyalty and this could hamper efforts to sell widespread cable phone service. Telephone customers are used to a reliability level in their telephone system that approaches 100 percent, a standard of dependability people are not used to in their cable system. According to one survey, 63 percent of consumers would not switch from their local telephone service if given an option, 26 percent would switch to a long-distance provider such as AT&T, and only 2 percent would switch to a cable provider (9 percent didn't know).[26]

Perhaps because of the many challenges faced by the cable industry in its hopes to provide phone service, some companies have scaled back previously ambitious plans. TCI has indicated it will move more cautiously into the home voice market, focusing its efforts on data communications in the near term. And the joint venture between TCI, Sprint, Comcast, and Cox—Sprint Spectrum—which originally sought to offer local and long-distance service around the country, dropped its wireline plans to focus solely on wireless telephone in the near term.

Industry-wide, there remains interest in providing voice service over the co-axial–fiber platform, but that service may evolve gradually as systems upgrade their two-way capacity and companies develop the business and technical expertise necessary to run the complex networks. In the meantime, cable and satellite companies will continue to pursue work on wireless phone service.

Wireless Telephone Service

Personal Communications Networks

Anyone who has used a cordless telephone at home can recognize the benefit of tetherless communications. A new generation of wireless services known as Personal Communication Services has the promise of making wireless telephony more affordable and more widely used. The aim is to provide telecommunication services any time, from anywhere, via lightweight, handheld transceivers. Conventional cellular telephone was introduced in the United States in 1984 with subscribership rising at a rate unprecedented for consumer electronics. From a base of zero subscribers in 1984, the industry grew to over 33 million subscribers at the end of 1995.[27]

PCS is the next step in cellular. The units can be made so small and light that some prototypes are actual Dick Tracy-like wrist telephones. Factions of an increasingly mobile society, like "road warrior" business executives, real estate agents, doctors, lawyers, service technicians, and couriers willingly pay metered rates of $0.25 to $1.00 a minute for the convenience and enhanced productivity provided by existing cellular telecommunications. PCS backers are so bullish on the technological and financial promise of the next step that they have spent over $20 billion in spectrum auctions for the privilege of providing the service.

The FCC defines PCS as "radio communications services that free individuals from the constraints of the wireline public switched telephone network and enable them to communicate when they are away from their home or office telephone."[28] This broad definition actually covers several services, including conventional cordless telephones, paging, and cellular, but primarily addresses developing technologies. These include a new generation of cordless telephones known as CT-2 (cordless telephone, second generation) that provides access in other locations outside the home (e.g., shopping centers, airports, and office buildings); PCS service that permits portability of telephone numbers and uses digital, speech-encoding software, and better protocols to achieve faster and more efficient transmission; and wireless private branch exchanges (PBX).

CT-2, PCS, and cellular radio all use technologies that make it possible for large numbers of users to share relatively small amounts of radio spectrum. The technologies achieve seamless access by overlaying cells of microwave transmissions operating at a low enough frequency to provide omnidirectional transmission. Because of the frequency used, the signal quickly deteriorates after reaching an expected cell diameter, making it possible to reuse the same frequency band only a few miles away. The cell size of this service ranges from twenty miles to about one mile in radius. New PCS ventures compress the size of the cell even further so that only a few city blocks are covered, making possible even greater frequency reuse and the operation of smaller transceivers with longer battery lives. Frequency reuse is essential to the business plans of cellular radio and PCS operators, because it dictates how many simultaneous operating channels a system can generate.

As suggested above, cable television operators have plans of their own for participation in this wireless revolution. The fiber–coax infrastructure so widely dispersed for video programming delivery also can provide an essential "backhaul" function for wireless telephone networks. Backhauling involves the carriage of traffic like telephone calls from a remote location, such as the site where a mobile telephone caller has connected to the wireless network, to a centralized switching facility where the call may be routed to another wireless transmitter or to the wireline facilities of the incumbent LEC. Because voice telephone calls occupy little bandwidth, cable operators can retrofit their fiber–coax plant to carry both video, wireless telephone, and data traffic.

Cable operators are already at work on several fronts. Sprint Spectrum has obtained FCC-auctioned PCS licenses for a number of markets, including New York and San Francisco. Comcast is delivering cellular and wireless data services in parts of New Jersey, Pennsylvania, and Delaware. Most cable operators do not have PCS licenses but can work with companies that do to provide traffic transport, or "backhauling," to local interexchange switches.

Satellite Delivered PCS

So far, wireless terrestrial systems have served primarily urban locales and highly traveled rural corridors, like major inter-city turnpikes. As PCS matures and expands, terrestrial systems will build out from densely populated areas. However, the cost of these technologies and technological characteristics, such as the small amount of land mass covered by each transmission cell, will leave vast expanses of rural areas unserved.

LEOs and MEOs.   Satellites can fill the gaps where terrestrial systems do not exist, or cannot provide adequate service. In contrast to the small cell transmission sizes of terrestrial systems, which can be limited to a few hundred yards, satellites transmit a much wider footprint. Conventional geostationary orbiting (GSO) satellites can provide PCS to terminals weighing about five pounds and ones installed in vehicles, but because of their high orbits and low power cannot yet provide strong signals to service the small, handheld transceivers like those used in common cellular phone service. New, primarily mobile telecommunication markets favor the use of satellites operating in low Earth orbit (LEO), middle Earth orbit (MEO), and inclined circular orbits (ICO). From these locations satellites can concentrate a satellite signal and avoid transmission delays and echoes that vex callers using geostationary options.

A number of proposals for LEO satellites have emerged to serve these markets. These systems will operate only a few hundred miles above the earth, thereby reducing the power needed to communicate. While more LEO satellites are needed to cover the globe than their GSO counterparts, they typically weigh less and can be launched more cheaply and in groups of five or more.

Constellations of LEO satellites provide the prospect of a global, ubiquitous wireless telephone service. Unlike terrestrial cellular service, where users physically move from one fixed cell site to another, LEO satellite footprints constantly change as the satellites orbit above. Users appear stationary relative to the fast-moving satellite footprints. Combining footprints from a satellite constellation makes it possible to engineer a global PCS network.

Despite the elegance and attractiveness of a global telecommunication infrastructure, critics question whether demand exists to support projects that will cost upwards of $9 billion. Will venture capitalists and incumbent carriers consider these projects overly expensive investments in first world technology primarily serving unprofitable third world niche markets? Alternatively, will they view these ventures as likely to serve high-end market demand for ubiquitous, wireless access to the rest of the world *and* low-end market requirements for basic telecommunication services in remote regions?

The Key Satellite PCS Players

Inmarsat.   Inmarsat has operated for over twenty years as a cooperative comprised primarily of government satellite monopolies. Its core service mission has been to provide telecommunications for operators located on the high seas and in aircraft. It now has authority to provide land mobile services. Inmarsat anticipates using a separate subsidiary to support a $2.4 billion investment in a new satellite constellation optimized to provide mobile PCS to land terminals.

Iridium.   Iridium plans to operate a $5 billion global constellation of sixty-six LEO satellites about 400 miles above Earth, able to provide voice, data, facsimile, and position determination services to handheld transceivers. Intersatellite links make it possible for the Iridium network to route calls between a number of satellites and on to a gateway Earth station located nearby the call recipient. The other satellite systems lack this function and therefore must rely on expensive switching and routing on Earth that may involve Earth stations far from the intended call recipient.

Motorola created the Iridium concept and has spent several years and several hundred million dollars developing the technology and soliciting investors to form a global consortium.

Globalstar.   Globalstar plans on operating an LEO constellation of forty-eight satellites in eight orbital planes. With fewer satellites operating in orbits about 800 miles above Earth, the $2.5 billion Globalstar network is projected to provide service at a cost of less than fifty cents a minute plus a monthly service charge of $60 to $70. However, less in-orbit resources means that the network will rely heavily on the widespread availability of gateway Earth stations to route calls.

Other Big LEO Ventures. The Ellipso MSS system will operate with up to twenty-four LEO satellites in high elliptical orbits that will maximize coverage of land masses. Organizers of this system claim the ability to bring the cost of satellite technology to within range of terrestrial system costs, i.e., fifty cents to sixty cents a minute. Mobile Communications Holdings, Inc., has secured financial or technical participation from Fairchild Space and Defense Corporation, a diversified aerospace and satellite manufacturer (a subsidiary of Orbital Sciences, Inc.), Harris Corporation, Westinghouse Electric Corporation, Israel Aircraft Industries, Interdigital Communications Corp., a terrestrial PCS manufacturer, and Barclays Bank.

TRW, a multi-billion dollar aerospace and satellite manufacturer, has announced plans for a $1.3 billion satellite Middle Earth Orbiting system comprised of twelve satellites. While the company has promoted its Odyssey system at trade shows, it has announced only one strategic partner, Teleglobe of Canada.

Little LEOs. The FCC also has granted licenses for nonvoice, nongeostationary systems applicants that include VitaSat, Starsys, and Orbcomm. Other nations, both developed and developing, have Little LEO satellite plans. These systems have generated little controversy in forums like the International Telecommunication Union on issues requiring consensus building, e.g., spectrum allocation and service definitions. They appear as worthwhile entrants in relatively narrow, but useful market niches.

Teledesic. Teledesic ups the ante and the anticipated power for LEO satellite constellations. Rather than provide ubiquitous narrowband (less than 4800 bits per second) capacity to mobile users, Teledesic will offer a global overlay of broadband capacity using Ka-band frequencies (20 to 30 GHz). The system will offer transmission rates in excess of 2 Mbps from 288 refrigerator-sized satellites at a total cost of $9 billion. Like its visionary backers, which include Bill Gates, head of Microsoft, Teledesic pushes the envelope with an eye toward providing a ubiquitous, broadband Global Information Infrastructure. The system will commercialize a technology, developed as part of the Strategic Defense Initiative, that deploys missile observer ("Brilliant Eyes") and disruptor ("Brilliant Pebbles") satellites into a seamless, global array. In 1997 Boeing agreed to invest up to $100 million in the venture for a 10% share.

Broadband Overlay Satellites. In 1997 the FCC authorized thirteen companies proposing to operate a total of seventy-three satellites in the 28 GHz portion of the Ka-band. The licenses permit the companies to provide a seamless web of wideband transmission capacity primarily to fixed users for use in such diverse applications as video, voice, data and Internet access. Hughes Communications, Inc. submitted two proposals: Spaceway, an eleven-satellite Ka-band constellation with the first launch scheduled for 1999 and Expressway, the first commercial proposal to use the 40–50 GHz frequency band. Loral Space and Communication Ltd. has proposed a comparatively modest three-satellite Cyberstar system with an eye toward being the first to commence service in 1999. The company also teamed up with Alcatel to propose a $3.9 billion video and data venture called Sky Bridge, comprised of sixty-four LEO satellites. Lockheed Martin Telecommunications has proposed a network of nine Astrolink satellites operating from five orbital locations providing global coverage. The first satellite is scheduled for the first quarter of 2000 with complete deployment by 2001. Motorola has proposed a $13 billion, Celestri network comprised of both geostationary and low earth orbiting satellites. The completed system will have capacity to transmit 80 gigabits per second.

Market Considerations

Satellite PCS operators hope to serve markets where wireline and wireless alternatives do not exist, or where service is unreliable. The ventures anticipate pricing the service well in excess of what conventional systems would charge, if available. Market surveys confirm that several different types of users with inelastic demand (i.e., a strong desire to access the rest of the world), will pay extraordinarily high rates. The long-distance calling rates from hotels and cruise ships, in the $5 to $10 a minute range, confirm this. However, with Iridium projecting (in its most optimistic estimates) service to as many as 3 million subscribers, the success of the ventures depends on market penetration beyond "road warriors" and business elites who have little concern for the cost of a telephone call.

Demand for service from satellite PCS operators will be dampened substantially if wireless networks like cellular radio build out into the hinterlands and if access to less elegant, but cheaper, satellite options become available. While many wireless technologies appear both capital intensive and appropriate for dense traffic routes, other terrestrial options, such as Basic Exchange Telecommunications Radio and Specialized Mobile Radio Service, may provide a cheaper alternative to satellite services.

Even with a steep and profitable rate of usage, cellular radio has achieved a market penetration of no greater than 15 to 20 percent, well short of the mass market penetration. The mobile service entrepreneurs expect terrestrial options, like cellular radio and PCS, to achieve mass market penetration.

Mobile satellite service operators can ride the coattails of terrestrial mobile service market success by providing service to "dual mode" transceivers that cut over to the satellite option when terrestrial service becomes unavailable. If terrestrial systems can achieve profitability with a market penetration of less than 10 percent, then it follows that global or regional satellite systems need only acquire a small portion of the total wireless market to achieve success as well.

Despite the relatively small number of subscribers needed, mobile satellite ventures present substantial risk, because of their cost (approximately $9 billion for Teledesic and $5 billion for Iridium), and the use of unproven technologies. LEO systems require extensive management information systems and network coordination to link as many as 288 fast-moving satellites. The Iridium satellite constellation will communicate not only with ground stations, but between satellites. Consumers may balk at a $3.00 per minute charge, but conditions already exist where access to the rest of the world comes at a price of $10 a minute or more (from hotel rooms, the high seas, and business communication centers in countries with unreliable conventional networks). As well, most LEO systems will provide voice and slow speed data without the capacity to meet broadband applications.

Satellites provide telecommunication service where wireline and other terrestrial options are economically infeasible or technologically inferior. Whether they provide additional services to a larger number of user groups in geographically diverse locales depends on the breadth and scope of terrestrial options. If the concept of "plain old telephone service" expands though infrastructure development initiatives, and if mobility, ubiquity, bandwidth on demand, and other concepts stimulate market development, then satellites will become an even more significant factor in the evolving telecommunications infrastructure.

DATA COMMUNICATIONS

Through 1995 and 1996 one of the hottest topics in communications, in fact in the business world at large, was the Internet. The World Wide Web was exploding. In homes and offices around the country everyone it seemed was going on-line. It was estimated that people were signing up for Internet or on-line services at a rate of 150,000 per month and 100 million people would be using the Internet by 1998.[29] Dozens of new Web sites were being constructed every day. A new industry sprouted up just to handle the business of creating Web sites for other companies. Broadband distribution industries were very excited.

Cable Data

In the Blue Sky 1960s, one of the projected uses of two-way cable was the simple alarm service, home fire alarms, burglar alarms, and emergency alert medical alarms. Some systems did and still do offer such extras, but they are not widespread. Telemetry functions associated with monitoring home utilities, especially in conjunction with local power companies, were discussed in the previous chapter. Like alarm services, they represent network applications beyond video and telephony. The Sega Channel is a kind of hybrid service combining data and video for home videogames. The game data is downloaded into a special box and players interact with the local intelligence, the software, in the set-top device. Sega uses very little bandwidth and can generate a reasonable cash-flow (estimated at about thirty cents per subscriber per month) for the cable system. As illustrated in Table 5-1, the relative importance of games to the bottom line is likely to grow in the next decade, but will remain a smaller piece of the pie. The more lucrative potential, according to most obsevers, lies in the link to the Internet.

The cable industry saw a business opportunity in the on-line gold rush. One of the most precious commodities to the cybersurfer is speed, or bandwidth, and bandwidth is cable's forte. Reports vary, but about half of all users do their surfing from home, and nearly all home computers use a telephone modem to connect to the Internet or on-line service.[30] But the telco twisted pair is a poor vehicle for the high capacity data needs of the Web. The typical consumer-grade modem has a top speed of 51 Kbps, a speed set primarily by the capacity of the standard telephone line, which tops out at 64 Kbps and cannot handle anything faster without special electronic conditioning (as noted below). The coaxial line can offer, as we've seen, downstream bandwidth a thousand times greater and can use telco return or its existing upstream path in the 5 MHz to 40 MHz band, when it is available. In contrast to the trickle of data possible over the standard home telephone line, a contemporary cable modem transmits data at up to 10 Mbps or faster.

These bit transmission rates make a significant difference in on-line performance. A moderately complex World Wide Web page that takes 32 seconds to download via a 28.8 Kbps modem and 16 seconds using a faster telco ISDN line (see below), requires only 2.7 seconds using a cable modem. The cable industry, in short, has seen the potential of selling broadband cable modems to speed-starved computer users.

Cable modems make it possible to link individual homes into a community-wide local area network. Contrary to other dial-up metered services, the connection is always on and available, because the data communications link is always available via the cable to be shared among users. In essence, the cable modems make it possible to attach one's personal computer into an ethernet data network. Because most cable television plant is not currently two-way interactive, some cable modems combine a conventional telephone digital to analog modem, in conjunction with an ethernet card, which is attached to the personal computer to give an address and the capability to process downloaded content. In systems that use the coax line for data flow in both directions, cable modems offer the additional attraction of freeing up a telephone line. For modern homes where a parent and teenager may both want to use the phone for a simple crosstown conversation, while a sibling wants to go on-line, the possible shortage of phone lines is a small but real issue, and one that cable providers can use to their marketing advantage.

Cable modems are not cheap. Initial retail prices ranged from $400 to $700 dollars. In 1996, however, companies like Motorola, LanCity, General Instruments, Intel, and Zenith introduced units costing $300 to $400. Even at that price, the units were significantly more expensive than traditional telco modems, but the demand for on-line service appears sufficiently high and the potential market large enough to justify the cost. About 35 percent of the nation's homes currently have a computer and as many as 20 percent of all households have a modem; as of mid-1996, some 13 percent used the Internet and its World Wide Web.[31] More than half of those accessing the Internet were doing so through commercial on-line services such as America On Line (AOL) and Compuserve. More than 12 million Americans subscribe to on-line services, paying $10 to $20 or more a month for news, sports, entertainment, information, and games, plus access to the more open universe of the Internet.[32] By one estimate there could be more than 40 million cable modem subscribers by 1999.[33] While projections vary, revenues from the cable on-line access business were anticipated to reach over a billion dollars by 2000 and $3.2 billion or more by 2004.[34] In the cable trials around the country, local operators have been successfully charging anywhere from $15 a month for a basic proprietary service and up to $40 a month for expanded services and Internet connection. Services included direct connections to existing on-line services such as AOL, Internet access, and proprietary local and regional content.

Telco Data

The attraction of a multibillion-dollar market has not escaped the notice of the telephone companies. While the standard twisted pair cannot compete with coaxial cable on its own, the telcos do have broadband capacity. Both ISDN and ADSL are seen as approaches to tapping into the broadband Internet business. ISDN has been available for several years as a means of providing data speeds of up to 128 Kbps, but it was expensive, $40 per month or more, and the telcos did not promote it heavily. While it was used in business, home consumers often found it difficult to get telephone companies to install and maintain ISDN lines. (Businesses also lease even higher-speed T-1 lines from the telephone company but these run several hundred dollars a month.) The surge in popularity of Internet services over the past several years and the incursion of cable into the market has prompted a revision in the telephone companies' thinking. In 1996 Bell Atlantic announced a reduction in ISDN prices and the start of a sales program to attract customers to the service. While an improvement over the twisted pair, however, coaxial connections are still one-hundred times faster than ISDN. Therefore ISDN looked only marginally competitive. With even greater capacity, ADSL also was being brought to market. While not the first choice for video distribution, it offered modem bandwidth comparable to cable, with data rates of more than 1.5 Mbps. Similarly, most of the telephone companies launched Internet access services of their own.

Satellite Data

Fiber-optic cables have generated most of the attention surrounding the anticipated two-way, broadband applications available over the "information superhighway." However, satellites can provide similar broadband functionality to users in widely dispersed geographical areas. Low Earth orbiting satellite constellations, like that proposed by Teledesic, and the larger available bandwidth in the Ka-band by LEO or GSO satellites, make it possible for satellites to provide access to cyberspace. A new phrase, *wireless fiber* (as an improved version of "wireless cable"), reflects the growing bit rate handling capacity of both existing and proposed satellites.

Ventures like Spaceway and Teledesic have targeted users in fixed locations who require "fiberlike" transmission capacity for highspeed, broadband applications. Even now GSO satellites, including ones providing Direct Broadcast Services, can easily handle the data transmission rates typically available to home personal computers, with some specialized applications ranging up to several hundred Kbps.

VSATs

Satellites provide an efficient means for sending and receiving data and for teleconferencing via inexpensive, Very Small Aperture Terminals (VSATs). As of 1996 approximately 300,000 such terminals operated throughout the world with North America constituting approximately 68 percent of the market. VSATs provide a low-cost way for corporations to deploy and manage a widely dispersed network. The terminals can be used to handle a variety of transactions on an immediate, real-time basis. For example, rather than install an expensive credit card verification network using dedicated or dial-up telephone lines, a company can use a VSAT network whereby a number of terminals share access to databases. Such shared hub networks make it possible to provide state-of-the-art transactional networking to installations in rural localities that may not generate a large amount of traffic. Primary users of VSATs include banks, retailers, automobile manufacturers and dealerships, utility companies, and governments. Banks and retailers use VSATs for low-volume services like Automated Teller Machines and credit card verification. Public utilities and oil and gas companies and mineral exploration companies use VSATs for Supervisory Control and Data Acquisition (SCADA) to monitor unsupervised locations and to transmit telemetry and seismic data. VSAT also can provide roof-top access to telecommunication services otherwise accessible using conventional wireline services that may be unreliable or fault-ridden.

Internet Access

Satellites can provide "virtual broadband networking" for high speed access to the Internet and other information sources. Hughes Network Systems has developed DirecPC, a sister service of DirecTV, for access to satellite-delivered data channels typically at 400 kilobits per second. The system uses an inexpensive 24-inch receive-only satellite dish and associated software, with upstream commands handled by a telephone line. Other DBS services were also looking to expand into Internet access. For users lacking telephone access and needing even higher speed transfer rates, VSAT technology can be adapted for two-way Internet connections.

Web Sites

Like the rest of the country, most companies in the telecommunications industry have put up a Web page. All the long-distance companies, the major MSOs, satellite distributors, the RBOCs, television networks, cable programmers, and equipment vendors have pages. A dozen community access centers have web pages. Industry service organizations like SCTE, NCTA, and Cablelabs are on-line. Scores, if not hundreds, of Web sites are available to the Web browsers interested in cable and telecommunications. Most are promotional. Cable programmers like the Discovery Channel and the Sci-Fi channel have very interactive sites, many are entertaining, some informative. TCI and Time Warner, in fact, have their own on-line services: TCI's @Home and Time Warner's Road Runner.

THE MULTIMEDIA FUTURE

In Chapter 1 the concept of a fully integrated system, delivering interactive video entertainment, video telephone, and sophisticated data communication services was introduced. Beyond even this, futurists see a world of multimedia innovations that promise the development of services that stimulate several senses using multiple modes of delivery. Multimedia promises to offer a three-dimensional picture complete with vivid resolution, sound, and graphics. With digitization and compression the emerging system can handle the bandwidth and throughput requirements presented by such applications. Some of the multimedia applications on the drawing board include: "virtual television," the ability of the viewer to select which camera angle the television set will display; on-line access to interactive programming and advertisements, voice-activated or intelligent agent selected program menus from an almost unlimited inventory of options; and "time shifting," the ability to select and view any programming at the viewer's convenience. VOD options that offer the ability to control programming in the same way as provided by a videocassette player—with stop, rewind, and fast-forward functions—will be mundane. Viewers will be able to watch live baseball games and, on the viewing screen, call up statistics on the team or the player at bat. While many of these applications are still on the drawing board, a host of companies and industries are competing to bring them to market.

MERGER MANIA

Is the cable, satellite, and telco television industry a highly contested and competitive market or is it naturally oligopolistic and characterized by a high degree of vertical and horizontal integration? Opinions differ. Critics of industry structure point to the web of interlocking ownership relationships and joint operating agreements that seem endemic in the business. Proponents of a free market philosophy note the increasingly competitive involvement of telco and wireless entrants in a field once dominated almost exclusively by cable. They argue that the deregulation brought about by the Telecommunications Act of 1996 has effectively opened the marketplace to a host of new providers. The critics, alternatively, call attention to the wave of mergers and consolidations that followed passage of the Act.

There are several underlying concerns. Concentration of ownership and concommitant market control may cause or exacerbate barriers to entry, making it difficult for new companies and new products to enter the market. Consumers are disadvantaged insofar as the diversity of possible goods is restricted and entrepreneurs are frustrated in their legitimate business ambitions. Goods and services are not efficiently, nor, some would argue, equitably, distributed by the normal forces of supply and demand, and prices are held artificially high by lack of competition. The problem is compounded in the media industries by their special role in society. There is a general cultural distrust of concentration of power in U.S. culture in all sectors and a special sensitivity to control over sources of news and information. Information is not just, or even primarily, a commodity, it is our political and cultural lifeblood. Our system of self-governance is dependent on an informed public that, in turn, relies on the free flow of information and opinion. It is democracy itself, and the open marketplace of ideas, that holds center stage in the debate over control of the media.

The question, of course, is not over the goal of a national forum for the exchange of ideas and opinions; the question is how best to achieve it. This is where people start choosing sides, advocating greater or lesser reliance on market solutions as opposed to state control. In analyzing the degree to which the industry is concentrated, a number of factors are typically considered. Ownership is examined in both its horizontal and vertical dimensions. A company that is vertically integrated owns or controls goods from the point of manufacture through distribution and into the retail outlets. A company, for example, that owns television production facilities that create TV shows, a cable programming network that distributes them nationally, and cable systems that show them in the home is vertically integrated. Horizontal integration concentrates ownership across one of these categories. Increasing consolidation of ownership of cable systems around the country is an issue of horizontal integration. The question of monopoly power also can be considered geographically, that is, at both the national and local levels. The latter is a good place to begin.

Competition in the Local Market

One of the long-standing questions in cable television is whether or not it is a natural monopoly. A natural monopoly tends not to lend itself to normal economic competition and its services and prices therefore are often subject to government control. Economists have differed on the issue of the status of cable and telephone as natural monopolies. Some have argued that cable's position in most markets as a monopoly provider is more the result of regulation than economics. By this argument, the practice of local authorities to issue exclusive franchises in order to reap the municipal benefits of franchise fees from monopoly profits historically prevented real competition.[35] To the extent this may have been true at one time, however, the 1984 Cable Act banned exclusive franchises and those barriers no longer exist.

Other economists contend that cable television is a natural economic monopoly. One of the indicators of a natural monopoly is a declining long-run average cost curve wherein the average cost of a unit of goods produced declines with each additional unit produced. The fixed capital costs especially are thereby distributed across a greater number of units and the production costs of each decreased. These constitute economies of scale in production and it works to the benefit of incumbent companies. Lower costs for a widely distributed and entrenched firm can be reflected in lower prices when the incumbent must beat off a competitive threat. As media economist Barry Litman points out, "Potential entrants will find it difficult to obtain the heavy capital financing and then capture the requisite share of the market to compete on an equal footing with existing firms. This is the way widespread scale economies fortify market concentration and function as barriers to entry."[36]

Scale economies are also reflected in the ability of the entrenched firm to hold down costs by striking favorable deals with suppliers and developing centralizing efficiencies in various aspects of management and operations. Litman explains, for example, that economies of scale are partially responsible for the predominance of local monopolies in the newspaper industry.[37]

A number of studies have concluded that the cable industry, like the newspaper industry, is subject to economies of scale sufficient to create monopoly structures in local markets.[38] Economist G. Kent Webb found declining average cost curves in the industry and concluded that, "From the perspective of costs, cable television systems are a natural geographic monopoly."[39] Moreover, the facts of cable history tend to support this view. There are more than 11,000 cable television systems in the United States and there have never been more than a handful of situations in which cable operators faced off in direct competition. Researcher Marianne Barrett noted in 1995 that there were about forty competitive cable markets in the United States, less than 1 percent.[40] She looked at one in Paragould, Arkansas, where the city, after a falling out with the local cable company, decided to build its own municipal system. The results, according to Barrett, were intense, real competition, lower prices, and improvements in customer service. On the other hand, she reported that both companies were selling services below cost and bleeding money. The city supported its operations with tax dollars. She concluded that the two companies eventually would have to enter into oligopolistic collusion, or one might eventually have to sell out. The modern history of the business is that when potential overbuilders come to town it is often a not-so-well-disguised form of "green mail" and the incumbent will purchase the overbuilder at a handsome price.

At the same time, there are confounding questions on the demand side of the equation. Some observers argue that cable is not a true "natural" monopoly, and raise sererval important questions. For example, are there competitive products or services that, for the consumer, would serve as substitutes for the monopoly services? If newspapers, for example, were potential substitutes for cable programming, the existence of a strong newspaper market would prevent or reduce monopolistic practices on the part of the cable operator. Again economists have argued whether or not local over-the-air broadcasting, videotape rentals, and other forms of entertainment serve as substitutes sufficient to hold down cable prices and maintain services. In the past, MDS, TVRO, and SMATV have been proffered as possible competitors in this sense. Until recently, the low penetration levels of such services have kept them as theoretical competitors only. Importantly, however, competitors in theory only may, in some cases, be sufficient. Owen and Wildman point out that, although locally a scant handful of competitive situations actually exist in the cable industry, historically cable prices to consumers have not demonstrated monopoly characteristics. "Adjusting for inflation and for the number of channels offered, the real price of basic service per channel has remained unchanged at about $.38, between 1986 and 1988."[41]

While wireline companies may exhibit the characteristics of natural monopolies they may nonetheless refrain from acting like monopolists if there is a credible threat that another company may seek to enter and contest for that market. The possibility that other firms might compete for the right to be the monopoly provider in that community can act to hold down prices and preserve reasonable service. Rand economist Leland Johnson concluded in 1994 that the cable television market was not contestable in this sense because of the high capital costs associated with competitive entry and the likely strategy of an incumbent provider to slash prices, even below cost, during the period in which an overbuilder was attempting to establish service. "In most cases, the incumbent," stated Johnson, "is protected because the prospective newcomer faces costs of entry and exit that are too high to render the threat of credible entry. For this reason, threats of overbuilding typically are empty or lead to a buyout."[42] While Johnson concluded that "the prospects for cable overbuilding [were] not bright," he also noted that any competition that did emerge would most likely come from local telephone companies offering bundled voice and video services.[43]

With the emergence of wireless cable, the clear evidence of the success of DBS, and the expressed intent of some telephone companies to be players in the broader telecommunications market, the concept of market contestability and even real head-to-head competition has gained new life. Whether serious local competition can sustain itself over time or whether, in the long run, the industry will revert to monopoly fiefdoms of service—the character of cable and telephone in the past—is an open question and will likely remain so for a number of years.

Horizontal Integration

Horizontal integration in the cable telecommunications business nationally is about the amalgamation of business across sectors, distribution or program production, for example. Insofar as it involves distribution facilities, either cable or telco, it is about Continental Cable selling to US West; it is about SBC buying PacTel and Bell Atlantic merging with Nynex. It is the underlying theme in the complex musical score that drives Hostetter's elephants' waltz. The premise, again, is that only companies of significant size will be able to compete on the national and international stage. To create the broadband networks that the information highway requires will take immense amounts of capital and the ability to sustain operating losses over long periods while businesses mature. Profit margins are shrinking and economies of scale will become increasingly important as a part of improved operating efficiencies.

In the cable industry there are several manifestations of the accelerating concentration of ownership. At the local level, there is an industry-wide movement to consolidate or cluster local and regional systems to achieve greater economies of scope and establish strong area-wide brand identification. It has led some MSOs to trade their systems in different parts of the country in order to establish ownership of all of the systems in a particular area; it also has led to some outright purchases. In the past few years TCI has swapped systems with Post Newsweek Cable, Multimedia Inc., Cox Communications, and Continental. Continental has been strengthening its presence in the northeast while TCI consolidated systems around St. Louis. Time Warner has traded systems with Century Communications, Jones Intercable, and Cox. TCI's purchase of Viacom's cable systems has given the cable giant control of all cable subscribers in the San Francisco Bay area and, in fact, in every sizable market between San Francisco and Seattle, with the exception of Sacramento (which is controlled by Comcast).[44]

Beyond clustering, the popular perception that only large companies will survive in the new economic order has motivated some medium and small firms, or larger companies with only marginal interests in cable, to sell their properties and leave the business. Cable MSOs spent $20 billion acquiring other cable systems in 1995 (see Table 5-4).

The result of this surge in MSO sales has been a constriction in the ownership structure of the industry. *Cablevision* magazine in 1996 reported that, for the first time, the number of MSOs had shrunk to below 200 due to the acquisition binge in the industry. MSOs had begun buying up MSOs; more of the country's cable systems were being held by fewer companies. This contraction is vividly illustrated by looking at industry concentration ratios over the past several years. Concentration is typically measured by the percentage of market share held by the top four and top eight firms. It has been calculated in the cable industry in two forms: one using figures based on the number of subscribers served by wholly owned cable systems (consolidated systems) and another measure that also includes subscribers served by systems in which an MSO has partial ownership interest (unconsolidated systems).

TABLE 5-4   Top 10 System Sales of 1995

Buyer	Seller	Subs	Price
Time Warner	Cablevision Ind.	1.4 mill	$2.7 bill
TCI	Viacom	1.2 mill	$2.3 bill
Comcast	Scripps	792,500	$1.57 bill
Time Warner	Houston Ind.	1.2 M	$2.2 bill
Continental	Colony Comm	773,700	$1.54 bill
TCI	Chronicle Publ	327,100	$654 mill
Charter Comm.	Gaylord Brdcstg	180,000	$360 mill
TCI/Jones	Columbia Intl.	189,000	$378 mill
TCI/Multimedia	TCI/Multimedia	90,000	$180 mill
Time Warner	Summit Comm.	168,500	$337 mill

Sources: "Cable Trading: A Big Deal," *Broadcasting & Cable,* 11 March 1996, 42; *Cable World,* 29 April 1996, 12.

An additional common measure of concentration is the Hirschman–Herfindahl Index (HHI), derived from the sum of the squares of the individual market shares of all firms. HHI, which gives disproportionate weight to the largest firms in the industry, is commonly used as a guideline by the Justice Department to judge the potential for anticompetitive behavior.

A number of scholars have looked at the growing concentration in the industry over time.[45] Most recently, Sylvia Chan–Olmsted has noted a pronounced acceleration in mergers and acquisitions (see Table 5-5).[46] In 1995 the top four firms held close to 50 percent of market share, 58 percent when folding in unconsolidated systems. In 1996 the top five operators controlled 66 percent of all subscribers; the top twenty companies served 85 percent of all cable customers. Chan–Olmsted declared that the changes in market concentration were due almost entirely to the top two firms, TCI and Time Warner. TCI alone held a 20 percent market share in 1995; in 1977 the largest firm accounted for only 8.5 percent of all subscribers.

The Justice Department classifies levels of industrial concentration using the HHI. Sectors with HH indices under 1,000 are considered "unconcentrated" and those with indices between 1,000 and 1,800 are "moderately concentrated." Despite the growing consolidation, the HHI for cable historically has been well under the level necessary to trigger antitrust restraints on mergers and acquisitions. Moreover, even though the HHI has recently moved into the "moderately concentrated" range it is unlikely that such action will be considered. Chan–Olmsted observed that Justice Department and Federal Trade Commission rules regarding horizontal integration have been relaxed in recent years, following a general deregulatory philosophy in Washington, D.C. The entry of competitive providers such as DBS and wireless cable weakens any arguments for state interference, and there appears to be greater governmental sympathy to the argument that construction of the information super-

TABLE 5-5   Concentration Ratios in the Cable TV Industry 1977–1995

	1977	1982	1987	1989	1992	1995
Top 4	24.5	N.A.	28.5	37.3	42.3	49.0
	(25.1)	(39.0)	(36.5)	(46.2)	(N.A.)	(58.0)
Top 8	36.4	N.A.	40.9	51.5	42.3	65.0
	(37.7)	(44.0)	(48.9)	(57.8)	(N.A.)	(73.0)
HHI	217	N.A.	350	528	603	935
	(231)	(316)	(576)	(576)	(N.A.)	(1292)

(unconsolidated systems)

Sources: David Waterman, "A New Look at Media Chains and Groups: 1977–1989," *Journal of Broadcasting & EM,* 35:2 (Spring 1991): 167–178; David Atkin, "Cable Exhibition in the USA," *Telecommunications Policy,* 18:4 (1994): 331–341; Sylvia Chan-Olmsted, "Market Competition for Cable Television: Reexamining Its Horizontal Mergers and Industry Concentration," *Journal of Media Economics,* 9:2 (1996): 25–41.

highway will require the resources available only to large multinational firms. Chan–Olmsted suggests the flavor of this philosophy is reflected in the government's revised 1992 guidelines on mergers and acquisitions that replaced the term *collusion* with the phrase "coordinated interaction."[47] While the 1992 Cable Act did require the FCC to impose an ownership cap on the cable industry, a cap the FCC set at 30 percent of the national subscriber base, that restriction was found unconstitutional in 1993,[48] and to date there has been no further effort to control cable consolidation.

While ownership in the cable industry therefore is gravitating toward the largest firms, especially TCI and Time Warner, it does not appear to be near the severity necessary to draw antitrust attention, although very large mergers between, for example, the top four firms, might attract government interest.

Vertical Integration

The question, in the first instance, is the extent of ownership ties between MSOs and programmers. Historically, the strong ownership interests of MSOs in cable networks is one of the most prominent features of cable industry structure. The ties are substantial, far-reaching and often complex. The cable industry has, on occasion, been described as incestuous due primarily to the tangled web of ownership lines that joins MSOs to programmers, MSOs to MSOs, and everyone, seemingly, to everyone else.

Many of the major cable networks are fully or partially owned by cable operators. The FCC reported in 1994 that 56 of the then 106 nationally distributed programming services had equity links to MSOs.[49] David Waterman points out that:

> The overwhelming proportion of equity ownership in nationally distributed cable networks was accounted for by the largest 12 MSOs or their parent companies. Eleven of those twelve MSOs (serving 67.4 percent of all U.S. cable subscribers . . .) had a 5 percent interest in at least one cable network.[50]

He further notes that a disproportionate amount of equity ownership was held by three firms: TCI, Time Warner, and Viacom. In fact, if one adds Cablevision Systems and two television network owners, Disney/Cap Cities and NBC, most of the ownership of the major cable networks is accounted for.

Further, joint participation of MSOs in the ownership of programmers is common, leading to the above-mentioned observation that, in the industry, eventually everyone is financially related to everyone else. Some striking examples include: "E!" network, jointly owned by Time Warner, Comcast Corp., Continental Cablevision, Cox, and Newhouse; The Golf Channel, with MSO participation by Times Mirror, Continental Cablevision, Cablevision Industries, Comcast, Adelphia, Newhouse, and Prime Cable; and CourtTV, jointly owned by TCI, Time Warner, and Cablevision. A&E is held by Disney, Hearst Corp., and NBC; American Movie Classics by Cablevision Systems and NBC; Comedy Central by Time Warner and

Viacom; the Discovery Channel by TCI, Cox, and Newhouse; ESPN by Disney and Hearst; The TV Food Network by Continental, Landmark Communications, Scripps-Howard, and Tribune Broadcasting. Appendix B offers a survey of ownership of some of the nation's top programming networks.

If there is a dominant programmer in the business it is probably Ted Turner and Time Warner. The list of Turner's properties is a long one: CNN, Headline News, TNT, The Cartoon Network, Turner Classic Movies, and WTBS. Prior to its acquisition by Time Warner, Ted Turner held only 29.2 percent of the company he founded; the rest was in the hands of cable operators, including TCI (22.6 percent) and Time Warner (18.6 percent). The merger with Time Warner gives the conglomerate full ownership over the Turner channels while TCI's interest (through its Liberty Media Group) converts to about an 8 percent stake in Time Warner.

Looked at from the perspective of the distributors, Time Warner holds full or partial ownership of Turner's properties, Cinemax, HBO, the Comedy Channel, CourtTV, and E!, to name a few. Of the major nondistributors, Disney has interests, full or partial, in A&E, ESPN, the History Channel, Lifetime and, of course, The Disney Channel. Viacom owns MTV, Nickelodeon, VH1, Flix, Showtime, The Movie Channel, and half of the USA and Sci-Fi networks, with MCA (Seagrams).

By far and away, however, the most impressive list belongs to TCI. The nation's largest MSO also has the most far-reaching interests in cable programming.

Issues and Concerns

These sorts of linkages, as noted above, have fostered concerns about the potential for anticompetitive practices in the industry. A number of cable channels, such as BET and Discovery, arguably could not have succeeded without substantial investment from MSOs such as TCI. In looking to create programming for their systems, cable operators invested, often heavily, in neophyte programming services. Cable operators today are often frustrated by public concern in this area, noting that some cable channels would not exist in the first place without their participation. Nonetheless, that concern persists. Specifically, there is worry that distributors today have unhealthy control over the creation and distribution of cable programming by virtue of these relationships. Waterman points out that while the indices of horizontal integration in cable would normally assuage concerns about undue monopoly power, the application of a "chain buying power" model (with or without vertical integration), in which the local monopoly character of the cable industry is coupled with a sufficient national market share by a given MSO, could result in significant bargaining power for that MSO.[51] According to Waterman, the result could be contractual agreements between MSOs and programmers that provide that MSO price and availability advantages would not be enjoyed by smaller cable operators, and through its market power "a chain might gain effective 'veto power' over individual products that attempt to enter the market."[52]

In this vein, most of the attention has been focused on Time Warner and TCI as the two dominant distributors. Without access to the 25 million plus homes served

TABLE 5-6   TCI–LIBERTY MEDIA GROUP Selected Holdings

Encore Media Group (90%)
Encore and Encore Multiplex (Love Stories, Westerns, Mystery, Action, True Stories, and Drama), WAM! America's Youth Network
Encore ICCP Inc. (International Channel) (45%)
STARZ! (47.9%)
Request TV (40%)
Viewer's Choice (10%)
CourtTV (33%)
Discovery Communications, Inc. (49%)
The Discovery Channel, The Learning Channel, Discovery Asia, Discovery Europe, TLC Europe, Discovery Latin America
BET Holdings, Inc. (22%)
BET Cable Network, BET Action PPV, BET on Jazz
The Box (5.5%)
DMX (11%)
E! Entertainment Television (10%)
International Family Entertainment, Inc. (20.3%)
The Family Channel, Fit TV, The Family Channel UK
Faith & Values Channel (49%)
Turner Broadcasting System (23%)
CNN, Cartoon Network, Headline News, TNT, Turner Classic Movies, TBS Superstation, CNN International, TNT Latin America, Cartoon Network Latin America, TNT & Cartoon Network Europe, TNT & Cartoon Network Asia TV!,
Home Shopping Network, Inc. (41.5%)
HSN, Spree!, ISN
QVC, Inc. (42.6%)
QVC Network, Q2, QVC-The Shopping Channel UK,
Prime SportChannel Network Associates (34%)
Affiliated Regional Communications Ltd., (68%)
Prime Sports Radio, Liberty Satellite Sports (DBS), Prime Sports Southwest, Prime Sports Midwest, Prime Network International
Liberty Sports, Inc. (100%)
Prime Sports Merchandising (75 sports clothing stores)
Prime Sports Rocky Mountains (78.5%); Home Team Sports (20.5%); Prime Sports Northwest (60%); Prime Sports Upper Midwest (38.6%); SportsChannel Chicago (50%); SportsChannel Pacific (50%); SportsChannel Philadelphia/PRISM (23%); SportSouth Network (44%); Sunshine Network (38%); LMC International, Inc. (50%)
Fox Sports (N.A.)
With News Corp., combines fourteen of the Prime Sports channels

---

by these two MSOs (43 percent of the national total), young programming services are unlikely to survive. According to Atkin:

> *In particular, TCI's 11 million subscribers can easily make or break a prospective network. Services that do not gain MSO support—such as ABC's (Satellite News Channel) and HSN's spin-off shopping network—are doomed to failure.*[53]

Beyond outright barriers to entry, integrated MSOs can create other favorable conditions in their affiliated relationships. It can, for example, give equity networks privileged channel positions, typically lower on the television dial. Or, it can bargain for deep discounts on prices, discounts not available to other distributors.

Complicating the issue even further is the problem of limited shelf space on most local systems. If the large MSOs exercised discriminatory practices in a universe of unlimited bandwidth, there would be justifiable public policy concerns. But in a another sense TCI, Time Warner, and other MSOs must make difficult decisions about which new networks to carry in an industry ironically characterized by channel scarcity. There have been, at any one time over the past several years, thirty or more fledgling cable networks hoping to launch. But insufficient channel capacity on most systems makes it impossible to carry all of them (even if they had compelling business plans and adequate capital). MSO latitude in selecting additional cable channels, of course, has been diminished further by the FCC's must-carry rules. As noted in Chapter 2, the broadcast networks, in lieu of direct payment for carriage of local affiliates, have chosen to bargain for carriage of network-backed cable channels, hence the creation of ESPN-2, the fX network, and what has become MSNBC.

In a world of too few channels and too many cable networks, MSOs are the gatekeepers, and would-be programmers need their carriage consent; if programmers can also pick up equity funding from an MSO, all the better from the point of view of the programmer. MSOs with a financial stake in a programming service traditionally will find space and promote that service. The success of Turner's TNN and the Cartoon Channel were due in part to the support and subscriber base provided by the MSOs on Turner's board, including TCI and Time Warner. Access to channel space is not the only criterion for a successful network launch (as we will see in Chapter 6), but a new entrant that fails to sign a sufficient number of systems will never generate the critical mass of subscribers necessary to survive.

While statutory and regulatory actions have made it possible for competitive providers to acquire cable programming, the forces of horizontal and vertical integration in the cable industry are likely to continue to privilege some companies over others, at least until additional channel space opens up through digital distribution. And even then, some observers suggest that public policymakers keep a close eye on the market.

The Big Dance

The trends toward concentration of ownership are not of course restricted to the cable industry in its formal, narrow sense, but as has been noted, cut across all media industries and now include the telephone companies, the computer industry, broadcasting, and a list of affiliate, and sometimes tangential, interests. The world's second largest media company (based on revenues), Disney, is a case in point. Through its participation in Americast it has a programming affiliation with several RBOCs. Disney owns cable networks and will help program the Ameritech cable TV systems in the midwest. It has several film production studios, it owns, through Cap Cities, radio and television stations and, of course, it has the ABC television network and the Disney theme parks around the world. Today, the notion of a "Mickey Mouse operation" has taken on an entirely new meaning.

TCI, too, has moved far beyond cable television hardware and software. An equity interest in Teleport has moved it into telephony; it has ownership interests in computer services through its @Home on-line service, a 20 percent stake in the Microsoft Network, and a 20 percent share of Netscape. It owns a majority share (67 percent) of McNeil–Lehrer productions, a dozen major market television stations following its acquisition of Silver King Broadcasting and, as previously noted, is joint owner of the PrimeStar DBS service. It is also worth noting again that the leading DBS service, DirecTV, is largely owned by General Motors Corp. through its Hughes subsidiary, with equity also held by AT&T.

As Table 5-7 indicates, the major media companies in the world today are integrated both vertically and horizontally, with companies or divisions in nearly every sector of media including broadcasting, film, records, cable, publishing, telephony, data, and merchandising.

Terms like *synergy* and *repurposing* have arisen in this context. It is the synergy created by the talents and resources of different corporate divisions being brought to bear on a particular problem or particular media property. It is where the magazine division and the television broadcast division of a media conglomerate collaborate on the development of, say, a public affairs reporting project that ultimately takes its form as a set of magazine articles and a series of TV news stories. Similarly, *repurposing* describes the practice of taking a given property developed in one media form and repackaging it for sale in all the other forms possible. This is necessary for new properties because of today's stratospheric costs of production, and it is easy with existing products because they do not lose their value. In fact, one of the interesting economic characteristics of media property is that it can be used over and over and still retain much of its original worth (see Chapter 7). In one of its simplest forms, it is illustrated by "Nick at Night" rerunning 1960s television shows and Ted Turner creating a successful network out of old cartoons. Turner's vast library of films acquired in the MGM purchase has been used to fuel first TNT and then Turner Classic Movies.

More typically, however, *repurposing* is used to describe the exploitation of media properties across a broader range of outlets. "It is no longer sufficient," according to one analyst, "to make a great movie and have it do well at the box office. You've got to be able to exploit every piece of revenue that you can, because the cost of creating and marketing the product is so great."[54] This involves, for example, taking a successful book, turning it into a movie, taking the main character from the movie and basing a television series on it, then creating a merchandising campaign based on the character that involves children's lunch boxes, T-shirts, key chains, pencils, bed sheets, toys, caps, and promotional tie-ins with fast-food companies. Disney, again, is one of the best at this, as any parent with a closetful of *Lion King* paraphernalia will attest. Time Warner, with its ownership of film, record, publishing, broadcasting, and cable properties is also very good. The popular *Batman* mo-

TABLE 5-7 Selected Holdings of Major Media Firms

Company	Progrmg	Bdcstg	Satellite	Films	Publg	Misc
TCI (13.9 mill cable subs)	Encore; RequestTV; Discovery; CourtTV; BET; QVC	Silver King Comm.	PrimeStar; Tempo			Teleport (CAPS); Netscape (20%)
Time Warner (12.1 mill cable subs)	Turner (CNN, TNT, TBS, CNNfn); HBO, Cinemax	WB Network; WB Television (*ER, Murphy Brown*)	PrimeStar	Warner Bros. films; MGM Library; New Line Cinema	Time-Life Books; Little, Brown & Co., Book-of-the-Month Club: *Time* magazine; *Sports Illustrated, People, Money*	Six Flags theme parks; WB retail stores; Turner Sports Teams: Atlanta Braves and Hawks
News Corp.	FoxNews; FoxSports; fX Network	Fox Brdctg	BSkyB	20th Cent Fox	Harper & Row; *TV Guide*	
Viacom	MTV; VH-1; Nickelodeon USA; Showtime	UPN		Paramount	Simon & Schuster; Allyn & Bacon	Blockbuster Video
Disney	Disney Ch., ESPN, Lifetime, A&E	ABC		Disney, Buena Vista, Touchstone	Newspapers Chilton Trade publs., Fairchild Publs.	Theme Parks, Mighty Ducks hockey; Anaheim Angels (25%)
GE/NBC	CNBC, Court TV, AMC, MSNBC, A&E	NBC	GE Americom			Appliances; Plastics; Medical Services
Westing-house/CBS	CMT (33%); CBS Ent.; Eyemark Ent.	CBS	Group W Satellite Comm's			Insurance; Investment Mngmt; Nuclear Power
Universal Studios (Seagrams, MCA)	Universal Television Group			Universal Studios	Putnam Berkley	Universal Studios Parks

tion picture series is an example. Time Warner owns D.C. Comics, which holds the rights to Batman. The *Batman* movies helped drive higher sales of the comics and spurred the development of "graphic novels," high-end comic books for an older demographic. For the first movie, Prince created some of the music on the Warner record label, and the marketing merchandise was, of course, voluminous. Companies will likely continue to both expand and integrate in order to advance these efficiencies, as well as to generate the size and access to capital markets that will allow them to complete globally.

Finally, the convergence of ownership extends to increasing numbers of joint ventures between many of these companies. In 1997 Microsoft spent $1 billion for an equity stake in the cable MSO Comcast. In addition to teaming with DirecTV to deliver data communications by satellite, Microsoft also was working with MCI to provide on-line services through the latter's long lines network. Both IBM and Digital Equipment Corp. (DEC) are working on partnerships with MSOs to deliver multimedia programming over cable. TCI has teamed with US West in national and international ventures, TCI has ties to News Corp., and News Corp is partnered with MCI. The ties between distributors and between distributors and content providers grow more complex every day as new pairings are announced, and the mergers and joint ventures are expected to continue in the rhythm of the interacting forces of competition and convergence. Proponents of amalgamation and globalization see the benefits that accrue with size, while opponents worry about concentrating control of the telecommunications infrastructure. Ownership issues will continue to raise some of the more challenging questions in the coming information age.

NOTES

[1]See, Ron Garay, "USA Network," in *The Cable Networks Handbook,* Robert Picard, ed. (Riverside, CA: Carpelan Publishing Co., 1993), 203–210.

[2]John Fryman and Jerry Hudson, "Turner Network Television," in Picard, 190–196.

[3]Ibid.

[4]Flemming Meeks, "What Brand Is Your Weather?" *Forbes,* 23 October 1995, 320–21.

[5]Rich Brown, "Turner on Murdoch: 'I'm Going to Squish Him Like a Bug,'" *Broadcasting & Cable,* 4 December 1995, 56.

[6]Charles Warner and Michael O. Wirth, "Entertainment and Sports Programming Network (ESPN)," in Picard, 90.

[7]Leonard Barchak, "Black Entertainment Television," in Picard, 23–33.

[8]Robert Ogles, "Music Television (MTV)," in Picard, 137–142.

[9]Susan Strohm, "The Discovery Channel," in Picard, 69–77.

[10]"PPV Revenue Pushes Half-Billion Mark," *Broadcasting & Cable,* 20 November 1995, 38.

[11]Kim Mitchell," Rope a Dope," *Cable World,* 13 May 1996, 1.

[12]"Databank," *Cable World,* 9 December 1996, 188.

[13]National Cable Television Association, *Cable Television Developments,* 1996, 5.

[14]The rules do not apply to systems serving fewer than 1,000 subscribers.

[15]Rules Relating to Exclusivity in the Cable and Broadcast Industries, 3 FCC rcd. 5299 (1988).

[16]*Television and Cable Factbook,* Services Vol. (Washington, DC: Warren Publishing, 1996), F-2.

[17]Linda K. Fuller, *Community Television in the United States,* (Westport, CT. Greenwood Press, 1994), 2.

[18]David Atkin and Robert LaRose, "Cable Access: Market Concerns amidst the Marketplace of Ideas," *Journalism Quarterly,* 68:3 (Fall 1991): 354.

[19]47 U.S.C. sect. 532.

[20]"Data Bank," *Cable World,* 19 February 1996, 46.

[21]National Cable Television Association, *Telecommunications and Advanced Services Provided by the Cable Television Industry,* April 1996.

[22]Mark Landler,"The Big Boys Come Calling," *New York Times,* 23 October 1995, D-1.

[23]"Data Bank," *Cable World,* 19 February 1996, 46.

[24]"Is Cable Telephony Here Yet?" *Cable World,* 25 March 1996, 37.

[25]Other issues involve unbundling of services for resale, virtual or physical co-location of equipment, dialing parity, directory listing, 611 repair service, call annoyance services, and hearing impaired services, just to name a few.

[26]"The Handbook for the Competitive Market, Blue Book Vol. III," *Cablevision* 1996, p. 26.

[27]"CTIA's Newest Report Shows 40 Percent Customer Growth," *Radio Communications Report,* 25 March 1996, 4.

[28]5 FCC Rcd. at 3995.

[29]James J. Lock, "The Internet as Mass Medium: The Media Enter the World of Cyberspace," *Feedback,* 36 (1995): 7–10.

[30]Peter Lewis, "Most Go On Line at Home, Study Finds," *New York Times,* 23 October 1995; Kim Mitchell, "World Wide Web Buying Power," *Cable World,* 6 November 1995, 30.

[31]"The Handbook for the Competitive Market," 28.

[32]Lewis, "Most Go On Line At Home."

[33]"Cable Plant's Two-Way Capability," *Cable World,* 26 February 1996, 25.

[34]National Cable Television Association, *Telecommunications and Advanced Services Provided by the Cable Television Industry,* April 1996, 35.

[35]See, e.g., Thomas Hazlett, "Private Monopoly and the Public Interest: An Economic Analysis of the Cable Television Franchise," *University of Pennsylvania Law Review,* 134 (1968): 1335–1409.

[36]Barry Litman, "Microeconomic Foundations," in *Press Concentration and Monopoly,* ed. Robert Picard, et al., (Norwood, NJ: Ablex, 1988), 20.

[37]Litman, 34.

[38]G. Kent Webb, *The Economics of Cable Television* (Lexington, MA: Lexington Books, 1983); Stanley Bensen, et al. *Economic Policy Research on Cable Television: Assessing the Costs and Benefits of Cable Deregulation* (Washington DC: Office of Telecommunications Policy, 1976); Mark Seiden, "An Economic Analysis of Community Antenna Television Systems and the Television Broadcasting Industry," in *Progress Report from FCC–1965, Hearings Before the Subcomm. on Communication of the Senate Comm. on Commerce,* 89th Cong., 1st sess., 1965; Eli Noam, "Is Cable Television a Natural Monopoly?" Research Working Paper #430A, Columbia University, 1982.

[39]Webb, 63.

[40]Marianne Barrett, "Direct Competition in Cable Television Delivery: A Case Study of Paragould, Arkansas," *The Journal of Media Economics,* 8:3 (1995): 77–93.

[41]Bruce Owen and Steve Wildman, *Video Economics* (Cambridge: Harvard University Press, 1992), 225.

[42]Leland Johnson, *Toward Competition in Cable Television* (Cambridge: MIT Press, 1994), 20.

[43]Johnson, 26.

[44]"Clustering the Cable Industry," *Cable World,* 27 November 1995, 81.

[45]See, e.g., David Waterman, "A New Look at Media Chains and Groups: 1977–1989," *Journal of Broadcasting & EM*, 35:2 (Spring 1991): 167–178; David Atkin, "Cable Exhibition in the USA," *Telecommunications Policy.* 18:4 (1994): 331–341; Herbert Howard, *Ownership Trends in Cable Television: 1985,* National Association of Broadcasters, Washington, D.C., Sept. 1986.

[46]Sylvia Chan–Olmsted, "Market Competition for Cable Television: Reexamining Its Horizontal Mergers and Industry Concentration," *Journal of Media Economics,* 9:2 (1996): 25–41.

[47]Ibid., 34.

[48]*Daniels Cablevision, Inc. v. U.S.,* 83 F.Supp. 1 (D.D.C. 1993).

[49]1994 Cable First Report, 9 FCC Rcd. 7442 at 73.

[50]David Waterman, "Vertical Integration and Program Access in the Cable Television Industry," *Federal Communications Law Journal* 47:3 (April 1995), 516.

[51]Waterman, "A New Look," 172–175. See also, David Waterman and Andrew Weiss, "The Effects of Vertical Integration between Cable Television Systems and Pay Cable Networks," *Journal of Econometrics* 72 (1996): 357–395.

[52]Waterman, "A New Look," 175.

[53]David Atkin, "Cable Exhibition in the U.S.A.," *Telecommunications Policy* 18:4 (1994): 331–341, 339.

[54]Rita Koselka, "Mergermania in Medialand," *Forbes,* 23 October 1995, 254.

6

Multichannel Business Operations: The Real World

While previous chapters have traced the tectonic movements of business and technology that are rearranging our map of broadband telecommunications, the reach of this chapter is more modest, although no less important. It looks at the business operations of cable and satellite television companies, the routines that characterize their typical daily and annual processes and functions. It examines the structure and operations of local cable companies, MSOs, satellite distribution firms, and programming networks. It looks at income streams and expenditures in cable, the production and distribution of programming, the buying and selling of advertising, customer service, acquiring new properties, and working with the public. While much is changing in the multichannel industries in the areas of technology, ownership, and regulation, many of the chores of daily business life have stayed largely the same for a number of years, with problems such as customer relations, network branding, shelf space scarcity, and signal theft among the ongoing challenges facing local and corporate managers. The chapter begins with a look at the operations of cable systems, both local and national, then considers satellite distributors, the new telco entrants, network programmers, and related organizations.

CABLE SYSTEMS

Structure and Operations

The organizational structure of a local cable system or national MSO is determined by the nature and number of its activities, usually as a function of its size. A small local operator running a thirty channel system with a few hundred subscribers may be able to handle normal operations with a staff of a dozen or fewer people and a very simple organizational chart. A top ten MSO with hundreds of systems, millions of customers, and business ventures that include Internet access, paging, telephony, PCS backhauling, or merchandising requires a much more complex and specialized structure. Figures 6-1 and 6-2 show sample organizational charts for a single cable system and an MSO.

Although organizational complexity increases with size, both large and small companies share some core functions. These include: general administration, programming, sales, and engineering. In a very small company there may be only a few people in each of these departments and some people may perform functions in several of them. Ten or twenty years ago, the person who sold you your cable service, a sales department function, might also have been the one to install it, an engineering task. Today, a large company may employ people in a wide variety of departments that represent specializations within each of the above areas.

Corporate structure can articulate into more complex forms to meet the demands and opportunities of new business. Some have centralized organization structures, others are more decentralized. TCI, as noted previously, spun its programming interests off into a separate holding company. Large MSOs may have corporate units in program production, competitive access, construction, Internet operations, even retail merchandising. Additionally, some MSOs are organized on a

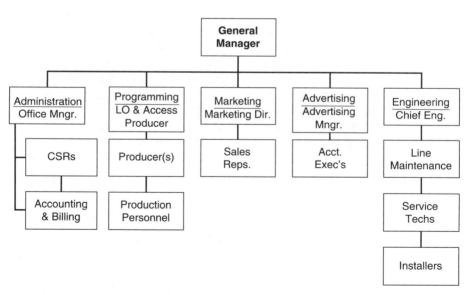

FIGURE 6-1   Local System Organizational Chart

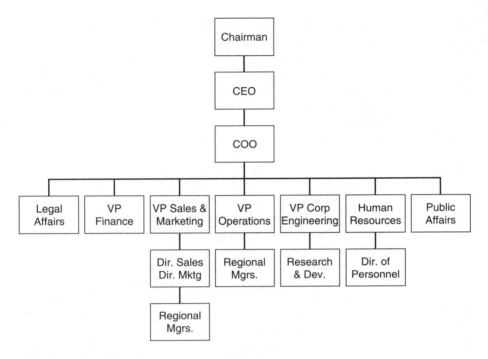

FIGURE 6-2   MSO Organizational Chart

regional basis, with vice presidents or managers responsible for programming, marketing, sales, or technology for all the systems in that area.

At the head of the organizational chart in a large, publicly held company are the Board of Directors, Chairman of the Board, Chief Executive Officer (CEO), and Chief Financial Officer (CFO). At the local level, a given cable system may be owned by a sole proprietor or a partnership. Whether the local system is one of the thousands held by a large MSO or whether it is held privately by local interests, its basic structure and functions are similar. Daily local operations are the responsibility of the general manager, who oversees all aspects of the business and reports regularly to corporate management or local owners. The following looks more closely at each service area.

General Administration

The general administration of the company typically includes its financial operations, bookkeeping and accounting, as well as office staff, secretarial support, and personnel. Larger companies will have separate departments for human resources (or personnel), which manage the hiring, firing, and training of staff. They also will have separate financial officers and departments, and may have legal departments to handle everything from contracts with suppliers, to lawsuits, to compliance with government regulations.

General Manager.   The general manager has direct authority over all departments and supervises daily local operations. The GM sets budgets, evaluates and approves marketing and sales campaigns, and is ultimately responsible for hiring and firing, personnel evaluation, and customer complaints. Central to the position is the goal of expanding the subscriber base, increasing revenues per subscriber, and generally improving profitability. He or she is the chief liaison with municipal officials, and in concert with the system's attorney, often will take the lead in working with local authorities on franchising and service issues. The GM also may spearhead initiatives for the improvement of customer and community relations through various public service campaigns. In larger companies, some of these roles may be filled by specialists in governmental and public relations departments. In an MSO system, much of the general manager's time is spent in consultation with regional and national corporate headquarters and in executing corporate policy at the local level.

Office Manager.   The office manager oversees the daily business functions of a local system. The office manager supervises customer service representatives and monitors billing activities, accounts receivable, delinquent accounts, and related financial matters. In smaller systems, the office manager also may be responsible for hiring and firing and double as bookkeeper. Most cable systems have fully automated billing and record-keeping systems (management information systems, MIS), often contracted out, that track customer accounts, provide computer-assisted budgeting and financial analysis functions. The office manager is often in charge of the computerized billing and finance systems.

Personnel or Human Resources Manager.   In systems large enough to support this position, the personnel manager is in charge of recruiting, interviewing, and hiring new employees, typically in consultation with the system manager. He or she may run employee training programs designed to introduce new hires to the job and to keep existing employees updated on industry trends and company initiatives. The personnel manager is responsible for employee moral and retention. In recent years many cable systems have developed alcohol and drug awareness programs. Health and insurance benefits, disputes between employees and personal problems that may affect the workplace typically come first to the doorstep of the personnel manager. In smaller systems, these functions are assumed by the general manager or office manager.

Customer Service Representatives.   CSRs are the cable system's front-line ambassadors to the public. Often an entry-level position in the industry, a CSR answers the telephones, takes orders for new service or disconnections, and responds to subscriber questions and complaints. CSRs also work the front office counter for walk-in customers. Customer service representatives work closely with the marketing department (in some cases they are part of the marketing department), and are responsible for selling services along with answering questions. Typically they are trained to discourage customer disconnects and encourage expanded services. In some systems they are known as CSSRs, or Customer Sales and Service Representatives, to underscore their role as sales agents.

Dispatcher.   Many systems have a person who schedules maintenance crews and installers. They assign field crews and monitor their status throughout the day, taking service orders from the CSRs and working with the engineering department.

Miscellaneous Positions.   Most systems have some secretarial support and larger systems may also have bookkeepers, accountants, clerks, public relations, and even legal personnel.

Sales and Marketing

This department is responsible for selling the service, acquiring new customers, and marketing expanded services to existing customers. The sales staff in a cable system can be divided into several groups because cable has several products to sell. Its primary job is to sell the cable television service to home subscribers. But a system may also have a sales staff to solicit and service local advertising for insertion into popular network programming (see below). Marketing and promotion of all the system's services, from basic cable to utilities monitoring, may be handled by a separate department or by the sales staff, depending on the size of the system. Programming and marketing are tightly intertwined in cable, and the marketing staff often has input into programming decisions. New services, such as Internet access or cable telephone, are likely to be given to the sales department or sales staff to develop, as well. The primary positions in this area include the marketing director, sales manager, and sales representatives.

Marketing Director.   The marketing director supervises all marketing activities, including promotion and advertising of new and existing services. He or she works with national programmers to coordinate campaigns for specific channels and consults with corporate headquarters in launching and evaluating system marketing programs. The marketing director also takes part in decisions about programming and program acquisition, how to bundle or tier channels, and pricing of different levels of service. He or she also may have a supervisory role in direct sales.

Sales Manager.   The marketing director and sales manager positions are closely related, often with one person serving in both capacities. The sales manager may report to the marketing director or share an equivalent position in the organization. The chief job of the sales manager is to supervise the activities of the sales staff, keep them apprised of changes in company activities and industry trends, to maintain records and track sales progress. The sales manager may be involved in decisions concerning programming, tiering, and pricing.

Sales Representatives.   The sales force, typically receiving compensation based on a combination of salary and commission (and sometimes commission only), plies the telephones and goes door-to-door to sell cable television to new customers. They also follow up on telephone calls taken by customer service representatives to maintain or upgrade old customers and solicit new ones.

Advertising Sales.   The local advertising staff sells commercial time on the system, soliciting new accounts and servicing existing ones. Much of this work is farmed out to advertising interconnect companies, as described later in this chapter. Positions in this area include the general sales manager, advertising sales or account executive, and, sometimes, traffic manager.

Advertising Manager.   Like the marketing director, the advertising manager supervises the advertising sales staff, setting goals, coordinating activities, and working with the general manager and corporate representatives.

Account Executives.   As with broadcasting and print media, these advertising sales representatives service existing accounts and prospect for new business, attempting to convince local merchants to advertise on the cable system. They often assist in the creation and production of the advertising.

Traffic.   Once an account executive receives an order for an ad, traffic is responsible for placing the commercial on the correct channel at the required time. In addition to scheduling the incoming spots, the traffic clerk or manager confirms it has run and may supervise billing of the client.

Programming

Unlike broadcast television stations, which have programming directors and programming departments, cable operations distribute this function across departments and management. Programming decisions tend to be made by committee with membership representing the highest levels of management, sales, marketing, and even engineering (especially when considering the system implications of new digital services). In most MSOs, decisions about which cable networks to buy are made at the corporate level, with local general managers having little input into program selection. Some MSOs grant local managers greater autonomy in determining a program mix appropriate to their community. Time Warner, for example, is known for allowing greater latitude at the local level than TCI.

Some cable systems have production studios, either because there's a market for local origination or because franchise agreements require them. In such cases, there may be a production staff to create or assist in the creation of programming and a local access coordinator to oversee use of the facilities and the scheduling of programs by public or governmental parties.

Engineering

The engineering department is responsible for the maintenance of the cable plant. Major construction of new cable systems often is contracted out to specialty firms that send crews around the country on a per-job basis, although some MSOs have their own corporate construction units. Engineering takes care of routine maintenance, such as replacing blown amplifiers and repairing downed cable. It ensures that the system meets FCC standards on signal emissions (leakage of electromagnetic signals that might interfere with broadcast services, aviation, or paging) and other technical requirements, and it must ensure compliance with state and local safety regulations. System technicians provide customer installation and disconnection service and are involved in system design and upgrading. With the evolution from the early days of twelve-channel analog television systems to interactive, digital fiber transmission technologies, the demands of the job have grown exponentially; even simple tasks like installation, when they involve digital technologies, call for technical backgrounds of increasing sophistication. At the MSO level, technology planning and evaluation are central to the business and these corporations have senior executives and associated staffs overseeing technology issues. As a result, there are specific job categories in engineering.

Chief Technician. Also known sometimes as headend technician or chief engineer, this person typically occupies a managerial job in larger systems with responsibilities for planning, budgeting, equipment acquisition, and personnel. In smaller systems the head of engineering may have actual maintenance responsibilities, such as ensuring the operational integrity of headend and microwave equipment. Engineering managers also play a key role in designing and supervising system upgrades, extensions, and new construction.

Line Maintenance Technicians. These technicians are responsible for system integrity from the headend to the customer drop. They monitor trunk and feeder lines for signal leakage, amplifier failures, and other transmission problems. They repair damaged lines, install new coax or fiber, and replace failed amplifiers.

Service Technicians. Service technicians are responsible for the line from the drop into the customer's home. They do the actual service work inside the house, responding to customer complaints about reception, connection, or outages restricted only to that residence. They also may do installation work.

Bench Technicians. Customer or headend equipment that needs repair or servicing in the shop will be attended to by skilled bench technicians.

Installers. Usually an entry-level technician position, installers hook up new service inside the home. During heavy marketing campaigns or with the development of a new cable system, operators frequently will contract for installation service, bringing in workers on a temporary basis.

Construction Personnel. Actual construction of new systems or extension of existing systems is typically done by independent firms on a contractual basis. Personnel will include hourly wage laborers who help string the wire or lay cable into the underground ditches, heavy equipment operators for digging trenches or operating "bucket trucks," and a construction foreman and supervisors.

Few systems can afford specialists in every area. As Table 6-1 illustrates, only the most central job categories are common in most systems. About 95 percent of all systems, for example, have a general manager, but only 6 percent employ a public relations or community affairs manager. The most common positions include general manager, chief technician, office manager, customer service representative, and service technician.

Income and Expenditures

Cable television is more like the newspaper industry than broadcasting in that it has two primary revenue streams, one from customer subscriptions and another from

TABLE 6-1   Frequency of Job Categories in Local Systems and Salaries

Title	%*	High Salary	Low Salary	Average
Gen. Manager	95	$90,000	$20,000	$44,915
Chief Technician	78	73,000	14,000	29,645
Office Manager	76	55,000	10,800	18,624
Customer Sales Reps.	80	21,000	9,400	14,526
Service Techs/Installers	77	35,000	12,000	18,374
Dispatcher	45	24,000	9,000	15,693
Secretaries	37	24,000	7,800	16,254
Construction Sup.	35	47,000	15,000	27,319
Installers (contract)	37	35,000	12,000	18,809
Marketing Manager	32	61,000	15,000	35,545
Subscriber Sales Rep.	30	35,000	10,400	19,609
Customer Service Mgr.	29	45,000	10,000	28,048
Chief Engineer	29	78,600	24,000	39,003
Accounting Clerks	26	27,000	8,600	17,307
Ad Sales Reps.	23	45,000	15,000	24,532
Product Technicians	24	20,000	11,000	16,445
Billing/Data Clerks	22	22,000	9,500	16,246
Prod./Prog. Sup.	22	45,000	14,000	26,132
Subscriber Sales Mgr.	21	50,000	12,000	30,316
Ad Sales Mgr.	21	70,000	16,000	36,067
Bench Techs	17	30,000	12,800	20,053
Human Resources Mgr.	8	55,000	16,600	36,950
Training Mgr.	5	35,000	16,000	26,200
PR/Comm Affairs Mgr.	6	50,000	32,000	42,500
Fiber Installer	4	30,000	18,000	24,824

*Percent employing

Source: Chuck Moozakis, "Working for Cable Today," *Cable TV Business,* 15 April 1990, 23.

advertising. Its dual revenue stream is one of the factors that has made it attractive to investors over the years.

Subscription Revenue.   Unlike newspapers, cable's dominant source of money historically has been subscriptions. In the newspaper industry, 70 percent or more of all revenue comes from advertising and the rest from subscription and single copy sales.[1] In cable, monthly subscriptions account for about 80 percent of total revenues. In 1995, for example, total cable revenue from subscriptions was $24.6 billion and income from advertising about $5.3 billion (see Tables 6-2 and 6-3).

Increases in subscription revenue over time have been driven primarily by climbing penetration and rate increases. Revenue gains were especially steep in the 1980s as a result of the proliferation of new cable services and the consequent expansion of cable plant into previously unserved areas, especially in many larger cities. Despite the higher profit margins of premium and PPV services, the lion's share of cable revenue continues to come from basic service fees (see Table 6-4).

In 1995, basic revenues represented about 68 percent of total income and pay services about 19 percent, but the ratio of basic to pay revenue has varied greatly over time. Premium service began in 1975 with HBO and slowly gained ground through the late 1970s. Subscriptions took off in the early 1980s along with the general growth in systems and subscribers, and by the mid 1980s, pay service was so popular that nearly 90 percent of all cable customers took some form and premium revenue nearly equaled that of basic. From that high-water mark, pay plummeted as

TABLE 6-2   Cable Subscription Revenue: 1980–1995 (in millions)

Year	Basic	Pay	Total
1980	$ 1,615	$ 765	$ 2,549
1981	2,061	1,317	3,656
1982	2,530	2,020	4,984
1983	3,048	2,747	6,425
1984	3,545	3,370	7,774
1985	4,145	3,727	8,938
1986	4,891	3,872	10,144
1987	6,014	4,112	11,765
1988	7,351	4,491	13,595
1989	8,670	4,896	15,678
1990	10,169	5,105	17,855
1991	11,414	4,943	19,463
1992	12,433	4,980	21,045
1993	13,528	4,628	22,782
1994	15,164	4,522	23,048
1995	16,863	4,800	24,619

Source: Paul Kagan Associates, Inc.(Carmel, CA), in *Cable Television Developments,* NCTA, 1996, 8.

a percentage of overall receipts, however. While basic continued to climb through the late 1980s and early 1990s, moving from about $5 billion to nearly $17 billion, pay income remained relatively flat at around $5 billion, and even suffered a slight decrease. The primary culprit in the consumer disenchantment was the introduction of the home videotape recorder and the rise of the home video rental market. Between 1980 and 1986 the percentage of television homes with VCRs rose from about 1 percent to 36 percent; by 1996 over 80 percent of all TV households had a VCR. In 1995, home video was a $16 billion dollar business, including $7.5 billion in rentals.[2]

It is, as previously noted, the hope of the cable industry that digital NVOD and VOD will restart the engine of premium service income by offering VCR rental convenience without the trip through the rain and snow to the neighborhood video store.

Advertising Revenue. Cable sells advertising at both the national and local level. National advertising time is purchased primarily from programming networks. Local advertising is made up of commercial spots purchased by area businesses and run on individual systems. In 1996, network advertising revenue was about $4 billion and local spot revenue was about $1 billion.[3] As Table 6-3 suggests, national advertising income has grown markedly since the mid 1980s. Local advertising revenue, while not growing as rapidly, started to accelerate in the early 1990s.

While cable television has attracted increasing numbers of advertising dollars, the medium still lags dramatically behind broadcast television and print as an outlet of choice for most businesses. Of total national advertising dollars spent in 1995, only about 2 percent went to cable. By comparison, the telephone directory yellow pages accounted for about 6 percent of all advertising volume and direct mail almost 20 percent.[4] The advertising money that does flow to cable is claimed primarily by the most popular national programming channels, such as CNN, USA, MTV, and ESPN.

TABLE 6-3   Cable Television Advertising Revenues

Year	Cable Net Adv. Rev.	Local Spot Adv. Rev.	Regional Sports Adv. Rev.	Total
1980	$ 50 M	$ 8 M	----	$ 58 M
1984	$487 M	$ 99 M	$ 9 M	$595 M
1988	$ 1.13 B	$374 M	$ 52 M	$ 1.6 B
1992	$ 2.3 B	$818 M	$140 M	$ 3.3 B
1994	$ 3.2 B	$ 1.2 B	$169 M	$ 4.6 B
1995	$ 3.6 B	$ 1.43 B	$215 M	$ 5.3 B

Sources: *Marketer's Guide to Media 1996–1997* (New York: Adweek, 1996), 11; *Cable World,* 6 May 1996, 42.; and © 1997, Warren Publishing, Inc., from *Television and Cable Factbook,* 2115 Ward Ct., N.W., Washington, D.C., 20037, Services Volume, I-13.

Cable is even less favored at the local level, where most advertising expenditures go for newspaper space and broadcast time. Local advertisers spent less than $1 billion on cable in 1995 compared to more than $8 billion on local radio and more than $30 billion on local newspaper advertising. In fact, the lion's share of local advertising dollars still go to the hometown newspaper. For reasons noted below, local cable systems do not make a great deal of money selling ad insertions.

Additional Revenue Streams. As Figure 6-3 illustrates, cable historically receives between 12 and 17 percent of its income from sources other than advertising and subscription fees for video programming. Figure 6-4 lists existing and planned income-producing services.

Some of these services, especially the ones that promise future large-scale growth, such as cable telephone and data transmission, already have been discussed. Operators charge separate fees for a host of items including digital audio services (about $10 a month) and the Sega game channel (around $13 a month). Some of the more mundane sources of income include charges for equipment rental and servic-

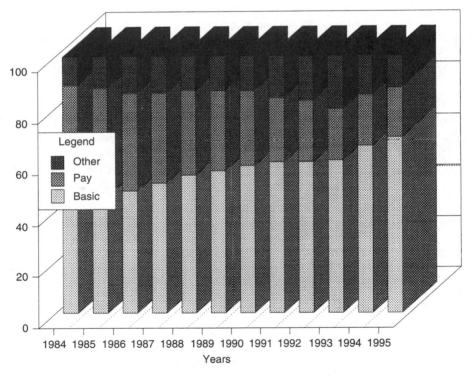

FIGURE 6-3   Cable Revenue Sources: Basic, Pay, Other

Source: Paul Kagan Associates, Inc. (Carmel, CA), in *Cable Television Developments,* NCTA, 1996, p. 8.

Basic Cable
Extended Basic, Premium, and PPV
Digital Audio Service
Sega Game Channel
Advertising: Local and National
Shopping Channel Fees
Equipment Rental: Converters, Remotes
Telemetry: Utilities and Emergency Services
Paging
CAPS & POTS
Leased Access Fees
Commercial Production Services
Service Charges: Installation, Repair
Cable Modems
On-Line Services and Internet Access

FIGURE 6-4   Selected Cable Revenue Streams

ing. Prior to federal rate regulation, which limited these types of fees to amounts that reflected the actual cost of the equipment, cable operators could levy fees of several dollars a month for set-top converters and the remote controls to run them. (In some cases, prior to cable-ready television, use of the converter would render the remote that came with the viewer's set largely useless and would require rental of a cable company remote control. Subscribers sometimes found they had to use both the television set remote and the cable remote to get full functionality out of their equipment.) Cable operators charge a fee for hook up of service and for service calls. Many systems charge to reestablish service in the event a customer is disconnected for failure to pay on time or other problems. Operators may assess a charge for each additional cable outlet in the home, for connecting a VCR to the cable, for installing an A-B switch, and for moving a cable outlet. The rate sheet for one large MSO affiliate lists more than thirty-five service items that accrue subscriber charges, including a $1.50 fee for exchanging the batteries in a remote control

Some MSOs, as noted previously, generate handsome revenue by backhauling PCS and wireline telephone traffic as competitive access providers. For local systems that carry home shopping channels, a portion of the purchase price of each item, about 5 percent of all purchases generated in the franchise area, goes to the local operator or MSO. In other cases, a shopping or infomercial channel may pay the local operator directly by taking system capacity on a leased access basis. Finally, some systems use their facilities and expertise to do commercial video production as a sideline business, and some rent out studio space on an hourly basis.

These auxiliary activities have accounted for a modest portion of cable's overall earnings, but as competitive multichannel providers begin to siphon away customers, the emerging telephone and data services discussed in the previous chapter may become a much more important part of cable's bottom line.

Expenses

After a cable system is built, the major operating expenses divide into a number of categories. In mature systems, primary expenses shift to those associated within any enterprise, raw materials, and personnel. Raw material in cable's case refers to programming, and the value added by manufacture is impressed on the material in the process of importation, carriage, and packaging. Other costs include advertising and promotion, upgrade and maintenance of the physical plant, various taxes and fees, and general administrative costs.

Programming Costs.   Cable's primary expenditure goes to programming. At least 32 percent, often more, of a system's costs typically go for the programs you watch.[5] Total expenditures for programming, industry-wide, have risen from about $1.8 billion in 1985 to nearly $5 billion in 1995 (the last year for which totals were available).[6] Differing payment models are used for different kinds of programming, including basic cable networks, premium services, and imported and local broadcast signals.

For advertiser-supported basic cable networks, cable operators pay a licensing fee ranging from a few cents to nearly a dollar per subscriber per month. When cable networks first sprang to life in the late 1970s and early 1980s, they paid the cable operators for carriage, a situation that was reversed beginning in about 1983 when programmers, beginning with ESPN, began to realize the value of their product and charge cable operators. The most popular networks today command the highest rates. A channel like ESPN may charge cable operators up to eighty cents a month per subscriber, the Family Channel about twenty-two cents, and BET fifteen cents, although contracts between programmers and MSOs vary. MSOs, especially large ones, usually negotiate discounted rates when purchasing programming for their systems. Start-up programmers seeking access to systems may ask less than five cents per subscriber. Some even try to acquire precious shelf space by paying operators to carry their signal (see discussion of startups later in this chapter), but most established programmers have been raising their license fees regularly for years. A typical cable system may pay anywhere from $4 to $6 per customer per month in programming fees. While the figure may not seem high, costs add up. A system with 20,000 subscribers and $5 per subscriber a month in licensing fees will pay $100,000 a month or $1.2 million a year for programming.

Distant broadcast television signals picked up off the air and imported by cable also cost the cable operator through the copyright fees paid to the Copyright Office of the Library of Congress. The amount of the fee is based on a complex formula that considers system revenues, number of signals carried, market size, and whether the signal is commercial or educational. Systems in the top one hundred markets additionally pay a syndicated exclusivity surcharge.[7] Small systems pay a two-tiered flat rate regardless of the number of signals they import.[8] Larger systems pay a fee based on the number and type of signals imported, although even those that import no signals pay a minimum, equivalent to just under 1 percent of gross revenues.[9] Fees for individual signals can vary from a low of 0.265 percent to a high of 3.75 percent, depending on how many signals the system imports and how they are classified under FCC rules.[10] The cable industry as a whole pays nearly $200 million in copyright fees annually.

Of the collected fees, 7.5 percent goes to the commercial broadcasters who originate the signal. Most of the money, about 55 percent, is distributed to the producers, writers, and others with contractual or copyright interests in the original programming (represented by the Motion Picture Association of America); about 29 percent goes to sports interests, including major league baseball, the NCAA, and the National Basketball Association, and 7.5 percent goes to noncommercial broadcasters.

MMDS and DBS operators also are subject to copyright fees. Congress extended the compulsory license to the wireless cable industry in 1994, making MMDS operators subject to the same copyright obligations as wireline providers. The 1984 Satellite Home Viewer Act granted DTH operators the compulsory license but set up a slightly different rate schedule.[11]

Advertising and Promotion.   Associated with programming costs are promotional costs, the money spent in advertising and marketing the system generally and specific channels in particular. Costs here take the form of newspaper or radio advertising and "bill stuffers," promotional material included in monthly billing statements sent to subscribers. Cable operators typically receive marketing support from the cable networks.

Personnel.   Cable television system operators, including MSOs, employ more than 100,000 people nationwide, of which about 42 percent are women and 26 percent minorities (the figures do not include program services). Salaries are the second largest expense category for cable operators and MSOs, accounting for about 18 percent of the budget, although this varies by system size with smaller operations paying out a higher proportion of the budget in salaries, up to 25 percent.[12] In 1993, the industry paid more than $3.7 billion in wages and salaries.[13] While there are a number of industry trade and professional organizations (see below), there are no unionized jobs in the cable industry, which has allowed owners to keep personnel costs down, although some unions, such as the Communication Workers of America (CWA), have an interest in the industry.

Salaries for different jobs in the cable business vary by market and system size, although local wages are, on average, lower than those found in broadcasting. Table 6-1 offers a summary of high, low, and average pay for different job titles. Compensation varies, of course, with the size of the local system; corporate jobs typically pay more than a system's positions. At the low end of the salary scale, construction crew laborers may be paid on an hourly basis, anywhere from minimum wage to $15 an hour or more. Some installers are paid for each installation and entry-level customer service representatives may earn annual salaries in the high teens to mid 20s. Salaries of advertising sales personnel, who may be paid fully or partially on commission, vary widely from a starting point of $20,000 to $100,000 or more. Chief engineers, marketing managers, and general managers may be paid $30,000 to $90,000. Corporate vice presidents of sales, marketing, legal affairs, and other major departments often earn salaries in six figures, again depending on the size and scope of the organization.

Construction and Maintenance. With nearly all of the United States wired, capital costs for new construction are aimed primarily at upgrading existing plant rather than wiring new neighborhoods. This does not necessarily result in a reduced need for capital funds. As previously noted, the majority of systems in the United States operate at well under the 750 MHz levels considered necessary to maintain a competitive advantage, and two-way capacity remains well below 50 percent. Cable will continue to require significant amounts of funding for the replacement of aging plant, the installation of HFC architectures, and the adoption of two-way technologies. This will include the purchase of equipment for telephone and Internet access, reverse amplifiers, switches, new testing equipment, and so on. The need to run the tighter system required by digital services also will mean increased maintenance costs. Capital depreciation, industry-wide, was reported at almost 17 percent of typical operating expenses in 1993.[14]

Pole Attachment. Telephone and utility companies rent space on their poles to cable companies. Like franchise fees, pole attachment rates are regulated by the FCC. Industry-wide, these charges range from about $4 to $6 per pole per year. A given system will allocate about 3 percent of its budget to pole fees, although costs will vary by system size and the amount of underground plant.

For years, during the 1960s and 1970s, the cable industry complained to the FCC about utility companies charging exorbitant fees for attachment. The complaints led the Commission to open a rule-making proceeding in the mid 1970s and eventually to attempt to broker a compromise between cable and telephone interests. The negotiated settlement fell apart, however, when the power companies declined to sign on and the FCC declared it did not have the jurisdiction necessary to compel their compliance (remember, the FCC has authority only over communications related companies such as telephone, broadcasting, and cable).[15] In 1978, Congress passed legislation granting the FCC authority to control pole attachment rates in all cases and the Commission soon thereafter enacted a formula (subsequently modified) for determining fair attachment rates.[16] A section of the Telecommunications Act of 1996 further opens up utility poles and other rights-of-way to cable operators, requiring just and reasonable negotiated rates. It also requires the FCC to adopt new regulations governing pole charges.

Franchise Fees and Taxes. Franchise fees are capped at 5 percent of gross operating revenues by the Cable Act of 1984.[17] Prior to the Act, the FCC limited fees to 3 percent[18] but municipalities often attempted to increase the revenue they received from the local operator by assessing fees in excess of 3 percent. An additional fee to fund public access facilities, for example, was not uncommon. Under the 1984 Act such additional charges beyond a total of 5 percent were forbidden. Franchise fees are usually passed directly on to consumers and show up as a separate line item on each subscriber's bill. Operators also must pay fees to the FCC to help fund the cost of federal regulation. In July 1996, the FCC raised regulatory fees from forty-nine cents per subscriber to fifty-five cents. The NCTA filed a petition for reconsideration, claiming the fees were unnecessary and unreasonable. Total taxes and fees, including any state taxes incurred, account for about 2 percent of a system's operating budget.[19]

Billing and MIS Systems.   Cable systems, telephone companies, and DBS operators must track customer usage of service, prepare and mail bills, and keep an accounting of the receipts plus any past due amounts. These activities are monitored by sophisticated management information systems (MIS) that contain information on each customer and may include detailed marketing data about past service usage in addition to simple data on the customer's address, phone number, level of current service, and number of cable outlets in the home. The cable and telco industries have hundreds of millions of dollars invested in computerized billing systems. As industries have taken on new services, the billing systems have been upgraded to monitor and assign charges to video, local and long-distance telephone use, and data communications for each customer. Integrating the new product mix, which includes everything from PPV movies to paging services, into a coherent and efficient billing system and database, has been expensive, but industry surveys show that customers prefer one itemized monthly bill. TCI reportedly spent up to $100 million to overhaul its back office system.

In addition to providing advanced, integrated billing functions and detailed information about subscribers, the new relational databases give customer service representatives access to real-time data about the system and its services. A CSR can, for example, call up a city map and determine where the nearest repair truck is and how long it will take to get to a customer who has called to report an outage. At the same time, that CSR can use the management information system and the opportunity to sell the customer any of the company's additional services and merchandise, everything from T-shirts to telephone service, then place the order or initiate the service while still on the telephone.

General Administration.   The general administrative budget includes, rent or mortgage on the building, utilities, supplies, and insurance. Office supplies, by some estimates, average about $1 per subscriber per year (sub/year); postage, $3 sub/year; travel and entertainment, $1.50 sub/year; telephone, $1 sub/year; and miscellaneous, $1.50 sub/year. General insurance is estimated at $50 per mile of plant and write-offs for bad debts at about 3 percent of gross revenues.[20]

Cable Financing and the Bottom Line

Historically, cable television has been a reasonably good business. Because of the high cost of construction and the heavy debt that many systems and MSOs have carried, it has not necessarily been a stellar performer in terms of annual gross profit margins, and its stock market track record has been uneven. Cable has performed well, however, in two important areas—cash flow and overall growth of assets. Cash flow is the measure of money moving through the system before deductions for depreciation, interest expenses, and taxes. One of the early and continuing attractions of cable TV, from a financial perspective, has been the steady monthly income generated by thousands of subscribers sending in a check on a regular basis. Cable systems have been described as "cash cows" because of this regular flow of income. Profit and cash flow margins can vary significantly from system to system and are influenced by a number of variables including penetration, housing density, channel capacity, and the competitive environment. With about $26 billion in revenue in 1995, most of it from basic subscriptions, the industry's average cash flow margin was about 43 percent, compared to 38 percent for broadcast TV, 34 percent for electric utilities, and 19 percent for long distance companies.[21] Moreover, annual cash flow has risen significantly over time, from about $20 per subscriber in the early 1980s to around $150 per subscriber in 1990 and $180 per subscriber in 1995.[22]

The second way in which the business has prospered is through the ever increasing value of most systems over the past forty years. Cable systems, when they are sold, are typically valued on the basis of either their historic or past cash flow or their total value, both measures being expressed on a per subscriber basis. In the early 1980s systems sold for eight times cash flow and around $800 per subscriber. By the late 1980s that had risen to twelve to thirteen times cash flow and as high as $2,500 (or more) per subscriber. The passage of rate regulation in 1992 cut into revenues and, along with escalating programming costs, helped drive down margins in the early 1990s, depressing the value of some systems. Market uncertainties have continued with the promise of increased competition brought on by the Telecommunications Act of 1996. In 1995 valuation averages were running around ten times cash flow and under $2,000 per subscriber.[23]

Cable companies have pursued differing strategies in nurturing the value of their holdings. TCI has aggressively sought to expand its subscriber base, using cash flow and acquiring debt to purchase systems, and sheltering operating revenue with the expanded depreciation. TCI head John Malone once described the company as an "asset accumulator." Glen Jones, on the other hand, built Jones Intercable through the heavy use of limited partnerships to buy and then manage individual systems, taking a management fee to run the operation and 25 percent of the profits when it was sold.[24]

One of the ongoing challenges for the cable industry has been acquiring financing for the high capital costs of system construction and, now, upgrading. The industry, especially those companies active in expansion, have historically carried a high level of debt that seems to grow every year. Total industry debt in 1990 was about

$41 billion. By 1995 it was more than $55 billion, although the ratio of average debt to cash flow has remained relatively steady at around five to one.[25] The ability of the industry to obtain financing has moved erratically over its history, influenced by broader economic trends such as inflation or recession, regulation or deregulation, and even bank mergers that have reduced the availability of capital. At one time banks were ready sources of financing; systems turned over frequently, sometimes doubling in value over a few years and existing debt was retired with the sale. In the late 1980s, however, controls on highly leveraged transactions (HLTs), which typified many cable financing deals, significantly reduced the industry's access to money. The industry turned to other sources of capital, including selling public and private equity (e.g., stocks, bonds, limited partnerships), and tapping into institutional lenders such as insurance companies, pension funds, venture capital firms, and foreign lenders. New public and private equity offerings rose from $10 million in 1990 to $2.4 billion in 1995.[26] As with most other things in the industry, corporate size makes a difference, mid-sized and smaller cable systems were expected to have greater trouble securing financing than the large MSOs. TCI, for example, reportedly had financial relationships with more than one hundred banks; small operators may only have standing ties with a few.[27] Still, heavy debt hurts the industry's ability to access capital and holds down stock prices. Investor disenchantment with cable in the mid 1990s kept stock prices low and contributed to severe cost-cutting measures at TCI. The company eliminated more than 2,000 jobs. It also raised subscriber rates. Both moves were aimed at improving profitability and reducing debt.

The following sections more closely examine cable programming practices, the packaging and pricing of services, marketing, sales, customer relations, and local advertising. However, in understanding the multichannel television industry, it is always important to keep in mind that the various processes of programming and marketing, strategic planning and technology development, Congressional lobbying, and public relations are all aimed at serving one end, the improvement of shareholder value. At the end of the day, owners and operators want to know if their interest in the company is worth more or less than it was the day before.

Programming

One of the most important tasks for a system operator is deciding what programming services to carry, to determine, in effect, what product to sell in the community. Nothing generates customer complaints faster than pulling a favorite channel, moving a programming service from one place to another on the dial (changing the channel lineup), or trying to add a controversial adult service. As noted, local general managers consult with regional or national MSO owners when selecting programming services and often the choices are kept almost entirely at corporate headquarters. Programming decisions are not made by isolated executives but through a collaborative process involving programming, marketing, audience research, and others.

A variety of factors are weighed in establishing a programming mix. Bruce Owen and Steven Wildman note that early models of program choice were driven, in part, by the limited universe of competitive channels; with only two or three choices, programmers (i.e., the broadcast networks) moved toward the middle of popular taste and demographics, offering programs of very similar types in an effort to capture as much of that middle as possible.[28] In contrast to a competitive situation, according to such models, monopolists who control all three channels will be inclined to program more broadly and with more diversity in an effort to capture minority interests as well as majority viewers.[29] Elaborations on models of program choice subsequently have incorporated the degree of customer demand as measured by willingness to pay for certain services, as well as the costs associated with programming. Therefore, channel capacity, the amount of competition, the nature and diversity of the local audience, and the costs of the programming all have become factors to be weighed when assembling a schedule of channels. In addition, operators must take into account legal constraints, equity interests in certain channels, and local culture. The following is a brief review of the elements that must be considered in determining which channels will be carried on a particular system:

Must carry: Under existing "must carry" rules, a cable system, in the first instance, is required to carry local broadcast stations, within the limits of the regulation (see Chapter 2). Even without the must carry rules, subscriber demand and basic business sense would compel carriage of most local signals, especially those of network affiliates, which remain the most popular channels in the television universe, although carriage might be contingent on the broadcast channels being available at a minimal or zero cost. The operator may additionally wish to import one or more regional broadcast stations, although latitude here is constricted by local broadcaster exclusivity guarantees.

Access channels: One or more channels may be required by the local franchise ordinance for the PEG access services. The system also may carry required leased access channels.

Basic networks: Systems typically will carry the most heavily viewed cable programming services, such as USA, Nickelodeon, ESPN, CNN, and MTV. After the heavily branded channels have been programmed, the operator will attempt to distribute other services in such a way as to cover as many demographic and interest or taste groups as possible. The goal is to strive to have at least a few services that appeal to everyone.

Channel capacity: Lack of channel capacity and the exploding menu of available and proposed cable networks have presented both a promise and a problem to system operators. The unbalanced supply and demand equation gives operators significant leverage in striking deals with programmers desperate for distribution, but it also poses a challenge in making the best market selection when adding new channels to the system. In keeping with the desire to program across market segments, operators typically seek to avoid network redundancy. That is, cable operators strapped for space are reluctant to add new services that duplicate existing ones. If a system already carries TNN it might be hesitant to add Country Music Television, especially if there are alternative available networks whose interests are not represented on the system line up. These considerations, however, can be overbidden by larger legal and economic realities. ESPN 2, for example, arose as a result of must carry, and Fox Sports constituted a third (or depending on the system, fourth) all-sports channel on TCI systems, due in part to the MSO's equity stake in the service. Similarly, there may be contractual tie-ins, such that the cost of one Turner service, for example, may decline if you take a second or third.

Equity interests: As the above suggests, then, if space exists on the system for a new service or an MSO is debating between similar competing services, the network that is partially owned by that MSO has an obvious advantage. As discussed more fully below, in a universe of limited shelf space, start-up networks without an MSO equity partner are handicapped at the outset.

Network price and performance: The paucity of open channels and large number of available networks also puts MSOs and system operators in a position to be more critical in evaluating existing network price and performance, and system operators have been complaining in recent years about the escalating cost of program services. System operators are reluctant to switch out networks, but are becoming more willing to pull an under-performing or expensive programmer in favor of a promising or less costly newcomer or competitor. In 1996, TCI announced it would be closely evaluating new and existing services, and soon dropped some channels it considered to be performing below expectations, replacing them either with services that were less costly, held greater promise of viewership, or in which the company held an ownership interest.

Programmers can exert pressure on their own behalf by offering the system operator special incentives to get on or stay on the system. Some well-heeled start-up networks have paid system operators $4 to $12 per subscriber for local distribution; more typical arrangements involve marketing incentives or additional advertising avails for the local operator. Nickelodeon's TV Land offered operators strong marketing support, attractive advertising time, regular promotional billboards, and free carriage for five years if they would carry the service.[30]

Local culture: Finally, system operators are sensitive to local and regional interests and values. Large cities on the East and West coasts have cultural characteristics different from agrarian communities in the midwest. The demographics of a town dominated by a major research university are going to vary from those dominated by agriculture or the mining industry. A system in a major metropolitan area may be more likely to program a high arts channel, such as Ovation, than a system in a small rural area. Adding CMT to a lineup that already has TNN may be appropriate in some parts of the country but not in others. Adult channels raise special problems, especially in locations outside major metropolitan areas. Proposed introduction of Playboy or Spice has sparked complaints by local conservative groups and sometimes prompted excited hearings before city councils. Where adult channels are introduced or already exist, system operators typically avoid drawing attention to them through traditional marketing techniques, although some have reported success with low key and "tasteful" marketing campaigns.

Channel Lineup

Channel surfing with the remote control and random access of services may eventually deprivilege some parts of the television "dial," but in the eyes of the industry and many consumers, the low end of the channel roster, channels 2–13, still constitute the choicest part of the television lineup. This is a holdover from the days when the VHF channels were the most common and powerful; they were the only channels on the dominant dial on the consumer receiver and they were the strongest local signals. Network affiliates were more often VHF than UHF stations, and UHF was seen as the poor, second cousin to "real" television. This psychology has bled through into the era of multichannel television to make the VHF band the more valuable numerical real estate. Existing VHF broadcasters jealously guard their channel position and UHF broadcasters and program networks seek to snuggle in next to the established stations on these channels.

Cable operators, by choice or technical necessity, have occasionally moved broadcasters from their over-the-air channel to a different spot on the cable dial. In the earliest days of cablecasting, operators had to shift stations on the higher VHF channels down to the low numbers to improve transmission quality (see Chapter 2). In latter years cable operators would sometimes move a weak local independent VHF station to a higher point on the dial to make room for a stronger nonbroadcast service. Moving a broadcaster to a new cable channel usually led to a howl of protest from the broadcasters and confusion among viewers who were used to finding a station at a particular place on the dial.

As part of the existing "must carry" rules, cable operators are required to carry broadcast stations, at least those covered by the must carry rules, on their normal on-air channel unless the broadcasters and the cable operator agree otherwise.[31]

Today, cable operators continue to privilege the lower part of the dial, maintaining local broadcasters, favored cable nets, and occasionally local access in the 2–13 range. The major broadcast networks, including Fox, plus HBO, USA, and similarly popular programming services are likely to be found on the VHF dial. Some systems are attempting to move toward clustering like services onto adjacent or nearly adjacent channels, so movie channels fill a certain span on the dial while news and documentary (CNN, Discovery, C-SPAN, and so on) take up a different segment. (Technical characteristics that make it preferable to put trapable pay-signals in the mid-band also contribute to this.) Systems have considered development of a more standardized formula for channel allocation so that BET, for example, is on the same channel in all the systems in a given MSO or on the same channel on all the systems in a particular metropolitan area. Currently, TNN may be on channel 34 in one city and channel 28 in another, or even on three different channels in the same metro area when different systems serve different parts of that city. While some clustered systems have moved toward a more uniform lineup, each city will have a different number of off-air stations on different channels, making a national uniform system difficult.

Tiering and Pricing

Cable channels are bundled into groups called *tiers*. If you look at your cable bill you may see a charge for a basic or lifeline tier, a separate charge for extended or expanded basic, plus charges for any premium or pay services you take. Each tier is offered at a separate, escalating price and historically has been subject to differing levels of rate regulation.

The basic tier by law includes only the locally available over-the-air and PEG access channels, although system operators may include additional channels on the basic tier if they wish. Some operators label this minimal level of service "lifeline" service, and sell it for $5 to $10 a month. All cable subscribers receive basic as an entry-level tier, but only a small percentage take only basic.

Most of the channels people typically associate with cable—CNN, USA, ESPN, and so forth—are bundled in the next level of service, called the expanded or extended basic tier. Rates for extended basic (which includes all the lifeline channels) average about $25 a month.

As noted in Chapter 5, premium channels and PPV channels are billed separately, on a monthly basis in case of the former and a program basis for the latter. Premium networks such as HBO and Cinemax split monthly revenue with the local operator, usually on a 50–50 or 60–40 basis. If the cable operator charges a subscriber $10 dollars for the Movie Channel, $4 may go to the network and $6 to the local system. PPV movies typically retail for about $4, a slight premium over rental store movies. PPV film prices are based in part on the license fees programmers must pay film studios. The price for a PPV event such as a concert is around $30 and a PPV boxing match about $37.[32] The local system receives about 50 percent of this. For special events, the PPV operator gets about 10 percent and the promoter 40 percent. Systems also can be expected to offer telephone and Internet services in discounted packages bundled with video services as the new services roll out.

One of the marketing tasks in the industry is to work out appropriate packages and price points for varying levels and types of service. The goal is to move subscribers to ever higher levels of service. Figure 6-5 shows the revenue progression.

Customers first need access to the cable line, accomplished when the plant reaches and passes their home. They then must be sold on the basic service. Once they become basic and extended basic subscribers, customers are encouraged to purchase monthly premium channels such as HBO or Cinemax and, if available, pay-per-view services. Prices for pay-TV channels range between $7 and $12 a month,

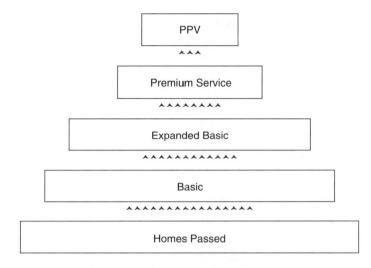

FIGURE 6-5   THE PAY PROGRESSION

although there are "mini-pay" services such as the $1.50 Encore. Several premium services are often marketed as a cluster, with the operator charging a discounted rate for two or three combined services.

Each higher level of service not only adds absolute additional income but it generates much higher levels of revenue on a per-channel basis. For example, the average basic rate, nationally, in 1996 was about $25 (see Table 6-4), well under $1 per channel. The average for monthly premium service was about $8 per channel and premium homes often subscribe to more than one premium service (multi-pay homes).

The numbers are even more attractive for pay-per-view. A home that purchases one PPV movie a week will generate $16 a month and a home that watches two movies per week will spend $32 a month or $384 a year, more than doubling the revenue over basic subscriptions.

Cable Rates and Rate Regulation
Over the history of the industry, cable rates have ridden a roller coaster of regulation and deregulation. As part of the comprehensive 1972 FCC cable regulations, the Commission required cable operators to obtain permission from their local franchising authority before raising rates for basic service, which at that time included all programming except premium pay channels.[33] As cable regulation was relaxed in the 1970s, the Commission began easing its 1972 requirements in a stated effort to encourage the development of and promote investment in the emerging delivery system. In 1974 it reiterated its position that pay channels were not to be regulated at the local level[34] and in 1975 preempted local regulation of rates for tiers consisting solely of imported signals (in an effort to advance the development of super-

TABLE 6-4   Average Monthly Cable Rates, 1980–1995

Year	Basic Rate*	Pay Rate	Total
1980	$ 7.69	$ 7.87	$15.56
1985	10.43	10.25	20.68
1990	17.60	10.30	27.90
1991	18.10	10.27	28.37
1992	19.08	10.17	29.25
1993	19.39	9.11	28.50
1994	21.62	8.37	29.99
1995	23.07	8.54	31.61

*Includes basic and extended basic.

Sources: "Data Bank," *Cable World,* 9 December 1996, 137; NCTA *Cable Television Developments,* Spring 1996, 3, from Paul Kagan Associates, Inc., *The Cable TV Financial Databook,* July 1995, 7, 9.

stations).[35] In 1976 it repealed its 1972 rules on local rate regulation,[36] but many local municipalities, through franchise agreements and other mechanisms attempted to exert rate control nonetheless.

A 1983 FCC ruling thwarted an attempt by the Nevada Public Service Commission to establish rate regulation for the state[37] and the Commission was supported by Congress a year later with passage of the 1984 Cable Act. Part of the legislation deregulated all cable rates in areas where cable faced "effective competition." Congress left it to the FCC to define "effective competition." The standard they chose was coverage by the grade B contour of at least three broadcast television stations, a situation that applied to about 97 percent of all cable systems in the country.[38]

The rate deregulation was part of the larger free market philosophy that drove policy thinking in Washington, D.C., in the early and mid 1980s. The failure of the assumptions of that philosophy, that subscribers would be protected by the rise of competing technologies, is traced in Chapter 2. The result was the Cable Act of 1992.

In response to the directives of the Act, the FCC moved to re-regulate and roll back cable rates. In a series of subsequent rule-making proceedings, the Commission issued reports, orders, and attempted clarifications that ultimately amounted to a dizzyingly complex, even bewildering, array of guidelines for controlling cable prices.

Cable systems would be subject to rate regulation in areas that lacked effective competition. Here competition was redefined to include only situations in which the system had less than 30 percent penetration, a competitive multichannel provider that reached 50 percent of the market and had a 15 percent penetration rate, or the local franchise authority operated a competitive system. Only a small percent of cable systems in the country met any of these standards. Rates for basic service, newly defined as local broadcast stations and access channels, therefore were subject to regulation by the local franchise authority, and rates for what became extended basic, or "programming services" tiers, could be regulated by the FCC. In the Spring of 1993 the Commission issued a freeze on all rate increases and proceeded to issue rules requiring a decrease in rates, initially of up to 10 percent.[39] The Commission later increased the amount of rollback to 17 percent when legislators and consumers complained that their local systems were holding their rates steady or in some cases increasing them despite the FCC action. In fact, some companies, prior to issuance of the rollback order, had re-tiered, moving channels from basic to extended or premium tiers and recalculating prices in expectation of the FCC cap. The FCC rate regulations were complicated and confusing, drawing complaints from both cable operators and local municipalities. Systems were permitted to challenge rate limitations by demonstrating that proposed increases were simple pass-through costs, but again the task of establishing the case was a daunting one. Rate regulation cost the industry, by some estimates, a billion dollars in lost revenue. Subsequently, to ease the burden of rate control and to promote new consumer services, the Commission adopted what it called "going forward" rules that allowed operators to offer new programming on unregulated tiers.[40]

Finally, passage of the Telecommunications Act of 1996, once again, relaxed the regulatory regime, promising operators even greater flexibility in packaging and pricing. The success of DBS, the reemerging promise of MMDS and the new possibility of telco competition prompted the Republican-dominated Congress to seek an end to rate regulation. As noted in Chapter 7, the Act fully exempted small systems (those with fewer than 50,000 subscribers and no ties to large MSOs),[41] and inserted a sunset clause to end rate regulation of the programming services (extended) tier for all systems by March 31, 1999. Systems that faced effective competition could be freed from regulation prior to that date, and effective competition was redefined as service offered by any comparable, unaffiliated, multichannel provider except DBS. Penetration quotas were eliminated. Moreover, the FCC, even before passage of the Act, was easing restriction of rates, permitting more generous allowance for passing along system costs including inflation, copyright fees, and regulatory costs.

With the relaxation of controls, cable operators were exploring new approaches to packaging and pricing. Following adoption of the Commission's "going forward rules," attempts to create and market "new product tiers" (NPTs), consisting primarily of start-up networks, met with mixed results. There was consumer resistance to an additional $5 to $6 charge for a tier of four or five new channels, sometimes related, sometimes not, and NPTs required costly addressable equipment for systems not already so equipped. Systems reported somewhat more success with "migrated product tiers,"[42] which consisted of one or two anchor services—existing branded channels moved or migrated from the extended tier—coupled with a few new services.[43]

Similarly, experiments with à la carte packaging, offering channels individually, has seen only partial success. Some consumers have shown interest in being able to select a single channel for 50 cents to $1.50, or to assemble a tailored package of services at a given price point. In general, however, acceptance rates for à la carte service have been low, and cable networks dislike the practice because it reduces or eliminates the chance of a viewer sampling channels, as with the extended basic tier. Some programmers have charged operators a penalty for à la carte carriage when it failed to meet minimum penetration levels. For many operators and most cable networks, the extended tier or a few extended tiers with a substantial number of established and new services remains the preferred mode. As digital capacity expands, operators may begin to more aggressively cluster like channels together. The model here could be existing DBS services that offer a variety of separately priced programming packages centered on themes such as movies, family viewing, or sports.

As to pricing, as previously noted, the industry has largely completed its construction phase with cable available to nearly all homes, and penetration for video services may have peaked. To pay off its significant debt, fund the technological expansion necessary to meet the competitive challenge, maintain cash flow, and expand the business, cable will move vigorously into the new product lines already outlined (telco and data) and most likely seek methods to increase rates across its range services. MSOs began raising rates for basic and extended service almost immediately after passage of the Telecommunications Act of 1996, as much as 20 percent in some cases.

Marketing, Promotion, and Sales

Rate increases, by themselves, have only limited power in elevating cash flow. Consumer resistance, competition from alternative providers, and potential political backlash all act to inhibit exorbitant price hikes. Cable additionally seeks to identify and tap new markets, markets defined both as new viewers and as new services for existing customers. Expanding the subscriber base and selling new services is largely the responsibility of marketing, promotions, and sales.

The market and promotion functions of both the local system and programming network encompass several goals, including:

- Acquiring new customers
- Retaining existing customers
- Encouraging migration to higher tiers
- Establishing brand identity and improving image
- Helping develop and test new products and services

New Subscribers

As long as cable plant was expanding, operators and networks could count to some extent on gaining new subscribers simply through increased penetration. In a mature system, however, marketing must work harder to acquire traditional nonsubscribers. Demographically, nonsubscribers are likely to be older and poorer than subscribers. Larger families are more likely to be subscribers and take a higher level of service than singles or couples. Enticing those who have never taken cable or purchased a PPV movie, the "nevers," to sample the service is often a chief goal of marketers. Recent attention additionally has turned to ethnic audiences. Penetration among Hispanics, for example, has historically been low, in part because of the lack of targeted programming. Yet Hispanic, African American, and other minority segments are a rising percentage of the U.S. population and by some estimates may constitute 47 percent of the population by the middle of the next century. Servicing the needs of this market, especially in regions where they already make up a significant portion of the audience, such as the Hispanic population in the Southwest, is seen as key to the industry's long-term prosperity.

DBS service began intensive marketing efforts in 1995, spending between $250 and $300 to acquire new customers. The satellite services were spending up to $150 in promotion for each new subscriber.[44]

Retention and Churn

The ability to hold a customer once he or she has signed up for the service has plagued the industry since its inception. Customers subscribe when the service initially comes to their neighborhood but some drop service as the novelty fades. Subscribers cancel service for various reasons: job layoffs, relocation, or a decision to read more, for example. Sometimes subscribers find themselves purchasing services, premium or PPV, beyond their reasonable means to pay and then default on payments and close their subscription or are disconnected by the operator. The problem of subscriber disconnects is called *churn*. The *churn rate* is the ratio of cancellations to total subscribers (disconnects/total subs = churn). Churn rates in new construction have run 30 percent or higher. In stable, rural areas, churn might be as low as 5 percent, and a 10 percent churn rate in many areas is considered reasonable. Churn rates are higher for pay services. In addition to the lost revenue, churn costs the operator in service time, administration associated with billing, and sometimes equipment not returned by the subscriber. DBS has discovered relatively high rates of churn in its first few years of service.

Encouraging Migration

The economic incentives to encourage existing subscribers to move to ever higher levels of service is noted above. The goal, again, is to increase per subscriber revenue, and it is the job of the marketing department to achieve it.

Building Image

The marketing staff also is responsible for helping polish the image of the company and the industry. TCI has run national television campaigns portraying the friendly cable installer and touting its commitment to quality service. Marketing helps publicize cable's various on-time and service guarantees in campaigns that, as noted, will become increasingly important as the industry goes head-to-head with alternative providers in the coming years.

New Product Development and Testing

One of the classic tasks of marketing is to probe consumers for unfulfilled needs, help develop product ideas to meet those needs, and test those products and possible price points. Positioning new products or repositioning existing ones away from potential competitors, either in real terms or in terms of the consumer's perception, is part of the task. Cable system operators and programmers are active in this area. The Fox News Network, for example, has been perceived by some as replicative of CNN and MSNBC, with some system operators and MSOs suggesting the market for news is saturated. The ability of Fox to position itself in the minds of viewers and advertisers as something different from existing services, perhaps appealing to an untapped market segment, could be critical to its success.

New product development also entails work on telephone and Internet services, and experimentation with different tiering schemes and pricing formulas for cable and DBS services. As distribution companies increase their reliance on bundled products, linking, for example, NVOD programming to discounted long-distance telephone service, the role of marketing will become increasingly complicated and central to the affected industries.

Marketing and Promotion Practices

Testing new service and product ideas often involves customer surveys and focus group interviews. Market analysts are normally among those involved in trials of new technology, such as the Bell Atlantic experiments with SDV in New Jersey and the Time Warner Full Service Network experiments in Orlando. Results of these efforts help guide planning for subsequent corporate ventures.

Marketers promoting existing services, most commonly program networks, summon a broad range of well-tested tools including the aforementioned "bill stuffers," glossy advertising brochures or cards stuffed inside your monthly cable bill, plus local or national broadcast, newspaper, and magazine advertising. The affiliate relations representatives for the networks work with local systems in most campaigns, supplying professional artwork for direct-mail programs, promotional television spots for on-channel and cross-channel insertion, as well as general advice and technical support. Telemarketing is also used in local and regional campaigns, promoting, for example, premium or PPV channels. When cable systems were still engineering their way into new cities, cable sales agents would go door-to-door soliciting subscriptions. Cross-channel promotions, cable guides, and the Web sites have also been used in promotional campaigns. These efforts frequently include some form of special incentive for potential customers. Operators may offer free hookup for new subscribers or a reduced introductory monthly rate. Premium channels might offer three months of free service, or a premium package of HBO and Cinemax may be discounted.

A marketing technique that caused special problems for the cable industry was the "negative option." Under the negative option, a cable system would provide subscribers with a new service and start billing them for that service unless the subscriber notified the company that he or she didn't wish to receive it. It created a situation in which customers were charged for a service they never requested. Attempts to implement the highly questionable tactic were often met with angry phone calls from subscribers and complaints to consumer bureaus and state attorneys general. In 1991, TCI attempted wide scale use of the negative option in rolling out its mini-pay network, Encore. The action prompted lawsuits by attorneys general in several states and a public relations thrashing in the popular press. TCI abandoned the effort soon after, and Congress specifically prohibited the negative option billing tactic in the 1992 Cable Act.[45]

Customer Service

The 1996 film *The Cable Guy,* starring Jim Carrey, featured a psychotic cable television serviceman that played off the popular image of the industry as something less than warm, friendly, and efficient. Many in the cable business were not amused. As has been noted, cable has suffered throughout its history with a poor reputation for service, and like many images, this one is not without some merit. The developmental, construction era of cable was dominated by engineers whose primary aim was to get a system built. As the early "pole climbers" who ran the business gave way to accountants and business graduates in the 1970s and 1980s, the focus of attention turned away from system construction and toward improving the financial health of the business, buying and selling properties, and negotiating deals for program acquisition, but concern had not yet shifted to the subscriber. Even those within the industry admit it took cable several decades to realize it was a service industry.

In 1990, the NCTA, seeking to reverse the poor public image and service record, instituted voluntary customer service guidelines. It called for improved response to telephone calls and appointments for installation, among other things. Promotion of and compliance with the guidelines was lukewarm, however. By 1993 only 2,000 of the nation's 11,000 systems had been certified as meeting the NCTA criteria. As part of the 1992 Cable Act, Congress authorized the FCC to develop stricter national regulations for customer service, which the Commission, with the NCTA's help, unveiled in 1993. Under the new FCC guidelines, cable operators were required to:

- Keep normal business hours
- Maintain a twenty-four-hour telephone hotline for customer questions or complaints
- Answer phones and transfer calls within thirty seconds
- Begin repairs on outages within twenty-four hours
- Locate service offices within convenient distance of customers
- Execute installations within seven days of an order
- Establish four-hour appointment windows for home service
- Publicize rate and schedule changes at least thirty days in advance

In 1995, the NCTA launched another public relations and service enhancement campaign called "The Future Is on Cable." Spurred by the prospect of yet another round of federal regulation and the growing competitive threat of alternative distribution providers, the industry offered a guarantee of on-time service to all customers as the centerpiece of its initiative. Customers would receive free installation if the installer failed to show up on time or a $20 credit for other service call failures. Industry-wide, cable moved more aggressively to train its customer service representatives and improve its track record and image, although as surveys noted earlier have suggested, they may face an uphill battle. Moreover, both industry surveys and the experience of head-to-head competition suggested that customers were not deeply tied to any particular industry (cable, satellite, or telco) and were much more sensitive to price and channel options than brand name. While customer service appears to be an important part of the equation for success, the quality and variety of the product itself along with its price may play the determinative role in consumer choice.

Theft of Service

While making service as convenient as possible and dealing with customer problems quickly and efficiently has become an important industry goal, cable also has had to deal with the contrasting issue of theft of service. Deterring cable piracy without invoking draconian measures that would irritate honest customers has been one of the challenges. Cable piracy and the manufacture and sale of equipment intended for such use are violations of federal law.[46] By recent estimates, cable theft costs the industry about $7 billion in lost revenues annually. Cable theft is manifest at all levels of service; customers illegally tap into basic service and access higher tiers, especially premium and PPV services, without authorization or payment. A 1992 NCTA survey estimated that nearly 10 million basic and 6 million premium cable households were receiving unauthorized signals. A Milwaukee system that reported 120,000 legal subscribers also estimated an additional 40,000 illegal users.[47]

Piracy is made possible in part by the growing gray market in illegal converter boxes. Since passage of the 1992 Cable Act, consumers have been able to purchase their own cable equipment instead of renting it from the cable system. Advertisements for unauthorized equipment are common in electronics magazines. Sales of unauthorized or counterfeit converters amount to an estimated $1 billion annually.[48]

Most MSOs and industry trade groups have adopted antitheft programs, and systems run regular promotion campaigns and security sweeps to detect illegal users. The goal in most cases is to convert the viewer to a paying customer, although fines have been levied. Soft-sell approaches include national advertising campaigns designed to make illegal users aware of the issue and hopefully make them feel guilty enough to stop. Harder campaigns include physical inspection of homes to detect illegal taps. In one "sting" operation, American Cablevision of Queens in New York City shot an electronic "bullet" through its system disabling illegal converters. When customers reported the service disruption they were encouraged to bring in the boxes for repair and were prosecuted when they did.[49]

The move to digitization and improve encryption of signals will likely reduce theft, but sophisticated pirates and enthusiastic customers will probably ensure that a healthy underground market continues.

Local Advertising

A New York City advertiser who wanted to run a commercial on cable television in the 1970s faced a daunting task. Like many large metropolitan areas, the city is served by many systems franchised to specific boroughs and neighborhoods. In the greater New York City area there are more than forty separate systems and eight MSOs. The 1970s advertiser would have to negotiate price and availability with each system or group of systems. Then, videotapes of the commercial would have to be distributed, either by microwave with the particular system recording the spot or by physically delivering a copy of the tape (a process known as bicycling) to the system. It was a nightmare of business and technical obstacles and one of the reasons local cable television advertising failed to make a significant contribution to overall industry revenues. Historically local spot sales have accounted for only about 3 percent of national cable income (although this varies by MSO and market, larger systems report up to 10 percent of annual revenue from local advertising).

Some of the more popular channels for local advertising are CNN, ESPN, USA, and other heavily viewed networks. The networks, as part of their contractual arrangements with the local systems, provide commercial availabilities, or "avails," of about two minutes per hour for local spots.

While cable ads are usually cheaper to produce and run than broadcast commercials, and they can be targeted more precisely to specific audiences, they nonetheless have drawbacks. A number of problems have hampered local cable advertising, including interconnection difficulties, unwieldy advertising insertion technologies, differences in pricing philosophies, merchant unfamiliarity and distrust, and weak ratings information.

Interconnection and Insertion

Efficient distribution of local advertising, especially in larger markets, is contingent on two things: system interconnection and advertising insertion equipment. Interconnection is an agreement between local, often adjacent, cable companies to combine their market for purposes of selling local advertising. It opens to local or national merchants the full penetration of the metro area, and helps to centralize and streamline all aspects of the process. Often interconnection is facilitated by a separate company that contracts with the various systems for sales, distribution, tracking, and billing services. The interconnect company sells the inventory of avails and splits the revenue with each system. The system is flexible; interconnect companies may have more or less involvement in packaging the commercials and tracking the schedule.

Advertising insertion equipment, especially in metropolitan markets, requires tremendous capacity and sophistication. The equipment may have to feed and monitor tens of thousands of commercials across a dozen or more channels and an equal number of systems every month. Older analog insertion devices are little more than computer-controlled banks of videotape recorders. Local spots are fed from these racks of VCRs to the different systems and routed to appropriate channels. Digital systems, on the other hand, can track millions of avails annually; they can increase turnaround time in producing and running a commercial and can increase flexibility by generating different versions of a given spot for different channels, systems, or programs. The Los Angeles interconnect, "Adlink," can customize commercials for twenty-seven regional "zones," so advertisers are able to target particular neighborhoods within the metro area, as well as certain demographic and psychographic markets using specific channels and programs. It makes cable a more attractive vehicle for advertisers who do not want to spend the money to reach the entire metro region. Eventually, advertisers see the possibility of using digital technology to deliver customized ads to individual homes.

The digital insertion equipment is expensive, several thousands of dollars per channel, and even older analog equipment is beyond the reach, or need, of many small systems. The bulk of local cable advertising is conducted by larger systems with the business market necessary to make worthwhile the expenditures for technology and sales staff. Nationwide there are about 160 interconnect operations;[50] only about 2,800 systems carry local advertising.[51]

Pricing

As noted earlier, local advertising dollars are much more likely to flow to community newspapers and even local broadcast stations than they are to cable. In addition to the logistics issues that have retarded local cable sales, pricing has also been a problem. Rates on small systems can be as low as $10 for a thirty-second spot; on metropolitan, interconnect systems as high as $100 or more depending on channel, program, and times. Local advertisers can purchase specified time slots on particular channels or, for a discounted price, buy "ROS" or run-of-system avails that appear at times convenient to the operators. In either case, the base price of the spot is determined, as in broadcasting, by the number of people watching the program; this is the cost per thousand or CPM. Advertisers complain that cable operators charge two to three times the CPM of local broadcasters. In fact, the actual cost of the commercial is substantially less on cable than on the local broadcasting outlet because the viewership of an given cable channel is a specialized fraction of a typical network broadcast affiliate. On a per-person basis, however, the cost may nonetheless be higher. Cable operators, seeking to charge as much as they can for advertising and striving for what they consider parity with local broadcasters, respond that they offer a premium not available through broadcasting: the ability to more closely target the advertising message to the appropriate audience. The debate between pricing on the basis of targeting or CPM will likely continue, but advertisers hold the trump card in the choice of cable versus other local advertising vehicles.

Cable advertising also has been hindered by a lack of familiarity, experience, and trust on the part of the business community. This is due in part to the aforementioned difficulties and in part because of weaknesses in the ratings systems. Cable advertising, both local and network, is plagued with measurement problems. As the price of advertising is contingent on viewership, the health of the advertising market is dependent on the ability to generate accurate information about the number and nature of the people watching cable television channels, and that ability has been elusive.

Ratings

Ratings are a measure, an estimate, of how many people have watched a particular program or channel. They are of central importance in cable, satellite, and broadcast television because they are the figures that largely determine the cost of advertising and hence revenues. Larger ratings translate into higher advertising prices and greater income. For example, one of the most heavily watched television programs of the year is the Superbowl. In 1997, the Fox Network, which carried the Superbowl, charged advertisers about $1.2 million for a thirty-second commercial "spot," generating over $70 million in total revenue for the program.

While numerous companies conduct specialized research into television viewing, only one company, A. C. Nielsen, provides the ratings data used nationally by the television and advertising industries. The company produces a variety of reports for broadcasters and cablecasters. It provides ratings measures for both national and local audiences. In either case, Nielsen selects samples of viewers to represent total viewing population. The national sample is 5,000 homes. The company does a separate measure of viewing in local markets.

In the national sample, the company uses a device called a *peoplemeter* to measure viewing. The peoplemeter box sits on a viewer's television set and is linked to the company's computers. Each member of the household is required to log their viewing periodically, using a special remote control. The box stores and later transmits to Nielsen the information on who was watching a particular program. Information on local viewing is gathered by diary method, with people listing on a paper diary what programs they watched for a particular week; passive meters, which only measure whether the set was turned on to a certain channel, also are used in the larger markets.

The data is reported as ratings and share. Ratings are the percentage of people or homes watching a certain program or network out of the entire population; one ratings point represents about 959,000 TV households. Share is the percentage of people or homes watching a certain program or network out of the population with sets actually turned on.

Cable programmers generally benefited from the introduction of Nielsen's peoplemeters in the late 1980s. The devices more accurately measured viewing of new and unfamiliar cable networks; in the diary method, people will often forget what they have watched and enter more familiar and established programs or channels. The Nielsen service has drawn criticism, especially from the broadcast industry. The primary concern is that the Nielsen sample fails to adequately represent the demographic makeup of the national audience. In an increasingly fragmented and targeted television and marketing universe, accurate estimates of audience characteristics are essential, and critics assert the existing system does a poor job in this area. The measurements are further flawed, according to some, by the failure of people to accurately enter information, in either the diaries or the peoplemeter. Nielsen and the major broadcast networks have been looking at ways to improve the service, including the possible adoption of "passive" measurement devices that can automatically determine if a given person is watching a particular program.

SATELLITE AND TELCO OPERATIONS

While still in their nascent stages. DBS, telco, and MMDS distribution organizations largely mimic MSOs in their functions and organization. All are dedicated to developing, securing, and distributing broadband programming, marketing and promoting content, and billing customers. DBS operators obtain and market programming in ways similar to cable operators. Sales of equipment and services differ, with DBS companies selling their product directly and through nationally based retailers. PrimeStar, for example, is sold through more than 6,500 Radio Shack stores, as well as by affiliate agents contracted by the company and its MSO members. TCI's distribution arm for PrimeStar, PrimeStar by TCI, employs a direct sales force of hundreds operating out of five regional offices. They solicit new customers door-to-door and by telephone. The company also maintains a national "call center" that takes new orders and supplies twenty-four-hour customer support services.

Bell Atlantic employs about 120 people at Bell Atlantic Video Services (BVS) in Reston, Virginia. BVS has run several operations including an ADSL trial in Fairfax. Virginia. Their SDV system in Toms River, New Jersey, began operation before the Baby Bell was permitted into the programming business and was run by the independent company FutureVision until Bell Atlantic bought the company in 1996. BVS also will be responsible for programming the ambitious Philadelphia broadband system. BVS worked in cooperation with the telco programming entity, Tele-TV, with which it shared facilities in Reston. Like DBS operators and MSOs, BVS is organizationally divided into functional departments, including: engineering and operations; marketing and sales; programming; business development; human resources, media relations, and finance.

Satellite Carriers

Grades of Service and Pricing

Satellite operators primarily differentiate services on the basis of the overall attractiveness of the satellite and the content carried vis à vis other satellites. Other factors, which we will consider here, pertain to the nature of the satellite's footprint, the availability of backup capacity that exists in the event of an outage and whether a transponder may be "commandeered" for use by another customer paying premium rates for a higher grade of service.

Footprints

From the discussion in Chapter 3, we know that satellite footprint can extend to cover one-third of the world, or concentrate signals to illuminate a single nation or region. Video and consumer electronics applications like DBS and Digital Audio Broadcasting (Digital Audio Radio Service) require concentrated spot beam signals or comparatively high-powered transmissions that make it possible for quite small dishes to capture an adequate signal. Customers seeking the widest possible coverage area will require global beam coverage. Generally a satellite will contain both wide beam and narrow beam configurations to serve different user requirement. A satellite operator can anticipate charging premium rates for users who so intensely prefer a particular beam configuration to the exclusion of what might an acceptable alternative for other users.

In economics, users are considered to have inelastic demand when second-best options do not meet their strongly held requirements. When users will not accept alternatives, which might be available at a significant discount, their inelastic demand means that they typically will not reduce consumption, or shift to another satellite even if the satellite carrier raises rates. Put another way, carriers can exploit the intensely held requirements of users with inelastic demand by charging higher per unit rates than for users who are more price sensitive and more willing to consider and use less than optimal service.

Backup Capacity

Satellite pricing also depends on whether users require the carrier to dedicate capacity to satisfy their requirements in the event an existing transponder fails. The most risk-averse customer will agree to pay premium rates for service that guarantees the near instantaneous cutover to another transponder in the event of an outage. This grade of service requires the carrier to designate "protection" transponders, that is, transponders that must remain vacant or available only to customers who agree that their service can be "preempted," or taken away almost instantaneously under certain circumstances.

Hence the most risk adverse satellite customer will require "protected, non-preemptible service." The satellite carrier can charge premium rates, because it protects such users with costly safeguards that all but assure continuous service. The service is nonpreemptible, meaning that the carrier agrees not to make the capacity available to others even when the premium service customer is not using the capacity. The service also is protected in the sense that backup capacity is available to restore service in the event of an outage affecting the transponder used or the entire satellite. Generally, all satellite services have backup capacity available over terrestrial or submarine cables. The premium grade of service makes it less likely that the customer will have to resort to a cable alternative, or even have to repoint each stations to another satellite.

The lowest grade of service includes preemptible, non-protected transponders. In this category, users typically pay significantly discounted rates, but run the risk that in the event of an outage or peak demand conditions, the transponders they may be using will be taken from them without much notice and assigned temporarily to a user with a higher and more expensive grade of service. The discount service attracts users who can tolerate the occasional disruption, or who have such confidence in satellite technology or in the user's importance to the carrier that any significant disruption appears unlikely. As one would expect, some video programmers opt for premium service, on grounds that they cannot tolerate outages of live feeds. On the other hand, other programmers may have acquired sufficient transponder capacity that they can shift traffic streams on the basis of their internal priorities. Still others have such confidence in their standing with satellite carriers to expect carriers to do everything in their power to prevent an outage from adversely affecting the delivery of time-sensitive content.

PROGRAM NETWORKS

In the simplest terms, the chief functions of any network are to: (1) create and acquire programming and package it in an appealing form; (2) expand distribution and increase subscriber base through the handful of DBS and MMDS operations, hundreds of MSOs, and thousands of individual systems; (3) sell national advertising time; and (4) market and promote the service. A host of ancillary activities are required to support these basic tasks. The typical departments in a programming network include administration and the office of the CEO, programming, advertising sales, affiliate relations, ancillary services, legal affairs, public relations, personnel, and finance.

Structure

Administration

The general administration or network management houses the offices of the Chief Executive Officer and related staff. The presidents and vice presidents of the different divisions or departments will report to the CEO and there may be a management team comprised of these officers. Strategic planning functions are also housed here.

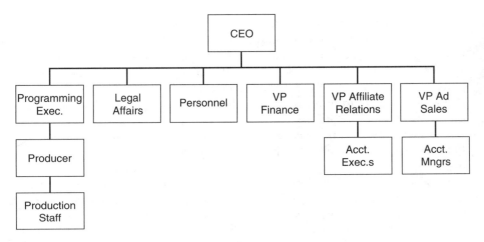

FIGURE 6-6   Programmer Organization Chart

Programming

The nature and scope of this department will depend largely on the type of programming run by the network. Services involved in heavy original production may have scores of producers, camera operators, editors, writers, technicians, and, in the case of news channels, reporters and anchors. Services that rely less on original material will have programming management staff that negotiate the purchase or creation of material, coordinate co-production ventures with independent film companies, and attend to the details of scheduling. In conjunction with management and the programming staff, the president or vice president in charge of programming has the responsibility of building a successful lineup of shows by selecting material and scheduling it to achieve the best fit for the audience. The various elements that go into this subjective and chancy process are discussed later in this chapter.

Marketing

The marketing staff works closely with programming and affiliate relations. Its assignment is the development of promotional campaigns for the network generally as well as for specific programs and new programming initiatives.

Advertising Sales

As with most media, programming networks have a staff devoted to advertising sales. Individual account managers, reporting to a vice president or president of advertising, services existing clients and solicits new ones. He or she may help develop creative ideas that match the advertiser's pitch to the channel's target demographic.

Affiliate Relations

Personnel in affiliate relations work with individual cable systems. Like advertising sales, it will have a staff of account executives and a department head, vice president or president (depending cn the particular company). In newer cable networks the primary challenge here is to sell the channel, that is, to convince systems to carry the service. In established networks with existing system affiliates, the main job is working with the local operators to promote the channel, coordinate marketing campaigns, answer questions, and respond to concerns.

Legal Affairs

Nearly all the business conducted by the network involves a contract and all contracts are written or reviewed by the legal staff or legal counsel. These include employment contracts with top management and on-air talent specifying wages and benefits; agreements with production companies for the creation of programming; advertising contracts; and carriage agreements with MSOs and individual cable companies.

Ancillary Services

As noted, many of the larger networks have expanded into new product lines. The Discovery Channel, for example, develops and markets CD-ROM software based on its programming. The range of activities and titles in these departments is wide, but at their core involve the development, promotion, and sales of new products and the creation of new revenue streams.

Additional departments may include public relations, sometimes called corporate communications, which handles interaction with the news media and the public; human resources or personnel, which handles most of the hiring and firing (below a certain level) and administers employee benefits and training; and the finance department, which keeps the books.

Profit and Loss

The chief expenses for programming services involve the cost of acquiring or producing the programming itself and personnel in the form of salaries and wages. Production and employee costs are included in the discussion of industry expenses above and vary widely from company to company, as do the income streams from licensing fees and advertising rates. As noted, per-subscriber fees can range from a few cents to a few dollars, depending on the service (basic or pay). Rates for advertising time on the commercial networks also run from hundreds to thousands of dollars, depending on a number of factors including network penetration, daypart, ratings, and demographics. The cost in 1995 of a thirty-second spot on A&E, for example, ran between $850 and $18,000; on CNN from $1,700 to $17,000; The Family Channel between $250 and $15,000. At the high end, Lifetime, with about 65 million subscribers, charged up to $30,000 in 1995, while the History Channel, with only 4 million subs, charged as little as $50 to $350.[52]

While advertising revenue for programming networks has been increasing and some of the more popular channels do very well, license fees still make up about half of all income for many of the programming services. The programming services recently reporting the largest revenues include: ESPN ($553 million); CNN ($491 million); TBS ($256 million); Nickelodeon ($205 million); Lifetime ($176 million); Discovery ($160 million); TNN ($137 million); A&E ($135 million); The Family Channel ($129 million), and CNBC ($78 million).[53]

Building Brand Identity

One of the primary marketing goals of all networks is to develop a clear brand identity. Each network needs to stand out in the mind of the viewer; the network seeks to present a distinct and favorable image both as a means to distinguish itself from the clutter of dozens of channels and to be considered the single source of television for a particular kind of content or a particular segment of the audience. An executive of Ted Turner's Cartoon Network once stated that their marketing goal was "to own the genre of cartoons the same way CNN owns the genre of news."[54] Even networks with broad appeal, such as USA, strive to establish a clear personality and develop a relationship with the audience. Marketers seek to increase the perceived value of their network, and measures of value—typically cast in terms of how much a subscriber would pay for the individual channel—become tools in promoting networks to system operators. Channels topping the list in perceived customer value over the last few years have included Discovery, ESPN, CourtTV, CNN, the Cartoon Channel, and Nickelodeon, with subscribers saying they would be willing to pay $1.50 to $2 each for these services.[55]

In addition, once a strong brand has been established it can be leveraged into new business venues. The Discovery Network, according to some surveys, is one of cable's most widely recognized and admired names. Discovery has tapped that popularity to move into the consumer products market, magazine publishing, feature film production, even theme parks, all sporting the Discovery label. "The heart and soul of the business is building brands," according to one Discovery executive.[56]

Programming

Program Sources

Programming for networks is generated or acquired in several ways. Channels that specialize in news or information, such as CNN, CNBC, and the Weather Channel, produce most of their own material. Premium channels such as The Movie Channel rely largely on recently released theatrical films. More broadly based entertainment networks and many specialized entertainment nets rely on a mix of syndicated programming, original productions, and film libraries. Examples include USA, TNT, Sci-Fi, and Lifetime.

Off-Network Syndication.   Early cable channels were sometimes criticized for being a retirement home for old broadcast television programs. No program ever really died, it was said, the show simply went to cable. And, as evidenced by earlier examples, a good deal of this is true; some networks have relied heavily and continue to rely on network reruns. The broader characterization is only partially accurate, however. Cable networks that specialize in news and current events, by definition, have always been substantial producers of original material. The programmers of dramatic and fictional material, on the other hand, have leaned heavily on syndication. In a 1986 study, Waterman and Grant found that nearly 97 percent of all informational material on basic cable was original, but over 95 percent of basic cable dramatic programming had previously appeared on commercial broadcast stations or in theaters.[57]

Syndication is the structure and process by which these old chestnuts find their way to services like Viacom's TV Land. Most programs produced for broadcast television are not owned by the networks that air them but by the firm that created them, usually a well-established Hollywood production company. Networks contract for these programs and acquire the rights to air them; program producers never actually relinquish ownership. The economics of television are such, however, that the money the networks pay the production company typically does not cover the production cost. If a program is canceled after several episodes have been aired, the production company normally has to bear the loss, which, given contemporary costs, can amount to millions of dollars. Producers, therefore, are gambling that they will have a successful program. If they do, then enough episodes are created that the company has a stock of material it can subsequently sell in the aftermarket. The aftermarket is composed of the many venues into which the program can be channeled following its network run. One of the primary aftermarket segments—and the chief distribution channel prior to cable network release—has been independent television stations. Syndication companies acquire the limited rights to the library of off-network shows and license them to local nonaffiliated stations.

In cable's developmental years, programming services were far down on the syndication food chain, as they had very little money with which to acquire recent, successful shows; cable nets purchased only material that had been sitting unused for years. Beginning in the 1980s, programming networks began to outbid broadcast outlets for the exclusive rights to off-network programs.[58] As many of the more established networks began to prosper in the 1990s, they were able to afford the most successful recent network programs. Turner, for example, purchased the syndication rights to several Warner Bros. programs, including *ER* for $1.2 million per episode, *Friends* for $300,000 an episode, and *Lois & Clark* for $275,000 an episode. The fX network purchased rights to the *X Files* from its corporate sister, Fox Television, at $600,000 per episode, and Lifetime paid NBC productions almost a half million dollars an episode for *Homicide: Life on the Streets.*[59]

In addition to network reruns, syndication includes "first-run" syndicated material. Talk shows, game shows, and tabloid programs are typical first-run syndication program types. *Oprah, Wheel of Fortune,* and *Jeopardy* are sold to local television stations as first-run syndication, as are programs like *A Current Affair* and *Entertainment Tonight.* Cable has been less heavily involved than broadcasting in first-run syndication.

Theatrical Films. Programming networks use thousands of feature films each year. Premium and PPV networks acquire the rights to recently released films, and basic cable channels buy or license libraries of older material. In the former case, the networks have to wait until the film is released into their market before they can show it. After screening in local theaters, current films are released into the various aftermarkets. Release is sequenced, a process called *windowing*, in an effort to maximize the total profit potential of the film. The windowing sequence in today's domestic distribution system begins with local theaters, then moves into video cassettes and DVD (digital versatile discs), pay-per-view channels (including cable and DBS), premium cable, basic cable, broadcast network television, and local television syndication. At each descending level, the license fees and the direct cost to the consumer drops. The windowing strategy is based in part on the observation that people are willing to pay more for the most recent films. Owen and Wildman explain, "Staggering releases forces buyers to sort themselves out according to how much they are willing to pay for the film or program close to its original release date."[60] Other factors, according to Owen and Wildman, that influence the sequence include:

(1) differences in the per viewer price earned in the different distribution channels; (2) differences in channels' incremental audiences, by which we mean differences in the number of new viewers they contribute to a program's total audience; (3) the interest rate as a measure of the opportunity cost of money; (4) the extent to which viewers exposed to a program through one channel are eliminated from its potential audience in other channels; (5) differences among channels in their vulnerability to unauthorized copying.[61]

Under recent windowing schedules, films are released into the home video market six to nine months following their initial theatrical run, and one to two months later into the PPV window. Premium channels get the films twelve to sixteen months after their theatrical run, although the sequence varies among studios and often by individual film. Cable networks and other distributors strike special arrangements with studios to acquire film rights prior to competitive outlets, paying a premium for the privilege.

Older films are acquired by cable networks either through syndication or outright purchase. In the first case, film syndicators license packages of movies to programming networks (and broadcast stations) for a period of several years, typically three to six, depending on the demand for the films. Higher demand for films by cable networks in the late 1980s led to a reduction in the licensing window offered broadcasters because the syndicators sought to turn the packages around more quickly for resale. Some programming networks have simply purchased huge Hollywood film libraries. The most prominent example here was Turner's purchase of the MGM library, used now for both Turner Classic Movies and TNT.

Original Production. Despite the historic reliance on syndicated dramatic programming, networks increasingly have tried to allocate resources to original production. Beginning especially in the 1990s, programmers moved more aggressively into original production. Networks today are making their own films, multi-part entertainment specials and documentaries, and even weekly series. From 1990 to 1995, programmers pumped more than $12 billion into original production and the spending was expected to grow. In 1996, Discovery spent $160 million on 800 hours of original material, primarily documentaries. A&E has run regularly scheduled series, including *A&E Biography, American Justice,* and *Investigative Report,* for several years. HBO, with 70 percent of its schedule in feature films, is aggressively developing its own programs, including comedy club specials and series.[62] Some networks formed their own companies to make feature material, others contract or coproduce with independent production companies, but most attempt in some way to develop their own content. There are several reasons.

Original programming promotes network branding. In 1996 USA began promoting its original programming by creating the fictitious on-air "USA Studios" to give viewers an opportunity to see actors and others in the process of production. The goal, according to the network was "to give the viewer a peek in (to) see how we tick, so they'll have a connection with us."[63] The Vice President of Programming and Production for Lifetime, Judy Girard, stated bluntly, "We certainly won't put dollars into it unless it brands the network."[64]

In addition to branding, original production leads to the accumulation of a valuable library of software wholly owned and controlled by the network. Instead of essentially leasing material through syndication, networks retain property rights to material that can be rerun as necessary. Ownership also offers the network the chance to deploy the material across alternative delivery platforms. Films and even successful series can be sold in overseas markets, through videotape and DVD outlets, and preserved for ancillary markets that have yet to develop. As software becomes the engine of revenue, companies will seek to amass their own libraries of material for subsequent exploitation.

Finally, for services that depend heavily on feature films, reliance on high quality product flow from the major studios has become something of a gamble. Huge box office hits represent only a fraction of the available material and a fragment of what is necessary to fill the schedule. HBO and others have sought to create their own movies in an effort to maintain consistent quality. The supply of high demand material also has been reduced by exclusive contracts struck between studios and specific programmers.

Infomercials. Infomercials have become a staple for some cable television networks. Infomercials, or program-length commercials (PLCs), are long format commercials, typically an hour or more. Most viewers are familiar with infomercials for exercise equipment such as Soloflex, Bowflex, Nordic Track, and scores of devices for working the abdominal muscles, the "abs." Infomercial pitches also have been created for a rainbow of wealth enhancement schemes from real estate to precious metals. They have promoted cosmetics, psychic fortune-telling 900/800 numbers, kitchen utensils and, among the more whimsical, spray paint to cover up bald spots.

The economics of infomercials are attractive. They are cheap to produce, as low as $50,000 for production and airtime, although they more typically cost several hundreds of thousand of dollars to create. Response rates reportedly run anywhere from 5 to 20 per 1,000 viewers and profit margins on the merchandise are high.[65]

Despite critical publicity and harsh government scrutiny of infomercials in the late 1980s, the industry has prospered. As noted in Chapter 5, there are several satellite distributed infomercial networks, including one, Product Information Network (PIN), owned by cable MSOs Jones Intercable, Cox Communications, and Adelphia. They are easy money for cable operators and likely to remain a popular and lucrative format. Moreover, digital interactive technologies promise to make direct purchases during infomercials even easier. Viewers will only have to touch a button or point and click on the screen to select an item. It should increase buy rates and perhaps enhance the breadth and power of the provider database that collects buyer–viewer information.

Niche Theory and Programming Strategies

Drawing on the above sources, program service executives must tailor a schedule sufficiently attractive to at least a large enough segment of the audience that it becomes a viable business enterprise. As we've seen, local cable system operators, dealing with dozens of channels and programmers, seek to assemble a something-for-everyone schedule. Individual programmers, alternatively, must develop their own unique brand or personality and this involves several choices.

Susan Eastman, in her excellent and exhaustive book on broadcast and cable programming, outlines five key elements in programming strategy: compatibility, habit formation, control of audience flow, conservation of program resources, and breadth of appeal.[66] While these themes reflect the traditions of broadcast television more than cable, they have some applicability in cable network programming practices.

Compatibility.   This involves scheduling programs to complement the daily routines of viewers, matching the activities of different parts of the day—morning "drive time" and evening "prime time"—with compatible programs. The Nickelodeon network is a good example. It schedules its heavily watched children's material during the day and switches to its stable of 1960s and 1970s off-network programs in the evening to capture a wider and older audience. Similarly, CNBC offers breaking business news and market information during working hours and switches to a lower key menu of consumer affairs and talk shows in the evening. Eastman also notes that compatibility arises naturally in cable programming insofar as narrowly niched services such as the Weather Channel make available specialty information that interested viewers can tune in to at anytime during the cycle of the day.

Habit Formation.   Research suggests that television viewers are creatures of habit; they settle into a comfortable routine of channel or program selection. Some sociologists have suggested that television viewing generally is more ritualistic than substantive, while others acknowledge the difference between content seeking and media seeking (see Chapter 9 for a more detailed discussion). Rubin, for example, proposed the labels "ritualized" and "instrumental" viewing.[67] The former is associated with habitual viewing (e.g., soap opera fans) or simple time passing; the latter is associated with purposive viewing, as in seeking information about the weather or current events (although watching news programs can also be a ritualized activity). The concepts of ritual viewing and media seeking behavior speak to the propensity of people to watch because the act of watching satisfies various personal or cultural needs or drives. This is not to say that content is irrelevant; there must be a match between the program and the interests of the viewer in the first instance to establish the link.

In cable, habit formation has been evidenced by the channel repertoires that people build.[68] Despite the availability of fifty or sixty channels and the widely discussed practice of remote control grazing, research has found that most viewers eventually develop a repertoire of five to ten channels that they watch regularly, bypassing the remainder unless a special event on a typically unwatched network attracts their attention. Cable-ready television receivers are programmed to allow viewers to delete or skip channels as they pan across the "dial," so a viewer may simply remove all the shopping or religious channels from their menu. The trick in cable network programming, as with broadcast networks, is to build a loyal following and habituate those viewers to specific programs or the channel as a whole. This has worked particularly well with certain audience segments, including sports fans who regularly turn to ESPN, and current affairs or news "junkies" who regularly tune in to CNN or C-SPAN.

Audience Flow.   The control of audience flow is a related concept. It attempts to capitalize on habit, or at least audience inertia, in an effort to get viewers to stay with a network through several programs, and, if possible, the entire evening. In broadcast television, programmers use a number of techniques to encourage audience flow, including promoting the upcoming program at the conclusion of the current one and, more recently, reducing or even eliminating the commercial breaks between programs so that the subsequent show begins directly on the heels of the previous one. Cable specialty channels again can often benefit from audience flow by featuring a long run of similar shows attractive to a given audience, such as several hours of cooking or home improvement programs. Channel grazing also is hopefully reduced in this manner.

Conservation of Program Resources.   This strategy was referred to in Chapter 5 in the observation that large media companies will attempt to exploit a given programming idea as fully as they can, repackaging or repurposing it in the form of books, films, television programs, Internet material, and merchandising activities. The point is to extend the original material and resources as far as one can. In meatpacking, they say that every part of the pig is used except the squeal. What is not sold in the form of ham and bologna ends up in pet food and tannery products. Media products, of course, can go this one better by reusing the same product over and over, as in the case of television reruns. Cable networks often will rerun programming more frequently than their broadcast counterparts.

Breadth of Appeal.   Eastman's strategy of breadth of appeal for broadcast programming is perhaps better recast in cable as "nature of appeal." While some of the most successful cable programmers, as we have seen, have adopted a broad format—USA and the Family Channel are examples—the majority of cable networks are more narrowly niched. Eastman offers a four-cell typology for thinking about niche services based on the relative breadth of both the content and the audience (see Figure 6-7).

A programmer can: (1) cast the net widely in both dimensions, mirroring the broadcast networks; (2) program broad content for a narrow audience (BET); (3) seek a broad audience with a narrow content (The Weather Channel); or (4) target a narrow audience with narrow content (MTV). No matter which personality or niche the service chooses, it will seek to position itself away from existing services and seek to establish some kind of link to its selected audience segment.

The problems associated with selecting a niche become more apparent and can be clearly illustrated in the process of attempting to develop a new programming service.

Starting Up

As we have seen, until digital deployment provides a critical market mass that can sustain additional networks, start-up programmers remain constrained by a lack of shelf space that puts local system operators and MSOs in control of the national distribution system. Even after distribution opens up, however, would-be program-

Dimensions	**Broad Audience**	**Narrow Audience**
Broad Content	(1) example, TNT	(2) example, BET
Narrow Content	(3) example, CNN	(4) example, MTV

FIGURE 6-7   Niche Dimensions

mers have substantial hurdles to clear. In 1996 News Corp. made industry headlines by offering to pay local systems up to $12 per subscriber in an effort to gain carriage for its all-news channel, Fox News. Cap Cities/ABC, which had announced plans for a similar all-news network earlier, dropped out, reportedly deciding that it didn't want to enter the bidding war for channel space. It may also have had doubts about the sustainability of three or more all-news channels in an increasingly fragmented market.

Fledgling cable networks must successfully meet a variety of challenges, some of them illustrated by the Fox News example. Proposed nets must acquire adequate distribution, secure sufficient financing, develop a reasonable business plan, locate an open market niche, and develop a brand identity. Ownership ties with MSOs or existing programmers can facilitate many of these goals.

In selecting a niche, programmers must evaluate the extent to which there exists a market demographic or psychographic large enough to support the service. By most industry estimates the "sacred break even point" is 25 million subscribers for a basic service.[69] Other estimates put the reach figure lower as the power to provide more research information on highly targeted markets grows and advertisers become more comfortable that they can reach specific groups of consumers. While fashioning an appeal to increasingly narrow niche markets, the so-called "slivercasting" strategy, is attractive, a certain critical mass of audience remains a prerequisite. The real question is: What is the break even point? The answer, especially for emerging services, hinges a great deal on the cost of programming and the value of the audience. One industry president suggested a new network could succeed with fewer than 15 or 20 million subscribers, given the right marketing information.[70]

While raw viewership is a necessary condition, it may not be a sufficient one. Whether or not the proposed service provides a demographically attractive advertising base (does anybody want to sell anything to the likely viewership?) also makes a difference. Sports, for example, attracts a certain demographic highly appealing to some advertisers, such as beer companies and athletic gear companies. The Discovery Channel was ultimately successful, in part, because many of its programs drew the male viewers prized by car companies, financial firms, and computer manufacturers. Disposable income is an important consideration. A&E attracts a more affluent and educated audience along with people who otherwise would be considered light viewers of television. One of the attractions for advertisers on the Golf Network was the upscale demographics of the audience.

Younger demographics are more appealing to many advertisers than older demographics because older viewers have established brand loyalty to products and are more resistant to advertising appeals. Younger audiences have not yet developed strong brand loyalties and are more open to experimentation, therefore more receptive to advertising.

Beyond the strategy associated with identifying a market and a niche are a host of related issues.

Competition.   Is there a market hole? Can a target audience or viable market niche be clearly identified that is not currently served by an existing service? Many in the industry have declared that all the good ideas for networks have been taken. Starting a new network is a sufficiently daunting task in the absence of real competition. Trying to unseat a dominant channel, or even carve a shared space, requires exceptionally deep pockets or a belief the market can support multiple services. And the market has not always been kind to challengers. Despite good connections and the backing of Liberty Media, the Music Zone, a would-be competitor to MTV, was short-lived. Liberty Media's President, Peter Barton, observed, "There are many aspirants (in music television) and there is this one huge omnipresent MTV wherever there is a vacuum. We decided that this was all we needed to learn in our experiment."[71] Satellite News Channel (SNC) failed to find a place alongside CNN in the mid 1980s. There is one dominant children's channel, one dominant channel for African Americans, one channel for science fiction, one for comedy. Whether or not the new wave of competitors, CNNfN, Fox News, Fox Sports, and MSNBC succeed presents an interesting question.

Branding and Brand Identity.   One of the hallmarks of a successful network is its ready identifiability. As noted above, networks view a strong brand identity as an essential element in building and maintaining a viable company, especially as competition increases and audience attention is splintered. MTV has one of the stronger brand identities. Other companies have struggled to establish a clear presence. The Arts and Entertainment Channel and The Learning Channel found early in their corporate histories that viewers had no clear concept of what the channel offered. Encouraging viewers of an established network to sample a new one through cross-promotion—the practice of advertising the new network on an existing one— is also seen as critical in the success of an emerging service, which is another reason ownership relationships between networks are an important aid in success.

Strategic Partners.   As has been pointed out, the cable industry is becoming increasingly integrated. The quid pro quo for carriage sometimes has been an equity position by the MSO, although only the very largest MSOs can exercise this kind of power. In other words, the start-up network must sell a percentage of the company to the MSO in order to acquire carriage. An executive of the young Outdoor Network observed in 1995: "The big fight is that the big MSO's want to own you before they'll carry you. Every service that's been launched . . . is owned by MSO's—it's a vertically integrated monopoly."[72]

Good Management.   Solid, intelligent management with clear, long-term goals and a detailed, realistic business plan are critical to the success of any business. Discovery's John Hendricks is frequently cited industry-wide not only as an astute businessman, but a benevolent and good-natured one as well. TCI's John Malone, while not always considered a warm and cuddly figure, is nonetheless an exceptionally capable leader with a sensitivity to both the details of the business and the broader perspective. On the other hand, failed services such as Financial News Network and the Satellite News Channel were hampered by management problems.[73]

Deep Pockets and Patience.   Start-up networks will typically bleed red ink for three to five years. The fledgling service needs the resources to sustain itself during this period and the patience or tenacity to hold on until the viewership and resultant advertising grows.

Estimates on the amount of money investors can expect to spend before they start to recoup their money range from $50 to $100 million to cover operating costs for the first three to five years, and it can go higher. ABC funneled more than $225 million into Lifetime before it became profitable, Ted Turner spent over $275 million on CNN, and USA was still unprofitable after $285 million in initial expenses.

Niche networks will need to find ways to keep costs down during their germination period, but at the same time maintain a reasonable level of production quality. Some new start-ups, such as the Food Network and Fit TV, lean heavily on low-cost studio production. Sci-Fi net is a good example of a network that found an open niche and filled it with low-cost programming. The Cartoon Channel offers a similar example. Both had strong financial backing from corporate parents (Turner and USA). One of the reasons for the failure of CBS Cable in the early 1980s was the large amount of money spent on programming; in contrast, MTV began with inexpensive programming including free concert footage.

Market Timing.   It can help to take advantage of cultural or social trends, or being lucky enough to benefit from them. The ecology movement help propel Discovery to success. Recently programmers have been looking at aging demographics and seeing ways to capitalize on an older audience. As one expert in network start-ups noted: "Network success is not a scientific process, it is a strategic process involving conventional business wisdom. No one formula works for all channels."[74]

INDUSTRY ASSOCIATIONS

Like all businesses large and small, the cable, satellite, and telecommunications industries have a plethora of associations and trade organizations that sponsor conventions and seminars, initiate public relations campaigns, lobby policymakers, and distribute information to their members. Some of the larger ones are noted below.

The National Cable Television Association (NCTA). NCTA is the cable industry's largest trade organization. Based in Washington, D.C., its chief function is political lobbying. It represents the industry before Congress, the FCC, and in the courts. It also sponsors the industry's principal annual convention, provides research and information for members, conducts workshops, and produces promotional material.

The Satellite Broadcasting and Communications Association (SBCA). SBCA is the national trade organization for the home satellite industry, including the direct-to-home business. It was founded in 1986 in the merger of its predecessor organizations, the Satellite Television Industry Association, Inc. (SPACE) and the Direct Broadcast Satellite Association (DBSA). Like NCTA and many of the other industry associations, it is based in the Washington, D.C., area and sponsors conventions, workshops, and publishes various reports and newsletters.

The United States Telephone Association (USTA). USTA is a century-old association of local exchange carriers and the dominant trade organization in the telephone industry. USTA, like NCTA, represents its industry in matters before Congress, regulatory agencies and the courts. It sponsors member services including technical and regulatory bulletins, general newsletters, education, and training workshops and industry-wide conventions.

Cable Telecommunications Association (CATA). Like several other cable associations, CATA changed its name in the early 1990s to reflect the growing convergence of technologies. Founded originally in 1973 as the Community Antenna Television Association, it was created to serve the pointed interests of smaller systems. Like NCTA, CATA represents the industry to policymakers and to the public, produces newsletters, and provides members information on all aspects of industry operations, legal, technical, and financial.

Cable & Telecommunications: A Marketing Society (CTAM). CTAM was formed in 1975 as the Cable Television Administration and Marketing Society. Initially a group representing the interests of marketers and management, CTAM in recent years has turned its attention more toward marketing and sales issues. Like the other industry organizations it conducts workshops, holds annual conventions, and publishes information on marketing, promotion, and sales trends.

The National Academy of Cable Programming. The Academy, founded in 1985, is sponsored by NCTA and is designed to promote cable programming. It created and runs the annual Ace Awards competition, the cable industry's version of the Emmys.

Society of Cable Telecommunications Engineers (SCTE). SCTE represents the special interests of cable and broadband engineers, providing information, seminars, and publications on the technical aspects of broadband television. It too changed the "television" in its title to "telecommunications" in the early 1990s.

Cable Television Laboratories, Inc. (CableLabs). Based near Denver, Colorado, Cable Labs, inaugurated in 1988, is the technical workshop for the industry. It tests and helps develop new technologies and plays a crucial role in helping fashion technical standards for the industry.

Women in Cable and Telecommunications (WICT). WICT is designed to support and promote women at all levels of the industry and especially to assist them in management and leadership positions. Membership is open to both men and women. It sponsors workshops and activities at the national and local levels, including a highly respected annual management conference and a year-long training program.

National Association of Minorities in Cable (NAMIC). Like WICT, NAMIC's goal is to advance opportunities for minorities in the industry, sponsoring conferences and workshops at the national and local levels. Both organizations have heavy support from the industry at large, which to its credit has been very active in supporting women and minorities at all levels of the business. While not a function of NAMIC, the Kaitz Fellowship program additionally encourages minority advancement in the industry. An annual class of forty to fifty Kaitz fellows is selected from the ranks of young management and given several weeks of special seminars that often feature the leaders in the industry.

The Alliance for Community Media. Formerly the National Federation of Local Cable Programmers, the Alliance represents local origination and community access groups. Based in Washington, D.C., it hosts national and regional conferences featuring business and legislation workshops and programming competition. It also publishes newsletters, promotes access and community programming interest in policy making.

Other industry organizations include: Wireless Cable Association International, representing MMDS operators; the Cable Television Human Resources Association, for personnel issues; the National Cable Television Cooperative, representing Independent system operators; the National CATV Institute, a training enterprise; and CTIA, a trade association for the PCS and cellular industry. There are, additionally, state-level organizations, such as the Pennsylvania Cable Telecommunication Association and the California Cable Television Association.

A CONCLUDING NOTE

The evolving delivery platforms and the services they will make possible raise interesting issues for programmers and distributors alike. Programmers have new options for getting their product to market; much of the recent growth in pay-per-view service, for example, has come from DBS. These prospects also bring complicated questions about the real-world mechanisms for creating and delivering twenty-first century services. The rise of advanced, interactive multimedia services of the type described earlier has implications for numerous business operations. Business plans, customer service, billing systems, program development, acquisition, and delivery conventions are all currently based on a traditional mode of one-way program distribution. Despite the fanfare about the interactive future, normal business operations remain largely based on simple sales of classic television entertainment. As true interactivity and increased viewer power to select and control programming does materialize, the business practices reviewed here will have to adapt accordingly. The cable industry has received a taste of this in its fledgling efforts to penetrate the telephone business. In many ways the interactive universe will be a new industry requiring new skills, systems, and strategies. Providing full VOD, multimedia, and virtual reality experiences requires much more than just technological advancement; it requires significant restructuring of many of the back-office routines that characterize cable and satellite television today, and success in these areas may prove as important as having the right technology.

NOTES

[1]Robert Picard and Jeffrey Brody, *The Newspaper Publishing Industry* (Boston: Allyn and Bacon, 1997), 40.
[2]"The Handbook for the Competitive Market, Blue Book Vol. III," *Cablevision*, 1996, 4.
[3]Ibid., 10.
[4]*Marketer's Guide to Media* (New York: Adweek, 1996–1997), 11.
[5]Bureau of the Census, Department of Commerce, *Annual Survey of Communication Services* (Washington, DC: Government Printing Office, 1995), 26.
[6]National Cable Television Association, *Cable Television Developments,* 1996, 7.
[7]Systems also pay less, about 1/4 normal fees, for carriage of imported educational or noncommercial stations.
[8]Systems with gross receipts under $292,000 pay 0.5 percent of the first $146,000 and 1.0 percent of revenue beyond that.
[9]0.893 percent.
[10]Specifically, whether carriage of the signal in question would have been permitted under FCC rules in effect between 1976 and 1981.
[11]Six cents per subscriber per month per signal for network signals, 14 to 17.5 cents for superstations.
[12]Bureau of the Census, Department of Commerce, *1992 Census of Transportation, Communications and Utilities* (Washington, DC: Government Printing Office, 1993).
[13]Bureau of the Census, Department of Commerce, *Annual Survey of Communication Services, 1993* (Washington, DC: Government Printing Office, 1995).
[14]Ibid.
[15]Memorandum Opinion and Order, 37 R.R.2d 1166 (1976). On a request to reconsider, the Commission further declared that it did not have jurisdiction over telephone pole attachments, 64 FCC 2d 753 (1977).
[16]Second Report and Order, Cable Television Pole Attachments, 77 FCC 2d 187 (1979); constitutionality upheld in *FCC v. Florida Power Co.*, 480 US 245 (1987).
[17]47 USC 542 (b).
[18]47 CFR 76.13.
[19]Department of Census, *Annual Survey*.

[20]Gerald Cahill, "Forecasting Operating Income in the Cable Television Industry," *The Journal of Business Forecasting*, (Winter 1990–1991), 7.

[21]"Databank," *Cable World*, 29 April 1996, 12.

[22]Walter Ciciora, *Cable Television in the United States* (Louisville, CO: CableLabs, 1995), 17.

[23]"Databank," *Cable World*, 19 February 1996, 46.

[24]"The Surprising Success Stories in Cable Television," *Business Week*, 12 November 1984, 81–88.

[25]"Databank," *Cable World*, 19 February 1996, 46.

[26]Ibid.

[27]K. C. Neel, "Who's Got the Dough?" *Cable World*, 27 November 1995, 190.

[28]Bruce Owen and Steven Wildman, *Video Economics* (Cambridge: Harvard University Press, 1992).

[29]Owen, 65–67

[30]Will Workman, "How Many Networks Does It Take to Fill a Niche?" *Cable World*, 6 May 1996, 50.

[31]47 C.F.R. sect. 76,57.

[32]Jim McConville, "Request Paints Rosy PPV Future," *Broadcasting & Cable*, 11 December 1995, 86.

[33]47 CFR sect. 76.31(a)(4) (1972).

[34]Clarification of the Cable Television Rules, 46 FCC 2d 175 (1974).

[35]Report and Order, 57 FCC 2d 625 (1975).

[36]Report and Order, 60 FCC 2d 762, 682 (1976).

[37]Community Cable TV, Inc., 95 FCC 2d 1204 (1983).

[38]The FCC's position was largely upheld by the courts in *American Civil Liberties Union v. FCC*, 823 F.2d 1554 (D.C. Cir 1987).

[39]This "benchmark" figure was based on rates from systems that faced effective competition.

[40]Technically all tiers remained regulated, but the FCC offered assurances that it would not interfere with product and pricing decisions on "going forward" services.

[41]Defined as MSOs with more than $250 million in annual income.

[42]Will Workman, "Dissing New Product Tiers," *Cable World*, 27 November 1995, 60.

[43]While moving channels out of the existing regulated tiers was technically out of keeping with rules, the FCC permitted MPTs for some MSOs under the terms of the "social contract" pacts.

[44]"Marketing New Media," *Cable World*, 19 February 1996, insert.

[45]47 U.S.C. sect. 543(f).

[46]47 USC sect. 553.

[47]Jim McConville, "Showtime Steps Up Anti-Piracy Efforts," *Broadcasting & Cable*, 24 June 1996, 54.

[48]McConville, "Showtime Steps Up Anti-Piracy Efforts."

[49]George James, "Cable TV Company Goes after Pirates, in One Zap," *New York Times*, 25 April 1991, A-1.

[50]Cabletelevision Advertising Bureau, *Cable TV Facts*, 1996.

[51]*Television and Cable Factbook*, Services Volume (Washington, DC: Warren Publishing, 1996), I-80.

[52]*Marketer's Guide to Meda*, 52.

[53]Paul Kagan Associates, *Economics of Basic Cable Networks*, Carmel, CA, 1993.

[54]Jennifer Pendleton, "Brand Names," *Cable World*, 1 July 1996, 14.

[55]"Marketing New Media," *Cable World*, 11 December 1995, insert.

[56]Pendleton, "Brand Names."

[57]David Waterman and August Grant, "Cable Television as an Aftermarket," *Journal of Broadcasting & Electronic Media*, 35:2 (Spring 1991): 179–188, 183.

[58]Ibid.

[59]Rich Brown, "Turner Pays $1.2 Million for 'ER,'" *Broadcasting & Cable*, 5 February 1996, 44.

[60]Owen and Wildman, 29.

[61]Ibid., 30.

[62]Rich Brown "Original Cable Programming," *Broadcasting & Cable*, 19 February 1966, 32.

[63]Richard Latz, "With New Look, USA Skeds More Shows," *Multichannel News*, 29 April 1996, 31.

[64]Brown, "Original Cable Programming," 36.

[65]Cyndee Miller, "Thirty Minutes Just Fine for Some TV Advertisers," *Marketing News*, 16 January 1989, 7.

[66]Susan Tyler Eastman, *Broadcast/Cable Programming*, 4th ed. (Belmont, CA: Wadsworth, 1993).

[67]Alan Rubin, "Ritualized and Instrumental Uses of Television," *Journal of Communication*, 34:3 (1984): 67–77.

[68]Carrie Heeter and Bradley Greenberg, *Cable-Viewing* (Norwood, NJ: Ablex, 1988).

[69]Will Workman, "The New Network Scramble for Shelf A Space," *Cable World*, 25 November 1995, 142; see also, Eastman, 290.

[70]Ricard Katz, "Madison Avenue Picks Hot New Nets," *Multichannel News*, 11 April 1994, 12.

[71]Michael Katz, "New Networks Fight for Space," *Broadcasting & Cable*, 29 April 1996, 61.

[72]Jim McConville, "New Nets: Tough Act to Open," *Broadcasting & Cable*, 27 November 1995, 74.

[73]Harold Fisher, "Finanical News Network," in *The Cable Networks Handbook,* Robert Picard, ed. (Riverside, CA: Carpelan Publishing, 1993); and Larry Collins, "Mizlou's Fall," *Inside Media*, 23 January 1991, 1.

[74]Laurie Jason, *The Art of a Successful Niche Programming Service*, Master of Arts Thesis, College of Communications, The Pennsylvania State University, August 1996, 61.

7

Law and Regulation

As the foregoing chapters illustrate, cable and satellite television, as well as the telephone industry, have been subject to a long history of regulation. The paths these industries took in journeying toward their present configurations have been cut in large part by the forces of government policy. It is the efforts of regulators that kept telephone and cable apart for many years and the work of deregulation now that brings them together. This chapter is about the philosophies, laws, and agencies that constitute the regulatory environment of the electronic media.

While the world of law and policy addresses itself to all the networks and businesses previously examined, it is worth noting that it does so differentially. That is, different kinds of telecommunications forms have been subject to different levels and types of regulation. The legal control of satellites, for example, has been vested primarily in the federal government and in international regulatory bodies, given the transborder nature of satellite communication. Regulation of broadcasting, likewise, has been held largely in the hands of the federal government and is influenced by international agreements. Telephone industry service and structure are controlled at the federal level through the Federal Communications Commission and by the states through their public utility commissions, which exercise often vigorous oversight, especially in the area of rate regulation.

Cable television, finally, has been subject to federal, state, and local regulation. At the federal level, Congress, the FCC, and other agencies have all had a hand in directing cable's development. Some states have been inclined to exercise cable oversight, usually through various regulatory bodies such as public utility commissions and an occasional state cable board, others have not. State interest, moreover, has waxed and waned through the years. Through the franchising process, local authorities have applied often strict control on cable operations. As Chapter 2 demonstrates, those controls have included rate regulation, service obligations, and content control. Municipalities require, in the first instance, that cable operators acquire a franchise, or permit, in order to string wire, access rights of way, and generally operate their businesses within the jurisdiction. The term of the franchise is typically fifteen years, although it can vary.

Despite the franchise requirement and the keen interest of local authorities in monitoring cable activity, most of the regulatory, or deregulatory, activity in recent years has taken place at the federal level. The following outlines the contours of law and policy as they affect cable and satellite television, and related media. It includes an examination of the legislative framework that currently serves to guide policy in this area, looking especially at the Telecommunications Act of 1996. It considers the governing bodies that are the major actors in crafting, implementing, and interpreting that legislation, including Congress, the FCC, the courts, and administrative agencies such as the National Telecommunications and Information Administration (NTIA). The issue of cable television's First Amendment standing and the role of freedom of expression in multichannel TV will be reviewed. And the structure and philosophy of international telecommunications policy, especially insofar as it affects satellite regulation, will be considered.

CONGRESS AND THE LEGISLATIVE FRAMEWORK

The Commerce Clause of the United States Constitution, Article I, Section 8, empowers the Congress to legislate on matters affecting interstate and foreign commerce. This provision affords Congress exclusive and preemptive power over commercial matters that impact more than one state or involve relations with other nations. Congress has ceded day-to-day regulatory authority to the Federal Communications Commission through the powers established in the Communications Act of 1934, as amended by the Telecommunications Act of 1996 and the Communications Satellite Act of 1962. However, Congressional committees with a budgetary or oversight role keep close track of FCC actions.

The power of the purse and the ability to convene oversight hearings on any topic confer substantial power to Congress. This means that legislators can stimulate regulatory activity and influence the decision making process through the questions posed in a hearing, via correspondence with the FCC, and by "unofficial" telephone calls. Congress cannot operate outside laws it created requiring government to operate "in the sunshine," that is, in public forums that allow all interested parties to observe, participate, and know the positions of other parties. Similarly, it cannot engage in "ex parte communications," or advocacy on matters before the FCC, but outside the conventional process in which all parties know of the communication and have an opportunity to comment on it. Nevertheless, the Congress has broad powers to affect the FCC decision making process, both officially and informally.

Primary Telecommunications Legislation

The Communications Act of 1934,[1] as substantially amended by the Telecommunications Act of 1996 and the Communications Satellite Act of 1962,[2] provide the basis for the structure and broad policies in telecommunications. The Communications Act created the FCC to serve as an expert regulatory agency with a mission to serve the public interest, promote the widespread use and availability of radio, and ensure that the enterprises it regulates likewise operate in the public interest. In telecommunications, the Communications Act initially contemplated service provided by common carriers, who operate as public utilities providing nondiscriminatory service on tariffed terms and conditions subject to FCC review. The Commission recently expanded the permissible range of regulatory classifications to include common carriers largely freed of regulatory burdens, following a philosophy that views marketplace conditions as favoring robust competition without domination by a single carrier. The Commission also uses a hybrid classification for service providers, including the local exchange telephone companies that own and operate telephone and cable television distribution channels, provided they lease a portion of the available capacity to competitors.

The Communications Satellite Act extends the common carrier model to satellite service,[3] and goes further by specifying that one carrier shall serve as the U.S. participant in the International Telecommunications Satellite Organization (INTELSAT) global cooperative. The Satellite Act affects the market composition in international telecommunications by creating a three-tiered satellite services marketplace: Comsat Corporation, as exclusive vendor of INTELSAT capacity, a handful of international carriers authorized by the FCC to deal with Comsat directly and other service providers, resellers, and users. Other satellite carriers have the option of leasing transponders, free of common carrier requirements.

The Telecommunications Act of 1996

Throughout the 1980s and into the middle 1990s Congress considered bills that would substantially revise the Communications Act of 1934. Until 1996 the law remarkably had not undergone substantial revision, despite massive changes in technology—including the onset of television, satellites, fiber optics, and digitization—and public policy, such as the migration from Roosevelt's New Deal to a market-oriented philosophy. While most legislators could agree that changed circumstances warranted a rewrite of the legislation, the lawmakers could not reach a suitable compromise. After generating thousands of pages, hundreds of hours of testimony and floor debate, and dozens of bills, The Telecommunications Act of 1996 was signed into law on February 8, 1996.

Objectives of Recent Bills and the Final Legislation

Until the broad-sweeping Telecommunications Act of 1996, throughout the late 1980s and early 1990s, Congress considered two types of bills:

1. Those designed to remedy a specific problem or related set of problems (such as the "Antitrust and Communications Reform Act of 1994" that proposed to supersede the MFJ and amend the Communications Act of 1934 to regulate the manufacturing of telecommunications equipment by the Bell Operating Companies);[4]
2. Broadsweeping bills designed to craft a complete overhaul of the Communications Act with the goals generally of promoting competition and reducing regulation in order to secure lower prices and higher quality services for American telecommunications consumers and encouraging the rapid deployment of new telecommunications technologies.[5]

The bills never came to fruition, primarily because affected groups, with comparable political clout, worked to stall progress or to add specific provisions they deemed essential. Until 1995 few in Congress considered the political value in tackling free speech and other Constitutional questions arising from efforts to restrict access by minors, and the public in general, to obscene or indecent programming over broadcast, cable television, and Internet sources. Only after several years of false starts, direct involvement by the President and Vice President and finely calibrated compromises was it possible for a single bill to reach the President for signature.

The Telecommunications Act of 1996 responds to the view that technological innovation and market entry can achieve the same public benefits that lawmakers previously thought available only through vigorous government oversight. Put another way, the legislation requires light-handed government involvement in lieu of heavy-handed "command and control" regulation. Rather than regulate the terms and conditions by which companies can enter and serve markets, the legislation relies on facilities-based competition among numerous carriers. This means that Congress eliminated virtually all "cross-ownership" restrictions that, for example, previously had prohibited telephone companies from providing cable television service in the same geographical area where they provide telephone service (except in rural locales).

Having assumed that the telecommunications marketplace can support numerous operators in the same locality, the legislation requires all operators to interconnect facilities so that users can enjoy the benefits of competition even by operators who have no intention of building a network completely parallel to what an incumbent carrier has available. This means that cable television operators, retrofitting their systems to provide telephone service, can secure direct interconnection with the distribution grid of the local exchange telephone company.

Congress reached closure on legislation because enough legislators and interested parties concluded that a new approach, no matter how flawed by legislative compromise, provided a better foundation than continuing application of the Communications Act of 1934. While the 1934 Act contains language supporting flexible and evolutionary regulation, most involved parties believed it nevertheless limited the scope of permissible competition and mandated pervasive government oversight, in spite of the increasing popularity of self-regulation. For example, language in the 1934 Act required all common carriers to file tariffs, notwithstanding the view of the FCC, most carriers, and many user groups, that individually registered contracts would generate superior dividends for consumers. Additionally, many believed that court formulation and approval of Consent Decrees to settle telecommunications antitrust suits, such as the Modification of Final Judgment (MFJ) that resulted in AT&T's divestiture of its Bell Operating Companies in 1982,[6] stifled competition by barring, or conditioning, market entry. Because of the expected onset of facilities-based competition for delivery of cable television programming from telephone companies, Congress also felt compelled to eliminate most provisions of the 1992 Cable Consumer Protection Act that had imposed regulation on cable's basic services.

General Provisions in the Telecommunications Act of 1996

The Telecommunications Act of 1996 seeks to stimulate competition in telecommunications by reducing barriers to market entry imposed by the FCC, consent decrees, prior legislation, and language in the Communications Act of 1934. It promotes market entry by foreclosing the states from frustrating the purposes of the law, specifying what constitutes full and fair interconnection between carriers, creating new opportunities for public utilities to enter telecommunications markets, and by largely eliminating prohibitions on "cross-ownership." The law encourages market entry on the view that, with proper safeguards and an emphasis on mandating interconnection between networks, an incumbent cannot prevent market entrants from thriving even when newcomers must use some of the incumbent carrier's facilities to provide service.

The Telecommunications Act of 1996 makes it possible for:

- Telephone companies to provide cable television services, including the creation and distribution of video programming in the same geographical region where they provide telephone services, provided the telephone company faces "effective competition" from another facilities-based operator;
- Cable television companies to provide telephone services with some assurances that the incumbent local exchange carrier would have to provide full, fair, and cost-based access to its facilities needed by the cable television operator to provide telephone services;

- The Regional Bell Operating Companies to provide long-distance services between Local Access and Transport Areas (LATAs) and to manufacture equipment after having satisfied a fourteen-point checklist to ensure that they provide full and fair interconnection (in January 1997, Ameritech filed an application with the FCC for authority to provide long-distance services, the first RBOC to state that it had satisfied the fourteen requirements and the first to be rejected by the FCC);
- Broadcasters to acquire a larger number of stations within the same market and to achieve a greater penetration of the total national market.

Fostering a Level Playing Field.   Mindful that expanding market entry opportunities create the potential for anticompetitive practices, Congress sought to ensure the development of competitive markets primarily by articulating what constitutes full and fair interconnection between the once dominant local exchange carriers and market entrants, such as cable television companies and competitive access providers that typically first install fiber-optic wire facilities only within major business districts. The Telecommunications Act of 1996 also seeks to ensue that competition does not handicap rural residents, small businesses, and the long-standing goal of providing universal service. Similarly, the law seeks to provide development in the telecommunications infrastructure to create a more robust, broadband digital highway extending to rural areas and available to schools, libraries, and medical facilities.

Creating a Deregulatory Environment.   The Act seeks to reduce the scope of FCC regulation and to permit the Commission to forbear from regulating markets and operators when it determines that marketplace competition will provide adequate safeguards. Courts previously had overturned several FCC deregulatory initiatives on grounds that the Communications Act of 1934 required the Commission to maintain government oversight of carriers that must file tariffs and comply with other common carrier regulatory duties. The legislation made it easier for the FCC to replace regulation with marketplace forces.

Violent, Obscene, or Indecent Programming.   Title V of the Telecommunications Act of 1996 Act, commonly referred to as the Communications Decency Act of 1996 (CDA),[7] created a great deal of controversy by expanding the scope of restrictions on access to violent or adult-oriented programming via both multichannel television providers and computer-based services like the Internet and America On Line. Section 506 of the Act gives cable operators authority to refuse transmission of obscene or indecent programming on public access channels. Section 505 requires any multichannel operator, including cable and MMDS, to fully scramble both video and audio components of any sexually explicit adult service to prevent reception of the signals by nonsubscribers. FCC rules permit restricting the hours of such services to a "safe harbor" period of 10 p.m. to 6 a.m. to prevent viewing by children.

The CDA also made the transmission of "indecent" or "patently offensive" material to minors via computer and the Internet punishable by a $250,000 fine or two years in jail. The Third Circuit Court of Appeals overturned that portion of CDA shortly after its passage, as an impermissible infringement of First Amendment rights of adult viewers and content creators, in view of lesser restrictive options to safeguard children. The court held that speech carried via the Internet deserved the same kind of protection from government intrusion as applied to the print media. This means that government must articulate a compelling reason to restrict a type of speech and do so in the least restrictive manner. While safeguarding children from indecent materials can warrant government intervention and regulation, the court rejected as either overboard or infeasible the methods established in the CDA: an absolute bar on such content combined with an exemption from prosecution for "Good Samaritans" who make reasonable, but not completely successful, efforts to block such content. In 1997 the Supreme Court unanimously affirmed the lower court's decision striking down the law, giving strong First Amendment protection to speech on the Internet.

Implementation of a ratings system for violent and indecent content in TV programming, in conjunction with the so-called "V-chip," also was mandated by the Act and is discussed in the next chapter.

Cable Rate Regulation and "Effective Competition."   In view of the anticipated facilities-based competition generated by telephone company entry into cable television, the Act created a new "effective competition test" for assessing when the FCC must refrain from regulating basic service rates charged by cable television systems. The standard pegs deregulation to the availability of at least twelve channels of comparable video programming (at least one of which is a nonbroadcast service like CNN or ESPN). Service must be directly available to subscribers from a telephone company (or its affiliate), or from another multichannel video programming distributor in the cable operator's franchise area offering an "overlay," an additional cable television system, wireless cable, or an Open Video System based telephone company facility. The availability of Direct Broadcast Satellite service does not satisfy this standard.

On satisfying the effective competition test, a cable television operator no longer has to charge uniform rates for service tiers and packages, or for à la carte or single channel services in a particular geographic area. Likewise, the exemption applies to bulk discounts for multiple dwelling units, provided the rate charges do not constitute predatory pricing. If a competitor presents evidence that one could reasonably conclude that the discounted rate is predatory (i.e., lower than other rates for similar service and designed to drive out competing systems, after which rates would rise), the cable operator will have to bear the burden of proving the contrary.

Subscriber rates for programming services tiers and basic tier rates of small cable operators who offered only a single tier of service as of December 31, 1994, are deregulated in any franchise area in which the operator serves fewer than 50,000 subscribers. A "small cable operator" is defined as a cable operator who, directly or through an affiliate, serves in the aggregate fewer than 1 percent of all subscribers in the United States and is not affiliated with any entity or entities whose gross annual revenues exceed $250 million.

Cable operators may use any reasonable written means to notify subscribers of rate and service changes. Prior notice is no longer required for rate changes resulting from a regulatory fee, franchise fee, or any other fee, tax, assessment, or charge of any kind imposed by any federal, state, or franchising authority on the transaction between the operator and the subscriber.

The Act eliminates the requirement that the FCC respond to and investigate complaints from individual subscribers about rates charged by cable television operators. Only franchise authorities may file such complaints, after having received one or more subscriber complaints about a rate increase within ninety days of a rate increase. The FCC must respond to a franchise authority complaint within ninety days, unless the parties agree to an extension. The Act "sunsets" all remaining rate regulation of cable programming services tiers on March 31, 1999.

Equipment Compatibility.   States and franchise authorities no longer may regulate in the areas of technical standards, customer equipment, and transmission technologies. Cable television consumers will have the option of buying their own set-top converter and other program access devices in lieu of the cable operator's rental or sale rate.

Telephone Company Provision of Video Services.   The Act eliminates cross-ownership restrictions on telephone company provision of cable television in the same area where it provides telephone service. However, local exchange carriers (LECs) and their affiliates may not acquire more than a 10 percent financial interest or any management interest in a cable operator providing cable service within the LEC's telephone service area. Likewise, cable operators and their affiliates may not acquire more than a 10 percent financial interest or any management interest in any LEC providing telephone exchange service within the cable operator's franchise area. Except for rural areas, the Act bars joint programming or telecommunications service ventures between cable operators and LECs whose service areas coincide. However, the companies otherwise can partner, including the construction of facilities for the provision of such programming or services. Local Telephone Companies have three regulatory options:

1. When operating a wireless cable system (e.g., MMDS), the LEC must comply with regulations applicable to that category of service, but will not also have to satisfy cable television operator regulations;
2. When providing cable television services as a common carrier, the LEC must comply with all applicable conventional common carrier regulations;

3. A new Section 653 creates an "Open Video Systems" option with less regulatory burdens than common carriage, but without total freedom to own and operate the channels made available to consumers.

Limited State and Local Regulation.   While conventional cable television franchise authority remains, states and localities cannot require cable television operators to secure a franchise to provide telecommunication services, nor can such authorities prohibit or limit the provision of such services. Franchise authorities may not require cable operators to provide any telecommunications services or facilities, other than institutional networks, as a condition of the initial grant of a cable television service franchise, or for its renewal or transfer. Franchise fees will continue to apply to cable television services but they cannot extend to revenues generated from telecommunications services.

Continuing Controls

Despite the significant deregulatory effect of the 1996 Telecommunications Act, cable, satellites, and telephone companies are still subject to a wide variety of structural, behavior, and content controls. Many of those previously discussed in this text include: copyright, must carry and retransmission consent, customer service obligations, signal leakage, and access channels. In addition to the restriction on telco purchases of cable systems in their own region, under FCC rules a cable system may not be owned by a television broadcaster in the same community; and in 1992 the FCC relaxed a twenty-two-year ban on ownership of cable systems by broadcast networks. The Telecommunications Act of 1996 directed the FCC to review its ownership rules in these areas with an eye toward further reducing or eliminating the controls. Cable operators are required to abide by Equal Employment Opportunity (EEO) guidelines and develop programs to recruit, maintain, and advance women and minorities.[8] The Children's Television Act of 1990 limited on commercial time on children's programming to 10.5 minutes per hour on weekends and 12 minutes per hour on weekdays. Operators also must maintain public records including franchise agreements, advertising logs, EEO records, and file annual reports with the FCC.

Social Contracts

In 1995, in order to settle a number of outstanding rate complaints against major MSOs, the FCC proposed "social contracts" with the operators. Under terms of the social contracts, the operators offered to cap rates, provide refunds to subscribers, invest in upgrades, and provide free hookups to schools. In exchange, proceedings on the rate complaints were dropped and some MSOs were allowed to adjust rates for inflation. Time Warner and Continental entered into such social contracts, other MSOs, including TCI, reached more limited settlements.

THE EXECUTIVE BRANCH

The President and Executive Branch agencies have powers created by the Constitutional separation of powers, such as foreign relations and operation of militaries. In addition, legislation can create additional Executive Branch responsibilities, including participation in shaping domestic and international telecommunications policy.

Executive Branch agencies have portfolios in trade policy, through the U.S. Trade Representative and Commerce Department, management of the federal government spectrum, through the Commerce Department's National Telecommunications and Information Administration, and telecommunication policy, through the Department of State and NTIA. While these agencies typically do not regulate, they can impact policy primarily through inter-agency coordination and by long-range planning. This frees them to consider issues in a larger context, and presents the opportunity, not always realized, to affect long-term policymaking and strategy.

The National Telecommunications and Information Administration

NTIA, an agency within the Department of Commerce, serves as the Executive Branch's principal voice in telecommunications policy.[9] The effectiveness of this agency depends in large part on the visibility and stature of its head, because it has no regulatory or licensing power. Likewise, NTIA only has a small staff involved in aspects of international policymaking.

Initially, NTIA constituted a department within the Office of the President. As the Office of Telecommunications Policy (OTP), it had a closer reporting line to the President, perhaps commensurate with the importance of telecommunications to the national economy. However, NTIA was spun off in 1978 to become an agency within the Commerce Department. In 1993, NTIA was threatened with a further downgrading in visibility and proximity to the President by a proposal to make it a part of the National Institute of Science and Technology, formerly known as the National Bureau of Standards.

NTIA participates in the policymaking process principally through advocacy in FCC proceedings, by studying issues like the National Information Infrastructure,[10] and by preparing thoughtful reports. Its statutorily conferred responsibilities address coordination and registration of the federal government's use of frequency spectrum,[11] including the identification of government used spectrum that can be transferred to private use as ordered by Congress[12] and participation in the oversight of Comsat's activities in INTELSAT and Inmarsat.[13]

Most of NTIA's responsibilities are shared with other agencies. The FCC has greater technical expertise and a larger staff. The State Department leads on foreign policy issues, and other trade offices in the Department of Commerce and the United States Trade Representative (USTR) hold more direct authority to formulate trade policy. Nevertheless, NTIA's studies and advocacy documents help shape the international telecommunications and trade policy agenda. Particularly in the trade area, staff technical expertise augments the more generalist USTR on telecommunications facilities, services, and equipment matters.

The Department of State

The State Department manages the foreign policy and international relations agenda of the United States. Substantive issues like telecommunications and aviation are subsumed within the Department's broad interpretation of its mission. In application this means that career Foreign Service Officers in the State Department will acquire a temporary portfolio in international telecommunications, and work with some civil servants dedicated to a career in telecommunication policy. Such a blend of general foreign relations and specific telecommunication policy skills sometimes does not result in the best product A 1993 reorganization within the State Department further diluted in-house expertise on the subject when the separate Bureau of International Communications and Information Policy (CIP) merged with the much larger Bureau of Economic and Social Affairs.

The goals of diplomacy and international comity with foreign nations can conflict with policy initiatives of other Executive Branch agencies. Depending on the personalities of the leaders at the FCC and NTIA, turf battles and spirited interagency debates can develop. Some critics allege that the State Department tends to emphasize "international comity" and cooperation over the nation's sometimes parochial concerns. Wisely or not, foreign policy concerns can dampen the tone and stridency of United States advocacy.

CIP attempts to coordinate international telecommunications and trade policy with all other involved agencies. It assembles the delegations that represent the United States at international forums like the International Telecommunication Union (ITU), often conferring the status of Ambassador to the delegation head. On matters involving INTELSAT and Inmarsat, it issues instructions to Comsat on what it should advocate and how it must vote on matters of national interest.

Despite perennial calls for better coordination between CIP, NTIA, and the FCC, the policymaking process can become disjointed. The potential for this is exacerbated by the fact that different Congressional agencies have oversight and budgetary responsibility for each agency. So far, proposals to unify the policymaking process and make it more coherent have failed to gain significant Congressional attention.[14]

THE FEDERAL COMMUNICATIONS COMMISSION

The Communications Act of 1934 authorizes the Federal Communications Commission to regulate interstate and foreign communications by wire and radio. The Commission's public interest mandate propels a regulatory portfolio into every aspect of telecommunications including the allocation of spectrum to specific uses, licensing operators to use the allocated spectrum, establishing policies and rules for various telecommunications services, including cable television, and adjudicating complaints filed by users and competitors.

The FCC operates as an independent regulatory agency, separate from the Executive Branch and the legislature. However, the President appoints the agency's five Commissioners (no more than three from one political party), subject to Senate consent. Terms are staggered to prevent a new President from appointing all new Commissioners. Congress votes operating funds and conducts regular oversight hearings to ensure that the agency accommodates the legislature's interest even in the absence of new laws.

FCC rules, regulations, and policies substantially affect the terms, conditions, and profitability under which telecommunications service providers operate. The Communications Act confers ample flexibility for the Commission to fashion new rules, regulations, and policies as the public interest so dictates. While subject to judicial review, the actions of this expert agency usually pass muster unless the Commission has violated procedural and fairness requirements.[15]

The Communications Act of 1934 authorizes the FCC to license facilities and service providers and to ensure that they operate in the public interest. The power to license and regulate also means that the FCC has ongoing responsibilities, under Title II of the Communications Act, to ensure that service providers do not operate in an unreasonable or discriminatory manner. Likewise, the Commission may require a licensee to operate as a common carrier,[16] thereby imposing a duty to hold itself indifferently to the public and to serve all who seek service, usually under a public contract known as a tariff.

FCC Practice and Procedure

Although courts defer to its expertise and Congress conferred substantial latitude in setting policy, the FCC cannot function with complete sovereignty. Because the legislature has the power of the purse and regularly conducts "oversight" hearings, it can "regulate by lifted eyebrow," and the FCC management is keenly attentive to the "will of Congress."

Procedurally the FCC must comply with the Administrative Procedure Act and other laws, like the Government in the Sunshine Act. These laws require the Commission to solicit input from interested parties, engage in open and reasoned decision making, and establish a factual record before promulgating rules and regulations. Typically this means that the FCC will initiate a Notice of Inquiry or Notice of Proposed Rulemaking that will serve as a forum for the Commission to articulate its initial view on how to proceed, pose questions, and seek comments from interested parties.

While the Commission cannot "make up its mind" before considering the views of the public, courts defer to the expertise resident in the agency. Unless a litigant can demonstrate to an appellate court that the FCC engaged in irrational decision making and ignored clear evidence supporting a contrary outcome, courts usually affirm the Commission's decisions. When courts reverse the FCC—as happens perhaps more frequently than for other agencies—the Commission typically failed to comply with procedural requirements, or reached a decision that the court considered "arbitrary, capricious or an abuse of agency discretion."

The FCC also must confer procedural and substantive due process to applicants for licenses and other types of regulatory authorization. Because more applicants typically file for licenses than the spectrum can accommodate, the Commission must conduct some type of administrative hearing to select licensees. The Commission initially determines whether applicants are legally, technically, and financially qualified to operate on a particular frequency, or to provide a specific service. This preliminary evaluation ensures that the applicant can legally operate in the United States, e.g., that the foreign ownership composition of the applicant does not exceed a permissible percentage, typically no more than 20 to 25 percent. The Commission also will make an initial determination whether the applicant has adequate resources to operate the service, both in terms of access to capital to construct, launch, and operate the service without any revenues accruing for at least a year, and in terms of whether the applicant's proposal is technically sound and that the applicant has sufficient technical resources to provide the service. After pre-qualifying the applicants, the FCC will issue licenses on the basis of a lottery, auction, or comparative hearing.

The FCC also has responsibility to ensure that equipment does not cause personal or technical harm, whether the devices use spectrum or physically attach to telecommunications networks like telephone handsets. Most devices are registered with the FCC after the manufacturer has tested them and has certified that they meet minimum technical standards. The FCC also has a program, in Part 15 of its Rules and Regulations, governing the use of equipment for unlicensed services that range from garage door openers to vehicle radars.

The Old World Order

Until about the late 1970s, the FCC engaged in "command and control" regulation. The Commission pervasively monitored and reacted to the practices of broadcasters, cable television companies, telephone companies, and other operators. The Commission used its mandate to "serve the public interest, convenience, and necessity" as justification for regulating the content of what broadcasters aired and the terms, conditions, and prices of telecommunication services. The FCC determined who would provide services and imposed a kind of "taxation by regulation" in the public service requirements and profit reducing policies it established.

Old World Order regulation of telecommunication service providers paralleled the nature and scope of public utility regulation. The FCC prohibited or limited market entry on grounds that only a single service provider, or a small set of carriers, could achieve optimal economies of scale and have the financial resources to provide nonremunerative services, that is, deliberately underpriced services.

The Old World Order maintained an implicit quid pro quo: The regulatory agency would confer a monopoly or substantial insulation from competition in exchange for the commitment by the licensed carrier to provide service to any financially qualified customer in the carrier's certificated service area. The carrier typically also had to agree to average costs among heavy and lightly traveled routes, which means that certain types of service received internal cross-subsidies.

In the Old World Order, the FCC used its expertise and mandate to serve the "public interest" as the basis for often intrusive regulation. The Commission did not use much economic analysis and if it had, the driving philosophy would have been the concept of market failure, such that the Commission would have to intercede to ensure that carriers operated in ways to achieve public interest objectives.

As noted in Chapter 2, cable television operators largely suffered under this regime. Aside from the period between 1984 and 1992, when the effect of the 1984 Cable Act was to reduce cable's regulatory burden, the FCC assumed the need to exercise substantial oversight in cable TV. Extensive government control stemmed from the view that despite its use of a closed circuit, coaxial cable medium, cable television had the potential to affect broadcast television adversely.

The New World Order

From the late 1970s and with increasing velocity, the FCC has abandoned heavy-handed regulation and seeks to lightly regulate as a referee of sorts. The Commission justifies its deregulatory initiatives on grounds that the marketplace can better regulate. The Commission views technological innovations, more choices for users, and heightened competition among the more plentiful operators as a better solution than having a government agency determine what would serve the public interest.

The FCC has migrated from a view that common carriers provide telecommunications services as public utilities, and often as exclusive "natural monopolies." The Commission now regards most telecommunications markets as contestable, that is, as ripe for market entry and competition, or as fully competitive already. In either case, the FCC now is inclined to refrain from determining who can enter and serve a particular market. Consistent with the tenor of the Telecommunications Act of 1996, the Commission and state public utility commissions cannot inhibit market entry on grounds that the public would benefit more by a monopoly, or by foreclosing certain types of enterprises from operating in two adjacent markets.

The scope and tenor of telecommunication regulation tracks the manner and pace of airline deregulation. While the FCC will not likely shut down, as was the case with the Civil Aviation Board, the nature of its mission and the scope of its regulatory oversight has changed substantially. The FCC will continue to allocate spectrum, but for some frequency bands it has resorted to market-driven assignments by auction rather than use an administrative process to determine who would best serve the public interest. The FCC no longer will determine whether telecommunications carriers have fairly priced services and whether they have accrued only a just and reasonable rate of return. Instead, the Commission will rely on carrier competition and the marketplace to relieve it of reviewing tariffs and imposing a cap on prices.

Despite a substantial trend toward deregulation, neither the Telecommunications Act of 1996 nor previous FCC policies point to "unregulation." The FCC will remain as a referee to ensure a "level competitive playing field," and to act more quickly than an antitrust court could. Extremely high financial stakes create incentives for companies to seek competitive advantages, including ones that violate the antitrust laws and the Communications Act. Because legislation cannot anticipate every strategy to create an unfair competitive edge, the FCC must remain vigilant and available to respond and resolve complaints.

The Telecommunications Act of 1996 created the need for the FCC to initiate over eighty regulatory and implementation proceedings. The rules promulgated by these proceedings and the potentially collusive and anticompetitive behavior of enterprises involved in telecommunications and information processing necessitate ongoing regulatory involvement.

THE JUDICIARY

Courts interpret, rather than make law. Their primary role in telecommunication policy and regulation is to resolve disputes by assessing whether the FCC has acted in compliance with applicable laws. In particular, courts determine whether the FCC has complied with the terms of the Communications Act, the Satellite Act and the Administrative Procedure Act (APA),[17] and the First Amendment. The substantive laws affecting telecommunications establish the FCC's powers and mission with broad and flexible terms to account for changed circumstances and technological innovation. The APA establishes procedural standards that agencies like the FCC must satisfy to ensure that the public has a full and fair opportunity to participate in the decision making process and that the agencies reach reasoned decisions based on the record of evidence and findings generated. The FCC cannot act arbitrarily or capriciously. It cannot abuse the discretion conferred on it by Congress, nor can it otherwise act outside the scope of authority vested with it by law.

CABLE TELEVISION AND THE FIRST AMENDMENT

The First Amendment prohibits Congress from enacting laws that abridge the right to freedom of speech or of the press, and that protection is extended to the states through the due process clause of the fourteenth amendment. Although some Supreme Court Justices have declared that "no law means no law," a majority of the Court has consistently ruled that the protection is not absolute. It does not, for example, extend to speech that might endanger the national security, it does not prevent government from placing limits on when or where someone might exercise their free speech rights, and it does not protect material held to be obscene within the legal definition of the term.

More importantly for present purposes, the Supreme Court has held that the First Amendment provides different levels of protection for different forms of media. Pure speech and print traditionally have been ceded the highest level of First Amendment protection against government interference. Electronic media, including all the forms dealt with here, have lesser levels of constitutional protection. Moreover, while there is a well established body of philosophy and a concomitant line of court cases, or judicial precedent, that has acreted around speech and print, the constitutional standard for much of the electronic media remains an open question. Like the technology itself, the law is still evolving.

Traditional broadcasting, as the oldest form of electronic mass media (despite the transient flirtation with telephone "broadcasting"), has the most fully articulated schema of First Amendment protection. Unlike print, broadcasters are subject to a host of governmental rules and regulations. Broadcasters, in the first instance, must obtain a government license in order to communicate. There are restrictions on who may operate a radio or television station and how many properties one can own.[18] There are controls on the operation of the business, and reporting requirements to government. While the FCC is formally prohibited from censoring program content, there are, nonetheless, restrictions on obscene and indecent speech and requirements to provide broadcast time for candidates for political office. Such regulation would, in most cases, be clearly unconstitutional if applied to newspapers or magazines. The justification for broadcasting regulation in the face of the First Amendment stems in part from the broadcasters' use of the airwaves. The spectrum has been held by the courts to be a scarce natural resource unavailable to everyone who wishes to use it. Further, the airwaves belong to the people, with the government as their surrogate. This "scarcity doctrine"—the idea that the airwaves are a scarce public resource and broadcasters are public trustees—is the constitutional underpinning of broadcast regulation, including the Communications Act of 1934.[19] In addition, broadcast regulation has been justified on the grounds of broadcasting's ubiquity and social impact, especially insofar as it involves children.[20] In this sense, broadcasters have been restricted in programming material that is not legally obscene but is nonetheless sexually explicit or legally indecent.

Broadcasters argue that in this age of multichannel television the scarcity rationale should be abandoned, and they should be afforded First Amendment rights equal to those of the print media. While still controversial, therefore, the structure of broadcast regulation at least has some constitutional stability. The same cannot be said for the more recent forms of electronic mass media.

Cable television has a longer judicial track record than does DBS or MMDS, but its First Amendment position remains far from settled. The constitutional evolution of cable TV has gone through several distinct phases. In cases involving cable and the First Amendment in the 1960s and 1970s, the medium was generally perceived as something other than a First Amendment speaker and constitutional rights were not typically an issue. In part, this was a conscious strategy on the part of the industry related to its political posturing on the copyright issue. If cable were held out as an active participant in the communication process rightfully deserving of constitutional protection, it could also be held liable for reperformance of protected broadcast signals in violation of copyright laws. The positioning of cable as a passive extension of the viewer's antenna insulated it from copyright accountability but also prevented active pursuance of First Amendment standing.[21] The success of the strategy is reflected, for example, in the Supreme Court's early examination of cable TV in *Fortnightly* in which it accepted cable's logic as a mechanism that simply facilitated better reception of the broadcast signal. The consequence, however, was that the FCC and the Court, as it did in *Southwestern*, could assign to cable a role as an adjunct to the national broadcasting system.

As cable started to provide services beyond those of simple broadcast retransmission and it secured its copyright protection, it began efforts to flex First Amendment muscle. The next phase in cable's First Amendment development began the mid 1970s, when, for example, the appeals court in *HBO* recognized a constitutional theme in cable distribution of programming.[22] There was a dawning realization that the scarcity doctrine, which had inappropriately been applied in some earlier cable cases, could not logically be invoked with the multichannel system. Other rationales for the restriction of cable First Amendment rights including the medium's use of city streets and thoroughfares to string cable were also becoming suspect as justifications for control of cable TV content and structure. The courts, however, remained divided. Some, as in *FCC v. Midwest Video Corp.*, which struck down FCC access requirements, granted cable a strong First Amendment status.[23] Other courts, however, determined that insofar as cable typically was a monopoly system in its market, there was an economic scarcity that mirrored the technical scarcity in broadcasting and provided the foundation for government control.[24] There was controversy over this. Some questioned whether cable truly was a local monopoly (see Chapter 5) and critics also noted that the Supreme Court had explicitly rejected economic monopoly as a rationale for the diminution of First Amendment protection as it applied to the newspaper industry in *Miami Herald v. Tornillo* in 1974.[25]

The Supreme Court had an opportunity to resolve these difference in 1985 when it heard a case involving a Los Angeles cable franchise. The cable operator in question, Preferred Communications, argued that the franchising process itself and the variety of requirements that typically appended to a franchise agreement were an unconstitutional restraint on its freedom of expression, it constituted licensing by the government in clear violation of the First Amendment. The High Court, for the first time, acknowledged that cable did have some level of constitutional protection.[26] It failed, however, to set an unambiguous standard for that protection. It could have held that cable, like print, deserved strict scrutiny of any attempt by government to interfere in its expression. The high level of the strict scrutiny standard offers substantial protection to the speaker. Instead, the Court chose an intermediate level of scrutiny based on a 1960s First Amendment case, *United States v. O'Brien*.[27] Under *O'Brien*, government controls that are held to be structural, or content neutral, are permissible if they further an important governmental interest and are tailored to be no more intrusive than is necessary to meet that interest. (Controls that clearly are based on the content of the speech, such as those that favor one form of ideology over another, must meet the greater burden of the strict scrutiny test, requiring a compelling government interest.) The problem with *O'Brien* is its malleability and uncertainty in application. It is subject to wide-ranging interpretation. Following *Preferred,* courts across the country heard cable television cases on issues ranging from the constitutionality of franchising to mandated access channels, and each applied the *O'Brien* test. Some jurisdictions held for cable and some against, depending on how they interpreted and applied the *O'Brien* guidelines.[28]

One of the recent cable First Amendment cases offers a telling illustration. The 1992 Cable Consumer Protection and Competition Act's reinstatement of the must carry rules, as previously noted (see Chapter 2), prompted an immediate First Amendment challenge from the cable industry. Twice before the appeals court had struck down the FCC's version of must carry, using the *O'Brien* test to find the Commission had not met the burden of proof necessary to overcome assumed First Amendment protection. In its 5 to 4 decision on the 1992 legislative version of must carry, the Supreme Court split on several issues including the foundational question of whether the must carry rules were, in the first instance, content neutral. In the first hearing of *Turner Broadcasting Co. v. FCC,*[29] Justice Kennedy writing for the court held that must carry was content neutral and subject to the intermediate level scrutiny of *O'Brien* (although again, the court sent the case back to the lower level for a deeper investigation of whether the standards of the *O'Brien* test had been met in this instance). In contrast, Justice O'Connor, writing in partial dissent, concluded that the must carry rules clearly privileged some forms of speech over others. Specifically favored were local broadcast programming, noncommercial educational broadcasting, and programming that promoted diversity. As worthwhile as the goals may have been, O'Connor found them insufficient to overcome the cable operators' First Amendment right to control their own editorial material. The rules, found O'Connor, were content based and called for application of a strict scrutiny standard of review. Justice Ginsburg also found the rules implicated content and called for a higher standard than *O'Brien.* On its next hearing, however, the Court finally upheld the must carry rules in a 5–4 decision that echoed the analytical differences of the prior review.

For at least a decade, since *Preferred,* cable television has been accorded some measure of First Amendment protection, but the nature and scope of that protection remains hazy. *O'Brien* is the nominal gauge for testing constitutionally suspect regulations, but it has provided little consistency in decision making.

Newer broadband providers ride even less settled First Amendment seas. Insofar as telephone companies have, until very recently, been legally classified as common carriers bound by law to hold out their services on a nondiscriminatory basis, First Amendment concerns have had little application. The telephone companies did not exercise editorial control over the system (for the most part) and were not considered First Amendment speakers. The desire by the Baby Bells to begin offering cable television service over their wireline systems muddied the waters. To prevent the Regional Bells from capturing and dominating the local video market, the 1984 Cable Act incorporated the long-standing FCC regulations prohibiting telephone companies form offering cable service in their market. In 1993 Bell Atlantic challenged this restriction as an unconstitutional infringement on its right to communicate over the network. The courts agreed, and in short order federal judges in jurisdictions across the United States had struck down the Cable Act prohibition as unconstitutional, helping pave the way for the telephone industry to enter the video market on its own terms.[30] In most cases, the courts called on the *O'Brien* test in reaching their decision, suggesting the constitutional benchmark for cable would become the standard for telco-delivered video as well. Adjudication in this area is, however, embryonic. It is not yet clear whether cable and the telephone companies will stand on the same First Amendment pedestal or how high the pedestal will be.

In broadcast broadband television, the picture is even less clear. With DBS operating for only a few short years and MMDS not much longer, there is little by way of court precedent. The fact that these services require open spectrum may argue for the application of traditional broadcast-based rationales. To the extent, however, that the scarcity rationale has been questioned in analog broadcasting, it becomes even more problematic in a digital world of hundreds of locally and nationally broadcast channels. The argument that economics creates a natural monopoly for the local distribution systems also looks tenuous in a situation in which consumers can receive digital video via the local cable system, the SDV telco operation, the area MMDS operator, or three or four DBS services. And while the Supreme Court has long noted that different standards for First Amendment protection may attach to different forms of media, the rule of *Tornillo*—that economic monopoly is no cause to override First Amendment protection—remains in the shadow of the debate.

The status of the First Amendment in the coming information age, therefore, remains one of the important unresolved issues.

SPECTRUM MANAGEMENT BASICS

Another pressing and controversial issue in telecommunications regulation is the control of the spectrum itself. As noted in Chapter 3, Congress authorized the FCC to manage non-government spectrum use. The efficient management of spectrum constitutes an essential element for effective use of a nation's telecommunications infrastructure.[31] The FCC realizes that spectrum has substantial, if unrealized value,[32] particularly when demand far exceeds the amount of bandwidth allocated.[33] Recently the Commission conducted a number of high visibility auctions that collectively generated over $20 billion for the U.S. Treasury. However, the FCC has yet to consider all spectrum as akin to real estate, and even for the slivers of quite highly valued auctioned spectrum, the Commission had previously determined the type of services for which the spectrum could be used.

Nevertheless the move to auctions for such services as Personal Communication Services (PCS) and for some satellite-delivered television to households, mobile radio, interactive video, and multipoint video distribution services signals a new trend. Simply put, the FCC has acted on the incentive to extract money from spectrum users, to fund the agency and to lower the national debt. Heretofore, the Commission has refrained from auctioning most types of spectrum, and it appears that if a public interest case can be stated for maintaining prior licensing procedures, i.e., the payment of a filing fee, but no auction competition, the Commission will continue to refrain from pursuing auction revenues.[34]

Background

Technological innovations have enabled productive use of progressively higher frequencies and the ability to derive usable channels with less bandwidth. But along with innovations, which conserve spectrum and provide more capacity, are new ideas and services that generate additional spectrum requirements.

Because of increasing demand for spectrum and the costs incurred by incumbents or newcomers to conserve it, international and national agencies must conserve and manage spectrum. This endeavor involves allocating spectrum among competing uses, and serving as a traffic cop of the airwaves to avoid interference and to resolve conflicts. Spectrum managers need to fashion compromises based on a number of factors including:

- **Technology**—the duty to prevent harmful interference and to achieve efficient activation of channels. As Chapter 2 noted, in allocating spectrum for broadcast television in the VHF band, the FCC had to create large geographical spacing between stations to prevent interference. This limited the number of available stations in any locality thereby generating demand for an additional allocation in the UHF band.
- **Regulatory policy**—regulation may direct spectrum allocations in ways designed to serve public policies. For example, the FCC sought to promote the doctrine of localism by allotting broadcast channels for as many different localities as technologically possible.
- **Commerce**—the need to conduct a comparison of spectrum requirements by services with an eye toward allocating spectrum to uses that will maximize social welfare primarily, and individual profitability of firms secondarily. For example, the FCC reallocated portions of the UHF television band for mobile radio services when it determined that most localities could not support a full inventory of UHF television stations, but desperately needed additional spectrum for public safety and private wireless services.
- **Social welfare**—the public interest merit in allocating spectrum for a particular service in the face of other requirements that accordingly have to make do with less, different, or possibly no spectrum. For example, in allocating spectrum for new wireless mobile services like personal communications networks, the FCC forced existing microwave users like railroads and public utilities first to share the spectrum and subsequently to move to higher, less congested frequencies.

- **National security**—compelling requirements for safety, public welfare, national defense, and emergency applications. For example, the ITU has allocated particular emergency calling frequencies that always are monitored.

Spectrum allocation decision making blends engineering with social science to provide the basis for making cost–benefit analyses. Policymakers need to determine who deserves spectrum allocations and what entitlements accrue to incumbent users. Managers must devise procedures for assessing new spectrum requirements and determining how to accommodate incumbent users and operators.

Currently, most nations generally allocate spectrum on the basis of consensus decisions reached at global or regional conferences convened under the auspices of the ITU. In the United States, the Federal Communications Commission uses the public interest as the basis for determining whether to implement ITU decisions by incorporating changes in the national table of spectrum allocations.[35] The FCC typically uses the public interest standard also to assign spectrum, but in 1993 it received Congressional authority[36] to auction portions of the spectrum (see below). The Commission also imposes user and licensing fees to compensate it for processing applications, granting licenses, and for the cost of regulation. Demand typically will exceed supply without a market mechanism[37] for clearing out spectrum inventory to the highest bidder.[38]

Spectrum Management in the United States

In the United States, the Communications Act of 1934[39] authorizes the FCC to regulate the nongovernmental use of radio spectrum, while the National Telecommunications and Information Administration holds delegated authority to administer the federal government's allocations.[40] Much of the frequency spectrum is shared on a coordinated basis by both federal and nonfederal users.

Spectrum management in the United States largely has been reactive.[41] Because adequate unused spectrum was available, managers could respond to new requirements, rather than plan for them. Growing commercial and governmental requirements and the proliferation of technological innovations that use spectrum require proactive planning.[42]

Private Spectrum Management

The FCC manages nongovernmental spectrum use in three fundamental ways:

1. *Allocating* blocks of spectrum that have propagational characteristics suitable for a particular class of user with specific service requirements;
2. *Allotting* channels for use in particular localities;
3. *Assigning* licenses to use spectrum subject to conditions and procedures to achieve fair, efficient, and noninterfering use, including the evaluation of applications from more than one party seeking a single license.[43]

Until the authorization for limited auctions in 1993, the Communications Act prohibited private ownership of spectrum.[44] The Act obligated the Commission to serve the public interest, convenience, and necessity in such broad matters as spectrum allocation as well as specific classifications of radio stations and prescribing the nature of service to be provided by such stations.[45]

The Commission's overall spectrum management mission remains to allocate, assign, license, and regulate "so as to make . . . a rapid, efficient, Nation-wide, and world-wide wire and radio communication service with adequate facilities at reasonable charges, for the purpose of the national defense, [and] for the purpose of promoting safety of life and property."[46]

This process remains one largely within the discretion of the FCC as tempered by procedural fairness requirements imposed by the Administrative Procedure Act,[47] international spectrum allocational efforts and the actual scarcity that occurs when consumer and government demand for spectrum exceed supply.

The Commission typically uses a rulemaking process to allocate spectrum or modify an allocation. In application the rulemaking process affords interested parties, including proponents of differing uses for a particular frequency band, a forum to articulate the public interest merits of a particular use.

Once it allocates spectrum, the Commission typically assigns frequencies on a first come, first served basis to individual licensees, with some rules on sharing, spacing of transmitters, and proof of adequate channel loading before assigning additional spectrum. However, in the event more applicants file for licenses than can be assigned, which regularly occurs in broadcasting and cellular radio, the FCC conducts a comparative hearing, lottery, or other proceeding to determine who shall receive an assignment.

In recent years the Commission has considered liberalizing its rules for some frequencies to permit use by more kinds of licensees.[48] The Commission also has expanded the type of services certain licensees can provide.[49] Additionally, the Commission reallocated spectrum for such new services as low earth orbiting (LEO) satellite-delivered mobile telephone service, position indicating and low speed data services from small LEO satellites,[50] digital audio broadcasting,[51] high definition television,[52] and personal communication networks.[53] The Commission conditions its assignments on periodic review and license renewal, and subject to technical regulations and standards, e.g., type of signal emission, signal strength, and bandwidth. Most FCC allocations are made on a nationwide basis, although the Commission has granted narrow exceptions, e.g., shared use of UHF television channels for land mobile communications in selected metropolitan areas. While the Commission's spectrum allocations process may reserve additional bandwidth to satisfy future demand, it generally does not consider possible future or alternative uses for the spectrum. When the Commission does reallocate spectrum from one service to another, it makes a judgment that existing or prospective demand and the public interest warrant the reallocation.

Government Spectrum Management

NTIA's spectrum management objective lies in guiding federal radio users and ensuring that the federal agencies "make effective, efficient, and prudent use of the radio spectrum in the best interest of the Nation, with care to conserve it for uses where other means of communication are not available or feasible."[54]

Both NTIA and the FCC must coordinate the spectrum management function, not only because of divided jurisdiction,[55] but also because much of the spectrum is allocated for shared private and government use.[56] The two agencies maintain separate databases of spectrum use authorizations. The FCC's database is comprised of its record of license grants. NTIA maintains the Government Master File, containing information on individual and group stations using government spectrum.

Governmental frequency assignment procedures are coordinated by an Interdepartmental Radio Advisory Committee (IRAC), convened under the auspices of NTIA and attended by representatives of most government agencies with significant spectrum requirements. IRAC's Frequency Assignment Subcommittee resolves spectrum differences between government agencies.

Block Allocations

ITU conferences and in turn, the FCC, allocate spectrum in blocks of frequency bandwidth earmarked for a particular service. This process often fails to consider the current and future spectrum needs of users, and to articulate the criteria used to determine the relative merits of one service versus others. The process places a premium on incumbency, and the acquisition of an allocation, that rarely have been eliminated. New services, technological innovations, or user constituencies with expanded spectrum requirements must vie for spectrum with incumbents. Faced with a growing population and diversification of services and devices that use radio spectrum, the FCC has the unenviable role of finding ways to accommodate every constituency. The Commission achieves this feat by forcing incumbents to share spectrum with newcomers on any frequency band where sharing is technologically feasible and will not generate unreasonable risks to life and property. It also forces incumbents and newcomers alike to use new, more efficient technologies, despite the cost, particularly for incumbents who must replace existing and fully functional equipment. Newcomers, however, typically must settle for shared spectrum allocations on an equal, "co-primary" basis, or on a subordinate, "secondary" or "tertiary" basis.

The block allocation process awards bandwidth at a particular point in time on the basis of the technologies, services, and user requirements effectively advocated. For example, satellite services have been divided as a function of transmitter and receiver location. There are separate allocations for maritime, land mobile, fixed, and aeronautical services. While there may have been a rationale for making such discrete service definitions and spectrum allocations, those justifications are unsustainable when users can easily move small terminals between fixed, mobile, land, water, and air locations.

Congressional Mandates to Transfer and Auction Spectrum

In 1993, both the President[57] and Congress[58] acted to make auctioning an alternative to freely allocated spectrum reality for a portion of the spectrum. Additionally, Congress codified a requirement for national spectrum allocation planning between the federal government's spectrum manager, the NTIA, and the private users' manager, the FCC.[59] NTIA was ordered to identify a minimum of 200 MHz of spectrum, half of which must be in band below three GHz, for reallocation from government to private use.[60]

As part of the Omnibus Budget Reconciliation Act of 1993,[61] Congress authorized the use of competitive bidding[62] for instances where: (1) the Commission has received mutually exclusive applications; and (2) the licensee is likely to receive compensation from subscribers. Rather than specify a particular type of auctioning method, the law requires the FCC to design and test multiple alternative methods appropriate to the class of license to be granted.[63] The law also requires the FCC to implement safeguards to ensure that new technologies are readily accessible by avoiding excess concentration of licenses and by disseminating licenses to a variety of applicants including small businesses, rural telephone companies, and businesses owned by minorities and women. A Supreme Court case subsequently invalidated preferential treatment of minorities and women.

Terrestrial Mobile Telecommunications

Much of the recent spectrum allocation and licensing activities involves terrestrial and satellite mobile telecommunications. The FCC has dedicated substantial, additional bandwidth to such services, because of the belief that "tetherless" communications will enhance productivity and efficiency while promoting safety and security.

Mobile services have so increased in importance at the FCC that a new Wireless Bureau was established as part of a major agency reorganization in 1995. The Commission had confronted a substantially greater demand for mobile radio spectrum in both commercial services like cellular radio and more specialized applications like public safety, such as police, fire, and other law enforcement services and industry-specific spectrum allocations like the Motor Carrier, Railroads, Taxicab and Automobile Emergency Radio Services.[64] Additionally, technological innovations have created new types of mobile radio services, e.g., dispatch taxis services that transmit messages and available fares via a silent terminal installed in individual vehicles. Innovations in satellite technology have also made it possible to provide essential navigational services, such as Global Positioning Service satellites. In a nutshell the following observations distill the nature of the FCC's role in mobile telecommunications:

- Increasing demand for mobile services has forced the FCC to consider ways to "refarm" spectrum by ordering incumbent users to reduce channel bandwidth through the use of modern, expensive, and more efficient technology, e.g., more selective and sensitive transceivers. Additionally, the FCC has ordered incumbents to share once exclusive spectrum allocations with newcomers, and in certain cases to relinquish spectrum and move to another frequency band so that providers of a new service can operate free of interference;
- The FCC and other stakeholders have recognized the key importance of global spectrum allocation and policymaking forums like the ITU in reaching consensus decisions that can favor or retard development of mobile satellite services with a direct and significant impact on employment, profitability and productivity;
- The FCC and other decision making bodies have come around to appreciating the potential for satellite-delivered mobile services to provide essential and profitable services, despite the multibillion-dollar cost of such ventures, the need to reallocate spectrum to accommodate such services, and the use of not yet commercialized technologies like nongeostationary orbits, inter-satellite links, and the deployment of satellite constellations comprising dozens of stations.

Satellite Spectrum.   The FCC's public interest assessment of Little LEO spectrum requirements concluded that up to 4 MHz of spectrum in the VHF/UHF bands should be made available. Low-cost data and position determination services can improve the efficiency of the oil exploration and transportation industries, enhance remote monitoring of weather and the environment, and provide a low-cost emergency and disaster recovery signaling system. The Commission concluded that Little LEOs could satisfy unmet service requirements and generate superior public benefits.

The FCC also granted a single license to the American Mobile Satellite Corporation, to provide geostationary orbiting satellite mobile services. The corporation is a consortium formed by most of the individual applicants. The Commission justified the grant of a single license to AMSC on the view that neither the available spectrum nor the market could support multiple licenses, and on grounds that it needed to act quickly to have a U.S. licensee available to negotiate spectrum sharing arrangements with Inmarsat.

PCS Spectrum.   In setting up the regulatory regime for PCS the FCC created three service categories:

1. Unlicensed low-powered operations that could provide voice and data services in closed, self-contained environments;
2. Narrowband applications for paging and slow speed data transmissions;
3. Wideband applications for voice and high speed data transmissions.

In seeking space for PCS in an already crowded spectrum, the Commission sought bandwidth that could be shared with existing and highly-used services with the possibility of relocating incumbent users. The Commission subsequently divided spectrum at around 2 GHz into six blocks to be auctioned to the highest bidder: three 30 MHz blocks, two of which are used throughout one of the 51 "Major Trading Areas," and one of which is licensed for use in one of 493 smaller "Basic Trading Areas." The Commission also created three 10 MHz blocks that were licensed for operation in one BTA.

In addition, the Commission allocated 20 MHz for use by low-powered, unlicensed PCS devices like Personal Digital Assistants, cordless telephones, and wireless PBXs,[65] and 3 MHz for narrowband PCS in the 900 MHz frequency band.

While the Commission refrained from creating nationwide PCS licenses and spectrum allocations, it allowed bidders to stitch together geographical areas and in effect create a winning nationwide bid. All bidders were limited to 40 MHz in any area.[66] The Commission treated cellular radio operators on the same basis as all other eligible applicants in areas where their cellular service area covers less than 10 percent of the population in the Market Trading Area or Basic Trading Area.

In 1995 and 1996, the FCC auctioned off the spectrum it had reallocated to PCS. The winning bids ranged from $1.3 billion for 30 MHz of wideband PCS spectrum in the New York Basic Trading Area, the largest in terms of prospective subscribers, to $100,000 for 30 MHz in American Samoa.[67]

In the reallocation, the FCC required the PCS newcomers to seek voluntary negotiations with incumbent operators to secure fair compensation for relocating to other frequencies or transmission media. The Commission provided for the involuntary relocation of an incumbent, provided that the PCS operators pay the cost of relocating the incumbent to a comparable facility.

INTERNATIONAL POLICY AND REGULATION

International Spectrum Allocation

Domestic spectrum management and policymaking cannot operate outside the context of a parallel and interdependent international process. The International Telecommunication Union, a specialized agency of the United Nations, serves as the international forum for establishing standards, harmonized frequency allocations, and common definitions of telecommunication services and regulations. Beginning with the onset of wireless telegraph service, spectrum management has constituted a key function of the ITU.[68] It convenes conferences to define services, allocate spectrum on a global or regional basis, and to promulgate binding regulations on frequency use. Nations typically implement the consensus decision reached at a conference, notwithstanding the sovereign right of domestic regulatory authorities to formulate their own rules and policies on spectrum issues.

Even if domestic regulatory action precedes the ITU process,[69] nations expect the ITU to establish an international, or at least a regional frequency allocation based on the consensus agreement of what frequencies best meet the requirements of particular services. The "Radio Regulations that result from ITU conferences have treaty status and provide the principal guidelines for world telecommunications operations."[70] In this way, other nations can make similar spectrum allocations and assignments, thereby coordinating spectrum usage and reducing the potential for harmful interference.

Conflict results when usage in particular nations exhausts the amount of spectrum allocated for a particular service, or when users find the operational rules unduly restrictive. For example, the ITU establishes a hierarchy of access rights whereby "secondary" service users are subordinate to both existing and future users of the "primary" service designated for the spectrum. Under this system, existing and prospective users of primary service have a superior right of access to the allocated spectrum. Existing or future secondary service users operate on a subordinate basis and must operate without causing interference.

In many instances, the spectrum allocation process involves a zero-sum situation. Spectrum is earmarked in blocks for specific services with an eye toward matching its technical characteristics with particular user requirements. Point-to-point microwave applications need extremely high frequencies (in the GigaHertz range) where radio waves are quite narrow and transmit in a line-of-sight pattern. Long-range broadcast applications need middle or high frequencies that are high enough to enable signals to bounce off the ionosphere. More numerous, geographically separated, local broadcasters can operate on the same frequencies at lower power, or at higher frequencies, as with FM radio band frequencies that typically do not skip off the ionosphere.

Matching technical characteristics of the spectrum with user requirements requires answers to the following questions:

1. What application(s) should occupy this frequency band? For any particular frequency band, certain uses appear best suited, but other commercial, social, or national security factors may prevail, particularly where more than one application can use a frequency band. Commercial interests supported allocation of Ultra High Frequency (UHF) channels to augment the number of television channels previously available in the Very High Frequency (VHF) band. But more compelling public safety and mobile communication requirements combined with incomplete use of the band by broadcasters have eroded the UHF band so that both the lower and upper portions are shared or have been reallocated.

2. Who should use this allocation and how should they be selected? The technical characteristics of the frequency band will target certain types of users for particular allocations. For example, militaries, telephone companies, and large, geographically dispersed corporations like railroads have requirements best

served by microwave allocations. National regulatory authorities have responsibility for assigning and licensing particular users.

3. How will the spectrum be used? The ITU Radio Regulations establish spectrum "rules of the road" that include specifications on what type of transmissions are permitted and what operators must do to avoid causing harmful interference.

4. Where can the spectrum be used? ITU conferences attempt to allocate spectrum on a global basis, but frequently allocations are limited to one of three regions (Europe and Russia, west of the Urals; North, Central, and South America, and Asia–Pacific). Nations may take a "Reservation" to any allocation, in effect refusing to go along with the consensus. Alternatively, they may request the ITU to attach a footnote to the allocation, contained in the ITU's Radio Regulations, specifying limitations to the consensus allocation, or a different allocation altogether.

The location of spectrum user is also important, because the first duly authorized, registered and operating user is entitled to continue operating interference-free when other operators subsequently seek to operate nearby. The propagational characteristics of the frequency band used will largely affect whether two nearby operators will incur harmful interference. Alternative uses for the frequency typically are permissible only on a restrictive, subordinate basis whereby the newcomer must not interfere with incumbents or future operators providing the service for which the band was allocated.

Incumbent users of spectrum are quite reluctant to relinquish spectrum or to agree that the spectrum can be shared with new services. However, technological innovations can make it possible for users to operate over less spectrum or to migrate to higher frequencies. For some, particularly users in developing nations, such technological innovations are too expensive, particularly where less efficient, but cheaper equipment recently has been installed. Users in developed countries are disinclined to change frequencies or share, based on the view that they should not have to incur additional expense merely to accommodate users in nearby developing nations.

The international spectrum allocation process primarily involves decisions on *how* spectrum will be used, and not *who* will use it. The process assumes that nations will register spectrum requirements on an a posteriori, "first-come, first served" basis, i.e., when and if they exist, or will soon develop. Developed countries typically will have a head start when it comes to actual spectrum use, because they will have the earliest requirements and the resources necessary to convert an allocation into a registered use.

Developing countries have voiced objections to the a posteriori system, and have proposed that the ITU allocate some spectrum and satellite orbital slots on an a priori basis, that is, that nations agree to a plan for allocating shared global resources in advance of actual requirements. While such a system might foster distributional equity, it could result in a glut of unused spectrum for developing countries and a scarcity for developed countries. The matter of equity versus efficiency in the spectrum allocation process, like that for satellite orbits, has on occasion generated a schism between developed and developing nations.

Spectrum management has become more controversial at both international and domestic levels, because of increasing demand for what is a finite resource by both incumbent users and proponents of new services. The ITU and domestic regulatory agencies must balance the duty to ensure that existing users do not experience harmful interference with the obligation to accommodate new spectrum requirements that will serve the goals of national interest and international comity.

WRC–95

The 1995 World Radio Communication Conference (WRC–95) followed up on many of the initial steps taken in 1992 to allocate new spectrum for satellite communication, particularly ones providing mobile telecommunication services operating at frequencies between 1 and 3 GHz.

While appearing quite technical WRCs are key forums that can make or break a business plan. Without adequate spectrum, a satellite venture cannot provide service no matter how attractive it might be. As virtually all spectrum has been allocated to one or more services, the proponent of a new service must persuade government officials that ample public dividends will outweigh the cost and inconvenience resulting from the need for incumbent users to share spectrum and perhaps even to vacate parts of a frequency band.

At WRC–97 the advocates for nongeostationary orbiting satellite-delivered Fixed Satellite Service had to convince nations of the need for large amounts of spectrum in addition to spectrum needed for FSS from geostationary orbiting satellites. As noted previously, both LEO and GSO ventures have announced plans for providing broadband services, including Internet access and compressed video from satellites operating in the Ka-Band. Both Teledesic and Hughes, along with their U.S. government advocates at WRC–95, needed to convince other nations that spectrum allocations would benefit the global interest and not simply the industrial interest of the United States or of individual companies. Such advocates confronted opposition perhaps based less on such global concerns, but on regional, industrial policy concerns that United States companies had a commanding lead in exploiting new technologies and frequencies. Some observers of WRC–95 and the preceding WRC–92 allege that European opposition to LEO ventures stemmed primarily from concerns that few European companies had any chance for profiting from the new services either by receiving a contract to manufacture components or to lead in the delivery of end-user services.

An international forum like the ITU primarily involves government delegates, but increasingly commercial concerns have stimulated private company involvement. United States based companies like Teledesic achieved success at WRC–95 by downplaying their citizenship and by not relying on official U.S. government advocacy. Global alliances also have helped make WRCs less an inter-governmental forum and more a blend of private and governmental advocates seeking a sufficiently large and geographically widespread constituency. A satellite venture that promises low-cost, state-of-the-art broadband access at little or no upfront investment can attract support from lesser developed countries.

The Great Parking Place Battle

All communication satellite operators licensed in nations that participate in the ITU need to comply with a lengthy and exhaustive registration process for the orbital slots from which their satellites operate. This process lacks any formal basis for assessing the credibility of the registrant in terms of its orbital slot needs and the likelihood of actually launching and operating a satellite. Likewise no mechanism exists for limiting applicants to a number of proposed registrations commensurate with actual or likely needs. Accordingly, just about every operator overstates its requirements and the ITU receives an onslaught of paper satellite filings now exceeding 1,000.

The ITU satellite registration process is based on the assumption that operators will file technical and operational data about prospective satellites well in advance of launch so that other existing or prospective operators can determine whether the satellite and its particular orbital occupancy will cause harmful interference. In theory the ITU has a straightforward and methodical process to administer: (1) receiving and "advance publishing" technical and operational parameters of new satellites; (2) overseeing the coordination of orbital slot occupancy so that harmful interference will not occur; (3) notifying all members of the ITU of a newly registered orbital use; (4) maintaining a master list of all orbital uses.

A satellite orbital registration process constitutes an essential component in what the ITU was structured to perform. While lacking enforcement powers, the ITU can lend its "good offices" to help manage a shared global resource. Presumably, ITU members would respect the process by complying with it and not abusing their registration privileges. Such respect largely did occur until the early and middle 1980s. Perhaps nations were slow to recognize the value of orbital parking places, or perhaps the current problem simply results when an increasingly large set of both governmental and private satellite operators seek to enter the marketplace.

The ITU registration process no longer works in a timely and definitive way. Without such processing, satellite operators face some degree of additional operational risk in that they have less certainty that once launched and operational a satellite can provide all of the services to all of the locations it was designed to offer. Such risk can translate directly into greater expense and lower profitability. Without successfully completed coordination, adjacent satellites operating in the same frequency band may interfere with each other, or may require the installation of larger, more selective earth stations. If interference can be abated only by turning off some transponders or reconfiguring footprints, assumptions made in business plans may prove overly optimistic. Such added risk may increase the cost of capital as the satellite operator may have to accept less favorable terms on loans, or it may have to offer a higher rate on its commercial paper and bonds.

The current registration process may take as long as two years before preliminary material filed with the ITU are examined and distributed to ITU members.[71] For the system to work on a timely basis, the ITU needed a "due diligence" mechanism to assess the bona fides of registrants and to determine their actual orbital slot requirements. Currently the ITU cannot disqualify a proposed registration based on the lack of progress in awarding a satellite construction contract and financial viability of the applicant. Some ITU member nations perceive the right of orbital slot registration as an exercise in national sovereignty. For example, the Kingdom of Tonga, a Pacific island nation of approximately 150,000 citizens attempted to register 31 satellites in 26 orbital slots. In 1995, The United Kingdom, on behalf of a Gibraltar-based subsidiary of General Electric, advance published 12 satellites. In the case of Tonga most observers objected to the proposed registration of satellites clearly not commensurate with the requirements of the nation. But in the case of Gibraltar, a foreign venture, perhaps with sufficient funds to invest in the construction and launch of 12 satellites, has chosen to rely on the sovereign registration rights of a country as a way to diversify beyond domestic or regional service. In both cases, the registration process becomes cluttered with clearly more satellites than the market could ever support, and the matter of sovereignty becomes nothing more than a "straw man."

The ITU may find its satellite and spectrum rules increasingly unsustainable. It makes no sense to allocate satellite spectrum on a service and geographically specific basis when the same transceiver can operate on in a fixed, mobile, land, maritime, and aeronautical environment. Likewise the ITU's priority based system vests incumbent services and operators of such services with such priority access to spectrum that newcomers will incur added delays, expense, and coordination burdens even for instances in which incumbents do not operate over the entire spectrum available and will not face interference.

The possibility exists for operators to resort to "self-help" if the ITU cannot resolve issues pertaining to orbital registration, spectrum allocation, and interference coordination. Already some carriers have launched satellites without completion of the orbital slot registration process. Some operators have incurred interference from adjacent satellites. Skeptics wonder whether the ITU can adjust its rules to accommodate LEO satellites. If nations will not rally under the banner of the ITU, then the nations of the world will lose the benefit of consensus rules or the road and visions of a GII become less feasible.

SUMMARY

The Telecommunications Act of 1996 was an attempt to address many of the long-standing and newly emerging issues in television and telecommuniations. Whether one agrees or disagrees with its guiding philosophy of market sovereignty or with its more controversial elements—such as the CDA—it can be recognized nonetheless as an attempt to adapt policy to the accelerating pace of technological and business change. At the same time, the law left many issues unresolved and new regulatory concerns seem to be created at every turn. As we have seen, the constitutionality of several existing statutes is in question, and the First Amendment status of the evolving infrastructure is still far from clear. Parties have contested and will continue to contest important sections of the Act. A host of issues will continue to press for legal attention, including telecommunication system access and universal service, control of program content, privacy, spectrum allocation, and intellectual property rights. Some of these issues are more fully explored in Chapter 9. All of them represent ongoing challenges to Congress, the courts, and the regulatory agencies, and likely are to be so for many years to come.

NOTES

[1]47 U.S.C. Secs. 151 et seq.

[2]47 U.S.C. Secs. 701 et seq.

[3]P. L. 104-104, 110 Stat. 56.

[4]HR 3626.

[5]See, e.g., S. 1822, the "Communications Act of 1994"; HR 3636, the "National Communications Competition and Information Infrastructure Act"; HR 1555, the "Communications Act of 1995"; and S 652, the "Telecommunications Competition and Deregulation Act of 1995."

[6]See *United States v. American Telephone and Telegraph Co.*, 552 F. Supp. 131 (D.D.C. 1982), aff'd sub nom. *Maryland v. United States*, 460 U.S. 1001 (1983).

[7]47 U.S.C. § 501 et seq. (1996).

[8]47 C.F.R. sect. 76.73.

[9]"The [Commerce] Department's telecommunications policy making functions are centered in the National Telecommunications and Information Administration (NTIA), which was created pursuant to Reorganization Plan No. 1 of 1977, with the responsibilities of the Secretary of Commerce under Executive Order 12046 [Fed. Reg. 13349-13357 (March 29, 1978)] delegated to it. *NTIA Telecom 2000: Charting the Course for a New Century*, Chapter 9, International and Domestic Policymaking in the Year 2000, 168, NTIA Spec. Pub. 88-21 (Washington, DC: Government Printing Office, Oct. 1988) [hereinafter cited as Telecom 2000].

[10]See, Information Infrastructure Tasks Force, Sec. Ronald H. Brown, Chairman, *National Information Infrastructure: Agenda for Action* (Washington, DC:Government Printing Office, September 15, 1993); *National Information Infrastructure: Progress Report September 1993–1994* (Washington, DC:Government Printing Office, September, 1994).

[11]Under Section 305 of the Communications Act of 1934, as amended, the President retains the authority to assign frequencies to all radio stations belonging to the federal government. The President has delegated authority to the Secretary of Commerce, who has in turn delegated it to NTIA. See Exec. Order No. 12046, as amended, 3 C.F.R. 158 (1978), reprinted in

47 U.S.C. Sec. 305 app. at 127 (1989); United States Dept. of Commerce, Dept. Organization Orders 10-10 and 25-7. The applicable Executive Order and an Office of Management and Budget Circular No. A-qq "provide NTIA with the power to assign frequencies and approve the spectrum needs for new systems." United States Dept. of Commerce, National Telecommunications and Information Administration, *U.S. Spectrum Management Policy: Agenda for the Future*, 20 NTIA Spec. Pub. 91-23 (Washington, DC: Government Printing Office, Feb. 1991).

[12]In 1993 Congress directed the Secretary of Commerce to identify at least 200 megahertz of spectrum currently allocated on a primary basis for Federal Government use that is not required for present or identifiable future use by the Federal Government, and that is most likely to have the greatest potential for productive uses and public benefit if allocated for non-Federal use. Omnibus Budget Reconciliation Act of 1993, Pub.L. No. 103-66, Title VI, § 6001(a)(3), 107 Stat. 312 (approved August 10, 1993); see also, H.R. Rep. No. 103-213, 103rd Cong., 1st Sess. (1993). On February 10, 1994, the Secretary of Commerce released *Preliminary Spectrum Reallocation Report (Preliminary Report)* NTIA Special Publication 94-27, identifying spectrum for reallocation from Federal Government use to private sector, including local government, use. See also Report to Ronald H. Brown Secretary, U.S. Department of Commerce Regarding the Preliminary Spectrum Reallocation Report, 9 FCC Rcd. 6793 (1994).

[13]"Functions relating to international communications satellite systems, vested in the President by the Communications Satellite Act of 1962, and the Inmarsat Act of 1978 have also been delegated to NTIA." Telecom 2000 at 169.

[14]See, e.g., Congress of the United States, Office of Technology Assessment, *Critical Connections—Communications for the Future*, Chapter 13, Jurisdictional Issues in the Formulation and Implementation of National Communication Policy, (Jan. 1990).

[15]Ibid., Sec. 706(2)(a).

[16]The Communications Act of 1934, as amended, defines a common carrier as "any person engaged as a common carrier for hire, in interstate or foreign communication by wire or radio. . . ." 47 U.S.C. Sec. 153(h) (1990). The Communications Act requires common carriers to provide service "upon reasonable request," at tariffed rates that are "just and reasonable," and "without unjust or unreasonable discrimination." 47 U.S.C. Sec. 201(a), (b) and 202(a). See, Note, "Redefining 'Common Carrier': The FCC's Attempt at Deregulation by Redefinition," *Duke Law Journal* (1987): 501.

[17]Administrative Procedure Act, as amended, 5 U.S.C. Secs. 701-706 (1990).

[18]At one time, television broadcasters were allowed to own only twelve stations each. As previously noted, ownership is now restricted by the 1996 Act by how many viewers a single owner can reach, 35 percent.

[19]See, *Red Lion Broadcasting v. FCC*, 395 U.S. 367 (1969).

[20]See, *FCC v. Pacifica Foundation*, 438 U.S. 726 (1978).

[21]Patrick Parsons, "Defining Cable Television: Structuration and Public Policy," *Journal of Communication*, 39:2 (Spring 1989): 10–26.

[22]*Home Box Office v. FCC*, 567 F.2d 9 (D.C. Cir. 1977); cert. denied, 434 U.S. 829 (1977).

[23]*FCC v. Midwest Video Corp.* (Midwest Video II) 571 F.2d 1025 (8th Cir. 1978).

[24]Patrick Parsons, "In the Wake of *Preferred*: Waiting for Godot," *Mass Communication Review*, 16:1 (Summer 1989): 26–37.

[25]*Miami Herald v. Tornillo*, 418 U.S. 241 (1974).

[26]*City of Los Angeles v. Preferred Communications, Inc.* 476 U.S. 488 (1986).

[27]*United States v. O'Brien*, 391 U.S. 367 (1968).

[28]Parsons," "In the Wake of *Preferred.*"

[29]*Turner Broadcasting Co. v. FCC*, 114 S.Ct. 2445 (1994).

[30]*Chesapeake and Potomac Telephone Company v. U.S.* 830 F. Supp. 909 (1993), 42 F.3d. 181 (1994); *Ameritech v. United States* 1994 U.S. Dist. LEXIS 15512 sect. 33 (1994); *U.S. West v. United States* 1994 U.S. App. LEXIS 36755 sect. 23 (1994).

[31]The United States government has begun to realize the need for effective and market-oriented spectrum management. See, United States Dept. of Commerce, National Telecommunications and Information Administration, *U.S. Spectrum Management Policy: Agenda for the Future*, 13, NTIA Spec. Pub. 91-23 (Washington, DC: Government Printing Office, Feb. 1991) [hereinafter cited as U.S. Spectrum Management Policy].

[32]In 1990, shipments of radio communication equipment generated over $55 billion. *United States Spectrum Management Policy*, Executive Summary. NTIA estimated the spectrum value of cellular radio services, which consumes 50 MHz, to be over $79 billion. *See Id.* at Appendix D, "Estimating the Value of Cellular Licenses."

[33]Sales of VHF television stations in major markets can exceed $500 million, far in excess of the physical assets involved. See H. Geller and D. Lampert, *Charging for Spectrum Use*, (Washington, DC: Benton Foundation Project on Communications and Information Policy Options, 1989), 13.

[34]For example, the FCC would like to auction spectrum to be used by broadcasters for a new generation of advanced, high definition television. But it appears that the broadcasters' public interest arguments for "free TV" will prevail. The advertiser-supported delivery of news, public affairs, and entertainment generates what economists call positive network externalities and free riders. This means that both consumers and nonconsumers of the advertised products can watch broadcast television and derive the benefits of viewership without having to pay the full cost.

[35]See, 47 C.F.R. § 2.106 (1995).

[36]103d Cong., 1st Sess., Omnibus Budget Reconciliation Act of 1993, Title VI, Communications Licensing and Spectrum Allocation Provisions, PL 103-66 (HR 2264), 107 Stat. 312, 379 et seq. (1993). See also H.R. 707, "Emerging Telecommunications Technologies Act of 1993"; United States Congress, House Report 103-19, "Emerging Telecommunications Technologies Act of 1993," 103d Congress (Feb. 24, 1993); Policies and Rules for Licensing Fallow 800 MHz Specialized Mobile Radio Spectrum Through a Competitive Bidding Process, 7 FCC Rcd. 8590 (1992) (denying petition for competitive bidding access to spectrum for mobile radio due to lack of explicit legislative authority). The FCC's in-house "think tank" endorsed spectrum auctioning for nonbroadcast spectrum, particularly for advocates of new services who need already used spectrum. See, e.g., Webbink, *Frequency Spectrum Deregulation Alternatives*, FCC Office of Plans and Policy Working Paper No. 2 (Oct.,1980); E. Kwerel and A. Felker, *Using Auctions to Select FCC Licensees*, FCC Office of Plans and Policy Working Paper No. 16 (May, 1985).

The Commission has authorized cash payments from newly licensed applicants to incumbent users for relocating to another frequency band before spectrum reallocations subordinated their status. See, Redevelopment of Spectrum to Encourage Innovation in the Use of New Telecommunications Technologies, ET Docket No. 92-9, Notice of Proposed Rulemaking, 7 FCC Rcd. 1542 (1992) (proposing to reserve 220 MHz in the 2 GHz band for new services like Personal Communications Networks while accommodating incumbent microwave licensees); Further Notice of Proposed Rulemaking, 7 FCC Rcd. 6100 (1992), 1st Report and Order, 7 FCC Rcd. 6886 (1992), 2d Report and Order, 8 FCC Rcd. 6495 (1993) (reallocating spectrum above 3 GHz to ease migration of incumbents in 2 GHz bands to accommodate emerging technology mobile services); 3d Report and Order and Memorandum Opinion and Order, 8 FCC Rcd. 6589 (1993) (adopting a plan for fair sharing in the 2 GHz band between incumbent microwave users and emerging technology services and for accelerated relocation by incumbents). The Commission also can collect fees to recoup the cost of regulation. See Implementation of Sec. 9 of the Communications Act, MD Docket No. 94-19, Report and Order, 9 FCC Rcd. 5333 (1994).

[37]Until passage of enabling legislation the FCC could consider marketplace forces when making spectrum allocations, but could not auction off spectrum to the highest bidder. "Nothing on Sections 303(A)–(C) [of the Communications Act] suggests that the Commission is not permitted to take into account marketplace forces when exercising its spectrum allocation responsibilities under the public interest standards." Amendment of Parts 2, 15, and 90 of the Commission's Rules and Regulations to Allocate Frequencies in the 900 MHz Reserve Band for Private Land Mobile Use, GEN Docket Nos. 84-1231, 1233, 1234, Report and Order 2 FCC Rcd. 1825, 1939 (1986).

[38]In 1959, R. H. Coase argued for a definitive spectrum ownership rights as a market-driven way to foreclose chaos and interference. R. H. Coase, "The Federal Communications Commission," *Journal of Law and Economics* 2 (1959): 1. In 1991, the Chairman of the FCC reported that the spectrum requested for new services exceeded 1200 MHz, while the FCC had only 3 MHz of unallocated spectrum available to accommodate such requests. *Emerging Telecommunications Technology Act of 1991: Hearings on H.R. 1407 Before the Subcomm. on Telecommunications and Finance of the House of Representatives*, 102 Cong., 1st Sess. (1991) (prepared testimony of Alfred C. Sikes).

[39]Pub. L. No. 73-416, 48 Stat. 1064 (1934) (codified as amended at 47 U.S.C.A. Secs. 151-610 (1990). For a legislative history of the Communications Act, see, Glen Robinson, "The Federal Communications Act: An Essay on Origins and Regulatory Purpose," in M. D. Paglin, ed. *A Legislative History of the Communications Act of 1934* (1989); see also, Note, "Allocating Spectrum By Market Forces: The FCC Ultra Vires?" *Catholic University Law Review* 37 (1987): 149.

[40]Under Sec. 305 of the Communications Act of 1934, as amended, the President retains the authority to assign frequencies to all radio stations belonging to the federal government. The President has delegated this authority to the Secretary of Commerce, who has in turn delegated it to NTIA. See, Exec. Order No. 12,046, as amended, 3 C.F.R. Sec. 158, reprinted in, 47 U.S.C. Sec. 305 app. at 127 (1990). See also, U.S. Dept. of Commerce, Department Organization Orders 10-19 and 25-7. The applicable Executive Order and an Office of Management and Budget Circular No. A-11 "provide NTIA with the power to assign frequencies and approve the spectrum needs of new [federal] systems." U.S. Spectrum Management Policy at p. 20.

[41]Because of the need to prepare for international conferences, which address particular spectrum allocation issues, "larger policy issues have been overlooked or neglected, and insufficient consideration is being given to the long term consequences of implementing new technologies and services. The result has been an often reactive and short-sighted approach

to spectrum policy. . . ." United States Congress, Office of Technology Assessment, "The 1992 World Administrative Radio Conference: Technology and Policy Implications," OTA-TCT-549 at p. 7 (Government Printing Office, May, 1993).

[42]NTIA, in a comprehensive study of spectrum management, proposed greater reliance on market forces and increased flexibility in management approaches. It identified four elements essential for long-term spectrum planning: (1) identifying requirements through the collection and dissemination of data concerning existing and anticipated use; (2) forecasting future requirements through both empirical methods and informed judgment; (3) publication of long-range plans; and (4) planning for unforeseen requirements. *U.S. Spectrum Management Policy*, 161.

[43]Procedural fairness requires the FCC to consider in a single proceeding all license applications deemed mutually exclusive. *Ashbacker Radio Corp. v. FCC*, 326 U.S. 327 (1945); *Johnston Broadcasting v. FCC*, 85 U.S. App. D.C. 40, 175 F.2d 351 (D.C. Cir. 1949) (a comprehensive comparative hearing is necessary for choosing between two or more mutually exclusive applicants); but cf. *United States v. Storer Broadcasting*, 351 U.S. 192 (1955) (a hearing is not necessary for purposes of determining whether to grant a waiver of limitations on the number of licenses held by an applicant).

[44]"The policy of the Act is clear that no person is to have anything in the nature of a property right as a result of the granting of a license." *FCC v. Sanders Bros. Radio Station*, 309 U.S. 470, 475 (1940); *Red Lion Broadcasting Co. v. FCC*, 395 U.S. 367 (1969) (approving regulations on the basis of scarcity and the view that broadcasters are public trustees); *Office of Communication of the United Church of Christ v. FCC*, 138 U.S. App. D.C. 112, 425 F.2d 543 (D.C. Cir. 1969) (broadcasters are temporary permittees of a great public resource). Both the FCC and commentators have begun to question whether a marketplace approach would better serve the public interest in lieu of the view that spectrum scarcity justifies pervasive regulation. See, e.g., Mark Fowler and Daniel Brenner, "A Market Approach to Broadcast Regulation," *Texas Law Review* 60 (1982):207.

[45]See Communications Act of 1934, as amended, 47 U.S.C.A. Secs. 302(a), 303, 307(a), 308, 309 and 316 (1990).

[46]Ibid., Sec. 151 (1990).

[47]Administrative Procedure Act, 5 U.S.C.A. Secs. 551-559, 701-706 (1990) (requiring federal agencies, *inter alia* to solicit public comment before issuing rules and regulations).

[48]See, e.g., Amendment of Parts 1, 21, 22, 74 and 94 of the Commission's Rules to Establish Service and Technical Rules for Government and non-Government Fixed Service Usage of the Frequency Bands 932-935 and 941-944 MHz, Gen. Docket No. 82-243, First Report and Order, 50 Fed. Reg. 4650 (1985), Second Report and Order, 4 FCC Rcd. 2021 (1989); Mem. Op. & Order, 5 FCC Rcd. 1624 (1990); Amendment of Part 90 of the Commission's Rules to Make Additional Channels Available for Private Carrier Paging Operations in the 929-930 MHz Band, PR Docket No. 85-102, Report and Order, 58 R.R.2d 1290 (Pike & Fischer) (1985) (ordering sharing between commercial, common carrier, and private use of paging frequencies).

[49]Amendment of Parts 2 and 22 of the Commission's Rules to Permit Liberalization of Technology and Auxiliary Service Offerings in the Domestic Public Cellular Radio Telecommunications Service, Gen. Docket No. 87-390, Report and Order, 5 FCC Rcd. 1138 (1990).

[50]Amendment of Part 2 of the Commission's Rules to Allocate Spectrum for Mobile–Satellite Services in the 1530-1544 MHz and 1626.5-1645.5 MHz Bands, Gen. Docket No. 90-56,

Notice of Proposed Rulemaking, 5 FCC Rcd. 1255 (1990), First Report and Order and Further Notice of Proposed Rulemaking, 8 FCC Rcd. 4246 (1993).

[51]Amendment of the Commission's Rules to Establish New Digital Audio Radio Services, Gen. Docket No. 90-357, Notice of Inquiry, 5 FCC Rcd. 5237 (1990), Notice of Proposed Rulemaking and Further Notice of Inquiry, 7 FCC Rcd. 7776 (1992).

[52]See, e.g., Advanced Television Systems and Their Impact upon the Existing Television Broadcast Service, MM Docket No. 87-268, Mem. Op. and Order, Third Report and Order, and Third Further Notice of Proposed Rulemaking, 7 FCC Rcd. 6924 (1992).

[53]Amendment of the Commission's Rules to Establish New Personal Communications Services, Gen. Docket No. 90-314, Memorandum Opinion Order, 9 FCC Rcd. 4957 (1994).

[54]U.S. Department of Commerce, National Telecommunications and Information Administration, *Manual of Regulations and Procedures for Federal Radio Frequency Management*, Sec. 2-1 (May, 1990); *see also* 47 C.F.R. Sec. 300.1 (1990).

[55]Section 305(a) of the Communications Act, as amended, provides that "Radio stations belonging to and operated by the United States shall not be subject to the provisions of sections 301 and 303 of this Act [that broadly state the scope of the FCC's regulatory mission]. All such Government stations shall use such frequencies as shall be assigned to each or to each class by the President." 47 U.S.C. Sec. 305(a) (1990). "Federal Government spectrum is delegated by The President under Executive Order 12046 to the Department of Commerce, NTIA, which is aided by other federal departments and agencies through an advisory group, the Inter-department Radio Advisory Committee (IRAC)." Telecom 2000, 657.

[56]63 percent of the spectrum below 30 GigaHertz is shared. "U.S. Spectrum Management Policy," 17.

[57]Executive Office of the President, *A Vision of Change for America*, (Feb. 17, 1993), 83.

[58]103d Cong., 1st Sess., Omnibus Budget Reconciliation Act of 1993, Title VI, Communications Licensing and Spectrum Allocation Provisions, PL 103-66 (HR 2264), 107 Stat. 312, (1993) [hereinafter cited as Spectrum Auction Law].

[59]Ibid., 107 Stat., 380.

[60]Ibid., 107 Stat, 380, codified at, 47 U.S.C.A. Sec. 923. The law tasks NTIA with identifying 50 MHz, half of which must be located below 3 GHz, within six months after the date of enactment. Ibid.. 107 State. 383.

[61]Ibid., 107 Stat. 388, codified at 47 U.S.C.A. Sec. 309 (j).

[62]See also, Implementation of Sec. 309(j) of the Communications Act Competitive Bidding, PP Docket No. 93-253, Notice of Proposed Rulemaking, 8 FCC Rcd. 7635 (1993).

[63]Ibid., 107 Stat. 388, 47 U.S.C.A. Sec. 309(j) (3).

[64]Addressed in Subpart E of Part 90 of the FCC's Rules and Regulations: 47 C.F.R. Part 90, Subpart E (1995).

[65]Wideband PCS Order, 8 FCC Rcd., 7738.

[66]Ibid., 8 FCC Rcd., 7728.

[67]Bear Sterns & Co., Inc. *Telecommunications Untethered, Vol. II: Battle on Two Fronts*, May 20, 1996.

[68]For a comprehensive history of the ITU, see, George A. Codding, Jr., *The International Telecommunications Union: An Experiment in International Cooperation*, (Arno Press, 1972); George A. Codding, Jr. and Anthony M. Rutkowski, *The International Telecommunications Union in a Changing World*, (Artech House, 1982). A more concise summary is available in James G. Savage, "The ITU and the Radio Frequency Spectrum: Use and Man-

agement of a Shared Universal Resource," *The Politics of International Telecommunications Regulation*, (Boulder, CO: Westview Press, 1989), 61–129.

[69]The prospect of an oncoming WRC can prompt the FCC to expedite its consideration of a spectrum allocation matter to ensure that the United States will have reached a position it can then advocate for other nations to endorse. "[I]t is necessary to make such authorizations now to clarify future United States domestic satellite interests at the upcoming Space WRC." Licensing Space Stations in the Domestic-Fixed Satellite Service, 101 FCC 2d 223, 224 (1985).

[70]U.S. Dept. of Commerce, National Telecommunications and Information Administration, *Telecom 2000*, Appendix A, 655.

[71]See Jorn Christensen, "The Great Paper Chase—The Rush for Satellite Frequencies Is On," *Via Satellite*, 11:2 (February 1996): 42–48.

8

Television without Frontiers

Cable and satellite-delivered television have begun to proliferate throughout the world. Television without frontiers makes possible the global distribution and marketing of all the programming and services described earlier. For many nations, this means satellite, as opposed to cable, infrastructures. In contrast to the United States and Canada, consumers in many nations have opted for predominantly satellite-based systems, or place greater emphasis on satellite delivery. This preference results primarily from the nonexistence or delayed market entry of cable, as well as the imposition of regulations that limited the attractiveness of cable television relative to powerful incumbent television broadcasters. Cable television typically develops quickly when operators have greater access to program options and have the technological wherewithal and regulatory freedom to add new channels. This freedom results when operators install new generations of equipment with broad bandwidth and the capacity to provide telephony and data services. It also requires governments to relax regulations that have constrained program access and the opportunities for foreigners to program channels and own systems. In many nations, access to diverse programming has been limited by incumbents, lags in regulatory change, demographics (often with a concentration of population and wealth in urban areas serviceable by conventional broadcast outlets) and the initial reticence of programmers to make service commitments to new regions.

WHY SATELLITES?

While 66 percent of the households in the United States subscribe to cable television, such heavy market penetration elsewhere has, with some important exceptions, yet to occur. Cable penetration is not evenly distributed around the globe; some European countries have high levels of cable subscription, more than 93 percent of all the homes in Belgium, for example, take cable TV. Other countries with high penetration include: Argentina, Israel, Japan, and Taiwan. Moreover, cable is expected to continue its rapid development in most parts of the world. To date, however, cable has lagged behind satellite-delivered or conventional terrestrial broadcast options in many regions.

In the United States satellite-delivered television had been limited to hobbyists and rural dwellers until the onset of DBS ventures like DirecTV in the middle 1990s. Elsewhere nations retained government ownership of a single channel or a limited group of broadcast channels well into the 1980s. A few nations permitted limited commercial television options, but restricted advertising minutes, the amount of foreign program content, and the percentage of ownership available to foreigners. Fewer nations still permitted commercial cable television enterprises to import foreign signals that could threaten cultural homogeneity and political stability.

Accordingly, in many nations government policies regarding broadcast station ownership and cable television deliberately limited the number and types of available programming. With few off-air programs to retransmit, cable television operators had a limited inventory of programming available without resorting to satellite-delivered imports. Lacking broadcast options, cable television operators had to pursue satellite-delivered program options, the very type of programming delivery mechanism that many national governments and their broadcast unions decided to monopolize. Contrary to the United States, where private enterprises compete in all sectors of the video marketplace, government agencies sought to serve exclusively the video program distribution markets for home viewers, including DBS and distribution to broadcasters and cable systems.

In Europe national governments joined in a cooperative structure, much like the global cooperative INTELSAT, to operate a pan-European constellation of Eutelsat satellites. Ostensibly for voice, data, and video, the Eutelsat system primarily serves video applications. With governments directly involved, the strategy appeared to find ways to incorporate satellites without conferring too many opportunities to private ventures. A nation might grant new broadcast licenses and it might permit DBS, but the favorable decision to franchise cable systems occurred much later. This meant that consumers, having long tolerated only a few broadcast television options, displayed substantial pent-up demand for video program options. The typically available new options came in the form of new conventional broadcast stations and satellite-delivered, pay television.

Rather than wait months for installation of a cable infrastructure, which could provide a greater inventory of channel options, operators can serve programming starved viewers with fewer, but quickly available options. In 1993 DBS served 3.5 million households in Britain compared to 443,000 homes served via cable.[1] By early 1996, the number of cable households in Britain had tripled to 1.4 million, but that significantly larger figure still represented only 6.1 percent of all television households in the country, with 6.4 million homes passed.[2]

Ironically, the reliance on satellites in time resulted in diminished opportunities for national governments to manage the flow of new video program options and to capture new revenue streams. Because satellite footprints typically traverse national borders, a single government has little control, shy of banning satellite dishes, over what its citizens view. What had been considered a way, perhaps, to expand the market wingspan of incumbents actually made it possible for a quicker and more pronounced consumer migration to private options, both in terms of new private broadcast stations and even the satellite delivery option. The majority of national governments, which sought to retain ownership and control of satellite delivery options, could not forestall a minority, such as Luxembourg, the United Kingdom, and Hong Kong, from authorizing the launch of private satellite ventures able to deliver video programming directly to consumers throughout the region.

The "Television without Frontiers" concept means that increasing numbers of nations, perhaps reluctantly, have recognized that consumers demand expanded viewing options and have the technical and financial resources to pursue them. Nations like the United States, Luxembourg, and the United Kingdom have been in a minority in terms of supporting transborder export and import of video programming. But more nations have agreed that video programming markets are porous and accessible, and that restrictive policies simply will not work.

For example, until the middle 1990s the Canadian government severely restricted access to foreign programming by requiring programmers to secure a license to operate, by capping foreign ownership of broadcast and cable facilities at 20 percent, and by setting Canadian program content quotas.[3] Ostensibly to guard against cultural imperialism, particularly from the south, these policies attempted to restrict access to one of the most heavily cabled nations on Earth. However, such restrictions did not prevent Canadian citizens from accessing foreign programming, through satellite dishes pointed to United States domestic satellites and through off-air reception of United States broadcasts, as the vast majority of Canadian citizens live within 200 miles of the border. Likewise, regional and global trade policymaking forums have begun to consider video program market access complaints. Increasingly these forums have decided that barriers to market access constitute an unjustified nontariff restriction unsustainable despite economic or cultural claims. As previously noted, in 1996, the FCC refused to permit a TCI proposal to use a Canadian satellite and orbital slot for direct broadcast service on grounds that Canada's content regulations denied U.S. ventures effective competitive opportunities. Satellite market access issues continue to prove daunting. While widely heralded as promoting substantial progress in telecommunications trade, the World Trade Organization Group on Basic Telecommunications in 1997 could not reach consensus on foreign investment rules for DTH and DBS.

A Global Gold Rush to Serve New Markets

Despite governmental concerns about national sovereignty and culture, many consumers have voted with their eyes and ears by purchasing television receive-only

Earth stations (TVROs), whether legal or not. Likewise, few popularly elected governments now can refuse to permit access to DBS as a speedy way to satisfy pent-up demand for greater diversity in video programming regardless of the national origin of programming. Some commentators have alleged that the upheaval in Eastern Europe was sparked in part by the ability to receive off-air television signals broadcast from nearby non-Communist nations, and the ingenuity of citizens to erect "homebrew" TVROs to receive satellite transmissions.

Given a whetted appetite for programming alternatives to the state's broadcasts, foreign governments have reconsidered prohibitions or restrictions on video programming. Some nations now permit private cable television ventures, rather than reserve the market for the incumbent telephone company or the national broadcast authority. In such diverse locations as the United Kingdom, France, Argentina, Israel, Poland, New Zealand, and Japan, for example, several of the Regional Bell Operating Companies (RBOCs) and U.S. cable MSOs have become equity partners. Despite some restrictions on the number of foreign channels and threats to impose quotas on the amount of foreign program content, video programmers and movie producers have experienced success in having their fare included in foreign cable service tiers.

The RBOCs initially may have pursued foreign cable television markets in view of domestic restrictions on ownership of cable television systems, former restrictions imposed by the AT&T divestiture decree on the provision of information services, and the opportunity to provide both cable television and other telecommunication services via a single wire in some nations. The runup of cable television system prices in the U.S. and penetration in excess of 95 percent provided another incentive as foreign nations offered a "ground floor" opportunity for the construction of new cable television facilities.

Despite language, cultural, and taste barriers, U.S. programmers, cable operators, and telephone companies have staked claims throughout the world. SBC has teamed with Cox Cable to build the cable television system in the Liverpool region of England, and also has acquired an interest in the Israeli company that serves Jerusalem and Tel Aviv. US West has heavily invested in European and Asian cable television with a stake in thirteen areas of France, including Paris, several U.K. locales, including South London and Birmingham, and locations in Hungary, Norway, and Sweden. TCI has teamed with US West, Comcast, and Compagnie General Des Eaux (CGE) to serve various locations in the U.K., and has other ventures in Argentina, Ireland, Israel, Hungary, Norway, and Sweden. TCI's international television ventures form a publicly traded stock, TCI International, and other publicly traded stock offerings include TeleWest, a joint venture of TCI, US West, Cox Communications, SBC Communications, and Bell Cable, the cable television venture of Bell Canada.

International programming activities by U.S. services have accelerated and become a competitive necessity for most companies. CNN's international service is a staple for many around the world. NBC (and the BBC) as well as others have followed CNN's lead. MTV and HBO are successfully penetrating foreign markets. Other services offer cartoons, children's programming, wildlife shows, documentaries, and more movies.

INTERNATIONAL CABLE
AND SATELLITE VENTURES

Asia–Pacific

The Asia–Pacific region has generated the highest percentage increase in demand for video programming over the last few years. This results from vibrant economic growth, and policy decisions designed to create an improved telecommunication infrastructure with increased telephone line penetration that in many countries in the region may not exceed single digits per one hundred inhabitants. The geographic composition of the region favors satellite usage: Many nations have large, sparsely populated hinterlands, spanning thousands of miles, or comprise hundreds of islands (e.g., Indonesia), all of which require interconnection with urban centers of commerce, government, and culture.

Consistent with such demand growth, the region also has become the site for the largest number of new satellite ventures and renewed efforts by incumbents to retain customer loyalty. The region's incumbents include:

> *INTELSAT, Intersputnik (Russia), Columbia Communications and PanAmSat (U.S.) for transoceanic traffic as well as Palapa (ASEAN nations), Optus Communications (Aussat–Australia, New Zealand), Asia Satellite Telecommunications, Co. Ltd. (Hong Kong-regionwide), the Chinese government, including the Ministry of Posts and Telecommunications, China Broadcasting Satellite Corp. and the Directorate General of Telecommunications and a quasi-private competitor Unicom (domestic, DFH, Chinasat and Sinosat), Japan Satellite Systems, Inc. (JCSat-domestic), Space Communications Corp. (Superbird-domestic), the Indian Space Research Organization (Insat-domestic and regional traffic), and several Russian government (Intersputnik) and private ventures.*

Recent entrants include:

> *Asia Pacific Telecommunications (Hong Kong-Apstar), Pacifik Satellit Nusnantara (Indonesia-used Palapa satellite), Satelindo (privatized operations of Palapa), Mediacitra (Indonesia-Indostar for DBS), Shinawatra (Thailand), Korea Telecom (Koresat), and Binariang (Malaysia-Measat).*

Other possible entrants include:

One or two Philippine ventures (Agila, Mabuhay), new operators in Pakistan, Singapore, and Taiwan and additional United States-based ventures (Orion and TRW Space and Electronics Group).

For all its potential, until a few years ago the Asia–Pacific region was slow to embrace both satellites and cable television. Much of the delay stems from the reluctance of governments in the region to support competition in the delivery of content. Few nations have adopted policies supporting unfettered access to programming from international sources, and fewer still haved authorized competition with the state-owned long-distance telephone carrier and broadcaster.

Likewise, the cable television and satellite master antenna television systems that exist have achieved only limited market penetration. This stems in part from the reluctance of video programmers to commit to packaging an Asia–Pacific channel until such time as the market showed signs of developing. The first sign of development occurred when new private satellite operators like AsiaSat commenced operations in 1990 and INTELSAT recognized the need to target the region for improved service. With more plentiful and cheaper distribution options, video programmers started to see market opportunities, even if national governments were slow in authorizing cable television and other operations needed to serve consumers. In what has turned out to be a smart and profitable gamble, programming pioneers like Cable News Network committed to distributing an Asia–Pacific feed, initially to hotels and SMATV systems serving individual condominiums and flats. As news spread of the satellite-delivered option, entrepreneurs pursued distribution to residences, with or without government approval. In India, for example, thousands of small cable television systems have evolved, despite the absence of a single, consistent national policy. In 1996, 33 percent of India's 48.5 million television households had access to some sort of cable-delivered video programming.[4]

As recently as ten years ago a survey of Asia–Pacific cable and satellite television activity would not take long. INTELSAT provided virtually all international, transoceanic services outside the Soviet Union, with a handful of domestic and regional players. Japan had launched U.S. manufactured satellites for domestic communications and DBS. China had a small constellation of Dong Fan Hong communications satellites. India had a number of Insats to serve its massive population. Indonesia, the third entrant in commercial satellite service, provided regional services to the Association of Southeast Asian Nations (ASEAN) via its Palapa network. The Aussat system in Australia provided domestic voice and video services. Terrestrial distribution occurred primarily by government-owned, national networks.

Currently, 55 million cable television subscribers in China, India, and Japan receive limited, primarily off-air programming. Only about 5 million households in the region have access to modern broadband systems. New, leading-edge technology systems are under construction in Australia, China, Hong Kong, Japan, the Philippines, Korea, Singapore, and Taiwan.[5] A prominent consulting firm predicts that cable and satellite television service revenues in the Asia–Pacific region will increase tenfold from under $5 billion to over $50 billion by the year 2005.[6] However, some industry observers predict a satellite transponder glut as a result of market entry from over a dozen new operators. Others believe liberalized policies regarding access to video programming and competition will stimulate adequate demand. The number of transponders in orbit over the region is expected to jump from 500 to 900 by the year 2000, provided orbital slots can be found for them. Set out below is a summary of cable and satellite ventures in several nations.

Australia

Australia's geography and demographics combined to delay the onset of pay and cable television in Australia until 1996. On rational public policy and economic grounds, the Australian government emphasized satellites as the preferred delivery vehicle for serving both urban areas and the sparsely populated Outback. But this policy, as well as government reluctance to privatize and subject both its broadcasting and telecommunication holdings to competition, resulted in the failure of a cable television industry to develop even in urban corridors. Belatedly the Australian government has encouraged cable television deployment by permitting operators to offer telephony and data services over the same network that provides video programming.

In 1996 Australia joined with the United States and Britain in offering commercially available cable/telephony service. Optus Vision, a venture of US West of the United States, Optus Communications Pty., Ltd, a subsidiary of the country's second long-distance telephone company and the Seven broadcast television network, expect to make available to three million households a two-way hybrid coaxial/fiber-optic cable network. This company will compete with Foxtel, a joint venture of Rupert Murdoch's News Corp. and Telstra Corp., the state-owned, incumbent telephone company. The companies expect to invest over $5 billion so that they can serve the pay television market, valued at $380 to $757 million, as well as the local ($3.8 billion) and long-distance ($12.1 billion) telephone service markets.[7]

Australia has been a long-standing user of domestic satellites, first through government ownership of the Aussat system and later through private ownership. As part of a major campaign to privatize government-owned ventures and to stimulate competition in telecommunications, Aussat was coupled with a franchise to operate as the second telecommunication carrier in the country. Optus was licensed as the second telecommunications carrier in early 1992, providing Australian consumers with a rival carrier to the government-owned Telstra, the name for the company representing the merger of the government-owned domestic monopoly Telecom Australia and the international monopoly Overseas Telecommunication Corp. (OTC).

Optus is owned by a consortium including Britain's Cable and Wireless (24.5 percent), BellSouth (24.5 percent), Mayne Nickless (20 percent), an Australian transport company, and a number of Australian institutional investors. The company paid $800 million (Australian) for the money-losing Aussat venture that had been envisioned as a domestic competitor to Telecom Australia. While Optus has concentrated on cellular radio and domestic long-distance services, it plans on using Aussat to provide regional video program distribution service and providing the satellites for pay television and cable television.

China

China presents a gigantic and largely untapped market for satellites, satellite-delivered services, and cable television. While individual ownership of TVRO dishes has been prohibited except for businesses, or hotels catering for foreigners, government-owned ventures have manufactured and sold them. At least one million "illegal" home dishes exist.

The Chinese government has operated geostationary satellites since 1986, commonly referred to as Chinasats, but officially called Dong Fang Hong (DFH, "The Sky Is Red"). In the mid-1980s, China appeared to invite foreign manufacturers to bid on a new third generation of more reliable DFH satellites with longer usable lives. A single DFH-3 satellite was launched in 1994, but it expelled all station-keeping fuel. Daimler-Benz, which had provided primarily technical assistance on the now-failed venture has returned to team up with the China Aerospace Corp. (CASC) in a joint venture called EurasSpace geared to construct a new satellite called SinoSat-1. Sino Satellite Communications, itself a joint venture between CASC and the People's Bank of China, will use the satellite primarily for VSAT links between bank branches throughout China. SinoSat will have sixteen low-powered C-band transponders and six higher powered Ku-band transponders. SinoSat will cover all of China, including Hong Kong and Taiwan.

To handle current satellite requirements, the Chinese government purchased an in-orbit GTE domestic satellite, repositioned it over China and renamed it Chinasat 5. In a recent deal with INTELSAT, the government sold 50 percent of the satellite's capacity, then agreed to lease all of it, as well, and to transfer its orbital registrations for a future satellite at 110.5 degrees east. INTELSAT will use this to launch its first satellite designed to serve land masses rather than provide primarily transoceanic service. INTELSAT also has shored up its satellite inventory in the region and now has 22 operational satellites over the region, translating into over 600 of the total 900 transponders available. It also cut a deal with the Indian Department of Space to lease, over ten years, capacity equivalent to eleven C-band transponders on India's INSAT 2-E satellite, due for launch in late 1997.

Hong Kong

Wharf Cable, a subsidiary of the large Wharf Holdings conglomerate, with interests in shipping, real estate and telecommunications, holds an exclusive pay cable television franchise in Hong Kong. The exclusivity was to terminate in 1996, but was extended for two years in view of Wharf Cable's poor financial performance. The company had only 200,000 subscribers in 1996, well short of its anticipated market penetration. Launched in 1993, Wharf Cable has encountered a market apparently satisfied with more limited satellite-delivered options.

Hong Kong serves as the home for the region's first primarily private commercial satellite venture, Asia Satellite Telecommunications Co. Ltd (AsiaSat), which began providing regional, primarily video program, distribution service in 1990. The venture combined a number of unlikely partners: Cable & Wireless PLC, of the United Kingdom, Hutchison Whampoa of Hong Kong, and the China Trust & Investment Corp. (CTIC), a government-owned enterprise. The company's first satellite was a Hughes HS-376, Westar 6, that had been stranded in a useless orbit along with Palapa B-2. The satellite was retrieved by Space Shuttle astronauts, refurbished for the bargain sum of $58 million and then relaunched. All twenty-four of AsiaSat1's transponders have been leased, primarily for video program delivery, either to home dishes or for cable/SMATV delivery. The satellite has two beams: a northern beam primarily serving China and Mongolia, and a southern beam ranging from the Philippines to eastern Turkey. AsiaSat2, a larger (three and one-half tons), more powerful (up to 115 watt transponders) Lockheed Martin Series 7000 satellite, was successfully launched in December, 1995. The satellite has twenty-four C-band transponders plus nine Ku-band transponders designed for high-powered video delivery. Digital compression capabilities will make it possible to generate as many as one hundred television channels to fifty-three countries from Africa to Australia.

Since 1992 Asia Pacific Telecommunications Satellite Co. (APT) has provided direct competition to AsiaSat using two Hughes satellites. Most of APT's transponders provide video program delivery, including the content of U.S. producers who have targeted the Asia–Pacific region for new cable television and SMATV networks. Chinese government agencies, headed by the China Telecommunications Broadcasting Satellite Corp., have a 75 percent ownership interest in the venture, though some equity is held by private companies based in Hong Kong, Macau, Taiwan, Thailand, and Singapore.

India

Aside from satellite master antenna television, India, for the most part, lacked much of a cable or satellite distribution infrastructure until the early 1990s. But in a few years both industries have taken off with satellite DTH rising from 400,000 households in 1992 to over 16 million (with a total viewership of 80 million) in 1995.[8] Key to marketplace success has been the availability and proliferation of mainly Hindi language programming, instead of English language programming.

India's four first-generation Insats, launched between 1982 and 1990, combine telecommunications, broadcasting, and weather-observation functions, in the 2 GHz S-band. Prior to the launch of the last 1-D satellite, the government found it necessary to lease capacity from Arabsat, a Middle Eastern joint venture led by Saudi Arabia. India acted on its desire to establish an indigenous satellite manufacturing capability by constructing its own second-generation Insat. The Indian Space Research Organization constructed two perfectly workable, but relatively low-powered satellites that have limited the broadcast footprint for the Indian state broadcaster Doordarshan to domestic audiences. The Indian Department of Telecommunications has ambitious plans to install over 300,000 VSAT terminals and improve telephone service to rural locales. India expects to launch more second-generation satellites and has plans for a third generation that will contain high-powered transponders for DTH television broadcasting.

The Indian Space Research Organization (ISRO) exclusively constructed the country's second generation of satellites. In late 1995, Ariane successfully launched Insat-2C, a 4,510 pound satellite containing seventeen C-band, six wide C-band, three Ku-band, and one S-band transponders. The satellite has an expected life of twelve years and will provide radio and television broadcast services, as well as business communications services.

Indonesia

Early in the commercial development of satellites, the Indonesian government recognized their potential to serve the 6,000 inhabited islands that span over 3,000 miles. The Palapa system was proposed in 1972 and became operational in 1976. A second generation was launched starting in 1983, and the first satellite of the third generation (Hughes-601 with thirty C-band and four Ku-band transponders) was launched in 1996. The Palapa system constitutes a regional system in view of the number of nations served by the satellite's footprints and the agreements among ASEAN nations (Brunei, Indonesia, Malaysia, the Philippines, Singapore, and Thailand) to use them.

Unlike most nations in the region, Indonesia has authorized limited facilities-based competition, although the scope of competition remains limited by interlocking investment. PT Satellite Palapa Indonesia (Satelindo), the owner of the most current Palapa satellites, remains 30 percent owned by the government telephone company, PT Telekomunikasi Indonesia (Telkom) with 10 percent held by PT Indosat, the state-owned INTELSAT signatory. PT Pasifik Satelit Nusantara (PSN) has received authority to market capacity on the first Palapa B-1 satellite that currently operates in an inclined orbit to extend its useful life. PSN has announced plans to pursue a mobile satellite venture called Garuda and may not continue marketing fixed satellite service transponders.

Additional facilities-based competition may occur if PT Mediacitra Indostar acquires the funding and ongoing governmental support to launch and operate small satellites to provide two channels of video using the S-band (2.6 GHz) with a number of digital audio channels transmitted via the L-band (1.5 GHz).

Japan

Despite a large, technologically sophisticated and financially prosperous population, Japan does not have a vastly successful cable television industry. This results from costly connection charges—in excess of $500—and "onerous limits" previously imposed by the Ministry of Posts and Telecommunications. [9] For the same amount of money Japanese citizens in 1998 will have access to one hundred DBS channels from three competing ventures: JSkyB, a News Corp. affiliate, DirecTV Japan, a venture of Hughes Communications and a Japanese video-rental chain, and Perfect TV Corp., a venture of four Japanese trading companies led by Itochu Corp and Sumitomo. News Corp. already distributes a Japanese version of the quite popular STAR TV DTH programming package.

Japan's satellite activity started in 1977, with the launch of the CS-1 Sakura communications satellite, a Ka-band satellite primarily built by Ford Aerospace. The National Aeronautics and Space Development Agency (NASDA) operated the CS-satellites for administration by the state-owned Telecommunications Satellite Corporation of Japan (TSCJ), which in 1992 was renamed the Telecommunications Advancement Organization. Japan pioneered the use of satellites for DBS in 1987 an experimental Yuri satellite built by General Electric as a subcontractor to Toshiba. The country launches its satellite in-country through the use of Delta rocket technology licensed from McDonnell-Douglas. The next two generations of CS satellites, launched in 1983 and 1989 respectively, contained two C-band transponders plus six in the Ka band (CS-2), increased to ten on CS-3.

Like the United States, the Japanese communication industry structure separates telecommunication from broadcasting with separately controlled satellites as well. Initially, there was only one license-financed public service broadcaster, Nippon Hoso Kyokai (NHK), one domestic telecommunications carrier, Nippon Telegraph and Telephone (NTT), and one international carrier, Kokosi Denshin Denwa (KDD). Japan has liberalized its communications policies to include multiple private broadcasters and telecommunication carriers. Currently NHK transmits four television channels (two via satellite) with 160, mostly local, broadcasters and ten other private DBS channels serving Japan's 44 million broadcast and 7.6 million DTH households. There are over 10.5 million cable-subscribing households, and two private satellite carriers: JCSat, formed in April 1985, and SCC, owned principally by a number of Mitsubishi companies. Both satellite ventures use U.S. manufactured satellites (Hughes for JCSat, and Loral Space and Communications for SCC). SCC has experienced incredibly bad luck in the launch and operation of satellites. Its first satellite lost all propellant after only eighteen months in operation; the second was destroyed in a 1990 launch failure.

In the DBS market, a consortium of NHK, Japan Satellite Broadcasting, and five other private operators, plus eight banks, joined in 1993 to create Broadcast Satellite Systems Corp. The venture planned to launch two Hughes HS-376 satellites in mid 1997 and 1998. JCSat and SCC also hold authorizations to provide DTH service. JCSAT-3, has Ku-band coverage that extends into India, East Asia, and Oceania, with C-band coverage from Iran to Southeast Asia and Siberia.

In the telecommunications area, the first Nstar advanced communications satellite was launched in 1995 for use by NTT and its mobile services affiliate. The Loral Space and Communications satellite has twenty-six transponders in four frequency bands: one at S-band (four beams), six at C-band, eight at Ku-band, and eleven at Ka-band.

Korea

Korea has ambitious plans to become a satellite manufacturer, first by acquiring satellites from an established manufacturer and then using technical assistance and training to develop an indigenous capability. Korea Telecom, the government-owned primary domestic and international carrier, ordered two Mugunghwa (Koreasat) satellites from Lockheed-Martin Marietta, with Matra Marconi Space as payload contractor. The domestic diversified manufacturer Goldstar was also involved. The first satellite failed to reach GSO and had to use most of its station-keeping fuel to reach the proper orbit, thereby reducing its usable life to about four years. The second satellite was successfully launched in January, 1996, and the third satellite will be launched in 1999. The satellite beams are concentrated over Korea with the primary purposes of delivering domestic television programming to compete with "illegal" reception of signals from Japanese satellites.

Malaysia

Malaysia joined the ranks of nations having their own satellites in 1996. The Malaysia East Asia Satellites (Measat) are owned and operated by Binariang SdnBhd and will be marketed under the Maxis trademark. The company hopes to compete with Palapa as the key satellite network for ASEAN nations. This would make Malaysia a key telecommunication hub for the region. The Philippines Long Distance Telephone Co. was reported to have leased capacity, but its plans for one or more domestic satellites may squelch the deal.

The Philippines

The Philippines may soon have a firm commitment for a satellite procurement. Long rumored as having such plans, two ventures have announced intentions to proceed: the eleven-member Philippine Agila Satellite Inc. (Agila) venture and the Mabuhay Philippine Satellite Corp., led by the Philippine Long Distance Telephone Company, which previously had participated in the Agila group. Both ventures had announced plans to launch a satellite by year end 1996. Recently Agila announced the issuance of additional stock so that it could avert a cash flow crisis. Mabuhay has abandoned plans to apply for a co-registration with Indonesia to acquire an orbital slot. Aerospatiale has been reported as building a satellite for Agila, and Loral Space and Communications is reported to have signed a construction contract with Mabuhay.

Taiwan

Taiwan has the highest cable television penetration in the region. This results from the government's early decision to permit the service as well as the nation's small size and urban concentration.

Taiwan will enter the ranks of satellite owners in 1998 with the launch of Rocsat-1, a $61 million TRW, Inc., satellite designed for physics, telecommunications and ocean research. This 880-pound experimental satellite will operate from low Earth orbit. Taiwan plans to put three satellites into GSO by 2006 at a cost in excess of $500 million. Rocsat-2, a Ka-band satellite, is tentatively scheduled for a launch in the year 2000.

Thailand

In 1991, Shinawatra Satellite Public Co. (Sattel) received a thirty-year concession to launch and operate satellite communications systems. Previously, Thai satellite users had to lease transponders from INTELSAT, Palapa, and Asiasat. Two Hughes HS-376s, (ten C-band and two Ku-band transponders) launched in 1993 and the following year generated an adequate signal for such adjacent nations as Cambodia, China, Laos, and the Philippines. The French firm Aerospatiale has been awarded the contract for Thaicom-3, which will have twenty-four C-band and twelve Ku-band transponders operating at high power.

Africa, Eastern Europe, and the Middle East

Africa, Eastern Europe, and the Middle East have somewhat belatedly joined the rush to embrace diversity and choice in video programming. While one can wonder whether particular ethnic, language, historical, cultural, and religious factors may limit the appeal of foreign programming, several new ventures have decided to serve the region with the expectation that millions of cable television subscribers and satellite dish owners in the region will view content mirroring that available in North America and Europe.

The early results appear favorable. For example, Star Television, which uses AsiaSat beams targeting viewers in nations east of the region, experienced a 230 percent increase in viewership from January, 1994 (593,777) to October, 1994 (1,364,350) in the Middle East and Pakistan. The Middle East Broadcasting Center, a subsidiary of the ARA Group International and the United International Holding Company, received authorization to provide video programming, via wireline and wireless cable, to 95 percent of the Saudi Arabian population.[10]

On the other hand, many governments in the region have evidenced significant ambivalence, if not outright opposition, to cable and satellite television. At one pole, nations like Iran have banned home access to satellites. At the other pole, Turkey has recognized the power of satellites to strengthen cultural ties by popularizing its dialect of Turkish in Azerbaijan and Central Asia. Since April, 1992, the Turkish government has authorized the copyright-free transmission of Turkish language programs, e.g., Avrasya (EurAsia) channel, throughout the region. The country has at least five earth stations capable of uplinking video programming.

The presently dominant satellite operators in the region include Arabsat, Insat, INTELSAT, PanAmSat, and Turksat. For the most part, however, reception in the region is provided by satellites designed to serve Europe to the west and north and Asia–Pacific to the east and south. Future satellite ventures will include Nilesat, a DTH venture of the Egyptian Radio and Television Union (ERTU). ERTU recently awarded the prime contractor role to Matra Marconi Space. Nilesat is scheduled for launch in late 1997. It will deliver up to fifty-six DTH channels to dishes only 60 centimeters in diameter as the transponders will operate at 100 watts. It is possible that Pakistan, Iraq, and Iran may launch satellites by the end of the century.

Until such time as an indigenous satellite capacity becomes widely available, most packagers of programming and individual operators will shop for capacity that serves multiple regions. For example, Orbit Communications Company has acquired three 72 MHz transponders on an INTELSAT VI satellite, one 150 MHz transponder on the INTELSAT IOR satellite at 63 degrees east, and four 36 MHz transponders on the INTELSAT 704, having migrated them from Arabsat 1D.[11] Orbit will extend incumbent Western programming already available via other DTH systems, such as the Discovery Channel, "America Plus" (Columbia Tristar), BBC World Service Television, CNN International, ESPN, E! Entertainment, and Orbit News (using content from the three major U.S. networks and the *Wall Street Journal*, C-SPAN, etc.).

Any nation in the region that embraces satellite telecommunication has to recognize the potential for political instability. Even Turkey, which has embraced satellites as a vehicle to bolster its cultural and political presence, has strongly objected to the transmission of Kurdish programming (MED-TV) via Britain.

Europe

Europe has a mature and extensive cable and satellite television industry still dominated or heavily influenced by government and incumbent telecommunication enterprises. The European Commission has attempted to eliminate telecommunications monopolies and to stimulate competition with only partial success. It issued a directive requiring all member nations to permit facilities-based telecommunication competition by January 1, 1998, and already requires member nations to permit cable television operators to offer multimedia services like home shopping and banking in addition to conventional video programming. However, the world's largest cable television company, Telekom Deutsche, remains a mostly government-owned company and not such visible enterprises as News Corp., TCI, Time Warner, or US West/Continental Cablevision. While scheduled for privatization, Deutsche Telekom[12] serves over 15.3 million subscribers and passes over 20 million homes.[13] Of the 150 million households in Western and Central Europe more than 60 million now have access to cable television with over 40 million taking service.[14] The European cable television market has an estimated value of $7 billion.[15]

In the satellite arena, a regional cooperative of forty-four nations, the European Telecommunications Satellite Organization (Eutelsat), predominates, with some competition from INTELSAT, PanAmSat, Orion, and government-owned systems in France (Telecom), Spain (Hispasat), and the Nordic countries. The primary DBS/ DTH operators in the region are Eutelsat, Luxembourg-based Societe Europeenne des Satellites (SES) that operates Astra, and Sweden's Nordiska Satellitaktiebolaget (NSAB). Medium powered services have been provided via INTELSAT and other systems like Hispasat and the German Kopernikus satellite.

Satellite operators in the region recently have concentrated on developing a large inventory of new generation, high-powered digital satellites to be used in DBS and other types of video program delivery. Some optimistic forecasters anticipate that European DTH demand will increase to 20 million by the year 2004,[16] and that the inventory of digital video channel capacity will exceed 1,000.[17] NetHold, a Netherlands-based international pay television company, recently ordered 1.1 million set-top decoders. Other premium DTH operators include: British Sky Broadcasting (BskyB), the UK pay-television group controlled by Rupert Murdoch, with 4.2 million paying customers; Canal Plus, France's leading pay television group with a total of 7.1 million pay-television subscribers in Europe and Africa; and NetHold, with as many as 8 million subscribers in Europe, Africa, and the Middle East. A European affiliate of Hughes Communications' DirecTV also expects to operate in the region.

BSkyB has leased capacity on Astra's all-digital television satellite and expects to have as many as 120 channels in its service package in early 1997 when three Astra satellites are launched into the same orbital slot. This strategy is designed to create a Hot Slot, which, as noted, is a preferred orbital location for pointing Earth stations where as many as 500 video channels can be received via one Earth station pointed at one orbital slot. The Hot Slot concept works in conjunction with an earlier coined concept, Hot Bird, used to reflect the most desirable satellite over which to transmit programming.

Astra and Eutelsat vie for Hot Bird supremacy in Europe. Astra claims that 85 percent of its capacity is already leased and negotiations over most of the rest are in their final stages. European television groups that have signed up include Canal Plus, the Munich-based Kirch organization that dominates German film and television program distribution markets, CLT, a Luxembourg-based international broadcaster, and BSkyB. Eutelsat has launched a new series of Hot Bird satellites that will deliver to 500 video channels and service dishes as small as 40 centimeters.

NSAB holds a distant third place in the DBS sweepstakes, but it too has ambitious plans. GE American Communications Inc., and NSAB have announced plans to offer pan-European and Nordic services via a thirty-two-transponder Sirius-2 satellite located at 5 degrees E, currently occupied by NSAB's Sirius-1. NSAB will market sixteen transponders in the Nordic region for a variety of satellite applications, including DTH, cable television distribution, and data services. GE will use its sixteen transponders to transmit video entertainment programming throughout Europe.

Both Astra and Eutelsat have impressive transponder leases to report already. For example, France's Canal Plus, Germany's Kirch Group and Pro 7, and Luxembourg's CLT have signed up for twenty-eight transponders on three new Astra satellites. Nethold has acquired eighteen transponders, split between Astra and Eutelsat. But questions remain whether too much capacity will become available from as many as eight new satellites for pan-European broadcasting in light of compression technologies and whether consumers will pay not only for the expensive premium programs, but also for the expensive set-top converters needed to unscramble signals (in addition to the Earth station). However, in the near term demand for video programming has matched or exceeded supply, so much so that the Astra management has considered leasing Ku-band capacity from Deutsche Telekom's DFS Kopernikus-1 satellite. Telekom is the largest shareholder of Astra with 16.67 percent of the company's investment shares.

The United Kingdom

The United Kingdom has become a favorite location for cable television investment by U.S. companies, primarily because of the favorable economic and regulatory climate. The nation still has relatively few broadcast television options and cable television operators have the option of providing both cable television and telephone services. The United Kingdom was the first country to permit cable operators to provide telephony. As of 1996 the only other countries were Sweden, Australia, Japan, and the United States.

TeleWest PLC, a joint venture between US West and TCI, has the largest market share in Britain with twenty-four separate franchises, and has access to over 6 million potential subscribers in the United Kingdom, France, Sweden, Norway, and Hungary. In June 1995 TeleWest agreed in principle to merge with SBC Cable-Comms (U.K.) (the fifth largest cable operator in the U.K.), with thirty-one franchises covering some 4.1 million homes. SBCC is jointly owned by SBC Communications and Cox Communications Inc. TeleWest offers its U.K. customers over thirty television channels, including BBC, ITV, and Channel 4, most channels available on satellite, and some channels unique to cable.

In late 1996, Britain's Cable & Wireless, one of the world's largest telecommunications companies, announced a merger with three other U.K. MSOs, Nynex Cable-Comms PLC, Bell Cablemedia, and Videotron Holdings PLC. The new company would be the nation's second largest cable provider, serving more than 400,000 subscribers and passing 6.3 million homes. Bell Cablemedia's major shareholders include: Bell Canada International Inc., (42 percent) a subsidiary of BCE Inc., Canada's largest telecommunications company, Jones Intercable, Inc., (13.4 percent) one of the largest U.S. cable television companies, and Cable and Wireless PLC, (12.8 percent).

General Cable PLC, a subsidiary of GUHL and its parent company, Compagnie Générale des Eaux S.A., is the fourth largest cable television operator in the U.K. The company's interests include three of the U.K.'s largest cable markets: Western

London (The Cable Corporation Limited), Yorkshire (The Yorkshire Cable Group Limited), and Birmingham (Birmingham Cable Corporation Limited). These markets represent 1.7 million homes, or approximately 11 percent of all currently franchised homes in the U.K., as well as 104,000 businesses. The systems currently provide 22 percent of all business telephone lines and 16 percent of all residential telephone lines in the U.K. cable communication industry and serve 14 percent of all cable television subscribers in the U.K. Cable television and residential telephone subscribers increased by 50 percent and 110 percent respectively, while the number of business telephone lines increased by 60 percent.

The Americas

Until recently video program distribution in Central and South American has been dominated by INTELSAT and domestic U.S. satellites whose footprints spillover into adjacent countries. In the middle 1980s, PanAmSat provided medium powered video program distribution service in the region forcing INTELSAT to improve the quality of service to the region. Other options now include domestic Brazilian, Mexican, and Argentine satellites. The area presents particularly attractive prospects, because fewer than 8 to 10 percent of all television households subscribe to cable television. This statistic reflects both a limited, existing cable television infrastructure as well as limited discretionary income in many households. Forecasters predict the Latin America DTH market to grow to 5 million households by the end of the decade.[18]

Canada

Canada has one of the highest cable television market penetration rates in the world with industry total revenues of about $2.5 billion.[19] The major players in the industry, Rogers, Shaw, and Videotron, expect to invest over $5 billion over the next five years to upgrade their networks to provide a broadband network for high speed data/Internet and voice applications.

Canada also has a mature satellite industry, having become the third country in the world to launch a satellite, after the Soviet Union and the United States. Satellites are quite important to this sprawling nation with a large land area and a commitment to serve all of its population no matter how scattered across a broad rural hinterland. The country became the first nation to operate a commercial satellite when it deployed Anik A in 1972, a three C-band transponder satellite launched on a U.S. rocket.

Canada has established world class expertise in many of the elements in satellite and earth station construction. The Anik satellite network provides extensive telecommunications and non-DTH video program distribution. In late 1995, the Canadian Radio-Television & Telecommunications Commission (CRTC) granted two DBS and five DTH licenses. This much awaited decision will help reduce reception of "grey market" U.S. programming that has not been authorized by the programming rights holders or the CRTC to be distributed in Canada. These services are frequently obtained using a false U.S. address.

ExpressVu, Inc. will offer forty DBS channels initially to the approximately 30,000 subscribers now receiving Canadian DTH programming services across Canada, using analog big-dish C-band systems. The company is owned by Bell Canada Enterprise, Inc. (33-1/3 percent), Tee-Comm Electronics (33-1/3 percent), Canadian Satellite Communications (Cancom, 19 percent) and Western International (14-1/3 percent). It expects to increase its programming line-up to over one hundred channels pending the availability of transponder capacity on the Anik-E1 satellite. When it can migrate to this satellite, the company will be able to provide digital DTH service to much smaller dishes.

As part of its licensing decision, the CRTC ended the policy of granting a video distribution monopoly. The Commission ordered the new DBS operators to maintain a predominance of Canadian programming in their consumer offerings. Toward the goal of maintaining the availability of domestic programming, the Commission will require all DBS basic and pay-per-view operators to contribute about 5 percent of their annual gross revenue to the production of Canadian programming in much the same way as is currently required of cable companies.

Central and South America

Hughes Communications has announced plans to offer to the 85 million television households in Latin America seventy-two channels of Spanish language programming and seventy-two channels in Portuguese, with an additional sixty CD-quality music channels. Partners in Galaxy Latin America include the Cisneros Group of Venezuela, MVS Multivison of Mexico, and Televisao of Brazil. The Cisneros Group had total annual revenues in 1993 of $3.6, billion much of it accruing from extensive broadcast, cable, and syndication holdings including Venevision, the leading Venezuelan broadcast television network, Chilevision, a television network in Chile, and the United States-based Venevision, a major distributor of Spanish-language television programming. MVS Multivision operates a major pay television venture in Mexico. Grupo Abril is one of the largest communications video and publishing conglomerates in Latin America with 620,000 subscribers in Brazil.

Galaxy Latin America will offer such established network channels as Fox, Cartoon, Discovery, CNN, HBO, CMT, and ESPN. Hughes will provide service via the Galaxy 3-R satellite that initially was designed for domestic service. The FCC granted the company permission to modify the Ku-band transponders to increase power and to provide international DTH services from an orbital location customarily slated for domestic service.

Rupert Murdoch's News Corporation has linked up with Organizacoes Globo (Globo), Grupo Televisa S.A. of Mexico (Televisa), PanAmSat, and Tele-Communications International, Inc. The strategic partnership will develop and operate a

DTH satellite service for the entire Latin American region and Caribbean basin. The partners bring a sizable degree of programming skill and capital. Globo is the largest media company in Brazil and Televisa is the largest entertainment conglomerate in the Spanish-speaking world. The venture will lease transponder capacity from both PanAmSat, which initially had teamed with Televisa in a separate venture. The venture will operate as many as forty-eight PanAmSat transponders on three satellites, two of which have not yet been launched. PanAmSat will share DTH revenues rather than simply lease transponder capacity.

Argentina

In contrast to the rest of the region, Argentina has a robust and commercially successful cable television industry serving approximately 45 percent of all households.[20] Unlike many other nations, where satellites would first serve interior locales, cable television has proliferated in both urban and interior localities, primarily because Argentine law limited the extent to which broadcasters could establish nationwide network affiliations. The nation's laws do not create disincentives to foreign investment, and companies like TCI and Continental CableVision have acquired large stakes in major cable television ventures.

Argentina launched its first satellite, Nahuel-C, in late 1996. Previously Nahelsat Telecommunications Satellites repositioned two aging Canadian Anik-C satellites, a cost-effective and quick way to secure a large block of satellite capacity in one transaction. The company secured initial capital investment through a consortium led by Germany's Daimler–Benz, France's satellite manufacturer Aerospatiale, and Italy's Alenia Spazio. It expects to launch two Aerospatiale Spacebus 2000 satellites that will have eighteen transponders each with 54 MHz of bandwidth.

Brazil

Brazil entered the satellite club in 1985 with the launch of the first Brazilsat by the country's international carrier Embratel. Currently the country has two B generation satellites with twenty-eight C-band transponders providing domestic and regional coverage and one X-band transponder (7 to 8 GHz) for military and government services. Deregulatory initiatives in Brazil may result in market satellite market entry and the elimination of both international and domestic services monopolies.

Mexico

Mexico has the Solaridad Morelos satellite network that provides C-, Ku-, and L-band capacity throughout Mexico, the U.S., Central America, and most of South America. The country's proximity to the United States tends to dampen demand for national systems.

NETWORK GLOBALIZATION AND PROGRAMMING

Liberalization of video program distribution regulations typically results in more outlets and greater demand for foreign programming. Programmers have exploited these opportunities first with regional services and later by pursuing markets anywhere on Earth. Business travelers have come to expect a hotel's satellite television system to offer an attractive complement of programming, including news from networks like CNN, NBC's international "Superchannel," and the British Broadcasting Company. They also look forward to high quality entertainment and sports like that provided by ESPN, Discovery, HBO, and MTV.

Increasingly such programming is available not only as a Satellite Master Antenna Television option, but as well to individual residences through DTH/DBS and cable television. Turner Broadcasting System's CNN began serving international markets in 1985 with service to a few European hotels. The company now uses eighteen different satellites to distribute CNN, Turner Network Television, and the Cartoon Channel throughout the world with dubbing in numerous languages. CNN International delivers news feeds to 210 countries and territories and serves a reported 85 million subscribers. It originates programming from Washington, D.C., London, New York, and Hong Kong.

Programmers have come to recognize that they cannot simply simulcast a single program feed over several different satellites or into cable systems serving different regions of the world. They calibrate their fare to the particular identities, tastes, and demographics of the target market, and as markets develop, they typically add channels to provide more choices and to occupy "shelf space" on choice satellites. MTV, for example, has different feeds to North America, Central and South America, Europe and Asia–Pacific, including MTV Mandarin. The Discovery Channel has nine different international feeds, including ones to India, Italy, Africa, and the Middle East.

U.S.-based MSOs, as suggested previously, also have wide-ranging international interests, in both distribution and programming. Most of the leading system operators have ownership interests in foreign cable properties. US West-Continental, for example, has partial ownership of systems in Argentina, Australia, and Singapore, as well as elsewhere. TCI International has holdings in over a dozen countries including the United Kingdom, Japan, New Zealand, Puerto Rico, France, and Chile. Time Warner is also active around the world. Sometimes, the properties are jointly held by a group of cable or telco firms. SKY Network Television, Ltd. in New Zealand, for example, has partners that include Time Warner, TCI, Ameritech, and Bell Atlantic.[21] The MSOs have similar interests in programming international ventures. Cox Communications is involved with BBC World and Gems Television, for exmaple. TCI International has a 50.9 percent share of Europe's Children's Channel, 15 percent of the European Business Channel, and 18 percent of Japan's Cable Soft Network.[22]

While these holdings shift routinely as alliances are made and old ventures break apart, they illustrate the spread and reach of the increasingly global media system and the activities of the international media companies that are an imporant part of its rapid development.

PRIVATIZATION OF SATELLITE COOPERATIVES

Privatization, corporatization, deregulation, and globalization have become predominant trends in telecommunications. Both developed and developing nations have eliminated or reduced the scope of government ownership in the industry. They have reduced regulations that have barred market entry or the scope of permissible competition. They also have freed incumbent carriers to respond to competition in a businesslike manner without service and financial handicaps.

Incumbent satellite carriers have embraced these trends, including the migration from a model contemplating extensive and ongoing involvement by governments, a simple pricing system based on averaged costs irrespective of the degree of competition, and preferential access to orbital slots and customers. When satellite technology was making its initial crossover to commercial applications, governments established cooperatives like INTELSAT and Inmarsat. The cooperative model helped spread risks, achieved scale economies, and ensured that lesser developed nations could access cutting edge technology with limited investment and without financial handicaps in view of their low demand for service.[24]

Now that the commercial satellite industry has matured, the managers at INTELSAT and Inmarsat seek to replace their cooperative status through "corporatization" or outright privatization. Even as their mission remains valid—to provide ubiquitous access to satellite service on a globally average cost basis—they must increasingly respond to competition and marketplace imperatives. The quasi-diplomatic status of these cooperatives has accorded them privileges and immunities that have translated into financial and competitive advantages. For example, the cooperatives have secured commitments from participating nations to avoid causing "significant" technical or economic harm when authorizing competing satellite systems.

Increasingly nations consider it possible to satisfy their commitment to global cooperatives while still authorizing some degree of competition. The managers of INTELSAT and Inmarsat believe that the organization must adapt to such changed circumstances by relinquishing its treaty-level privileges and immunities in exchange for greater latitude to operate as a commercial enterprise that can respond to competitive necessity with selective rate reductions.

A CONCLUDING NOTE

Deregulatory, procompetitive, and efficiency-enhancing initiatives result when nations recognize that revamping the telecommunications sector can stimulate a nation's economy. A strong correlation exists between having a state-of-the-art telecommunication infrastructure and the ability to participate in information age markets like financial services and data processing. Increasingly, nations of the world are seeking to join the global information economy while domestic and transnational telecommunications conglomerates extend their global market reach.

NOTES

[1]"Cable-Ready—With America Pretty Much Wired, U.S. Companies Begin a Cable Land Rush Overseas," *The Wall Street Journal*, Global Entertainment, 26 March 1993, R-14.

[2]National Cable Television Association, *Facts at a Glance: International Cable*, Spring 1996, 3.

[3]See, *Interactive Video News*, 15 April 1996; *The Reuter Business Report*, 16 January 1996; *Broadcasting & Cable*, 1 January 1996, available in LEXIS-NEXIS, Curnws file.

[4]Ibid., 3.

[5]See, *PR Newswire*, 28 June 1995, available in LEXIS-NEXIS, Curnws file.

[6]Ibid.

[7]See, *Multimedia and Videodisc Monitor*, 1 August 1996; *Electronic Media*, 9 October 1995; *The Reuter Asia–Pacific Business Report*, 19 September 1995, available in LEXIS-NEXIS, Curnws file.

[8]See *WorldPaper*, December 1995, available in LEXIS-NEXIS, Curnws file.

[9]*The Washington Times*, 9 July 1996, available in LEXIS-NEXIS, Curnws file.

[10]*Moneyclips*, 24 July 1996, available in LEXIS-NEXIS, Curnws file.

[11]*The Hollywood Reporter*, 5 July 1995, available in LEXIS-NEXIS, Curnws file.

[12]See, *Financial Times*, 7 November 1995, available in LEXIS-NEXIS, Curnws file.

[13]*The Reuter European Business Report*, 11 October 1995, available in LEXIS-NEXIS, Curnws file.

[14]Ibid. At the end of 1994 the Netherlands had 5.8 million subscribers; Belgium 3.6 million; France 1.4 million; and Britain just over 1.0 million.

[15]Ibid.

[16]Ibid.

[17]*Financial Times*, 6 October 1995, available in LEXIS-NEXIS, Curnws file.

[18]*Video Age International*, October 1995, available in LEXIS-NEXIS, Curnws files.

[19]*Interactive Video News*, 15 April 1996, available in LEXIS-NEXIS, Curnws file.

[20]*The Reuter European Business Report*, 30 June 1996, available in LEXIS-NEXIS, Curnws file.

[21]National Cable Television Association, *Facts at a Glance: International Cable*, Spring 1996.

[22]Ibid.

[23]For more extensive discussion of satellite cooperative privatization, see Rob Frieden, "Privatization of Satellite Cooperatives: Smothering a Golden Goose?" *Virginia Journal of International Law* 36:4 (Winter, 1996), 1001–1019; Rob Frieden, "Should INTELSAT and Inmarsat Privatize?" *Telecommunications Policy*, 18:19 (December 1994), 679–686.

9

Social Issues in Cable and Satellite Television: The Broadband Society

Imagine a world without cable, without DBS, without VCRs. Imagine an evening of television in which your only choices are NBC, CBS, and ABC. There is no remote control. To change channels you must get up, go to the set, and turn the dial. You know exactly what's on each channel at every hour and every program looks pretty much the same. There is no MTV, no CNN, Weather Channel, or ESPN. To watch the U.S. House of Representatives in action, you must go to Washington, D.C. To watch a recent movie, you must go to a theater. Computers are housed in huge underground, air-conditioned buildings and data is fed into them using long decks of punched paper cards. A telephone with a push-button keypad in place of a rotary dial is a thing of wonder.

For most people this was the world of communication and information technology thirty years ago. People were talking about the "wired city" but nobody was really doing much about it. It was a communications environment very different than the one today. Critics lamented the lack of diversity on network television and some worried about a "mass society," others were just starting to talk about a coming information age.

Societies change over time and they do so for many reasons; sometimes change is gradual, sometimes dramatic. Technology is one of the important forces that has the potential to effect both subtle and radical social development. Communications technologies have accounted for some of the most significant changes in human history, including the invention of the printing press, the telegraph, and the introduction of television. None of these occurred in a social vacuum; the interaction between communication technology and society is complex and inter-causal. Society today is different, not solely because of changes in the nature of television, but those changes have in many cases modified the way we go about our daily affairs and the way we think about the world.

While few question the simple observation that communications technologies and the information they convey play a powerful role in social evolution, the extent and nature of that role are subject to debate. This chapter is about the interaction between the emerging telecommunications system and society. It looks at theories of technology and social change, the effect of existing social forms on the development of the broadband systems, the reciprocal effect of the emerging system on existing institutions and individuals, both as viewers and citizens. It considers important policy issues that the developing system raises about the quality of media content, the ownership and control of information, and the long-term social implications of a multimedia world.

The role of cable and satellite television in our social lives can be examined from a variety of perspectives and at a number of levels. At the most applied and pointed level, one can look, for example, at the issue of children and television violence. At a broader level we might probe the issue of the relationship between politics and the emerging information system, asking questions about the role of instant global news reporting on international diplomacy. At one of the most abstract levels we can consider the general interaction of technology and society, considering issues of technical innovation and social change. It is this level at which we will begin.

THE INFORMATION SOCIETY

The gradual expansion of channel capacity and the increasing flexibility of a telecommunications system grounded in a digital standard have been cited as crucial components of the information age. Popular and scholarly writers have expounded on the changes they view as a consequence of technological innovation and the dawning of the information society. But what, exactly, is the information society and what are its implications for everyday life?

Many see the information age as a disjuncture with previous historical periods, each earmarked by their technical–economic base. Prior to the information age were the industrial and agrarian ages. Information economists such as Fritz Malchup and Marc Porat have detailed the growing contribution of the information sector to economic life, arguing that the percentage of gross national product attributable to the "knowledge industries," such as entertainment, telecommunication, research, and education, have been steadily growing over the last few decades.[1]

Similarly, Daniel Bell has argued that we have, for some for some decades now, been in the midst of a fundamental social transition from an economy based in the manufacturing of goods to one based in the provision of services, and that fundamental to the change is the increasing reliance on information processing and distribution.[2] Characteristic of this "post-industrial society" is a decline in the number of traditional agrarian and "blue collar" industrial occupations and a concomitant rise in middle-class, white-collar occupations associated with office work. Around the turn of the century, agricultural laborers made up more than 30 percent of the workforce; today they represent about 3 percent. The information sector, meanwhile, supplies more than 45 percent of all jobs in the United States, up from about 10 percent one hundred years ago. The market value of Microsoft surpassed that of General Motors in 1992. The service industries, including communication and telecommunications, have become an ascending component of the national and international economy. This, in turn, may signal a reduction in the economic and social distance between classes, according to Bell.

A host of other popular writers have addressed the topic, from Alvin Toffler, author of *Third Wave*, to management consultant Peter Drucker, each arguing for the revolutionary nature of the changing information environment.[3]

At the same time others question analyses of the information age that place their emphasis on disjuncture as opposed to continuity. Instead of characterizing the information society as a revolution or a new era, they view it as a more fluid outgrowth of existing social and economic structures. While the importance of the information sector has accelerated in recent decades they nonetheless stress the relationship and connectedness of communication systems and information markets with their antecedents in social, industrial, and political history. Representing a classic Marxist analysis, Herb Schiller argues that capitalism constitutes the underlying theme in technical development and that the internal dynamics of a capital economy make mandatory the regular improvement of technology to increase efficiency and profitability.[3] Information theorist Jorge Schement adds to the role of capitalism what he considers a requisite element of industrialization—the organizing principle for capitalism—in explaining the expansion of the information economy.[4]

Other sociologists have offered alternative, albeit complimentary, analyses. Anthony Giddens, for example, cites the surveillance requirements and activities of the developing nation states of the modern world as a fundamental contributor to the rise of information technics.[5] James Beniger sees the new information technologies as the most recent manifestations of a "control revolution" that stretches back to the industrial revolution and constitutes the effects rather than the causes of underlying socio-economic change premised on the need to control production, distribution, and product markets in the modern era.[6]

Whether one views broadband communication as an evolutionary occurrence or a revolutionary one, no one doubts that it constitutes a significant change in the national and global telecommunications system.

In the late 1960s and early 1970s, social planners, urban sociologists, and assorted academics and policymakers wrote voluminously about the potential of cable television to revolutionize communications—the "Blue Sky" era discussed in Chapter 2. One of the core visions was that of a newly democratized communications system, an electronic forum for the exchange of ideas and commentary. It would be free to all and provide a voice for the common man and woman. It was to be the electronic equivalent of the town square. With it would come instant voting, and electronic plebiscites, both local and national. Services, too, would abound; health care would be electronically provided and improved, two-way interactive services would offer enhanced opportunities for education, child care, and any number of services, all of the same dreams now recast as a function of the Internet and the information highway.[7]

This outpouring of praise and hope for the potential of early cable television to reshape the urban environment and help remake civic life illustrated the two larger aspects of the long-standing debate about the role of technology and society noted above. The first point deals with the causal relationship between the two. The question, as economic historian Robert Heilbroner bluntly phrased it in a classic 1967 article, is "do machines make history?"[8] To what extent is technology a uniformly dominant force in social change? The second related question is whether technological change or even technology generally is beneficial or detrimental to society. Quite often the two questions are intertwined, as in the blue sky prophesies that assumed (or at least hoped) that cable would open new avenues for local self-expression and that such a technological trajectory would in turn disperse political and social power more equitably.

The theme of technological utopia is an old one and the idea of a democratic technic has been particularly strong in American ideology. Technology, especially in popular writing, has been seen as the force that would break the shackles of heavy manual labor, freeing citizens from the drudgery of subsistence employment to pursue philosophy, the arts, community beneficence, and a host of self-actualizing and socially enhancing activities. Technology meant progress, and progress, by definition, was good. Numerous writers have traced this theme in American cultural history, noting, for example, the perceived promise of the coming of electricity to "exorcise social disorder and environmental disruption, eliminate political conflict and personal alienation, and restore ecological balance and a communion of man with nature."[9] Similar promises have been held out for the telegraph, telephone, and television. Utopian writers such as Edward Bellamy, in his classic *Looking Backward,* describe a world made comfortable and secure by the wonders of technical innovation, including a telephone-based mass media system that delivered live twenty-four-hour music into everyone's home.[10]

While many writers in both fiction and nonfiction have described a technological Garden of Eden, however, just as many have seen a technological concentration camp. George Orwell's *1984* is a model of technological despotism in which everyone's move is monitored electronically and repressive control is enabled by unceasing surveillance.

It is not only the blunt trauma of authoritarian rule that has concerned critics of technology, but the dehumanizing possibilities of the industrialized workplace and the stultifying routines that accompany it. In Charlie Chaplin's famous 1930s film, *Modern Times,* he portrays the common man trapped—figuratively and literally—in the crushing cogs of the social–industrial machine where people become little more than replaceable parts themselves and the human spirit withers. It was the assembly-line rationalism, the "Fordism," of the industrial age that worried many. Lewis Mumford, a prominent scholar of technology and society, joined the pessimists in his latter years, dejectedly predicting "man will become a passive purposeless, machine-conditioned animal whose proper functions . . . will either be fed into the machine or strictly limited and controlled for the benefit of depersonalized, collective organizations."[11]

One of the most influential contemporary technological pessimists is the French social philosopher Jacques Ellul. For Ellul, the problems of society and technology are much more subtle, much more powerful, and much more ubiquitous than those captured by Fordism. It is not just the technology itself, its use, development, or the technological process that is of greatest concern for Ellul, but rather the mindset, the philosophy of life that rests behind the technology, that he sees as dangerous. It is what he calls "technique," the ruthless principle of mechanical efficiency that permeates all contemporary thinking, the cold machine-driven rationalism of modern management, the consistency of fast food, and the prearranged "playdates" for suburban children.[12]

Ellul sees little hope of overcoming the cultural bondage of technique, in part because he locates it so centrally. He is significantly, if not completely, a technological determinist. Technological determinism describes social thinking that privileges the technological component of a social system over all others. There are variations on this theme, as well as endless debates. There are hard determinists and soft determinists along with scholars who reject any form of determinism as an oversimplification of a complex social process. Mumford, for example, while expressing dismay at the possibilities of a technocratic civilization, saw culture as antecedent to technology in social formation.[13]

Debates about the role of communications technology, as contrasted with technology generally, follow along similar lines. The predominant examples of technological determinism in communications are Harold Adam Innis and his more widely known student Marshall McLuhan. Both centered communications technology in the process of social formation. McLuhan's admonition that "the medium is the message" was intended to point people's attention away from the content of television and the endless debates about sex and violence and toward the phenomenon of the technology of television itself and its power to reshape how we interact with the world.

Against McLuhan are scholars such as Brian Winston, who sees technology as only a piece of a larger social puzzle developing within the context of existing social and economic forces.[14] Social conditions act to retard or suppress any potential that a communication technology might have to radically alter the social relations in a society, according to Winston.

Similar differences in perspective are apparent in the views on the social impact of new communications technology, which one writer has labelled "Technologies of Freedom" and another "The Electronic Nightmare." In the first instance, communications scholar Ithiel de Sola Pool has argued against undue governmental restraint on new media forms, especially those such as cable television, because of their potential to foster increasingly pluralistic political life, reminiscent of the Blue Sky language noted above.[15] He has lauded the diversity of voices that hundred-channel cable systems and on-line networks would make possible and has argued that only political error would prevent the blossoming of the system. Conversely, Robert Wicklein's *Electronic Nightmare* sees cable television and other interactive technologies as the modern equivalent of *1984*, carrying the capacity to deprive citizens of privacy, security, and, ultimately, freedom.[16]

Even more alarming are the concerns of some observers that the information age will usher in not an era of freedom and creativity but a tidal wave of meaningless and disconnected information that will inundate and drown us in social irrelevancy. Ellul, again, leads the way in worrying about a kind of information overload that the broadband system may unleash. The majority of news and information on television, according to Ellul, is superficial and trite and distracts from meaningful thinking and discussion about important issues. The pastiche of two-second flashing images born by remote-control grazing only exacerbates the tendency to mistake disconnected data points with understanding. In this way, broadband, interactive media providing access to a million databases of news and entertainment become a form of popular delusion; they are inherently undemocratic and in their own way subtle forms of totalitarian control.

The debate between the pessimists and the optimists no doubt will continue. A middle ground suggests that the emerging global information infrastructure will affect many things dramatically, some not at all, will benefit some individuals in a myriad of subtle and overt ways, and work to the detriment of others. There will be intended and unintended effects as the tools of the information utility open opportunities we dare not even speculate about today.

The question of the interaction between society and technology, generally, and society and communications technology, specifically, is an exceptionally complex one that does not lend itself to sweeping generalizations. In addition to the broad theoretical and philosophical views outlined above, television touches our lives in scores of ways, both good and bad. Different questions and varying situations tend to call on particular theories or sets of theories to help explain the relationship. There is, as yet, no unified field theory in media studies, but there are some clear-cut avenues of thought. To examine how information technologies may help shape the world it is useful to move from the more general level of analysis to look at specific issues.

USING MULTICHANNEL TV

Why do people watch television, and why do they watch certain kinds of television? Why do they subscribe to DBS instead of the local cable operation or why do they switch from cable to an MMDS service? The answers are as varied as the individuals themselves and not always as obvious as they seem. Communication researchers and market analysts have been looking at these issues for many years both to better understand the role media plays in our lives and to improve the competitive position of their respective businesses.

Among the approaches used, primarily by social scientists, is "uses and gratifications" theory, along with several related approaches such as "expectancy value" research and the concept of "para-social interaction." All attempt to address the question of motivation, and by implication the effect of certain media use patterns on individuals and society.

Uses and grats is best understood against a backdrop of concern about the powerful effects of mass media. Earlier in the twentieth century, one popular view of mass communication was that of a powerful, ubiquitous propaganda machine capable of political persuasion on a mass scale. What has been dubbed the "magic bullet" or "hypodermic model" of media effects saw individuals as open, ready vessels, easily swayed by political messages from those who controlled the means of communication. The rise of the new mass media in the early 1900s, movies and radio in particular, a concern about mass society and the loss of individual attachment to social moorings, the increasing popularity of philosophical irrationalism and the rise of Freudian approaches to psychology all fed into the belief among some that exposure to media messages could quickly alter one's attitudes and beliefs.[17] Important research programs starting in the 1940s and 1950s soon helped belie those concerns, demonstrating that individuals, especially adults with well-developed ideologies, were significantly more resistant to short-term political propaganda than some feared.

Uses and gratifications research has its roots in this notion of the active audience, an audience of individuals with reasonably well-formed ideas about how the world works and certain needs they think can be satisfied by certain patterns of media use. Attention here is turned to what people do with media and is informed by the appreciation that viewers are directed agents with conscious, as well as unconscious, motives. People evaluate and select media content based on specific criteria. Instead of asking "what does media do to people," uses and gratifications asks "what do people do with media?"[18]

Some of the motivations and categories of motivations for television viewing have already been discussed in Chapter 6. This list of uses to which media is put include information seeking and learning, self-discovery and self-actualization, context for social interaction, diversion, and escapism. Various researchers have categorized motivations in different ways. Some, as noted, invoke the idea of instrumental versus ritual or habitual usage. Watching a home improvement show to find out how to fix a door or catching a few minutes of the Weather Channel to see if it is going to rain are examples of instrumental viewing. Habitual or ritual viewing is what others have labelled "media seeking." Watching a particular prime-time television show because you have watched it for years and because that is simply what you and your family do at a particular time is ritual viewing; it becomes part of the fabric and rhythm of your daily life.

By offering new and varied delivery and content alternatives, multichannel television has altered many use patterns. Families that might have been drawn together in the evening in the context of watching a movie on NBC or CBS now may be split into different rooms in the house watching ESPN in the den, MTV in the bedroom, and the Home and Garden channel in the kitchen.

Alternatively, some families may be drawn more tightly together or drawn toward closer contact with others across the nation through the development and use of the targeted demographic and subject channels. A family that shares an interest in hiking and the outdoors might join to watch programming on one of the outdoor channels. Religious families might gravitate toward the Family Channel's *700 Club*. Moreover, those watching the targeted content tend to identify and relate to the unseen thousands or millions of other viewers who share that life interest or perspective. An inherent human need for social contact or perceived social contact can drive much of one's media activity.

For individuals with little real-world contact with others, people who by choice or circumstance lead more isolated lives, television can even become a substitute for human interaction. The concept of para-social interaction suggests that some people treat television, its programs, and characters, as if they were real, thereby satisfying an innate need for social intercourse. Para-social interaction helps explain why some soap opera fans treat the program characters as if they were real, sending letters to praise or condemn characters' on-screen plots and small treacheries, even going so far as to send money or food when a character is portrayed in difficult straits.

De-linking or separating from human interaction can, for many, be just as important as making contact and media serves as a simple and effective means of escape and diversion from the stresses and demands of everyday life.

A related, and to some degree consequent, approach to motivation and use is expedience-value research. Expectancy value theory extends the uses and gratification concept by noting the differences between gratifications sought and gratifications obtained and tying them to the consequent level of viewer satisfaction. If a given cable channel or program exceeds a viewer's expectations, satisfaction with that program and its perceived value increases. The converse, of course, is also true. The expectancy value model has been particularly popular with some marketing researchers who see it as a tool for analyzing levels of cable subscription or repeated viewing of specific channels. The focus often is on level of viewer satisfaction. LaRose and Atkin, for example, found that levels of cable subscription, especially consumer motivations for disconnecting, were explained more fully through expectancy value analysis than they were through demographic variables, such as age or income, or through simple cost of service.[19]

VIEWING HABITS AND FRAGMENTATION

One of the first and most obvious effects of cable and satellite television or any media is the basic fact of their existence. Because people spend time with multichannel TV, by definition they do not engage in alternative activities. And by virtue of the way people reallocate their television time to cable and satellite programming, new questions about social formation and cultural cohesion have arisen.

We can start with the observation that people have only so much time to spend on certain life activities; there are only twenty-four hours in a day. Over the years television viewing time has steadily increased in American homes, from about five hours per household per day in 1960 to about seven hours per day now.[20] Increasing channel capacity, further, has been related to increased viewing time. The average amount of television viewing in a noncable TV household is about 45.2 hours per week, in a cable TV household it is about 59.2 hours per week.[21] According to recent time budget studies, the activities that occupy most people's time in an average day include, in order, work, sleep, and watching television.

The advent of broadcast television is held chiefly responsible for the dramatic changes in people's moviegoing habits in the 1950s, as people stayed at home to watch instead of going out, and attendance figures at theaters plummeted from over four million in 1946 to about one million by the 1970s. Television also was held responsible for the decline in attendance of minor league baseball. Visiting neighbors and even comic book reading suffered in the glow of the blue-green screen.

The introduction of cable television was seen by some, as Chapter 2 points out, as a threat to local broadcasting, as audiences fragmented and viewership was siphoned away from over-the-air television to cablecasting. The ongoing slide of network ratings bears witness to the movement of viewers from three channels to thirty or more.

The fragmentation of the broadband audience has implications beyond the competitive arena of the news and entertainment industry. Social observers have expressed concern about the potential decline or even disintegration of a common social language and ideology. As early as 1969, media scholar James Carey commented on the centripetal and centrifugal functions of mass media.[22] The former acted as a social glue that helped bind the culture in a common rhetoric. That is, no matter what one's ethnic or political background, everyone watched pretty much the same kind of television. The nation shared three channels of news and entertainment and, because of the economic nature of the mass appeal system of programming, the differences between those three channels in terms of actual cultural content was negligible. Television constituted a relatively unified vision of the American landscape, one which few people could, or chose to, escape. Cable and satellite services today program to micro-levels of taste and interest. As audiences and sub-audiences gravitate to these slivercast channels, goes the argument, the centripetal force that brings people together is not just lost but replaced by a centrifugal, expansive force that pushes people apart. Viewers now watch ESPN or BET or the Family Channel instead of ABC. And to the extent that those specialized channels offer a different vision of and language about the outside world, viewers' collective perceptions are concurrently divided and, perhaps, isolated. While people do not, in the multichannel world, watch only one channel, the limited channel repertoire of most families probably does exhibit some kind of internal consistency with respect to values and norms. One is unlikely to find many viewers devoted simultaneously to the *700 Club* and the Playboy Channel. The fabric of a common political heritage that holds us together thereby begins to loosen and unravel at the ideological seams.

Heavy empirical support for the substantive existence of a centrifugal force is as yet undeveloped, however. The proposal assumes that the discrete channels themselves in fact speak different ideological languages, that despite the above *700 Club*–Playboy Channel example, the underlying norms and values of most channels exhibit wide variance, that ESPN differs radically from A&E. While the ideology of MTV may arguably be distinct from that of the Family Channel, how far do such differences extend? One recent study suggests there has been relatively little change, for example, in the use of historically underrepresented groups, such as African Americans and Hispanics, in primary program roles, as a consequence of the new channels. While the study acknowledged the contribution of BET and similar channels, it concluded that cable channels were, on balance, no better than the major networks at offering representation of minority groups comparable to their population distributions or that cable had helped improve levels of representation over time.[23] While this is bad news from the perspective of a more accurate and socially desirable representation of all groups on television, it does not, at the same time, support a notion of broad-based cultural fragmentation.

INFORMATION RICH AND INFORMATION POOR

There is yet another dimension to this issue of cultural differentiation, one that has less to doing with content and viewing habits and more to do with general access to and control of the system. One of the frequently discussed fears in the conversation about the emerging information age is the possibility that the economic and social gap between classes will widen as a consequence of the evolution of the emerging system. The concern goes by a number of names: information rich–information poor, information haves and have nots, information apartheid. It is the fear that there will be an increasingly wide social distance between those who can afford access to information and those who cannot.

The possibility, observers point out, is important for several reasons. Full and equal access to information is critical to informed self-governance. Our political system is premised on the assumption that everyone has sufficient information about the working of the government to make rational decisions about representation and policy. Moreover, as all observers note, knowledge is power. In countless ways, from politics to economics, access to information means access to power. Knowing more than someone else about stock prices, the potential impact of a legislative proposal on the environment, or where the best supermarket deal on laundry soap is, provides an advantage to those who have the information.

The argument for information equity is not that everyone should know everything, but that everyone should have opportunities to access the same information, especially information relative to self-actualization and self-governance. There is also a deeply held cultural belief in social equality and its darker side, the fear of social or political power being too heavily concentrated in one source, be it an individual or a social class. Morally and politically our system rests, in part, on the notion of equal opportunity to sources of social power such as the vote, social services, the open economic market, and information.

Like the social fragmentation theory, the worry about information apartheid is somewhat counter-intuitive insofar as one might expect the increased flow of information and the enhancement of the nature and detail of raw data to help make knowledge more accessible to everyone, to help democratize a process by breaking down centralized and tightly held repositories of information jealously guarded by the government or private interests. In fact, the jury is still very much out on the question of information equality. The system is not sufficiently developed and the empirical data not widely enough gathered to declare all the concerns fully justified. Nonetheless, there are enough real-life signs and enough good grounding in theory to suggest that the fears are not without merit.

The potential for an information-based division of classes can be seen in several social and economic arenas, including research into a phenomenon known as the knowledge gap hypothesis, in economic trends that raise fears about privileged access to the system, and in legal concerns about control over information.

The Knowledge Gap

The introduction of television in the 1950s was greeted with a host of happy social expectations, along with the normal measure of fear that accompanies such innovation. One of the hopes for the new medium was that it would constitute an educational and information resource for people previously deprived of broader educational opportunities. It was seen as being capable of extending to everyone the benefits of lifetime education, news, and the panoply of local, national, and global events and ideas. It was to be a democratizing force that would make more equitable the levels of knowledge and understanding held by the different social strata. Researchers subsequently set out to test this hypothesis. The results were disappointing to those who hoped television might constitute the great leveler. At the University of Minnesota a team of social scientists—Phillip Tichenor, Clarence Olien, and George Donahue—began publishing a series of studies on what they called the "knowledge gap" hypothesis.[24]

According to the knowledge gap hypothesis, the introduction of greater amounts of information about public affairs into a social system not only fails to equalize the amounts of knowledge that members of that system hold about the topic, it in fact makes matters worse by increasing the gap between certain segments of the community. More specifically, as increasing amounts of information on a subject flow into, say, a small town, everyone does learn more about that topic, but some groups learn at a faster rate and acquire relatively more information over time.

In other words, the difference between groups grows larger as the fast-acquisition group takes on knowledge at a quicker rate—the knowledge gap grows. Unsurprisingly, the groups in question are characterized by socio-economic status. High-income, high-education groups become disproportionately better informed about things relative to socially disadvantaged groups. The reasons, at least in retrospect, are clear. People with more money have greater access to information that typically comes in the form of newspapers, books, magazines, and similar retail materials. In addition, more highly educated groups (and income and education have always been correlated) assimilate complex information more quickly because they have the educational skills to translate certain kinds of information, and they have the socio-cultural context, the background in history or economics, that permits faster contextualization of information.

The knowledge gap hypothesis is subject to a variety of factors that can moderate these effects. It is often situation specific, with information about sports, for example, rendering different kinds of results. But knowledge centrally important to local and national self-governance is likely to reflect this pattern and it has obvious implications for broadband, interactive media systems and an information age.

Access: The Pay-Per Society

There are several ways in which access to the emerging system is important: access to get on the system and have one's voice heard, access to two-way real-time communication, as in simple POTs service, and access to information. In the first case, it has been observed that the freedom of the press belongs to the person who owns one. For social "out groups" seeking to get their message, their story, on the system, the possibility of censorship by those in control of the system is of concern to some. The political requirement of public access channels on many cable systems has been one response.

Whether the problem is transmitting information or receiving it, the underlying issue is usually one of economics. In 1988, critical social researcher Vincent Mosco coined the phrase "pay-per society." For Mosco the paperless society of electronic data becomes once again a pay-per society in the sense that there is no such thing as free or even cheap information: A monetary value can be and is attached to every viewer, every program, every keystroke entered into a computer, every bit in the digital stream.[25]

There are two significant ways in which the information highway becomes a toll road: the first is an entrance fee, the toll one pays to get on, the second comes in the price of the information itself. You pay to get into the venue and you pay again to purchase the goods. In cable, you pay a monthly fee for access to the system, even at lifeline rates. If you want on-demand movies, you pay another, albeit small, access fee in the form of a monthly charge for the converter box. Finally, you pay for the film itself.

The problems of ownership and the control of the telecommunication system, discussed in Chapter 5, become important here. Cable, satellite, and telco providers may compete, but access to any of these systems by consumers is limited by their financial resources. There are two major ways to limit access, one simply by not running a wire past one's house and another by charging unreasonable rates when the wire does come by. In the first case, cable operators and other telecommunication providers have occasionally been accused of cream-skimming and redlining. Cream-skimming, a term usually attached to cable overbuilders or telco access providers, describes the practice of targeting only the most affluent or accessible markets in a community, a high-density, high-income condominium complex might be one example. The cost of wiring is relatively lower than for other areas and the potential rewards higher. Redlining, as in real estate, refers to avoiding certain neighborhoods, typically lower income areas where profit potential is smaller and operational costs higher. There are, in fact, sound business reasons to service some neighborhoods in favor of others. In the better sections of town, a higher portion of people are likely to sign up for service meaning less stranded investment in plant. Residents are likely to be more economically stable with higher rates of on-time payment and lower rates of churn. But the social consequences of those decisions do not evaporate because the motivations are economically reasonable. Something as simple as housing density affects access. It is more efficient and so more profitable to wire areas of high density. Rural homes and farms are the last to be wired, if at all, because it is economically unjustifiable to run a wire several miles to serve one subscriber.

These are the nutrients that feed the debate over universal service. Universal service has long been a norm in the telephone industry. This is the social obligation to run that single wire miles to the lonely prairie farmhouse even though it costs several thousand dollars to do so. The telcos have been compensated by being permitted to charge higher rates for some customers than others. Rural service rates, for example, are below costs because telcos charge businesses rates above cost. Some residential service is thereby underwritten and universal service supported through differential pricing.

Even with access to a wire, some fear that system operators will charge monopolistic rates, foreclosing service for the financially disadvantaged. Legislative and policy guidelines that encourage or mandate basic and low-cost levels of service are designed to give those who can least afford it the assurance that they have some basic access to telecommunication facilities. But even with lifeline service, statistics reveal that income level remains one of the primary determinants of cable television subscription. As income level increases so does cable penetration; over 82 percent of homes with incomes of $60,000 or more subscribe to cable while only 54.2 percent of homes with incomes under $20,000 subscribe. And the income gap between subscribers and nonsubscribers widens every year. In 1985 the aggregate national income of cable and noncable homes was very close, $1.34 versus $1.12 billion, respectively. In 1995 the figure for cable homes had risen to $2.75 billion, while for noncable homes it had dropped to less than $1 billion.[26]

The most recent incarnation of this concern has come in debate about access to the Internet. Access to the electronic system requires a certain level of home technology, which is never cheap. If the Internet is to become a primary form of social and political information, the question is how to provide access for those who cannot easily afford the price of the ticket, and insofar as nearly all possible solutions will require some financial support, who will pay the fare? Should broadband services, including cable television, be subject to rate regulation and universal service obligations similar to those of the telephone companies? In the United States the National Information Infrastructure initiative seeks to promote ubiquitous access to a telecommunication infrastructure that can support broadband, digital services like access to the Internet, large file transfer, remote access to databases, telemedicine, video teleconferencing, and the like. The U.S. initiative seeks to promote private sector investment through appropriate tax and regulatory policies. Through passage of the Telecommunications Act of 1996, the concept of universal services has been expanded to promote the NII by expressly identifying the special service and access needs of schools, libraries, and medical facilities. The Act calls for a special fund to finance universal service for telephony and relies on competition and market forces to provide equitable service in broadband communications. The efficacy of these initiatives will only be assessed over time.

Information as a Commodity

Gaining access to the system and the question of how much access costs is only one part of the concern about information rich and poor, an additional issue involves the costs of the information itself. Information has long been a commodity, an item of value that can be bought and sold. Colonial newspapers were often vehicles for commercial information on shipping news. But information and mediated forms of expression have traditionally been more than that as well. Art and literature serve as local and global forms of self-expression, the provision of information is a social service and a social responsibility for members of the institutional press, and information used in formal and informal education is an essential part of a civilized society. The rising tide of commodifiction of information has been seen as a threat to much of this. Commodification describes the increasing stress on information as a fungible as opposed to social good. Part of this debate is captured in the notion of "infotainment." It is the concern that news and public affairs programming in particular are increasingly sensationalized and trivialized in order to draw larger audiences and more advertising or subscription dollars. News and information that previously was low-cost or free and relatively clean of pure commercial intent increasingly becomes a part of the infotainment and advertainment environment. Advertiser-supported entertainment and information is increasingly the only kind available to economically disadvantaged segments. Low-cost information becomes embedded with explicit and implicit commercial pitches. Access, therefore, to less commercialized and arguably higher quality fare requires additional payment. To get an uncut, commercial-free movie, you pay a fee. To obtain in-depth, sophisticated business or political information, some individuals pay very high prices for specialized newsletters or trade journals, or in the broadband world, database access. Similarly, retiering practices in the cable industry that relocated popular services into higher-cost tiers, along with general rate increases, will move cable programming farther away from some families' ability to pay. And even when those families do pay for the more expensive services, they will allocate a greater proportion of their income to television than those with greater means. The quality of the information available to some segments of society decreases, it is argued, while only the affluent retain access to undiluted material.

Copyright

The debate about control of and access to information in the digital age has especially focused in recent years on the problem of copyright. In 1994 media analyst Anne Branscomb looked closely at the question "Who Owns Information?"[27] No question is more central in the information age than the ownership and control of the information. We have seen how companies are aligning themselves industrially to exploit to the fullest extent the expanding demand for software, content, and information.

Because programming or information is increasingly a commodity, those who control it are increasingly vigilant in guarding against what is considered unauthorized use. In legal terms, multichannel television programming is intellectual property, property that some would argue is equivalent to personal property or real estate. In economic terms, however, information is largely a public good. That is, it can theoretically be used and reused without diminishing its value to the next person—a magazine can and is handed around to many people; unlike a soft drink or machinery that wears out over time, information is not "consumed" in this sense. This characteristic gives it significant social utility, but those who own and seek to exploit information justifiably note that it can lead to a situation in which information used or enjoyed by many people—as in the case of pass-around magazine reading—denies the owners compensation for their efforts in producing the material. Publishers receive subscription revenue from the first reader but not the second, third, and so on. (In fact, in the magazine industry, pass-around circulation is figured into advertising rates, but it nonetheless illustrates the problem.)

Therefore, because information is increasingly a product for sale, there is a keen interest on the part of program producers to move it out of the public sphere insofar as it might in any way be available to large numbers of people for free or at low cost. The advent of the information age has, ironically, made this ever more difficult. The power of contemporary information technology, and especially the digitization of all information, makes real-world control of content somewhere between difficult and impossible. The advent of the photoduplication process, the ubiquitous copying machine, made it relatively easy to reproduce at reasonable expense any written or published work, an ability millions quickly took advantage of. Information from books and magazines that consumers would otherwise have had to purchase is now easily copied.

But even the copying machine can print only a few copies at a time and usually not in the same format (e.g., hardcover and glossy pages) as the original. Videotape machines upped the ante in the tug of war between producers and consumers by giving anyone with a VCR the ability to tape and copy television programs and films. In fact, the illegal copying and distribution of music CDs and theatrical videotapes has become a billion-dollar business for pirate companies based in some Pacific Rim countries. It has been such a large problem that it became a major issue in trade negotiations, for example, with China. The VCR can make copies that look more like originals than is true in photoduplication, but limits on quality and production capacity remain.

The digital revolution is to photoduplication and analog video copying what the stealth bomber is to an ox-drawn cart. Duplicating a book via "xerography" takes some amount of time, paper, and money, even copying a videotape requires a blank cassette and a bit of time, and in both cases the copy is never exactly the same or as good as the original. Downloading digitized video or text onto a floppy disk or posting it on a Web site for global distribution takes so little time, effort, and money that it is almost pointless to try to measure them, and each copy is indistinguishable from the original. In the digital age, information is money, but that information can be "counterfeited" by nearly anyone, perfectly and instantly, and distributed to everyone at practically no cost.

Technology, in short, makes widespread easy copying possible. Information democrats, with a small "d," argue that information, including sometimes television programming, is a necessary public resource and ought to be made as widely and cheaply available as possible. They further argue that a great deal of information in the form of art, literature, the moving image, is our cultural heritage and ought to be a part of the public record. Writers, creators, and owners of information argue they ought to be compensated for their work out of basic fairness and out of the incentive it offers to continue producing creative works.

As Branscomb asks above, then, what sort of information ought to be made public and widely accessible, what sort of information ought to be protected, and toward what end? Existing law is not always helpful in answering these questions.

The 1976 Copyright Act discussed previously is the legislative extension of Article 1, Section 8 of the U.S. Constitution that gives the government the power to issue copyrights and patents. The intent of the Constitutional protection was not ultimately to protect the property interests of authors and creators but rather to protect the greater social good of assuring a continuing stream of innovation and artistry.

But the law of the mid 1970s has not kept pace with technological change. For example, copyright holders are protected from infringement in cases involving public performance of their work, that is performances typically for profit that would deny the authors royalties they would otherwise receive if the viewers or readers had to purchase the work. It is the notion of public performance, you may recall, that helped the cable industry avoid copyright liability in the mid 1960s. The Supreme Court determined that retransmission of broadcast programming was not a reperformance of the work; cable wires were a passive extension of the private home aerial. Attempts by organizations representing copyright holders to expand the protection beyond public performance and into private use of copyrighted material have met with mixed results. In 1984, the Supreme Court ruled against the idea when it held that private individuals could videotape material off the air (or cable) without violating the law, in situations involving time-shifting of copied material.[28] By a 5 to 4 decision, the Court, in the "Betamax" case, held that VCR taping fell into the "fair use" exemption that permits copying a limited amount of material for certain noncommercial and educational purposes. The decision was seen at the time as a major setback for film studios who were deathly afraid that home VCR taping would erode the value of their vast program holdings and threaten markets for new programming.

Conversely, in 1995 the Clinton administration revealed a proposal to update copyright law to protect the authors and creators of digital material or information distributed in digital form. The heart of the proposal was to classify electronic transmission of documents and information as copies protected under existing law. The catch in the proposal was that it would therefore make any individual liable for copyright infringement when they downloaded any information for nearly any purpose, commercial or private. Insofar as access to an Internet Web site, for example, is in reality copying that information onto the RAM or hard drive in your home computer, the proposal would require permission and arguably a potential fee for accessing the database. To insure that every piece of digital information generated compensation for its owners, the proposal also suggested electronic "watermarks" that would attach to digital documents, tracking their location and use anywhere on the system. Illegal, that is unpaid, use of copyrighted material could be spotted and violators prosecuted. Finally, the proposal would reduce or eliminate the exemption for the fair use of material. The meter could start ticking no matter how much information was used or for what purpose. As broadband television programming migrates to digital servers and set-top boxes take on the characteristics of high-end computers, a similar logic could be extended to the protection television programming, reversing the holding in the Betamax case. The proposal generated significant debate and opposition from those who sought a more open arena for information and interchange on the information highway.[29]

Another complicating facet of the existing law is that it protects only the form of expression, not the actual facts or ideas. A newspaper, for example, can copyright only the way in which it tells the story, the style, and structure of the material; it cannot copyright the facts of the story, such as the results of a presidential election. This can lead to curious situations. A private firm may spend a great deal of money collecting raw information on, for example, marketing trends. A rival firm may buy one copy of the final report or database and, arguably without violating copyright, turn around and market the same information under its own name. One market firm, in fact, borrowed liberally from freely available academic studies on Internet use, repackaging the information and selling it to private clients for a hefty fee.[30] The Supreme Court has ruled that a local telephone company that had collected names and phone numbers for its phone book could not protect that information and allowed a rival company to repackage and market that data without having had to spend the time and money to collect the original information.[31]

There is a heavy tension in this area between the rights of the individual and the rights of the collective, between the rights of authors and creators to control their own work and reap the rewards of their efforts on the one hand and the interests of the public in open and equitable access to art, information, and even entertainment. Balancing too far on the side of copyright protection could once again push economic groups apart in their ability to enjoy the fruit of the broadband harvest. There are reasonable arguments on all sides. It makes for few easy answers to a set of important difficult questions. One of the legal and ethical challenges of the information age will be to sort out the competing interests and issues into a framework of law and policy that meets a wide range of needs in an equitable manner.

PRIVACY IN THE INFORMATION AGE

Another issue related to the broad question of access and control of information has do to with privacy in the information age. In 1981 Wicklein warned people about what he saw as a threat to their personal privacy as a result of information age technology and techniques.[32] Surveillance of our public and private lives, directly and indirectly through the data that business and government has accumulated, were at the heart of the threat. It was not a new concern. Privacy as a concept in American jurisprudence made its debut in 1890 when legal scholars Samuel Warren and Louis Brandeis wrote a now famous article suggesting that privacy should be counted among the indispensable rights of modern life.[33] They wrote presciently that:

> Instantaneous photographs and newspaper enterprise have invaded the sacred precincts of private and domestic life; numerous mechanical devices threaten to make good the prediction that "what is whispered in the closet shall be proclaimed from the house-top."[34]

They argued that the law should recognize the threat to personal privacy pregnant in the new communications technologies. People, they declared, should have the general right "to be let alone." More recently, media scholar Oscar Gandy, Jr., has compared modern communication and information technology with the nineteenth-century Panopticon, an architectural design for use in prisons that would permit the jailer to keep constant surveillance on the inmates.[35]

Concern about privacy and the broadband information highway takes at least two major forms, one involving direct surveillance, another involving data privacy. The first speaks to the popular fear that government or business can surreptitiously watch or listen to people via the agency of an interactive communication system. One of the popular myths against which cable television had to battle in its formative years was the fear that people had of running a television wire into their home. Some felt it would allow the television to watch them in their living room (or bedroom) and transmit pictures back to the cable company. The fear became even more pronounced following early talks about two-way and interactive TV. In what some would consider an Orwellian nightmare come true, surveillance cameras are now commonplace in businesses and some public areas. They are ubiquitous in supermarkets, department stores, and government offices. Cameras are used to monitor traffic flow on highways. Baltimore, along with other cities, has placed cameras on tall poles in downtown areas giving police a twenty-four-hour, bird's-eye view of pedestrian traffic. High schools have experimented with video cameras in cafeterias and hallways to help maintain student order. Some see the day when many if not most of these cameras will be connected to a broadband, interactive television system and anyone will be able to tune into the shopping aisle at the local market, the traffic camera above the freeway, or the "neighborhood watch" camera in anyone's neighborhood.

The law generally protects one's privacy against intrusion and surveillance in private places such as your home. But there is no such protection in public places and there are unresolved questions about which sorts of business spaces constitute private as opposed to public venues and under what conditions.

Less obvious but considered of greater concern by many observers is data privacy. The process of collecting and selling information about individuals is a multibillion-dollar business. In the information society, a permanent record is made nearly every time a person makes a financial transaction, replies to a Web site survey, calls a business-related 800 number, subscribes to a magazine, or fills out a warranty card on a consumer electronics device. Marketing firms know who you are, where you live, what you do, what you wear, what you eat, and how you spend your leisure time. The cable company keeps information on the channels you buy, the phone companies keep records of the calls you make, the video store keeps records of the tapes you rent. Within certain legal safeguards, all the information can and is packaged and sold to people who have an interest in you, an interest usually tied to efforts to separate you from your money.

As the broadband system becomes increasingly interactive, the capacity to identify, record and collate information on discrete uses by individual citizens will increase dramatically. Databases will include the specific TV programs you have watched, the Web sites you have visited, the news articles you have requested, and the commercials you either watched or avoided.

Critics worry about the uses to which such detailed and private information can be put. Marketers will use it to target not just small groups but specific individuals; commercial pitches will be tailored specifically for you. Some, like Warren and Brandeis, worry about the news media getting its hands on private information and shouting it from the broadband rooftops.

The government has always been a primary source of concern in the extent to which it could monitor and control citizens' lives. In the early 1990s, the National Security Agency proposed that a special data encryption chip be installed in all telephones in the United States. The "Clipper Chip" would help secure data transfers through a highly sophisticated encoding process, but it would also contain a computerized "back door." The back door was a key to the encryption code held in "escrow" to protect data security but available to government agencies with a court order. Government agencies, therefore, using this electronic back door, could gain access to the computer conversations of anyone in the United States. The rationale was that law enforcement needed a way to crack the increasingly sophisticated computer systems of drug smugglers, organized crime, and terrorist groups. The fear was that the measure would have made nearly everything on any computer in the country subject to government inspection at the drop of a proper court order. Public outcry over the proposal forced its withdrawal, but similar ideas are still being considered by law enforcement agencies.

There is some legal protection, although critics are concerned it does not go far enough. The Privacy Act of 1974 requires that there be public knowledge of government data banks and that citizens have a right to correct inaccuracies in their record. More specifically, the Cable Act of 1984 requires cable companies to inform customers about any data that is collected, and it prohibits the company from collecting any information on an individual unless the information is necessary in the provision of a service, such as pay-per-view, or to detect signal theft.[36] Selling or releasing the subscriber information to a third party without subscriber consent also is prohibited, although systems can collect aggregate data that does not provide for individual identification. A similar law protects data on video store rentals.

Privacy, as with many of the other issues addressed here, involves important goals in conflict. The trick in a world of pay-as-you-go broadband communication is to strike the proper balance between competing worthwhile claims. It will be one of the more important policy challenges in the information age.

TELEVISION VIOLENCE

In late February of 1996 a prestigious group of television executives gathered at the White House to discuss with President Bill Clinton the problem of violence on television. Included in the meeting were TCI's John Malone; Gerald Levin, head of Time Warner; Ted Turner; Walt Disney's Michael Eisner; Rupert Murdoch; the heads of the other major broadcast networks, and others. The goal of the Presidential summit was to solicit an industry pledge to implement a television ratings system for program content. The system would be used in conjunction with a new technology, the V-chip. The V-chip reads a code television producers inscribe into each program and it blocks out those programs that parents deem unsuitable for their children. The "V" in V-chip stands for violence, and while an assortment of parental worries including language and sexual content dance around the problem, violence stands in center stage. Implementation of the V-chip proposal was mandated by the Telecommunication Act of 1996. It had the backing of the President and bi-partisan support in the Congress. The outcome was the current television ratings system, following the MPAA's age-based movie rating formula, with six viewing categories: TV-Y, all children; TV-Y7, children 7 years old and above; TV-G, General Audience; TV-PG, parental guidance suggested; TV-14, suitable for children 14 years old and above, and TV-M, for mature audiences only. When numerous citizens groups and politicians criticized the rating scheme for its lack of content-specific information, the industry proposed an amended plan, adding designations for sexual content (s), violence (v), objectionable language (l), adult dialogue (d), and fantasy violence (fv). Television news programs are exempt.

Media violence has been a public concern since the rise of mass media itself. Parents especially have worried that what their children see in films and on television might adversely affect their behavior. Literally thousands of books and articles have been published by sociologists, psychologists, and communication researchers. Two modern studies stand out as the most far-reaching and influential in this area. The 1971 Surgeon General's Report on Television Violence and the follow-up review of research conducted a decade later by the National Institute of Mental Health (NIMH).[37] The 1971 report is a collection of more than forty commissioned studies and literature reviews. Behavioral studies indicated that children clearly learned aggressive behavior from watching it on television, and could replicate the behavior when asked to do so. Whether viewing violence made them more inclined to behave aggressively or incited aggressive behavior also was studied. Results suggested that there was, for children, a positive relationship between watching TV violence and an inclination to behave more aggressively in certain situations. A positive albeit mild relationship between viewing and aggression also was found among adolescents.

The 1982 update by NIHM did not sponsor any original research but reviewed more than 3,000 articles and studies. The focus of the report was much broader than just TV violence, encompassing the pro-social effects of television viewing, general learning from television, and specific topics such as television and health. With respect to TV violence, however, the findings of the report reinforced previous conclusions of a causal relationship between viewing and behavior. The general consensus among social scientists today is that there is evidence to support a causal link between TV violence and the increased probability of subsequent aggressive behavior, especially in children. That conclusion must be carefully qualified however. The underlying models used in explaining this relation offer wide latitude in applying the findings to specific individuals and specific circumstances. Research suggests that some people will be affected in some conditions, but not everyone is affected all the time.

The principle theory used by researchers today is Social Learning Theory. In its simplest form it is what is more commonly known as modeling, the tendency for people, especially children, to mimic the behavior of others. In a classic experiment in 1965, social psychologist Albert Bandura demonstrated that children could learn aggressive behavior from television.[38] Children were shown television program segments in which aggression was both rewarded and punished on screen. Children who had seen the aggressive behavior rewarded were more likely than the alternative group to act violently later when given the opportunity. Importantly, however, even those children who did not replicate the aggressive behavior in the laboratory setting could demonstrate it if asked to; everyone learned from the models. The likelihood that this observational learning will actually lead to aggressive behavior is contingent on variety of factors. Children, for example, are more likely to act aggressively if they identify with the aggressive character, if the on-screen violent behavior is not punished, if the depictions are more realistic or lifelike (as opposed to, say, cartoon violence). Related concepts involve the use of aggressive cues in modeling and the state of arousal in the subject. Some researchers suggest that television provides cues to viewers about when and under what conditions violence is appropriate. Aggressive behavior in subjects also has been found to increase during periods of emotional arousal; children who are frustrated or angry are more likely to replicate an aggressive act than those who are not.

The set of qualifying criteria makes broad generalizations about any individual's response to television violence difficult; television, for example, is one important role model or influence in social learning, but it is not the only one. Countervailing influences include parents, schools, family, religious institutions, and cohorts. Children from abusive homes, where parental violence is the norm, are understandably more likely to have television violence reinforce their real-world experience than children from loving, supportive environments where the difference between the television world and the real world is a daily lesson.

This sensitivity to context has been taken up as a more prominent theme in recent research.[39] In a study sponsored by the cable television industry in 1995, researchers at the University of California at Santa Barbara looked closely at the context in which television violence was portrayed.[40] They found that, overall, almost three-fourths of all acts of television violence were likely to go unpunished and only 15 percent of the violence perpetrated by the "good guys" was likely to be negatively reinforced, thus "the characters that viewers, in particularly children, are most likely to identify with are rarely discouraged for acting aggressively."[41] The study also found that children's programming was less likely than other types to depict negative consequences of violence and most likely to depict unrealistically low levels of injury as a result of violence, increasing the risk for children who watch those programs.

The study, in addition, compared levels of violence in broadcast versus cable television programming. Public broadcasting was found to have the lowest overall amount of violent content, the broadcast networks had a slightly lower than average amount of violence. Basic cable programming showed amounts close to the industry average. The highest levels of violence were found on premium cable channels. Premium channels also revealed the heaviest use of warnings or content advisories. While this may help mitigate the violence findings, a companion study in the set funded by the cable industry reported, in initial findings, that warning advisories on violent television content seemed to have little or no effect on adolescents' interest in watching TV violence or their attitudes about violent programming, although MPAA ratings and some advisories were used by some young girls in choosing programs.

While controversy still surrounds the issue of television violence and how to deal with it, most social scientists have concluded that there is a relationship worth worrying about and Congress and the President through their endorsement of the V-chip have concurred.

MULTICHANNEL TV AND SOCIALIZATION

Modeling and social learning theory address the question of how media influence our behavior, especially certain forms of behavior. Media sociologists Melvin DeFleur and Sandra Ball–Rokeach include social learning theory among several different approaches that more broadly include the impact of media on how we come to understand the world.[42] These models of media socialization consider the "indirect, subtle and long-term influences [media] have on human culture and the organization of social life."[43]

In the broadest sense, various theories see media as one of several agents that help shape our perception of reality. Our cognitive universe, in the language of one approach, includes everything from the existence and nature of physical reality to social norms, political ideology, and personal values. Mediated channels of communication help teach you what it is like to be on the bottom of the ocean, how different politicians propose to handle the national debt, and whether it is good form to burp at the dinner table (it is not). Much of this is socializing information, the information that deals pointedly with social norms and values, bringing individuals into conformity with the existing social order and thereby maintaining social continuity over time. Television, newspapers, radio, books, and computers all play a role in the process, but they do not play the only role nor in most cases the most important role. As DeFleur and others have long noted, among the most important sources of socializing information are parents, educational institutions, peers, and religious agencies. The relative degrees of influence from these sources will vary by individual and circumstance. While most theoretical approaches agree that media is an actor in the play, they often diverge on the issue of how much influence it exerts and how the actual process operates.

For students interested in a deeper understanding of the important similarities and differences between and among these and other camps of media theory, there are a number of good surveys including *Mass Communication Theory* by Stanley Baran and Dennis Davis,[44] and *Mass Communication Theory* by Denis McQuail.[45] The discussion here will limit itself to a sampling of topics most commonly at issue in telecommunications drawing as necessary on the theoretical heritage behind them.

In cable, one of the first serious questions about the effect of the new channels on our attitudes and beliefs accompanied the introduction of MTV. In 1984, the National Coalition on Television Violence released a report condemning what it found to be increasing levels of violence in rock videos, and a host of academic studies followed. The concern was particularly pronounced as it interacted with the portrayal of women in the videos. Women, said many observers, were seen primarily as sex objects and often the victims of aggression. These concerns were not particular to MTV, the objectification of women and the issue of sex role stereotypes is a long-standing one in media, but cable seemed to push the boundaries and exacerbate the concerns. Cable was perceived as somehow less "public" than broadcasting because people had to pay for it, making it somehow less accountable to public sensitivities about these issues. Broadcasters had to be more careful in how they presented sexual situations, for example, following the desire to avoid offending any group too much. Cable channels were often more liberal in their treatment of sensitive subjects, especially channels such as HBO, which showed uncut theatrical movies that were frequently much more graphic than prime-time network television. MTV targeted a youth market for which sex and action were natural draws.

While the concern in some quarters was the simple portrayal of sexual activity and the fear that it would encourage young people to follow suit, especially teens and preteens, an additional worry centered on the power relationships between men and women that had characterized television for most of its history.

Studies have shown that women historically have been underrepresented in television, with men appearing in twice as many roles as women. In research on televising through the 1960s and 1970s, women who were shown on television typically held less powerful or prestigious positions than men and were too often cast as either domestic helpers or in purely sexual roles.[46] In most cases they were deferential to men. Research further confirmed that children learned from such portrayals what was socially appropriate for men and women—men, for example would be doctors and women were always the nurses.[47]

Researchers who studied MTV music videos, largely in the 1980s, concluded that women were frequently shown as sex objects, subject to various forms of physical and symbolic domination by men, portrayed as less active, and less worthy than men and confined to social roles inferior to men.[48]

Pro-Social Effects

Horace Newcomb and others, responding to criticisms of television content, have called television a cultural forum, pointing out that there is a wide variety of content, some of it angry and hostile, but some of it educational and uplifting.[49] People engage this content in a variety of ways and take away a breadth of lessons. To the extent that people learn about violence from television, some researchers also note they can learn cooperation. In fact, the pro-social aspects of television have been widely studied, although less so than the problems of TV. Much of the research focuses not on the usefulness of information, such as news or weather, but rather on the positive social messages that can accrue. They start from the same point as studies on sex role stereotyping or violence with the view that people, in one fashion or another, learn from television and that they can learn altruistic norms and values as readily as they can learn aggression. In the 1982 NIHM report, researchers looked at more than forty studies of television learning that sought to promote attitudes such as altruism, friendliness, self-control, and coping with fear. As expected, the findings suggested TV could be effective in these areas.[50] Pro-social behavior can take a variety of forms, including the intentional promotion of socially desirable behaviors such as those cited above, or in the reduction of antisocial activities, as in campaigns to reduce or prevent drug use. The children's television program *Sesame Street* is often cited as an example of successful educational programming for children. There also has been evidence that children can learn from the positive messages commercial broadcasters include in such fare as Saturday morning cartoons, although whether the brief homilies dedicated to sharing toys and playing fair balances the preponderance of the more questionable content remains problematic. Directed advertising campaigns aimed at increasing seat belt use or promoting AIDS awareness have mixed track records. Success, as interpreted by the people behind the campaigns, has depended on initial expectations, and the professionalism of the campaign itself.

Further, multichannel television, by expanding the choices and detail of available information has increased the utility of the media system. To the extent that programming services such as BET and GEMS provide opportunities for cultural self-expression and social visibility not previously possible, they constitute a pro-social outcome of cable and broadband TV. Similarly, the ability to access current information on local weather and breaking national news, provided by the Weather Channel and the various news programming services, is of great utility to individuals and society. C-SPAN's live coverage of the U.S. Congress has been widely lauded as a contribution to the process of governance. Cable and satellite television have structurally opened new avenues to content and much of the content has real-world utility. Distance education and the wider access to Internet resources that broadband-to-the-home can make possible further expand the benefits derived from the emerging system.

MULTICHANNEL TELEVISION AND POLITICAL LIFE

The 1996 Republican presidential nominating convention in San Diego was a made-for-television event unlike anything before it. The major broadcast networks had determined that it was unlikely there would be any surprises; there was no real competition for the Bob Dole–Jack Kemp ticket; audience interest, as ratings would later confirm, was lukewarm. Therefore, the networks limited their coverage to an hour in the evening. Political strategists, weaned on the importance of television coverage, used that hour to their best advantage with fully scripted and meticulously prepared for-television, multimedia presentations. More importantly, for the first time, the Republicans put on their own television show and distributed it themselves. Creating what they called GOP-TV, complete with anchors, interviews, and self-promoting commentary, they ran their own gavel-to-gavel coverage, then they acquired time on the Family Channel and USA, bypassing the networks and their reporters.

Television, almost from its inception, has been a powerful tool in politics and a powerful influence on political life. It opens the political arena to more people, at least as observers, and offers more information about political activity than was easily accessible before TV. It has become one of the primary influences in the process of political socialization. Most observers acknowledge that it has changed radically the nature of how political campaigns are run and who can enter. Most of the money spent on campaigns is spent on television time. Television is held partly responsible for the decline in the power of political parties, opening up, for example, the process of selecting candidates, helping move decision making out of the closed and "smoke-filled rooms" and onto the stage of heavily televised primary elections. Whether the shift from politics dominated by party machine to politics dominated by television is all for the better is a subject of debate.

Television's role in politics also has come under sharp attack. Candidates must present well on camera. The days of the dynamic orator with sweeping gestures and booming voice are gone, replaced by the quiet, sincere candidate who can use the intimacy of the living room television set. Television's form, therefore, acts as a filter for who can and cannot compete for office. Detailed descriptions of campaign platforms and policy positions have given way to the MTV pastiche of quick cuts, appeals to visceral emotions and personal attacks on opponents. Critics like Neil Postman point out that television has displaced writing, the image has replaced substance, public discourse has become jest and we are, politically, "amusing ourselves to death."[51] The made-for-television candidate is packaged, marketed and sold like any other commodity, except, of course, that toothpaste does not determine foreign policy.

In what ways, then, does the introduction of multichannel television change even further the nature of political life? There are several important, related characteristics of the emerging system that have implications for political communication: It provides a vastly expanded wealth of instant, global information; it opens direct channels between the audience and the source of the information; it gives the viewer greater control; it offers opportunities for targeting audiences; and it promises greater interactive capacity.

Nonstop News

Social theorists like Ellul see the tidal wave of cable-delivered news and information as a threat to rational, deliberative thought and democratic self-governance. The disparate and disjointed bits and bytes of political information, in their view, do more to confuse and disorient than to clarify. Others, however, with greater faith in the human ability to digest and collate information, note that CNN, C-SPAN, CNBC, Fox News, and the many local news channels have brought millions instant access to the world's events. Multichannel television is a capacious resource for social and political information. Nonstop news is not just a convenient utility that gives the viewer greater control over how and when they watch, it expands the amount and variety of available news. While there is substantial consonance in the kind of news shown by cable and the broadcast networks, there are also importance differences, by simple virtue of the requirement that the cable channels fill so much time. CNN made its mark on the world in its coverage of the Gulf War; the world watched and its ratings soared. C-SPAN has given the electorate access to congressional deliberation once reserved for only a small minority of citizens. With broadband television and the Intenet, one can argue that citizens have access to greater information resources than ever before. While knowledge gap effects need to be acknowledged, on balance more people have the opportunity to be better informed.

Unfiltered News

All of this is not to say that the new media are an unalloyed boon to public discourse. The fact that the cable-satellite system affords more direct connections between senders and receivers has both positive and negative implications. Viewers today often tap into news events directly, bypassing the traditional structures of selection, interpretation, and packaging performed by television news departments or the sources themselves. C-SPAN, along with other cable networks, carries news conferences live, unedited and complete. Speeches and debates from the floors of Congress can be seen in their entirety. CourtTV offers full-length coverage of trials. Live coverage of breaking news is common. In creating this direct connection, the organizational structures that select and shape some kinds of coverage are arguably bypassed. The quality of the information takes on a different character. For some citizens it is a benefit insofar as they become their own editors and interpreters; for others, as the critics suggest, the information may become a cacophony and increase even more the need for trained journalists to help make sense out of the stream, to reinsert themselves into the channel of communication.

In addition, politicians and news makers are keenly aware of their ability to contact audiences without having to go through the sometimes critical filters of journalistic interpretation. Political scientists Jeffrey Abramson and his colleagues have noted that politicians who wanted to reach mass audiences at one time had to find ways to catch the eye of the reporter or simply buy the time themselves.[52] There is less need under the new system to depend on the gatekeepers of television news. Congressmen and Senators create their own videotape news releases and beam them by satellite to their local TV news station where they are often run with little editing. Candidates for office are making increasing use of local cable channels to buy advertising time, targeting specific markets and groups in the same manner as business. Politicians are talking directly to audiences through programs such as CNN's *Larry King Live*. The suggestion is that the professional journalistic community, at least for some purposes, may play a reduced role in social surveillance and political discourse.

Some observers suggest a similar effect on political party structure. Political party identification has been on the wane for decades; people are much less likely today to vote in the shoes of their parents, so to speak, than was true forty years ago. By giving freshman Congressmen and Congresswomen direct access to their home audiences, C-SPAN is said to have helped reduce the influence and control of party leadership in the House of Representatives in recent years, leading in part, to increased division and greater inefficiencies in the legislation process.

Participants in the process are also using the media to form more direct links among themselves, creating new patterns of communication and organization. Again, freshman Republican representatives found in the 1980s they could obtain rare direct access to President Ronald Reagan because he would watch their floor speeches on C-SPAN.[53] Special interest groups have used teleconferencing, videotapes, and the Internet to maintain ties with their members across the country, to keep them up to date on events, to maintain their enthusiasm for the cause, and to mobilize them to action when necessary. Media has long been seen as providing a mobilizing function for citizens, giving them the information necessary to take action in the context of a specific policy issue and even encouraging them to do so. Targeted mobilizing communication becomes even more efficacious in the context of special interest groups using internal one-way and two-way media to marshall the troops.

Tele-Democracy

Finally, one of the older visions for cable in politics is the notion of the instant referendum, the ability to poll citizens using the two-way technology of the cable–satellite system, moving governance more toward a direct democracy and away from a strictly representative structure. The practical problems with such an idea have been noted often, the inability in the real world to assure that a representative sample of adults, each voting just once, actually make up the plebiscite. A true referendum would afford polling access to everyone, and, as has been shown, this is unlikely ever to be the case. Controlling voting from the home is problematic: Teledemocracy proposals have always been haunted by visions of the family dog stepping on the "vote" button five or six times. Codes and passwords could alleviate some of the difficulties, but the deeper problem is that instant opinion is often uninformed opinion. One of the traditions in political theory is the value of quiet, thoughtful, and deliberative decision making, a careful gathering of facts and assaying of policy alternatives. Instant polls, whether by two-way cable or Internet, may have some value but should be treated cautiously.

A CONCLUDING NOTE

Insofar as the emerging system will alter our communication patterns in myriad ways, many of them yet to be discovered, the impact on our political, social, and cultural life could be substantial. The possible variations and permutations are so great, however, as to make hard forecasts a fool's business. We have intentionally avoided trying to make detailed predictions about the future of the information age. As noted in this chapter and Chapter 1, the human imagination is limitless and is likely to steer the information infrastructure into many uncharted domains. Moreover, history has shown the marketplace to be a sometimes fickle and often unpredictable place. Many apparently sound business plans have crashed on the rocks of consumer-based reality. That leaves us, perhaps, with only the possibility of making best attempts at gauging long-term trends and forces and staying open to the possibilities that might arise from the churning mix of technology, economics, and human inventiveness. With respect to the anticipated and unanticipated problems that might accompany the evolving system, a mixture of sound principles and flexibility may be the best prescription. To a large extent, the information age will be what we make it. Establishing clear principles of equity, fairness, and freedom and keeping close watch on the evolving system may the best we can strive for, dealing with specific problematic manifestations of that system as they arise. Cable and satellite television have changed dramatically in the last twenty-five years and, as we have seen, are likely to change just as dramatically in the next twenty-five. For better or worse, we will continue to live in interesting times.

NOTES

[1]Fritz Malchup, *The Production and Distribution of Knowledge in the United States.* (Princeton, NJ: Princeton University Press, 1962); Porat Marc Uri, *The Information*

Economy: Definition and Measurement, OT Special Publication 77-12(1), (Washington, DC: U.S. Dept. of Commerce, Office of Telecommunications, May 1977).

[2]Daniel Bell, *The Coming of Post-Industrial Society* (New York: Basic Books, 1976).

[3]Herb Schiller, "Old Foundations for a New (Information) Age," in *Competing Visions, Complex Realities: Social Aspects of the Information Age*, Jorge Reina Schement and Leah Lievrouw, eds. (Norwood, NJ: Ablex, 1987).

[4]Jorge Reina Schement and Terry Curtis, *Tendencies and Tensions of the Information Age* (New Brunswick, NJ: Transaction Publishers, 1995), 39.

[5]Anthony Giddens, *The Nation State and Violence, Volume Two* (Cambridge: Polity, 1985).

[6]The development of organizational bureaucracies, polling and survey methods as well as marketing science would also be included as forms of the control revolution. James Beniger, *The Control Revolution* (Cambridge: Harvard University Press, 1986).

[7]Thomas Streeter, "The Cable Fable Revisited: Discourse, Policy, and the Making of Cable Television," *Critical Studies in Mass Communication*, 4(1987): 174–200; New York City, Mayor's Advisory Task Force on CATV and Telecommunications, *A Report on Cable Television and Cable Telecommunications in New York City*, 1968; President's Task Force on Communications Policy, *Final Report* (Washington, DC, Government Printing Office, 1968).

[8]Robert Heilbroner, "Do Machines Make History?" *Technology and Culture* 8(July 1967): 335–345.

[9]James Carey and John Quirk, "The Mythos of the Electronic Revolution," *The American Scholar*, 39(Spring 1970): 219–41, and (Summer 1970): 395–424.

[10]Edward Bellamy, *Looking Backward*, (New York: Penguin Books, 1982).

[11]Lewis Mumford, *The Myth of the Machine*, vol. 1., *Technics and the Human Development* (New York: Harcourt Brace Jovanovich, 1966).

[12]Jacques Ellul, *The Technological Society* (New York: Vintage, 1964).

[13]See Merritt Roe Smith, "Technological Determinism in American Culture," *Does Technology Drive History: The Dilemma of Technological Determinism*, Merritt R. Smith and Leo Marx, eds. (Cambridge: MIT Press, 1995), 23–42.

[14]Brian Winston, *Misunderstanding Media* (Cambridge: Harvard University Press, 1986), 1.

[15]Ithiel de Sola Pool, *Technologies of Freedom* (Cambridge: Belknap Press, 1983).

[16]John Wicklein, *Electronic Nightmare, The New Communications and Freedom* (New York: Viking Press, 1981).

[17]See Shearon Lowery and Melvin DeFleur, *Milestones in Mass Communication Research*, 3rd ed. (White Plains, NY: Longman Publishers, 1995).

[18]Elihu Katz, "Mass Communication Research and the Study of Popular Culture: An Editorial Note on a Possible Future for This Journal," *Studies in Public Communication*, 2(1959): 1–6.

[19]Robert LaRose and David Atkin, "Satisfaction, Demographic, and Media Environment Predictors of Cable Subscription," *Journal of Broadcasting and Electronic Media*, 32(1988): 403–413.

[20]*Trends in Viewing* (New York: Television Bureau of Advertising, 1991).

[21]*1996 Cable TV Facts* (New York: Cable Advertising Bureau, 1996), 15.

[22]James Carey, "The Communications Revolution and the Professional Communicator," *The Sociological Review Monograph*, 13(1969): 23–28.

[23]Robert Kubey, et al., "Demographic Diversity on Cable: Have the New Cable Channels

Made a Difference in the Representation of Gender, Race, and Age?" *Journal of Broadcasting and Electronic Media* 39(1995): 459–471.

[24]Phillip Tichenor, George Donohue. and Clarence Olien, "Mass Media Flow and Differential Growth in Knowledge," *Public Opinion Quarterly* 34(1970): 159–170.

[25]Vincent Mosco, "Introduction: Information in the Pay-Per Society," in *The Political Economy of Information*, Vincent Mosco and Janet Wasko, eds. (Madison, WI: University of Wisconsin Press, 1988).

[26]Cabletelevision Advertising Bureau, *Cable TV Facts, 1996.*

[27]Anne Wells Branscomb, *Who Owns Information: From Privacy to Public Access* (New York: Basic Books, 1994).

[28]*Sony Corp. of America v. Universal City Studios, Inc.* 464 U.S. 417 (1984).

[29]Pamel Samuelson, "The Copyright Grab," *Wired*, January 1996, 135.

[30]Steve Lohr, "Rethinking Copyright and Ethics on the Net," *New York Times*, 9 October 1995, D-3.

[31]*Feist Publications, Inc. v. Rural Telephone Service Co.*, 111 S.Ct. 1282 (1991).

[32]Wicklein.

[33]Samuel Warren and Louis Brandeis, "The Right to Privacy," *Harvard Law Review*, 4:5 (1890): 193–220.

[34]Warren, 195.

[35]Oscar Gandy, Jr., "The Surveillance Society: Information Technology and Bureaucratic Social Control," *Journal of Communication.* 39:3 (Summer 1989): 61–76.

[36]47 U.S.C. sect. 551.

[37]Surgeon general's Scientific Advisory Committee on Television and Social Behavior, *Television and Growing Up: The Impact of Televised Violence.* Report to the Surgeon General, United States Public Health Service. Washington, DC, 1971; *Television and Behavior: Ten Years of Scientific Progress and Implications for the Eighties*, Vols. I and II. (Washington, DC: U.S. Government Printing Office, 1982).

[38]Albert Bandura, "Influence of Models: Reinforcement Contingencies on the Acquisition of Imitative Responses," *Journal of Personality and Social Psychology*, 1(1965): 589–95.

[39]Dale Kunkel, et al., "Measuring Television Violence: The Importance of Context," *Journal of Broadcasting & Electronic Media*, 39(1005): 284–291.

[40]Barbara Wilson, et al., "Violence in Television Programming Overall," *The National Television Violence Study* (Washington, DC: National Cable Television Association, 1995).

[41]Wilson, 15.

[42]Melvin DeFleur and Sandra Ball–Rokeach, *Theories of Mass Communication*, 5th ed. (White Plains, NY: Longman, 1989).

[43]DeFleur, 202.

[44]See, e.g., Stanley J. Baran and Dennis Davis, *Mass Communication Theory: Foundations, Ferment and Future* (Belmont, CA: Wadsworth Publishing, 1995).

[45]Denis McQuail, *Mass Communication Theory*, 3rd ed. (London: Sage, 1994).

[46]See, e.g., Gaye Tuchman, Arlene Kaplan Daniels, and James Benet, eds. *Hearth and Home: Images of Women in the Mass Media* (New York: Oxford University Press, 1978).

[47]See, e.g., Robert Liebert and Joyce Sprafkin, *The Early Window*, 3rd ed. (New York: Pergamon, 1988).

[48]Steven Seidman, "An Investigation of Sex-Role Stereotyping in Music Video," *Journal of Broadcasting and Electronic Media*, 36:2 (Spring 1992): 209–216.

[49]Horace Newcomb and Paul Hirsch, "Television as a Cultural Forum: Implications for Research," in *Interpreting Television: Current Research Perspectives,* Willard Rowland, Jr., and Bruce Watkins, eds. (Beverly Hills: Sage, 1984), 58–73.

[50]Philipe Rushton, "Television and Prosocial Behavior," in Pearl et al., eds., *Television and Behavior*, vol. 2, 249.

[51]Neil Postman, *Amusing Ourselves to Death* (New York: Penguin Books, 1985).

[52]Jeffrey Abramson, F. Christopher Arterton, and Gary Owen, *The Electronic Commonwealth: The Impact of New Media Technologies on Democratic Politics* (New York: Basic Books, 1988).

[53]Abramson, 145.

Appendix A

Selected Programming Networks

Video Services	Start Date	Subscribers (millions)
Action Pay Per View	Sept. 1990	7.2
A&E Television	Feb. 1994	66
AMC	Oct. 1984	60
Asian American Sat. TV	Jan. 1992	0.3
BETJan. 1980	44.3	
BET on Jazz	Jan. 1996	0.8
The Box	Dec. 1985	5.0 (19 million broadcast)
Bravo Cable Network	Dec. 1980	22
Cable Video Store	Apr. 1986	2.8
Cartoon Network	Oct. 1992	24.7
CBS Eye on People	1996	—
Channel America	June 1988	7.8
Cinemax	Aug. 1980	8.9
Classic Sports Network	May 1995	5
CMT	March 1983	32.9
CNBC	April 1989	55.6
CNN	June 1980	67.8
CNN International	Jan. 1995	5.5 (United States)
CNNfn	Dec. 1995	5.5
Comedy Central	April 1991	37
CourtTV	July 1991	25
C-SPAN	March 1979	64.5
C-SPAN 2	June 1986	43.4
Discovery Channel	June 1985	67
The Disney Channel	April 1983	16.1

(continued)

Video Services	Start Date	Subscribers (millions)
E! Ent.Television	June 1990	37
Encore	April 1991	6
ESPN	Sept. 1979	67.9
ESPN-2	Oct. 1993	30.8
EWTN	Aug. 1981	39.5
The Family Channel	April 1977	64
Fit TV	Dec. 1993	11.2
fX June 1994		20
fXM: Movie from Fox	Nov. 1994	—
FoxNews	1996	—
Galavision	Oct. 1979	5.17 (including MMDS)
GEMS International	April 1993	6
The Golf Channel	Jan. 1995	1.5
HBO	Nov. 1972	20.8
	(Dec. 1975 via sat.)	
Headline News	Jan. 1982	60.2
The History Channel	Jan. 1, 1995	15
Home and Garden TV	Dec. 1994	10
Home Shopping Network	July 1985	47.9
Home Shopping Spree	Sept. 1986	12.4
The Independent Film Ch.	Sept. 1994	3
The International Channel	July 1990	7.5
Jones Computer Network)	Sept. 1994	1.5
Kaleidoscope	Sept. 1990	14.5
KTLA	March 1988	6.9
The Learning Channel	Nov. 1980	45
Lifetime Television	Feb. 1984	64
Madison Sq. Garden Net.	—	4
Mind Extension University	Nov. 1987	26
MOR Music TV	Sept. 1992	16
The Movie Channel	Dec. 1979	14.8
MSNBC	1996	—
MTV: Music Television	Aug. 1981	65.9
Nick at Nite's TV Land	April 1996	—
Nickelodeon	April 1979	64
Nostalgia Television	Feb. 1985	9
Odyssey	Oct. 1993	24.1
Playboy TV	Nov. 1982	10.5
Prevue Channel	Jan. 1988	43.5
Prime Sports	Jan. 1993	49.4
Product Information Net.	April 1994	5.4
QVC	Nov. 1986	54.6
Q2 Sept. 1994		10.6
Request Television.	Nov. 1985	35
Sci-Fi Channel	Sept. 1992	29
Showtime	July 1976	13.3
Spice	May 1989	11
Starz (Encore 8)	Feb. 1994	3.3
TBS	Dec. 1976	67.6

(continued)

Video Services	Start Date	Subscribers (millions)
Television Food Net	Nov. 1993	15.3
TNN: The Nashville Net.	March 1983	63.1
TNT: Turner Network TV	Oct. 1988	66.6
The Travel Channel	Feb. 1987	19.3
Trinity Broadcasting Net.	May 1973	30.9
Turner Classic Movies	April 1994	8.8
Univision	Sept. 1976	6.3
USA Network	April 1980	67
ValueVision	Oct. 1991	14
VH1 Jan. 1995	54	
Video Catalog Channel	Oct. 1991	10.9
Viewer's Choice	Nov. 1995	32
The Weather Channel	May 1982	62
WGN	Nov. 1978	38.4
WPIX	May 1984	11.6
WWOR	April 1979	12.5
Z Music Television.	March 1993	27

Subscriber figures as of 1996.

Audio Services	Start Date	Subscribers (millions)
AEI Music Network	Oct. 1979	4
Beethoven Sat. Net.	1986	—
Cable Radio Network	March 1982	10
C-SPAN (Audio 1 and Audio 2)	Sept. 1989	6.2
Digital Music Express (DMX)	Sept. 1991	0.35
KJAZ Satellite Radio	Dec. 1994	1.8
Moody Broadcasting Network	May 1982	0.76
Music Choice	May 1990	11
SUPERAUDIO Cable Radio Services	Sept. 1987	10
WFMT	March 1979	0.85
Yesterday USA	1985	3

Subscriber figures as of 1996.

Appendix B

Selected Programming Network Ownership

Network	Owner	%
A&E	Walt Disney Co.	37.5
	Hearst Corp.	37.5
	NBC	25
American Movie Classics	Cablevision Systems	75
	NBC	25
BET	Bob Johnson	55
	TCI	17.5
	Time Warner Inc.	15
	Others	12.5
Bravo	Cablevision Systems	50
	NBC	50
Cartoon Network	Turner/Time Warner	100
Cinemax	Time Warner	100
CMT	Gaylord Enterprises Co.	67
	Group W Satellite Co.	33
CNBC	NBC	100
CNN	Turner/Time Warner	100
Comedy Central	Time Warner	50
	Viacom, Inc.	50
CourtTV	TCI	33.3
	Time Warner	33.3
	Cablevision Systems	33.3
Discovery Channel	TCI	49
	Cox Cable	24
	Newhouse	24
	John Hendricks	3

(continued)

Network	Owner	%
The Disney Channel	Disney	100
Encore	TCI	90
	JJS Communications	10
E!	Time Warner	50
	Comcast Corp.	10
	Continental Cablevision, Inc.	10
	COX	10
	Newhouse	10
	TCI	10
ESPN	Disney	80
	Hearst	20
Odyssey	National Interfaith Cable Coalition	51
	TCI	49
Family Channel	IFE, Inc.	100
Fit TV	IFE, Inc.	90
	Jake Steinfeld	10
fX	News Corp.	50
	Liberty Media Corp.	50
HBO	Time Warner	100
Headline News	Turner/Time Warner	100
History Channel	Hearst	37.5
	Disney	37.5
	NBC	25
Home & Garden TV	E.W. Scripps Co.	100
HSN	TCI	80.4
	public	19.6
Independent Film Channel	Cablevision Systems	50
	NBC	50
Lifetime Television	Hearst	50
	Disney	50
Mind Extension University	Jones Education Network	51
	Jones Intercable	38
	Glenn Jones	11
The Movie Channel	Viacom	100
MTV	Viacom	100
Nickelodeon	Viacom	100
Outdoor Life	*Cox	45
	Comcast	22.5
	Continental	22.5
	Times Mirror	10
QVC	Comcast	57
	TCI	43
Sci-Fi Channel	Seagram	100
Showtime	Viacom	100
Starz!	TCI	90
	JJS Communications	10
TBS SuperStation	Turner/Time Warner	100

Network	Owner	%
Turner Classic Movies	Turner/Time Warner	100
The Learning Channel	TCI	49
	Cox	24
	NewHouse	24
	John Hendricks	3
TNT	Turner/Time Warner	100
TV Food Network	Providence Journal Co.	N/A
	Continental Cablevision	N/A
	Landmark Communication	N/A
	Scripps–Howard	N/A
	Tribune Broadcasting	N/A
USA Network	Seagram	100
VH1	Viacom	100
The Weather Channel	Landmark Communication	100

*Outdoor Life's current ownership is Cox 50 percent and Times Mirror 50 percent, but a Comcast/Continental deal is pending.

Sources: Paul Kagan Associates (Carmel, CA) in "Who Owns What," *Cable World*, 27 November 1995, 64–65; "Liberty Media Group Programming Interest," *Broadcasting & Cable*, 22 April 1996, 29; Mark Crispin Miller, "Free the Media," *The Nation*, 3 June 1996, foldout.

Bibliography

Abramson, Jeffrey, F. Christopher Arterton and Gary Owen. *The Electronic Commonwealth: The Impact of New Media Technologies on Democratic Politics.* New York: Basic Books, 1988.

Bagdikian, Ben. *The Media Monopoly*, 4th ed. Boston, MA: Beacon Press, 1992.

Baldwin, Thomas, D. Stevens McVoy, and Charles Steinfield. *Convergence: Integrating Media, Information and Communication.* Thousand Oaks, CA: Sage, 1996.

Baldwin, Thomas and D. Stevens McVoy. *Cable Communication.* Englewood Cliffs, NJ: Prentice-Hall, 1983.

Baran, Stanley and Dennis Davis. *Mass Communication Theory: Foundations, Ferment and Future.* Belmont, CA: Wadsworth Publishing, 1995.

Barnouw, Erik. *Tube of Plenty*, 2d ed. New York: Oxford University Press, 1991.

Bartlett, Eugene. *Cable Communications: Building the Information Infrastructure.* New York: McGraw-Hill, 1995.

Bell, Daniel. *The Coming of Post-Industrial Society.* New York: Basic Books, 1976.

Bellamy, Jr., Robert, and James Walker. *Television and the Remote Control: Grazing on a Vast Wasteland.* New York: Guilford, 1996.

Beniger, James. *The Control Revolution: Technological and Economic Origins of the Information Society.* Cambridge, MA: Harvard University Press, 1986.

Besen, Stanley and Robert Crandall. "The Deregulation of Cable Television," *Law and Contemporary Problems* 44(1981): 77–124.

Besen, Stanley, et al. "Copyright Liability for Cable Television: Compulsory Licensing and the Coase Theorem," *Journal of Law and Economics,* 21(1978): 67–98.

Beville, Jr., Hugh Malcolm. *Audience Ratings: Radio, Television and Cable*, revised ed. Hillsdale, NJ: Lawrence Erlbaum, 1988.

Bracken, James and Christopher Sterling. *Telecommunications Research Resources: An Annotated Guide.* Hillsdale, NJ: Lawrence Erlbaum, 1995.

Brand, Stewart. *The Media Lab; Inventing the Future at MIT.* New York: Viking, 1987.

Branscomb, Anne Wells. *Who Owns Information?* New York: Basic Books, 1984.

Brenner, Daniel L. and Monroe E. Price. *Cable Television and Other Nonbroadcast Video: Law and Policy.* New York: Clark Boardman, 1986.

Brenner, Daniel. *Law and Regulation of Common Carriers in the Communications Industry.* Boulder: Westview Press, 1992.

Brock, Gerald. *Telecommunications Policy for the Information Age.* Cambridge, MA: Harvard University Press, 1994.

Carey, James and John Quirk. "The Mythos of the Electronic Revolution," *American Scholar* 39 (Spring 1970): 219–41, and (Summer 1970): 395–424.

Chan–Olmsted, Sylvia. "Market Competition for Cable Television: Reexamining Its Horizontal Mergers and Industry Concentration," *Journal of Media Economics* 9:2(1996): 25–41.

Codding, George A., Jr. and Anthony M. Rutkowski. *The International Telecommunications Union in a Changing World.* Artech House, 1982

D'Agostino, Peter and David Tafler. *Transmission: Toward a Post-Television Culture*, 2nd ed. Thousand Oaks, CA: Sage, 1994.

DeFleur, Melvin and Sandra Ball–Rokeach. *Theories of Mass Communication*, 5th ed. White Plains, NY: Longman, 1989.

Dizard, Wilson P. *Old Media/ New Media.* White Plains, NY: Longman, 1994.

Dordick, H. and G. Wang. *The Information Society: A Retrospective View.* Beverly Hills: Sage, 1993.

Eastman, Susan Tyler. *Broadcast/Cable Programming: Strategies and Practices*, 4th ed. Belmont, CA: Wadsworth, 1993.

Egan, Bruce. *Information Superhighways: The Economics of Advanced Public Communications Networks.* Norwood, MA: Artech, 1991.

Ellul, Jacques. *The Technological Society.* New York: Vintage, 1964.

Emord, Jonathon. *Freedom, Technology and the First Amendment.* Pacific Research Institute for Public Policy, 1991.

Firestone, Charles and Jorge Reina Schement. *Toward an Information Bill of Rights and Responsibilities.* Washington, DC: The Aspen Institute, 1995.

Forester, Tom. *High-Tech Society: The Story of the Information Technology Revolution.* Cambridge, MA: MIT Press, 1987.

Gandy, Oscar. *The Panoptic Sort: The Political Economy of Personal Information.* Boulder: Westview, 1994.

Garay, Ron. *Cable Television: A Reference Guide to Information.* New York: Greenwood Press, 1988.

Gershon, Richard. "Pay Cable Television: A Regulatory History," *Communications and the Law,* June 1990, 3–26.

Gilder, George. *Life After Television: The Coming Transformation of Media and American Life*. New York: W.W. Norton, 1992.

Goodale, James and Morton Hamburg. *All about Cable: Legal and Business Aspects of Cable and Pay Television*. Law Journal Seminars Press, 1981.

Gross, Lynne Schafer. *The New Television Technologies*, 2nd ed., Dubuque, IA: W. C. Brown, 1986.

Harlow, Alvin Fay. *Old Wires and New Waves, The History of the Telegraph, Telephone and Wireless*. New York: Appleton-Century, 1936.

Head, Sydney W. and Christopher H. Sterling. *Broadcasting in America*, 5th ed. Boston, MA: Houghton Mifflin, 1987.

Heap, Nick, et al. *Information Technology and Society*. Thousand Oaks, CA: Sage, 1995.

Heeter, Carrie and Bradley Greenberg. *Cable-Viewing*. Norwood, NJ: Ablex, 1988.

Hilliard, Robert and Michael Keith. *The Broadcast Century: A Biography of American Broadcasting*. Boston, MA: Focal Press, 1992.

Hollowell, Mary Louise, ed. *The Cable/ Broadband Communications Book*, Vol. 1, 1977–78. Washington, DC: Communications Press, 1977.

Horwitz, Robert. *The Irony of Regulatory Reform: The Deregulation of American Telecommunications*. New York: Oxford University Press, 1989.

Inglis, Andrew F. *Behind the Tube: A History of Broadcasting Technology and Business*. Boston, MA: Focal Press, 1990.

————. *Satellite Technology: An Introduction*. Boston, MA: Beacon Press, 1991.

Jansky, Donald M. and Michel C. Jeruchim. *Communications Satellites in the Geostationary Orbit*. Boston, MA: Artech House, 1987.

Johnson, Leland. *Toward Competition in Cable Television*. Washington DC: American Enterprise Institute Press, 1994.

Jones, Kensinger, Thomas Baldwin, and Martin P Block. *Cable and Advertising: New Ways to New Business*. Englewood Cliffs, NJ: Prentice-Hall, 1986.

Jones, Steven. *Cybersociety: Computer Mediated Communication and Community*. Thousand Oaks, CA: Sage, 1994.

Klingler, Richard. *The New Information Industry: Regulatory Challenges and the First Amendment*. Washington, DC: The Brookings Institution, 1996.

Le Duc, Don. *Cable Television and the FCC: A Crisis in Media Control*. Philadelphia: Temple University Press, 1973.

————. "A Selective Bibliography on the Evolution of CATV: 1950–1970," *Journal of Broadcasting* 15:2(Spring 1971): 195–235.

Lundstedt, Sven, ed. *Telecommunications Values and the Public Interest*. Norwood, NJ: Ablex, 1990.

Malchup, Fritz. *The Production and Distribution of Knowledge in the United States*. Princeton, NJ: Princeton University Press, 1962.

Mansell, Robin. *The New Telecommunications*. Thousand Oaks, CA: Sage, 1994.

Marvin, Carolyn. *When Old Technologies Were New, Thinking about Electric Communication in the Late 19th Century*. New York: Oxford University Press, 1988.

McChesney, Robert. *Telecommunications, Mass Media and Democracy*. New York: Oxford University Press, 1993.

Mirabito, Michael and Barbara Morgenstern. *The New Communications Technologies*, 2nd ed. Boston, MA: Focal Press, 1994.

Mosco, Vincent. *The Political Economy of Information*. Madison, WI: University of Wisconsin Press, 1988.

Negroponte, Nicholas. *Being Digital*. New York: Alfred Knopf, 1995.

Noam, Eli M., ed. *Video Media Competition: Regulation, Economics and Technology*. New York: Columbia University Press, 1985.

————. *Asymmetrical Deregulation*. Norwood, NJ: Ablex Publishing, 1994.

Owen, Bruce and Steve Wildman. *Video Economics*. Cambridge, MA: Harvard University Press, 1992.

Parsons, Patrick. "In the Wake of *Preferred*: Waiting for Godot," *Mass Communications Review* 16:1(Summer 1989): 26–37.

————. "Two Tales of a City," *Journal of Broadcasting & Electronic Media*, 40:3 (Summer 1996): 354–365.

Pavlik, John. *New Media and the Information Superhighway*. Boston, MA: Allyn and Bacon, 1996.

Phillips, Mary Alice Mayer. *CATV: A History of Community Antenna Television*. Evanston, IL: Northwestern University Press, 1972.

Picard, Robert, ed. *The Cable Networks Handbook*. Riverside, CA: Carpelan Publishing, 1993.

Poole, I. De Sola. *Technologies of Freedom*. Cambridge: Belknap Press, 1983.

Postman, Neil. *Technopoly: The Surrender of Culture to Technology*. New York: Random House, 1992.

Pringle, Peter, Michael Starr, and William E. McCavitt. *Electronic Media Management*, 3rd ed. Boston, MA: Focal Press, 1994.

Reed, Maxine K. and Robert M. Reed. *Career Opportunities in Television, Cable, and Video*, 3rd ed. New York: Facts on File, 1990.

Rheingold, Howard. *The Virtual Community: Homesteading on the Electronic Frontier*. Reading, MA: Addison-Wesley, 1993.

Roman, James W. *Cablemania*. Englewood, Cliffs, NJ: Prentice-Hall, 1983.

Salmon, Charles, ed. *Information Campaigns: Balancing Social Values and Social Change*. London: Sage, 1989.

Salvaggio, Jerry, ed.. *The Information Society: Economic, Social and Structural issues*. Hillsdale, NJ: Erlbaum, 1990.

Schement, Jorge Reina and Terry Curtis. *Tendencies and Tensions of the Information Age*. New Brunswick, NJ: Transaction Publishers, 1995.

Seiden, Martin. *Cable Television U.S.A.: An Analysis of Government Policy*. New York: Praeger, 1972.

Singleton, Loy A. *Telecommunications in the Information Age*, 2nd ed. Cambridge, MA: Ballinger, 1986.

Slack, Jennifer Daryl & Fred Fejes, eds. *The Ideology of the Information Age*. Norwood, NJ: Ablex, 1987.

The Sloan Commission on Cable Communications, *On the Cable: The Television of Abundance*. New York: McGraw-Hill, 1971.

Smith, Merritt Roe and Leo Marx, eds. *Does Technology Drive History: The Dilemma of Technological Determinism*. Cambridge: MIT Press, 1995.

Smith, Ralph Lee. *The Wired Nation, Cable TV: The Electronic Communications Highway*. New York: Harper and Row, 1972.

Sterling, Christopher and Michael Kittross. *Stay Tuned: A Concise History of American Broadcasting*, 2nd ed. Belmont CA: Wadsworth, 1990.

Sterling, Christopher H. *Electronic Media: A Guide to Trends in Broadcasting and Newer Technologies, 1920–1983*. New York: Praeger, 1984.

U.S. House Committee on Small Business. Small and Minority Business Ownership in the Cable Television. Industry. 97th Cong. 2d. Sess., 1982 H. Rept. 97-976. Subcommittee on General Oversight and Minority Enterprise of the House Committee on Small Business. Media Concentration (Part 2). 96th Cong. 2d. Sess., 1980. Hearing.

U.S. Senate Subcommittee on Telecommunications, Consumer Protection, and Finance of the House Committee on Energy and Commerce. *Telecommunications in Transition: The Status of Competition in the Telecommunications Industry*. Report by the Majority Staff 97th Cong., 1st sess., 1981. Committee Print. 97th Cong.

U.S. Senate. *Television Inquiry: Special Problems of TV Service to Small Communities*. Hearings before the Senate Committee on Interstate and Foreign Commerce, 85th Cong. 2nd sess., part 6. (1958).

U.S. Senate, Senate Commission on Interstate and Foreign Commerce. *Television Inquiry, Television Allocation*, 86th Cong. 2d Sess., pt. 6, 1960.

Webb, G. Kent. *The Economics of Cable Television*. Lexington, MA: Lexington Books, 1983.

Webster, Frank. *Theories of the Information Age*. London, New York: Routledge, 1995.

Wicklein, John. *Electronic Nightmare: The Home Communications Set and Your Freedom*. Boston, MA: Beacon Press, 1982.

Williams, Frederick. *The New Telecommunications: Infrastructure for the Information Age*. New York: Free Press, 1991.

Williams, Frederick, and John T. Pavlik, eds. *The People's Right to Know: Media, Democracy and the Information Highway*. Hillsdale, NJ: Lawrence Erlbaum, 1994.

Wilson, Barbara, et al. "Violence in Television Programming Overall," *The National Television Violence Study.*Washington, DC: National Cable Television Association, 1995.

Winston, Brian. *Misunderstanding Media.* Cambridge: Harvard University Press, 1986.

Wood, James. *Satellite Communications and DBS Systems.* Boston, MA: Focal Press, 1992.

Wriston, Walter B. *The Twilight of Sovereignty: How the Information Revolution Is Transforming Our World.* New York: Scribners, 1992.

Index